THE UNITED STATES SINCE 1945

The Ordeal of Power

D0217196

THE UNITED STATES SINCE 1945

The Ordeal of Power

Dewey W. Grantham

Vanderbilt University

McGraw-Hill Book Company

New York   St. Louis   San Francisco   Auckland   Düsseldorf
Johannesburg   Kuala Lumpur   London   Mexico
Montreal   New Delhi   Panama   Paris   São Paulo
Singapore   Sydney   Tokyo   Toronto

THE
UNITED STATES
SINCE 1945
The Ordeal
of Power

4 5 6 7 8 9 0   DODO   8 3 2 1 0

This book was set in Times Roman by Black Dot, Inc. The editors
were Robert P. Rainier and Michael Weber; the designer was
Joseph Gillians; the production supervisor was Dennis J. Conroy.
R. R. Donnelley & Sons Company was printer and binder.

Library of Congress Cataloging in Publication Data

Grantham, Dewey W
    The United States since 1945.

    (The Modern America series)
    Includes bibliographies and index.
    1. United States—History—1945-   2. United
states—Foreign relations—1945-   I. Title.
I. Series.
E813.G68   973.92   75-20221
ISBN 0-07-024116-3

For Diane,
Wes,
Clint,
Gayle,
and Laurie,
who started out in
the Age of Aquarius

CONTENTS

PREFACE

The World War II years form a watershed in recent American history. The war acted as a catalyst for social change and accelerated the pace of such change. Almost overnight the nation was ushered into a new era of revolution—an age that seemed incredibly different from the prewar period. Many thoughtful scholars now tell us that we are living through one of the great divides in human history. "The gulf separating 1965 from 1943," the cultural anthropologist Margaret Mead has written, "is as deep as the gulf that separated the men who became builders of cities from Stone Age men." Although there are strong continuities between prewar America and our own day, the years since World War II in the United States, as elsewhere, essentially constitute an age of extraordinary change and disruption in the national experience.

It is still hard to see the broad shape of the postwar period, to understand how it is related to the prewar epoch, and to perceive the pattern of its evolution through time. This book represents a modest attempt to help organize and interpret the tumultuous years since 1945, and thus to bring new perspectives to our recent history and a better understanding of modern times. I hope this work will be helpful, to use Felix Gilbert's words, in "reconstructing a historical consciousness that integrates the present with the past." Without some awareness of the complexity, ambiguity, and burden of the past, one is surely ill prepared to deal with the kaleidoscopic present and the onrushing future.

I am deeply indebted to J. Leonard Bates and Richard S. Kirkendall, my associates in writing the new three-volume history of modern America of which this book is a part. I am grateful for their comradeship as well as their many contributions to the formulation of the series and to the improvement of this particular book. I also wish to thank Robert P. Rainier of McGraw-Hill for his long-time assistance and constructive advice as History Editor. Miss Martha H. Swain of Texas Woman's University helped me in a variety of ways as an able research assistant. I am also happy to acknowledge the support of my colleagues in the department of history at Vanderbilt University.

Dewey W. Grantham

Chapter 1

The Transit
from War
to Peace

When the Japanese formally surrendered to the Allies on September 2, 1945, the United States was vastly different from the nation that had been propelled into war by the surprise attack on Pearl Harbor on December 7, 1941. To most Americans in the late summer of 1945, the war seemed very old, its beginnings already shrouded in the mists of the retreating past. Part of this feeling was an illusion produced by the sacrifices and weariness of wartime, abetted by the tumultuous events of a global conflict. But the impression was also based on the reality of alterations that had taken place in the United States during the past four years. It is clear that the myriad developments of World War II inaugurated a new age of revolutionary change in America.

World War II: The Great Transformation

The first part of the war was a grim and sobering experience for Americans, and in those dark days it sometimes seemed that it would be impossible for the Allies to stem the powerful tide of the Axis onslaught. Yet the people and their leaders set about the forbidding task in a spirit of remarkable unity. Although the extravagant idealism that attended the nation's involvement in World War I was noticeably absent from that of World War II, most people would have agreed with Vice President Henry A. Wallace's characterization of the conflict as "a fight between a slave world and a free world." Divisions and disagreements in the United States continued to be evident, as might be expected, but there was little intolerance or hysteria compared with 1917–1918, and except for the treatment of Japanese-Americans on the West Coast violations of civil liberties were relatively few.

The war resuscitated the American economy and brought a new era of prosperity in place of the devastating Depression of the previous decade. In spite of serious flaws in its mobilization schemes, the United States became, in the phrase of the day, an "arsenal of democracy." So great was its increase in plant capacity that production almost doubled between 1939 and 1945. By late 1943 an incredible flow of tanks, airplanes, ships, and guns was pouring out of American factories, and the national output was more than twice that of the combined Axis Powers. The economy was transformed in many ways: in the growing industrialization of the South and the Western regions, the massive internal movement of workers, the mounting strength of organized labor, the development of greater industrial concentration, and the increase in agricultural productivity despite a substantial decline in farm population during the war.

Governmental intervention during World War I and the period of the New Deal appeared limited when compared with the mobilization of manpower, industry, finance, and technology during the early 1940s. Although the American home front was not subjected to the thoroughgoing controls imposed by most of the major belligerent powers, the extent of the federal government's involvement in the economy was unparalleled in United States history. The war enhanced the power of the President and the federal bureaucracy, thereby accustoming people to Washington's expanded role. This development was associated with a revolutionary change in the national government's fiscal policy; wartime expenditures were so enormous that they amounted to twice as much as *all* federal appropriations before 1941! The heightened wartime influence of the national government centered on Franklin D. Roosevelt, in whose deft hands the responsibility for coordinating mobilization and production rested. Roosevelt's leadership symbolized the nation at war, and his influence and personality were indelibly stamped on the great transformation of American life during these hectic years.

Although the Roosevelt administration continued to win the support of a majority of the voters, the war weakened the influence of liberals and intensified the strength of conservatives. Power in the Democratic party shifted in the direction of more moderate and conservative elements.

Political alignments began to change, and new issues like inflation, foreign policy, and civil rights came to the fore.

No feature of the war years contrasted more sharply with the situation in the 1930s than the abandonment of isolationism in the United States. Unlike its involvement in World War I, America now became a full-fledged partner in the Allied struggle against Germany. The United States became a leader of the Grand Alliance and was intimately involved in formulating the great military and diplomatic decisions of the war. Under President Roosevelt's leadership, the nation appeared to be united on the wisdom of creating an international organization to settle disputes and preserve peace.

Wartime had other repercussions as well. The new prosperity and economic mobility began to reshape the fabric of social institutions. Cultural changes were accelerated. A vast redistribution of population took place during the war years, with millions of soldiers and civilian workers moving around the country, large numbers of Southern Negroes[1] migrating to the North and West, and many rural inhabitants going to cities and towns. Women assumed a much more important place in the industrial labor force.

Americans in 1945 seemed to be better prepared for the postwar period than they had been in the autumn of 1918. As Franklin D. Roosevelt remarked at a press conference in May 1944, "Today, we are a little older; we have gone through some pretty rough times together. And perhaps we are not saying that we can devise a method of ending all wars for all times." After the signing of the formal surrender documents on September 2, 1945, on the deck of the battleship *Missouri* in Tokyo Bay, General Douglas MacArthur spoke by radio to the American people, warning them of the "utter destructiveness" of war in the new atomic age and urging the need to devise "some greater and more equitable system." The General noted that "a new era is upon us." How the United States would adjust to the new era only the future would tell.

Demobilization and Reconversion

Although the anticipated blessings of peacetime did not come easily or quickly, many of the mistakes of the heedless demobilization process in 1918 and 1919 were avoided in the aftermath of World War II. For one thing, the War Production Board and other agencies began to plan for reconversion as early as 1943, and before the end of the war the President and Congress had approved an essential blueprint to guide the economy in the transition from wartime to peacetime. The widespread fears of a

---

[1]"Negroes" and "blacks" will be used interchangeably in this book, since both terms have been widely employed in the black community during the postwar years.

major postwar recession proved to be unfounded, and despite momentary uncertainty the nation experienced continuing and expanding prosperity. Industry adjusted quickly to civilian production, and by the end of 1945 its reconversion had largely been completed. Unemployment did not become a severe problem, and by August 1946 the number of men and women at work in the United States had reached the breathtaking figure of 60 million!

Even so, the strains of resuming normal peacetime arrangements were very great. The first order of business, dictated by an irresistible demand, was the demobilization of the armed forces. The process went forward so rapidly that some military and civilian leaders became alarmed at the prospect of a complete disbandment of the mighty force created to fight Germany and Japan. The pressure to "bring the boys back home" was inexorable, however, and by April 1946 almost 7 million men had been released from the armed forces. In one respect, at least, the government had given thought to the future needs of those who had served in the armed forces. The Servicemen's Readjustment Act—soon dubbed the G.I. Bill of Rights—had been enacted in June 1944, providing support for education and training; loans for homes, farms, and business-es; unemployment benefits; and veterans' hospitals. By 1947 more than 4 million young men and women were receiving benefits from this legisla-tion, and by 1950 the annual expenditures of the Veterans Administration had reached a peak of over $9 billion. Of all the reconversion plans, none received more popular approval or proved more beneficial in human and social terms.

Governmental planning in many other respects worked out less well. The structure of the mobilization machinery was rapidly dismantled after the war. Billions of dollars worth of war contracts were canceled immediately, many wartime agencies were soon abolished, and numerous controls were removed early in the postwar period. In October 1945 the War Production Board was replaced by the Civilian Production Adminis-tration. In January of the next year the War Assets Administration was established, and it proceeded to dispose of hundreds of government-owned war plants, often at bargain prices to corporations which had operated them during the war. The government also showed its concern for business in other ways; in November 1945, for example, Congress reduced taxes by almost $6 billion, thereby providing a further boost to the peacetime economic lift-off.

President Roosevelt's annual message to Congress in 1944 had included an "Economic Bill of Rights," in which Roosevelt looked ahead to the establishment in postwar America of "a new basis of security and prosperity." In the campaign of 1944 the Democrats had talked about full employment in peacetime as well as in war, and early in the Truman administration Congress began to consider a so-called maximum employment bill. The Employment Act was passed in 1946 and became a landmark in recent United States history. It provided for a three-member Council of Economic Advisers to study economic trends and to recommend to the President policies to alleviate downturns in the business cycle. It required the President to make an annual report on the economy, and it created a congressional joint committee on the economic report to recommend stabilization steps. While it did not guarantee government action against recessions, Section 2 of the act declared it to be "the continuing policy and responsibility of the Federal Government to use all practicable means . . . to promote maximum employment, production, and purchasing power."

The Struggle over Economic Controls, 1945–1946

Following V-J Day most Americans wanted a quick return to "normal" conditions, but they disagreed over what constituted normality and over the best means of bringing it about. The strong pressures for higher prices and increased wages, coupled with continuing shortages of many critical products, presaged a serious inflation unless effective governmental controls could be maintained during the reconversion period. The Truman administration hoped to provide such controls. But the task was fraught with complexities and difficulties. Organized interest groups were determined to throw off governmental restraints. Businessmen and farmers were eagerly buying new equipment and machinery. Consumers, with billions of dollars in wartime savings and plenty of credit, were in no mood to delay the purchase of long-sought durable goods. The Office of Price Administration (OPA), the heart of the postwar stabilization program, was widely disliked. According to Cabell Phillips, "It inspired a devious, illicit sort of gamesmanship not unlike that of the prohibition era, with black marketers taking the place of the bootleggers." There was also the "politics of inflation." The administration's honeymoon period ended with the war; the President was now expected both to remove wartime controls and to prevent inflation.

Industrialists, businessmen, and farm representatives pressed Congress to abolish all controls. Such action, they contended, would enable the "natural forces of the marketplace" to bring abundance and low prices within a few months. Businessmen argued that controls were delaying full production, encouraging the black market, and preventing producers from getting their rightful profits. Many trade association executives denounced the OPA as a "socialistic" bottleneck that was damaging production, employment, and the heart of the free enterprise system. The business community mounted a concerted campaign to destroy the agency.

Organized labor tended to favor price controls, but only if it could secure higher wages. Labor had acquired great strength and confidence during the war. At the same time, its leaders believed that workers had not shared equally with capital in the war prosperity. Concerned over the return to a forty-hour week and the loss of overtime pay after the war and apprehensive over the alternate possibilities of massive unemployment and drastic inflation, they fiercely insisted upon the protection of labor's interests in the postwar era.

Labor's restiveness quickly manifested itself. Half a million workers went out on strike within a few weeks of Japan's surrender, and the following autumn and winter witnessed widespread work stoppages when union demands for wage increases and other benefits were not met by management. A series of strikes in the steel, automobile, meat-packing, and electrical industries threatened to disrupt the entire economy. Although a Labor-Management Conference in late 1945 failed to reach agreement on reconversion wage policies, a recommendation by a Presidential fact-finding board eventually provided the basis for the settlement of the great industrial strikes in the winter of 1945–1946. In general, labor received a little over two-thirds of what it sought, while management was allowed substantial price increases in return. A new round of labor-management disputes began in the fall of 1946, with an agreement in April of the next year providing for an hourly wage increase of about 15 cents. A third encounter was settled in 1948. In these and subsequent confrontations, management showed a willingness to accede to labor's demands, but with the understanding that the added costs would be passed on to the consumer in the form of higher prices.

The general settlement of 1946 did not end the Truman administration's problems with organized labor. A national emergency was created when John L. Lewis of the United Mine Workers led 400,000 miners out of the coal pits on April 1, 1946. The strike continued until the government finally decided to take over the mines. Eventually a settlement gave the UMW most of what it wanted. Lewis made new demands the following October, and when negotiations failed, the labor leader called another strike. In December 1946, Lewis and his union were fined for contempt for disregarding a temporary restraining order. But when the mines were returned to their owners in July 1947, Lewis secured a new contract that provided virtually all he had sought.

Meanwhile, the troubled spring of 1946 had confronted the administration with still another labor controversy. When the railroad brotherhoods called a nationwide railroad strike in mid-May, the President seized the railroads under the provisions of the Smith-Connally Act and won a compromise settlement with most of the unions. But two of the brotherhoods—the Engineers and Trainmen—decided to strike anyway. "If you think I'm going to sit here and let you tie up this whole country," Truman exclaimed to the leaders of the two unions, "you're crazy as hell." When they went ahead with the strike, Truman made a dramatic appearance before Congress on May 25 to request authority to prevent the paralysis of transportation and to curb labor disputes in essential industries. The railroad unions gave in just before the Chief Executive spoke, and the crisis ended.

A large number of congressmen applauded President Truman's get-tough policy toward John L. Lewis and the railroad brotherhood leaders. Yet many of these same men were critical of Truman's economic controls in 1945 and 1946. As Senator Edward H. Moore of Oklahoma declared in June 1946, "A controlled economy leads to an authoritarian psychology which results in the oppression and destruction of individual rights and liberties under a gestapo system." Truman sought "continued stabilization of the national economy" through a policy of gradually relaxing the wartime regulation of prices, wages, and commodities in short supply. Unfortunately, there was considerable conflict within the administration over the implementation of this policy. Chester Bowles, the head of the OPA, wanted to follow a more stringent program of price ceilings than the more conservative John W. Snyder, the director of the Office of War Mobilization and Reconversion. The President leaned toward Snyder's position and allowed higher prices, a concession he described as a "bulge in the line." Bowles became discouraged and soon resigned. Nevertheless, the administration's anti-inflation record during the ten months following the war was fairly good; wholesale prices during that period rose only 7 percent.

The brunt of the Truman administration's battle against inflation in 1946 was carried by the OPA, whose statutory authority would expire on July 1, 1946. The administration urged that the agency be continued for another year, and a congressional struggle ensued during the spring of 1946 over the issue of extension. A price control bill was finally passed on June 27 providing for a one-year extension, but it gave the agency little power and ordered it to decontrol prices "as rapidly as possible." The President vetoed the measure, which he described as "a sure formula for inflation," and allowed price controls to end on July 1. Prices immediately zoomed, climbing 25 percent in a little over two weeks—an increase almost twice as great as that of the previous three years. Congress then passed a second bill on July 25, almost as weak as the first, authorizing a one-year extension of price and rent controls. The damage had been done by that time, however, and thereafter the administration could do little to halt the inflationary spiral. Soon after the November elections, the President ended all controls over wages and prices except on rents, sugar, and rice.

If the Democrats had won the 1946 elections, President Truman might have continued the fight against inflation. But the Republicans won a sweeping victory in 1946. During the campaign they had indicted the administration for inept and discriminatory price control policies, high prices, and continuing shortages. As they put it to the voters, "Had enough? Vote Republican." The Democrats were also vulnerable in other ways. Union labor was disaffected. Truman was unpopular with many members of his own party—conservatives because of his liberal domestic proposals and his economic policies, liberals because of certain of his appointments and his support in some instances of conservatives against liberals within his own administration. The President's popularity with the public was at a low ebb, for he presented a spectacle of executive incompetence. There was a rash of Truman jokes going around, including the quip that "to err is Truman." The Republicans won majorities in both houses of Congress and would control the legislative branch for the first time since 1930.

National Defense and a New Role in World Affairs

When the guns finally stopped firing in the summer of 1945, the United States had to deal with the issue of reducing the size of its armed forces. The country had the most powerful military force in the history of mankind. A vast army and navy had been created within a few short years, American military bases had been established all over the world, and in the postwar years American soldiers occupied parts of Germany, Austria, Japan, and other foreign countries. The question of how much to reduce the army and navy following the war was, to some extent, taken out of the hands of military and political leaders. The pressure for rapid demobilization was, as we have seen, an irresistible tide that quickly returned most men and women to civilian life. President Truman and the military representatives urged the maintenance of larger forces, but there was little support for such a policy in the early postwar period. Congress reluctantly agreed to continue Selective Service but refused to adopt the administration's plan for universal military training. Notwithstanding a couple of temporary increases, the size of the army had declined by the spring of 1950 to 600,000 men.

No aspect of national defense could now be considered without taking the atomic bomb into account, and the American monopoly of this awesome power made it imperative that policies be adopted for its control at home and abroad. The need for governmental control over the production and use of atomic energy was accepted by most political leaders, but sharp disagreement developed over the nature of such regulation when Congress debated the matter in the fall of 1945. Brien McMahon of Connecticut, the chairman of a special Senate committee investigating the problem, prepared a bill with the backing of the administration to establish an atomic energy commission with exclusive civilian control. Senator Arthur H. Vandenberg of Michigan, also a member of the special committee, and others insisted that military representatives be given a key role in the work of the commission. This position won the approval of the special committee. President Truman strongly opposed this approach, as did much of the public, and the issue was heatedly debated in the spring of 1946. A compromise was finally worked out that resulted in the Atomic Energy Act of August 1, 1946.

The law created a five-member Atomic Energy Commission, with civilian control but with provision for a military liaison committee to work with the Commission. Complete control over fissionable materials was vested in the government, and the act stipulated that the President alone would have responsibility for ordering the use of atomic weapons in warfare. Meanwhile, the administration was giving thought to the need for international control. Early in 1946 the United Nations Assembly established a UN Atomic Energy Commission, and soon afterward the so-called Acheson-Lilienthal plan was formulated under the aegis of the Truman administration.[2] In mid-June 1946, an American proposal based on this plan was submitted to the UN by Bernard M. Baruch. It constituted a comprehensive design for the international control and inspection of atomic energy. American spokesmen hoped that it would win quick approval in the United Nations.

The administration also made progress in solving another problem, the need to reorganize and unify the country's armed forces. The disaster at Pearl Harbor had revealed fundamental defects in military organization, and the war provided much more evidence of duplication, waste, and inefficiency resulting from overlapping and competing services. Many informed people urged the creation of a common command and a more streamlined organization. But a major reform of this character was not easy to effect; a bitter controversy swirled around the question for two years following the war's end. Representatives of the Navy were especially recalcitrant, since they feared that unification would diminish the role of seapower and eliminate the Marine Corps. President Truman worked actively to secure a workable arrangement, and the unification legislation was enacted in July 1947.

The National Security Act, as it was called, provided for a Secretary of Defense with Cabinet rank, under whom there would be Secretaries of the Army, Navy, and Air Force. The Joint Chiefs of Staff, representing the three services, would assist in coordinating the armed forces and be responsible for defense plans and matters of strategy. The act created a

[2]Under Secretary of State Dean G. Acheson and David E. Lilienthal, former Chairman of the Tennessee Valley Authority Board, were the principal authors of the American scheme.

Central Intelligence Agency to take charge of intelligence work at the highest level. It also established a National Security Council and a National Security Resources Board to advise the President and Congress on policies and plans. The great expectations for the reorganization of 1947 were not realized in practice; unification did not do away with interservice rivalry and bickering, despite the eventual mushrooming of power in the Pentagon.

In the meantime, the American posture toward other nations was also revealed in the organization and early operation of the United Nations. The United States was, from the very beginning of its involvement in World War II, the leading advocate of a new world organization. President Truman was as enthusiastic as his predecessor had been in supporting the creation of the peace organization. Congress was also strongly in favor of the idea, and the Senate's ratification of the UN Charter by a vote of 89 to 2 on July 28, 1945, made the United States the first nation to approve the plan. The American public welcomed the new organization, whose permanent headquarters were located in New York City.

While the UN was impressive in design, experience soon demonstrated that it could work only to the extent that its members voluntarily cooperated. Although empowered to use force against aggressor nations, the organization was unable to force compliance over the opposition of its strongest members. Permanent members of the Security Council had the right to veto all but procedural questions, and the Charter permitted "regional" agreements and agencies. The United States, despite its ardent efforts to create the new world organization, had insisted on both the veto and the legitimacy of regional defensive associations, and these two features of the UN Charter played an important part in the troubled international history of the postwar era.

In some respects, however, the United States followed a generous and cooperative policy in the early operation of the United Nations. Its financial support was indispensable in launching the UN's far-flung activities. American contributions channeled through the UN and other agencies were vitally important in bringing a measure of relief and rehabilitation to millions of starving and homeless people in war-ravaged Europe and Asia. Relief was also afforded in generous amounts through the aid of such private groups as the Red Cross. The United States, moreover, made funds available to needy nations through such agencies as the Export-Import Bank, and in 1946 the American government extended Britain a $3.75 billion loan. Meanwhile, the United States worked to ease restrictions on trade, to stabilize foreign currencies, and to stimulate American investments abroad.

While these relief and rehabilitation efforts were being made, the

United States was deeply involved in the formulation of peace treaties with the Axis Powers and in their political reconstruction. In the case of Germany, the United States occupied one of the four zones agreed upon by the Allies, proceeded with the task of destroying the German military potential, and joined in the victors' policy of "denazification." The Americans were also instrumental, between November 1945 and October 1946, in the trial at Nuremberg of a group of leading Nazi officials by an International Military Tribunal. Twelve of the Reich leaders were sentenced to death for war crimes and atrocities. The United States alone controlled the occupation and reconstruction of Japan. General MacArthur was appointed Supreme Commander for the Allied Powers (SCAP), and under his imperious control a thoroughgoing program was carried out to demilitarize Japan, to establish a system of social democracy there, and to reconstruct the country's economy. Twenty-eight top officials of wartime Japan were tried before an International Military Tribunal for the Far East, and seven of these men were executed.

Peacetime Pursuits

International problems and matters of statecraft did not much concern the majority of Americans during the immediate postwar months. They were too preoccupied with the exhilaration of coming home, throwing off wartime restraints, and settling down in familiar surroundings. As jobs were found and new business ventures undertaken, the fears of a crippling depression in the reconstruction period soon dissipated, and most people began to achieve an unaccustomed sense of security and to be aware of marvelous possibilities in the future. "Times have changed," one labor representative remarked early in the new era. "People have become accustomed to new conditions, new wage scales, new ways of being treated." In the prosperous transition from war to peace, Americans busied themselves with the myriad plans of an energetic people in a society that still seemed uniquely open and promising.

One evidence of postwar America's social buoyancy was the sharp increase in the birthrate. There was a trend toward earlier marriages, and the marriage rate (as well as the divorce rate) rose sharply. The growing number of new households and the large crop of new babies gave a strong impetus to the economy. But they also produced social problems. For example, the veterans' return, the growth of population, and the rapid movement of people to the cities and suburbs caused a severe housing shortage, a shortage that was not relieved for several years after 1945. The educational system also experienced a major crisis during this period. Wartime neglect, the shift of many teachers from the classroom to better paying jobs, and the crowded schools resulting from an expanding and migratory population confronted many educational districts with an impossible situation. Higher education was also entering a period of remarkable expansion, caused in part by the influx of veterans studying under the G.I. Bill of Rights. The nation's campuses had never witnessed anything like this G.I. invasion, but the veterans generally proved to be serious and hard-working students, who adjusted well to the requirements of academe.

There was considerable evidence in 1945 and 1946 that the United States had entered a new and radically different stage in its historical development. Just how different the new era was became more apparent in 1947, when the cold war became fixed as a dominant concern in the nation's policy and consciousness. It is to that extraordinary development that we must now turn.

SUGGESTIONS FOR FURTHER READING

Richard Polenberg, *War and Society: The United States, 1941–1945** (1972), offers a fresh and balanced analysis of the impact of World War II on the American government, politics, economy, and society. Less scholarly but useful are Geoffrey Perrett, *Days of Sadness, Years of Triumph: The American People, 1939–1945** (1973); Richard Lingeman, *Don't You Know There's a War On? The American Home Front, 1941–1945** (1970); and Francis E. Merrill, *Social Problems on the Home Front: A Study of War-Time Influences* (1948). James MacGregor Burns, *Roosevelt: The Soldier of Freedom** (1970), while emphasizing foreign policy and military affairs, is valuable for developments on the home front.

For inflation and economic issues in the postwar period, see Lester V. Chandler, *Inflation in the United States, 1940–1948* (1951), and George A. Steiner, *Government's Role in Economic Life* (1953). Stephen Kemp Bailey's *Congress Makes a Law: The Story behind the Employment Act of 1946** (1950) is a classic study of the techniques and processes involved in the enactment of Public Law 304. For the G.I. Bill and other veterans' benefits, see Davis R.B. Ross, *Preparing for Ulysses: Politics and Veterans during World War II* (1969). The movement to control atomic energy is described in Richard G. Hewlett and Oscar E. Anderson, Jr., *The New World: A History of the United States Atomic Energy Commission*, vol. I (1962).

Eric F. Goldman's *The Crucial Decade—and After: America, 1945–1960** (1960) contains some intriguing glimpses of the domestic scene after 1945. Broad perspectives are provided in John Brooks, *The Great Leap: The Past Twenty-five Years in America** (1966), a lively social history, and William E. Leuchtenburg, *A Troubled Feast: American Society since 1945** (1973), a perceptive interpretation of United States domestic history since World War II. *Congress and the Nation, 1945–1964: A Review of Government and Politics in the Postwar Years* (1965), by the Congressional Quarterly Service, is an invaluable reference work.

*Books marked with an asterisk are available in paperback editions.

Chapter 2

The Cold War and the Revolution in American Foreign Policy

After the war Americans settled down to enjoy the fruits of the Allied victory, confident that the major threats to international peace and stability had been destroyed. But to their dismay they soon discovered that the United States faced a new time of testing—a far-reaching conflict with the Soviet Union that seemed ready at any moment to precipitate a worldwide holocaust. This "cold war," as it was labeled, polarized many nations of the world into Communist and anti-Communist blocs, produced a generation of recurrent crises and confrontations, and profoundly influenced almost every consideration of foreign policy and national politics on the part of the principal protagonists. Most Americans thought that it was both possible and desirable for the United States to use its immense power to help reshape the world along the lines of their own democratic capitalism. And they eventually came to believe that drastic steps must be taken to counter Soviet moves, that vast amounts of aid were required by friendly allies, and that United States military power must be available around the globe.

America Faces Russia

The immediate origins of the momentous struggle that developed between the United States and the U.S.S.R. lay in the wartime relations between the Russians and the Americans and British, in the way the war changed the earlier balance of power in Europe and Asia, and in the fact that the United States and the Soviet Union had emerged as the two most powerful nations on earth. In July 1945 at the Potsdam Conference, the last wartime meeting of the Big Three heads of state, the fundamental differences between the U.S.S.R. and the Western Allies became clear. Agreements were finally reached on the questions of reparations and the occupation of Germany, and the Russians reluctantly conceded permission for British and American observers to move about freely in occupied countries in Eastern Europe. But these agreements were not self-enforcing, and even at Potsdam they scarcely concealed the deep cleavage that now divided the former allies. At the Potsdam Conference the West accepted Polish occupation of German territory as far as the Oder-Neisse line and approved the Russian annexation of eastern Poland. President Truman and his advisers were unhappy about the Soviet spheres of influence in Eastern Europe, but they had no real alternative in view of the fact that the Red Army already occupied most of these areas. They could only hope that Stalin would live up to his earlier commitments to permit free elections and minority rights in the East European nations.

Figure 1   The Big Three at Potsdam *(U.S. Army Photograph, Courtesy Harry S. Truman Library)*

At Potsdam a Council of Foreign Ministers was approved to draft definitive peace treaties with Italy and the former Axis satellites. The Council held numerous conferences and struggled between September 1945 and the end of 1946 to overcome the chronic disagreements and hostility between East and West. Treaties with Italy, Finland, Hungary, Rumania, and Bulgaria were finally concluded. The Italian settlement was favorable to the Western Allies, but in the other treaties the Western Powers acquiesced in Soviet control of Hungary and the Balkans. No agreement could be reached in the case of Austria, part of which was being occupied and exploited by Russia. A Russian regime was also imposed on Albania, Marshal Josip Tito's Communists controlled Yugoslavia, and a Communist movement shared power in Czechoslovakia.

The United States gradually adopted a firmer posture in its dealings with Russia. In October 1945, President Truman delivered what some officials described as a "getting tough with the Russians" speech. American policy, he declared, was "based firmly on fundamental principles of righteousness and justice." The United States would "refuse to recognize any government imposed on any nation by the force of any foreign power." In early January 1946, an exasperated Truman told Secretary of State James F. Byrnes: "Unless Russia is faced with an iron fist and strong language another war is in the making. Only one language do they understand—'how many divisions have you?' . . . I'm tired of babying the Soviets." In March 1946 came Winston Churchill's famous speech at Westminster College in Fulton, Missouri, an appearance Truman helped arrange. The former Prime Minister warned his audience that an "Iron Curtain" had descended across Europe "from Stettin in the Baltic to Trieste in the Adriatic," and he asserted his conviction that there was nothing for which the Russians had "less respect than for weakness, especially military weakness."

A series of incidents in 1946 heightened the increasing tension between Russia and the West. While doubtless fortuitous in their timing, several of these developments appeared almost as a direct response to Truman's stiffening position and Churchill's Iron Curtain warning. The Russians created a crisis over Iran by refusing to withdraw their troops from that country in accordance with a previous agreement. They made demands on Turkey for naval bases and a "joint defense" of that country. They refused to become a member of the World Bank and the International Monetary Fund, agencies that were strongly supported by American economic strength. They launched a new five-year plan and made a significant change in their economic policy toward East Germany. And they timed their evacuation of Manchuria in such a way as to leave valuable materiel to benefit the Chinese Communists in their struggle with Chiang Kai-shek's Nationalist forces. The Soviet reaction to the plan for international control of nuclear energy which the United States presented to the United Nations in June 1946 was incomprehensible to Americans. The Russians refused to accept the provisions calling for international management and supervision, while vociferously demanding that the United States show its good faith by unilaterally destroying its atomic weapons. Meanwhile, as the world soon learned, the U.S.S.R. was rapidly completing the development of its own atomic bomb.

The major bone of contention between the Soviet Union and the West, however, was the "German question." The Russians were fearful of a reunited Germany which they could not control; the West was afraid of a Soviet-dominated Germany that would destroy the possibility of a balance of power in postwar Europe. Russia's obstructionist tactics soon produced friction within the four-power Allied Control Council, and with help from France, still uneasy about German power, the Soviet Union blocked all efforts to unite Germany economically and politically. The Russians also stripped the eastern zone of industrial equipment and exploited its economy, while claiming a share of the industrial plant in the other three zones. In May 1946 the Western Powers ended German reparations to the Soviet Union, and in the autumn of that year the United States gave up the attempt to secure a united Germany. Within a short time, the U.S.S.R. and the Western Allies were involved in a propagandist and ideological contest to win the support of the Germans—the dreaded enemy only two years before!

Neither side fully understood the objectives of the other, and neither appreciated the source of the other's suspicions and fears. American leaders were genuinely alarmed by the Soviet Union's expansion into regions of Eastern and Central Europe formerly dominated by Germany. Deprecating power politics and highly moralistic in their approach to international questions, they expected the Russians to live up to the Yalta Conference's "Declaration of Liberated Europe," which affirmed the principles enunciated in the Atlantic Charter and pledged its signatories to self-government through free and open elections. Americans may have been concerned about the Russian threat to foreign investments and open markets in Europe, but they were also committed to traditional United States values of self-determination, democracy, and humanitarianism. Nor should we minimize the weight of their distrust of the communist ideology.

The situation that existed two years after the close of World War II was startlingly new to Americans. As Dean Acheson expressed it in June 1946, "We have got to understand that all our lives the danger, the uncertainty, the need for alertness, for effort, for discipline will be upon us. This is new for us. It will be hard for us." It proved to be a remarkably accurate forecast.

The Architects of Containment

The containment doctrine that President Truman urged Congress to approve in the spring of 1947 was the product of no single leader, group, or party, though it rightly came to be identified most closely with Truman and his administration. The consensus that quickly formed in support of containment may tempt one to assume that, given the Russian position in postwar Europe, such a policy was inevitable, almost foreordained. The question arises as to whether containment would have become a national policy had Franklin D. Roosevelt lived to serve out his fourth term. It is impossible to know. Perhaps Roosevelt's supreme confidence and great flexibility would have made possible a broad settlement with the masters of the Kremlin. Roosevelt's view of the world was more Wilsonian than Churchillian, and he believed that the interests of the great powers in the postwar era could be reconciled. Yet when Roosevelt died, he was moving toward a position of insisting that the Russians honor their agreements. One suspects that the cold war would have come even had FDR lived on in the White House. He would have asserted America's new role in world affairs, and it is likely that he would have sought to uphold the principle of the open door; to oppose spheres of influence and balance-of-power politics; to insist upon the traditional American ideals of justice, self-government, and international cooperation.

Harry S. Truman continued Roosevelt's policy of cooperation with the wartime allies and his efforts to work out an accommodation with the Soviet Union. He lent wholehearted support to the organization of the United Nations; sent Harry L. Hopkins, Roosevelt's most trusted adviser, on a special mission to talk with Marshal Stalin in May 1945; and helped arrange the conference of the Big Three at Potsdam during the following summer. But he came to the presidency with an abiding distrust of communist ideology, and when suddenly faced with awesome responsibilities for which he had virtually no preparation, he was naturally less patient, flexible, and confident than his illustrious predecessor. Although his transition from wary friend to implacable foe of the Russians was gradual, he became increasingly steadfast in his relations with Moscow in 1946. In September of that year he dismissed Secretary of Commerce Henry A. Wallace when Wallace openly criticized the administration's policy toward Russia. Truman was influenced, like many other American leaders, by the assumption that the Soviet Union's great need for economic assistance in the postwar period would make Stalin more amenable to United States demands. His "get-tough" posture was also bolstered by the immeasurable weight of the American monopoly of the atomic bomb in all calculations involving the national interest and perhaps by his frustrating setbacks on domestic issues in 1946 and 1947.

The principal spokesman for the Truman administration's foreign

policy during the crucial eighteen months between the Potsdam Conference and the end of 1946 was James F. Byrnes, who succeeded Edward R.
Stettinius, Jr., as Secretary of State in June 1945. Although the genial,
quick-witted, and debonair Byrnes, a South Carolinian, was never overly
sanguine about the prospects of reconciling differences between Washington and Moscow, he intended through compromise to maintain the
Grand Alliance and to achieve a stable world order after the war. But like
the President, he gradually adopted a harsher line in dealing with the
Russian leaders, a toughness, Richard D. Burns observes, "anchored, not
to military and economic strength, but to a moral rhetoric which created
the illusion of ultimate success."

Byrnes was succeeded in January 1947 by George C. Marshall, a
distinguished military officer who had served as Army Chief of Staff
during the war. While Marshall shared the fundamental assumptions of
President Truman and Secretary Byrnes about the nature of the East-
West split, he was not one of the major architects of containment. Rather,
his role was that of presiding over the process of transforming the
doctrine into a national policy. A more important contribution was made
by Under Secretary of State Dean G. Acheson. A diplomatic "realist,"
Acheson did not accept Wilsonism as an adequate foundation for
American foreign policy or the achievement of stability in the world; nor
did he agree that the purpose of United States policy abroad was "to carry
out a 'crusade' or 'mission' to bring about equal justice or to vindicate
international law." The great task in the conduct of American foreign
policy, he believed, was to apply morality *and* power in handling
international relations. As for the Soviet Union, Acheson had long been
distrustful of its policies, which he termed "aggressive and expanding."

No member of Congress contributed more to the creation of an
American consensus on the doctrine of containment than Senator Arthur
H. Vandenberg of Michigan, Chairman of the Senate Foreign Relations
Committee in the Eightieth Congress (1947–1948). A Republican and a
staunch isolationist before Pearl Harbor, Vandenberg experienced a
dramatic change of heart during World War II, becoming a strong
supporter of a world peace organization and his party's leading advocate
of an internationalist foreign policy. Vandenberg more than any other
Republican leader prepared the way for the bipartisan foreign policy that
flourished during the early years of the Truman administration. The
Michigan Senator was in complete agreement with the get-tough policy
that Truman and Byrnes gradually adopted in dealing with the Russians in
1945 and 1946. And he played a key role in congressional approval of the
containment program in 1947. Vandenberg, as well as such internationalist Republicans as Thomas E. Dewey and John Foster Dulles, sometimes
differed with Truman over tactics, but he was no less critical of the Soviet

Union and no less insistent that American strength be exerted to counter Russian expansionism.

The American who provided the ideological base for the containment doctrine was George F. Kennan, a Foreign Service officer who was serving in Moscow when the war ended. Kennan, who believed in the diplomacy of "reality," had become convinced of the Soviet Union's deep-seated expansionist aims. In a long cable to the State Department in February 1946, the diplomat outlined the strategy that later became official national policy. In explaining Soviet behavior, he expressed the increasingly strong feeling among American leaders that it was futile to seek further agreements with the Russians. The Soviet leaders, Kennan warned, had a "neurotic view of world affairs. And they have learned to seek security only in patient but deadly struggle for total destruction of rival power, never in compacts and compromises with it." Yet Soviet power was "neither schematic nor adventuristic," Kennan contended. "It does not take unnecessary risks. For this reason it can easily withdraw—and usually does—when strong resistance is encountered at any point." The main element of any United States policy toward the Soviet Union, Kennan later wrote in a famous article published in *Foreign Affairs,* "must be that of a long-term, patient, but firm and vigilant containment of Russian expansive tendencies." This would increase "the strains under which Soviet policy must operate," force the Kremlin to show more "moderation and circumspection," and promote tendencies which "must eventually find their outlet in either the break-up or the gradual mellowing of Soviet power."

Kennan's cogent and eloquent language expressed the views and predispositions that had come to prevail among American leaders by early 1947. The formulation of specific policies to implement the containment doctrine awaited only the formal decision of the Truman administration. And the precipitant of such a decision would almost certainly be another in the recurring crises in East-West relations.

The Truman Doctrine and the Marshall Plan

The crisis came in the eastern Mediterranean early in 1947. Russian pressure on Iran continued, despite the withdrawal of Soviet troops from that country in the spring of 1946. Nor had the Russian leaders given up their demands on Turkey for territorial cessions and naval bases in the Bosporus. Although the U.S.S.R. was not active in Greece, the Greek royalist regime was encountering mounting pressure from Communist-dominated rebels in the northern part of the country. In late February 1947, the British quietly informed Washington that they could no longer bear the burden of supporting the Greek government; British troops would soon be withdrawn, thus ending that nation's historic role as a great power in the eastern Mediterranean. Greece and Turkey turned for financial and military assistance to the United States, which was keenly aware of the vital importance of the region in the East-West conflict. "If Greece was lost," Truman later wrote in his *Memoirs,* "Turkey would become an untenable outpost in a sea of Communism. Similarly, if Turkey yielded to Soviet demands, the position of Greece would be extremely endangered."

President Truman and Secretary Marshall were determined to prevent the Russians from taking advantage of the British withdrawal to move into the eastern Mediterranean. After being informed of the British decision to withdraw from Greece, Truman conferred with congressional leaders of both parties, obtaining their backing of his plan of action. Senator Vandenberg was later quoted as saying at that conference, "Mr. President, if that's what you want, there's only one way to get it. That is to make a personal appearance before Congress and scare hell out of the country." Truman took Vandenberg's advice, and in an appearance before a joint session of Congress on March 12, 1947, he requested approval of a $400 million program of military and economic assistance to Greece and Turkey.

The President proclaimed what came to be called the Truman Doctrine. He described in grim words and dark colors the way in which "totalitarian regimes" were threatening to snuff out freedom in various parts of the world. The United States, Truman declared, must "support free peoples who are resisting attempted subjugation by armed minorities or by outside pressures." If Americans faltered in their leadership, Truman warned, "we may endanger the peace of the world—and we shall surely endanger the welfare of our own nation." Congress approved the administration's request, and the Greek-Turkish Aid bill became a law in May 1947.

The Truman Doctrine worked. The United States spent over $650 million in aid to Greece and Turkey between 1947 and 1950, and the eastern Mediterranean remained within the Western sphere. Turkey was able to strengthen its economy and modernize its armed forces. The Greek problem was more difficult, but the government there succeeded in reorganizing the army and accelerating its campaign against the Communist insurgents. After Yugoslavia broke with the Soviet Union in 1948, the Greek guerrillas were deprived of a major source of support, and the civil war was finally ended in the fall of 1949.

The Truman Doctrine cleared the way for a gigantic American aid program abroad. The former was essentially a military program, and its application was intended to be specific and limited. But it was a natural first step in the evolution of a much more comprehensive and imaginative

Figure 2 The Cold War *(From A History of the American People by Norman A. Graebner, Gilbert C. Fite, and Philip L. White. Copyright © 1970 by McGraw-Hill, Inc.)*

enterprise to strengthen European nations against the challenge of Communist domination. This broader and more audacious undertaking emerged not only from the Kremlin's growing recalcitrance, the bitter conflict between the Western Allies and Russia over the future of Germany, and the precedent for bold American action provided by the

Truman Doctrine, but also from the terrible internal conditions that existed in the countries of Western Europe in 1946 and 1947. Although the United States had already committed $11 billion in postwar relief, grants, loans, and other kinds of aid to these countries, they were still suffering from the paralyzing effects of the war, their economies appeared on the verge of collapse, and they were experiencing severe food and fuel shortages. Their leaders were also haunted by the specter of social upheaval. Europe, declared Churchill, had become "a rubble heap, a charnel house, a breeding ground of pestilence and hate."

Soon after Secretary Marshall returned from Moscow, where a Council of Foreign Ministers meeting on Germany ended in failure in late April 1947, the Truman administration began to develop a program to provide further aid to Western Europe and at the same time to resist Russian expansionism. Much of the work on this European aid program was done by the Policy Planning Staff in the State Department, a special committee recently created by Marshall and headed by George F. Kennan. This group worked at a furious pace in May. It recommended that short-term assistance be provided to arrest the deterioration of the European economy and that a long-range program be launched to encourage the economic integration of Western and Central Europe. Kennan and his colleagues had devised a bold plan to contain communism by eradicating the poverty and misery that provided much of its sustenance.

The essentials of what was soon labeled the Marshall Plan were set forth in Secretary Marshall's famous commencement address at Harvard University on June 5, 1947. The Secretary proposed a gigantic reconstruction of the European economy, to be financed largely by the United States but to be worked out as a joint plan between the United States and the European nations. Marshall spoke less in tones of anticommunism than of humanitarianism. But there was no mistaking the diplomatic and ideological objectives of the scheme. "Our policy is directed not against any country or doctrine but against hunger, poverty, desperation and chaos," Marshall declared. "Its purpose should be the revival of a working economy in the world so as to permit the emergence of political and social conditions in which free institutions can exist."

The response of Western Europe was immediate. Great Britain and France took the lead in convening a European conference in Paris in July 1947. The Soviet leaders hesitated briefly and then decided to boycott the Paris meeting; they were joined in doing so by their satellite nations and by Finland and Czechoslovakia, where Russian influence was great. But the representatives of sixteen nations met in Paris and prepared an elaborate plan for European recovery, estimated to cost $22 billion over a period of four years. In December 1947, President Truman submitted this plan to Congress, with his own recommendation for an appropriation of $17 billion over a four-year period.

The novelty of the request and the enormous amount of money it called for shocked many Americans and provoked sharp criticism in Congress. The strongest congressional opposition came from Senator Robert A. Taft of Ohio and his supporters, whose ranks included some of the nation's traditional isolationists. Men of the Taft persuasion feared that the Marshall Plan would wreck the American economy and lead to a third world war. It was a huge "international WPA," one critic asserted. The support for the proposal was impressively large, however. Liberals of both parties backed it. A powerful array of business, farm, and labor organizations endorsed the plan, recognizing the beneficial effects it would have on the national economy. Vandenberg led the bipartisan supporters of the administration measure, calling it a "calculated risk" to "help stop World War III before it starts." Events in Europe also contributed to congressional approval, particularly the Communist coup in Czechoslovakia, a nation to which Americans had a strong sentimental attachment.

Congress approved the aid program in March, and it was signed by the President on April 3, 1948. Under Vandenberg's leadership the four-year commitment sought by the administration was eliminated and the first installment was reduced somewhat, from $6.8 billion to $5.3 billion. But no one could doubt that the Truman administration had won a great victory and that its foreign policy had been given an overwhelming vote of confidence. The law established a European Recovery Program (ERP) to be carried out by the Economic Cooperation Administration (ECA), which in turn was supposed to work with the Committee of European Economic Cooperation (CEEC). By the end of 1952 the United States had spent about $13 billion on this program. The results were strongly encouraging. Industrial production in the Marshall Plan countries had increased by 64 percent within three years. An impetus was given to the economic integration and unification of Western Europe—to such eventual developments as the European Steel and Coal Community and the Common Market. West Europeans had regained their confidence, and the Communist threats in France and Italy were substantially lessened.

The Truman Doctrine and the Marshall Plan constituted a revolutionary shift in American foreign policy. For the first time in a period of peace, the United States, by these policies, committed its military and economic strength to the defense of nations outside the Western Hemisphere. The United States had involved itself directly in the internal affairs of countries like Greece, and a host of American experts and advisers were soon swarming over Europe to help implement a vast program of reconstruction. Even more significant, perhaps, was the primary justification for these drastic new policies. Their purpose, it was endlessly proclaimed, was to prevent the expansion of the Soviet Union and to halt the spread of international communism.

Forging New Coalitions

The Marshall Plan exacerbated the differences between the United States and the Soviet Union and, in combination with the worsening controversy over Germany, provoked the Russians into drastic action and created still another crisis in East-West relations. The Kremlin denounced the European Recovery Program as an example of American imperialism and an effort to establish continental bases for aggression against the U.S.S.R. The Soviet leaders had not been idle in the face of American and Western European activities in 1946 and 1947. They had formed their own coalition by bringing their satellite nations together in the Warsaw Alliance of September 1947. They had set up a new Cominform (Communist Information Bureau) to ensure unity throughout Eastern Europe. In February 1948 Communist workers in Czechoslovakia had carried out a successful coup and forced that country into the Russian orbit. Nevertheless, the Russians were profoundly disturbed by the Marshall Plan and the unity it inspired in Western Europe. Moscow had also suffered a setback when Yugoslavia, its strongest satellite, had refused to follow the Soviet line and succeeded in striking out on an independent course. Then there was the acute problem of Germany, where the Western Powers were moving rapidly to effect an economic and political consolidation of their zones.

Early in June 1948, the three Western Allies announced the consolidation of their zones. The resulting "Trizonia" constituted a rich industrial area with a population of 50 million people, in contrast to the 17 million residents of the Soviet zone. The consolidated western region was brought into the recovery machinery of the Marshall Plan, and a drastic reform of the West German currency was carried out. The Russians resisted these efforts to unify western Germany, and in the early spring of 1948 they began to obstruct the traffic between the western zones and Berlin, located a hundred miles inside the eastern zone. There were violent scenes in the four-power Control Council for Berlin. When the Western Powers extended their currency reform to their sectors of Berlin on June 23, Soviet leaders responded by stopping all surface traffic between the western zones and the capital city. They cited the fact that the Western Allies had never secured a written agreement guaranteeing land access to Berlin. Although the Russians maintained that they were blockading the city because of the new currency reform, it was obvious that they were trying to force the Western Powers to abandon their plans for a united West Germany, or, failing in that, to bring about their withdrawal from Berlin and thus achieve a great symbolic victory in the cold war.

American leaders refused to give ground. General Lucius D. Clay, Deputy Military Governor of the American zone, wanted to use an armed convoy to break the blockade. "When Berlin falls, western Germany will be next," the General warned. President Truman was equally adamant, declaring, "We [are] going to stay period." But Truman did not resort to the provocative action recommended by General Clay and some other advisers. He imposed a counterblockade against the Russians in Germany, and with the British supported the non-Communist majorities on the Berlin City Council, forcing the Soviet representatives to set up a separate administration for their sector of the city. But most important of all, he decided to prevent the starvation of the West Berliners by using air transport to supply their needs. This continuous airlift, operated by the U.S. Air Force and the British Royal Air Force, was maintained for 324 days, with 277,264 flights in all and a total cargo of 2.5 million tons of food, coal, and other supplies. The airlift was a spectacular success; it saved West Berlin and lifted the morale of its people. Early in the blockade, the Truman administration did resort to a little saber rattling: the President ordered two groups of B-29 bombers—planes designed to carry atomic bombs—sent to England.

In the end, Western resistance and the success of the airlift caused the Russians to give in. They agreed to lift the blockade if the Western Powers would reopen the whole German question and discuss the Austrian peace treaty at a new meeting of the Council of Foreign Ministers. After more than ten months, the blockade was ended on May 12, 1949, on the same day the foreign ministers met in Paris. The Paris conference made no real progress on the German problem, but it provided the Soviet Union with a diplomatic pretext for abandoning the Berlin blockade. In the meantime, the United States and its West European allies were completing the formation of a West German state, the German Federal Republic. The Russians also acted. In October 1949 they created the German Democratic Republic, with its capital in East Berlin. Thus, instead of a single reunited Germany, there were now two German nations.

While these developments were taking place, Western Europe and the United States had formulated and adopted an extensive military alliance that was designed to counter Soviet expansionism. The Truman Doctrine and the Marshall Plan had pointed the way. But the Western European nations had also done their part. France and Belgium had signed a mutual defense agreement in March 1947. Great Britain had indicated a willingness, in January 1948, to join in a Western European union. And in Brussels on March 17, 1948, Britain, France, and the Benelux countries had entered into a fifty-year treaty of economic cooperation and military alliance. Early the following year the Council of Europe was established. The Council, which included the German

Federal Republic, had broader representation than the Brussels Pact. These agreements stimulated the interest of American leaders in a still broader military alliance, for despite this evidence of West European unity, they were dubious about the effectiveness of military strength in Western Europe. At the time of the Brussels agreement, there were only about a dozen inadequately equipped and poorly trained divisions in the whole region. A significant indication of American interest and intent came from Washington in June 1948, when Arthur H. Vandenberg introduced a resolution in the Senate to encourage "the progressive development of regional and other collective arrangements" for defense and to promote the "association of the United States" with such organizations. The Senate swiftly approved the Vandenberg resolution, by a vote of 64 to 4.

The Truman administration, which was already searching for means to this end, took advantage of the Vandenberg resolution to begin discussions the following month with the Western European Powers. A conference of most of the Marshall Plan countries met in Washington early in 1949 and drafted the North Atlantic Treaty Organization (NATO). It was formally adopted on April 4, 1949, by the United States, Canada, and ten West European countries. Greece and Turkey joined NATO in 1952, and three years later West Germany became a member. The treaty constituted a twenty-year military pact. Each member pledged itself to lend military support, which was to be jointly organized and supervised by a North Atlantic Council, a Secretary-General, and a Military Committee. The members also agreed that

> an armed attack against one or more of them in Europe or North America shall be considered an attack against all of them and that in the exercise of the right of individual or collective self-defense, recognized by Article 51 of the United Nations Charter, they will take action as deemed necessary, including the use of armed force, to restore and maintain the security of the North Atlantic area.

The United States Senate confirmed the treaty on July 21, 1949, by an overwhelming majority of 82 to 13. In late September, while Congress was still considering the initial appropriation for NATO, President Truman informed the public that the Soviet Union a few weeks earlier had exploded an atomic device. Within six days Congress voted a billion dollars for NATO arms and equipment under the Mutual Defense Assistance Act, with an additional $211 million for Greece and Turkey.

The effort to construct a formidable military force under the North Atlantic Treaty Organization began in earnest in 1950. Late that year General Dwight D. Eisenhower was appointed Supreme Commander, and soon afterward the Supreme Headquarters of the Allied Powers in Europe (SHAPE) were established near Paris. President Truman had also directed that the development of a more powerful nuclear weapon, the hydrogen bomb, be accelerated. American military authorities, acting within the framework of the administration's policy, were determined to build a large conventional European army, an army that would include German military units. The United States frontier now stretched across Central Europe. As Secretary Acheson put it, the United States had learned "that the control of Europe by a single aggressive unfriendly power would constitute an intolerable threat to the national security of the United States."

While American leaders concentrated on European reconstruction and the containment of Russian communism on that continent, they tried to devise policies and machinery in other parts of the world that would strengthen the nation's position in the cold war. The United States was eager to present a united front in the Western Hemisphere toward the Soviet Union and the challenge of international communism. Canada, whose relations with the United States had grown closer during World War II, became an ally in NATO. Latin America was less predictable, although the Good Neighbor Policy of the 1930s had resulted in some relaxation of tension between the United States and the twenty nations to the south, and all of the Latin American countries except Argentina had cooperated to some extent in waging war against the Axis Powers.

The United States took the first step in the direction of postwar unity in Latin America by arranging a special conference in Mexico City in February 1945. The result was the Act of Chapultepec, which was eventually signed by all Latin American states; it stipulated that any attack upon one American state would be met by the combined forces of all of them. In June 1947, after the Truman Doctrine had been announced, President Truman indicated that the United States was seeking a mutual defense agreement that would guarantee concerted hemispheric action. In the late summer, delegates from twenty-one American republics met at Rio de Janeiro to consider enforcement machinery for the Act of Chapultepec. On September 2, 1947, they adopted the Inter-American Treaty of Reciprocal Assistance. This agreement established a broad security zone around the North and South American continents, declared that an attack anywhere in this zone would constitute an attack against all American states, and provided for collective self-defense for the Western Hemisphere, as a regional association permitted under Articles 51 and 52 of the United Nations Charter. In the spring of 1948, at the Ninth Inter-American Conference at Bogotá, a charter for an Organization of American States was drafted, giving full constitutional status to the inter-American system. As David Green has written, "All non-American military and political power had been successfully excluded from the hemisphere."

In spite of this evidence of hemispheric unity, Latin America was a bubbling caldron of social misery and potential upheaval. Economic colonialism flourished, the gap between rich and poor continued to widen, the army assumed an even larger role in politics, and few countries were able to maintain political stability for any length of time. Many Latin Americans remained suspicious of the United States, which was clearly giving priority to European recovery over Latin American development. Truman's Point Four program, announced in his inaugural address in January 1949, promised United States technical aid "to supply the vitalizing force to stir the peoples of the world into triumphant action, not only against their human oppressors, but also against their ancient enemies—hunger, misery and despair." This new program to make the benefits of American scientific and industrial progress available for the improvement of underdeveloped areas was aimed primarily at Latin America. But one of its goals was the stimulation of private investment in the region, and ironically, it had the effect of helping to perpetuate the colonial and extractive character of the Latin American economy.

During the early months of 1950, the National Security Council, in response to an order from the President, carried out "an over-all review and re-assessment of American foreign and defense policy." The resulting study—NSC 68—was a comprehensive statement of the nation's defense strategy. After reviewing the various policy alternatives in the cold war, the authors of NSC 68 concluded that the only logical course open to the United States was the development of free-world military capabilities. They advocated an immediate and large-scale buildup in the military and economic strength of the United States and its allies in order to meet "each fresh challenge promptly and unequivocally." NSC 68, Stephen E. Ambrose writes, "represented the practical extension of the Truman Doctrine, which had been worldwide in its implications but limited to Europe in its application. The document provided the justification for America's assuming the role of world policeman."

The Cold War Consensus

As the rift between the Western Powers and the Soviet Union widened during the first eighteen months after V-J Day, American opinion seemed to be divided into three fairly distinct positions. At one extreme was the view that the breakup of the Grand Alliance and the intransigence of the Russians required a resort, by the United States and its European allies, to balance of power politics to protect Western interests. At the other extreme stood those who believed that British and American aggressiveness was provoking Soviet hostility and that the United States had no business interfering with Russian control in Eastern Europe. The United

States government and the largest part of the public, representing a third position, seemed to waver between the two extremes. Yet by early 1947 a large number of Americans, probably a majority of the population, had come to approve a get-tough policy toward the U.S.S.R.

Nevertheless, a national consensus on the containment of the Soviet Union did not emerge overnight, and several obstacles had to be overcome before such a consensus was created. At the end of the war most Americans were unprepared for the demands of the new international age—for the responsibilities of world leadership, the complexities of European politics, the enormous costs of national defense and foreign aid that containment entailed, the imposition of internal security controls, and the powerful effect that foreign policy came to have on almost every domestic consideration. The idealism associated with the vision of "one world" and the strong faith in the United Nations challenged the assumptions that supported the containment program. There was also some reluctance in the United States to support reactionary governments like that of Greece in the name of democracy and morality.

The most spectacular dissent from the Truman administration's hardening opposition to the Russians was led by Henry A. Wallace, who was dismissed from the Cabinet after calling for a softer line toward the Soviet Union. Wallace and his supporters saw no reason why the wartime collaboration with the Russians could not continue. They discounted the charges of Soviet aggression and contended that the U.S.S.R. would cooperate with the Western Powers if the West recognized the Russian sphere in Eastern Europe and otherwise showed that it had no intention of "encircling" the Soviet Union. Wallace lost much of his support when he attacked the Marshall Plan, and as a Progressive party nominee for President in 1948 he was tellingly assaulted by Democratic spokesmen, including the Americans for Democratic Action, for opposing the containment policies and allegedly making common cause with Communist groups in this country. Meanwhile, however, there had been some conservative opposition to the Truman policies. At the beginning of 1947, just before the Truman Doctrine was made public, East-West tensions seemed to ease somewhat following the completion of the Big Three peace treaties with Nazi Germany's former puppet states, Bulgaria, Hungary, and Rumania. The Republicans, led by such economy-in-government advocates as Robert A. Taft, controlled Congress. They were suspicious not only of costly foreign aid programs but also of aggressive foreign policies in general that were sponsored by the administration.

Thus a series of events, plus the deep division over foreign policy in the Republican party, played a vital role in undermining potentially powerful opposition to the containment doctrine. These developments included the Russian pressure on Iran and Turkey in 1946, the Soviet Union's chronic obstructionism in the UN's Security Council, the crisis atmosphere surrounding the eastern Mediterranean in early 1947, the Communist coup in Czechoslovakia in 1948, the Berlin blockade of 1948–1949, the fall of Nationalist China in 1949, the Russian explosion of an atomic bomb in 1949, and the mounting fear of a Communist conspiracy in the United States. These events provided the Truman administration with several dramatic issues, cleared the way for the announcement of the containment policy, and contributed mightily to the emergence of a cold war consensus. Truman's startling electoral victory in 1948 also strengthened the emerging American consensus on foreign policy. The administration, frustrated in its domestic policies, made skillful use of foreign policy to increase its support during the campaign, and such alarming developments as the Czech coup and the Berlin blockade enhanced its credibility.

The national consensus that emerged by 1949 was one of the most remarkable aspects—and manifestations—of the revolution in American foreign policy in the 1940s. Even so, there were limits to this consensus. It did not extend to China and the Far East. Also, the bipartisanship of the late 1940s began to break down by 1950, as Republicans mounted an attack on the Democratic administration for being "soft on communism" at home and abroad. In 1950, for example, Senator Taft and former President Herbert Hoover strongly indicted the Truman administration for its plans to use American ground troops in Europe, for its neglect of the Western Hemisphere, and for the heavy financial burden of its foreign programs. Other critics, including George F. Kennan and Walter Lippmann, were deploring what they regarded as the excessive moralism and legalism of United States policy makers.

Despite such criticisms, the broad agreement on the policies adopted to contain the expansion of Russian communism continued after the end of Democratic control in 1952. The consensus did not break down until the bitter divisions over the war in Vietnam brought a reassessment of American policy in the late 1960s. In the long interim the radical transformation that had occurred in American attitudes and policies soon after the war determined the nation's role in international affairs.

SUGGESTIONS FOR FURTHER READING

The best general works on the American side of the cold war are John W. Spanier, *American Foreign Policy since World War II* * (4th ed., 1971); Walter LaFeber, *America, Russia, and the Cold War, 1945–1971* * (2d ed., 1972); and Stephen E. Ambrose, *Rise to Globalism: American Foreign Policy since 1938* * (1971). The first book (Spanier) is generally favorable in its evaluation of containment; the

*Available in paperback edition.

latter two are quite critical of American policy. Other useful general studies include Norman A. Graebner, *Cold War Diplomacy: American Foreign Policy, 1945–1960** (1962); Louis J. Halle, *The Cold War as History** (1967); and Seyom Brown, *The Faces of Power: Constancy and Change in United States Foreign Policy from Truman to Johnson** (1968).

The most authoritative treatment of the genesis of the cold war is John Lewis Gaddis's *The United States and the Origins of the Cold War, 1941–1947** (1972). Other useful books on this problem include John L. Snell, *Wartime Origins of the East-West Dilemma over Germany* (1959); Herbert Feis, *From Trust to Terror: The Onset of the Cold War, 1945–1950** (1970); George C. Herring, Jr., *Aid to Russia, 1941–1946: Strategy, Diplomacy, the Origins of the Cold War* (1973); and Thomas G. Paterson, *Soviet-American Confrontation: Postwar Reconstruction and the Origins of the Cold War* (1973). Among the important revisionist studies are William Appleman Williams, *The Tragedy of American Diplomacy** (2d rev. ed., 1972); David Horowitz, *The Free World Colossus: A Critique of American Foreign Policy in the Cold War** (1965); Gar Alperovitz, *Atomic Diplomacy: Hiroshima and Potsdam* (1965); Joyce Kolko and Gabriel Kolko, *The Limits of Power: The World and United States Foreign Policy, 1945–1954** (1972); and Diane Shaver Clemens, *Yalta** (1970). Critical evaluations of cold war revisionism are made by Robert W. Tucker, *The Radical Left and American Foreign Policy* (1971), and Robert James Maddox, *The New Left and the Origins of the Cold War** (1973). Thomas G. Paterson (ed.), *The Origins of the Cold War** (1974), is a helpful anthology. An invaluable introduction to the scholarship on the Truman years is provided by Richard S. Kirkendall (ed.), *The Truman Period as a Research Field: A Reappraisal, 1972* (1974), and an earlier edition of the same work published in 1967.

Lloyd C. Gardner presents a series of enlightening biographical studies in *Architects of Illusion: Men and Ideas in American Foreign Policy, 1941–1949** (1970). Four of the postwar Secretaries of State are assessed in Norman A. Graebner (ed.), *An Uncertain Tradition: American Secretaries of State in the Twentieth Century** (1961). For the views of several key actors in the drama of recent United States foreign policy, see Arthur H. Vandenberg, Jr. (ed.), *The Papers of Senator Vandenberg* (1952); Harry S. Truman, *Memoirs** (2 vols., 1955–1956); George F. Kennan, *Memoirs, 1925–1950* (1967); and Dean Acheson, *Present at the Creation: My Years in the State Department** (1969).

The German problem in the early postwar period is dealt with in John Gimbel, *The American Occupation of Germany: Politics and the Military, 1945–1949* (1968); Lucius D. Clay, *Decision in Germany* (1950); and W. Phillips Davison, *The Berlin Blockade* (1958). Joseph M. Jones, *The Fifteen Weeks (February 21–June 5, 1947)** (1955), is an absorbing account of the formulation of the Truman Doctrine and the Marshall Plan. The best book on the latter plan is Harry B. Price's *The Marshall Plan and Its Meaning* (1955). For the North Atlantic Treaty Organization, see Robert Endicott Osgood, *NATO: The Entangling Alliance* (1962). Theodore H. White's moving *Fire in the Ashes: Europe in Mid-Century** (1953) throws light on the recovery of Western Europe. Several important revisionist essays on foreign policy are included in Barton J. Bernstein (ed.), *Politics and Policies of the Truman Administration** (1970).

Chapter 3

Truman and the Politics of Stalemate

The postwar scene that started unfolding in the United States in the fall of 1945 promised to be very different from the prewar period, and many Americans anticipated a marked change in politics. For one thing, the Age of Franklin D. Roosevelt was over. Contemporaries found it difficult to conceive of national politics without Roosevelt, so vital and all-encompassing had been his influence on the political culture; yet it seemed clear that one era had ended and another was beginning in American politics. The new era, it was widely assumed, would be one of Republican dominance, and most people hoped that it would also be a time of relaxation and normality after the long years of national emergency and crisis. These hopes were soon frustrated. The postwar period was dominated by confusion, political division, and pressing problems related to such issues as demobilization, inflation, the role of organized labor, and civil rights, not to mention the unaccustomed pressures of foreign problems.

FDR's Legacy: The New Deal Coalition

The 1930s had witnessed the coming of political age of the urban minorities, the emergence of organized labor as a powerful factor in politics, the shift of a majority of Negro voters into the Democratic column, and the development of strong loyalties to Roosevelt and the Democratic party by millions of white-collar workers and middle-class Americans. The results of this political revolution were spectacular. Franklin D. Roosevelt had been elected President four times, and the Democrats had ended the one-party domination that had long prevailed in many parts of New England, the Midwest, and the Far West and had won control of both houses of Congress in every election since 1930.

But all of this had changed—or appeared on the verge of changing— by the end of World War II. Bereft of the magnetic and compelling Roosevelt, the Democrats appeared to be leaderless and confused. Harry S. Truman, the new President, seemed even less prepared to assume the mantle of Roosevelt's leadership than Martin Van Buren had that of the mighty Jackson. The Democrats, moreover, had been in power a long time, were badly divided along ideological lines, and faced the inevitable discontents and irritations that accumulated with lengthy tenure. A conservative coalition, led by Southern Democrats and Midwestern Republicans, had emerged in Congress in 1937, and while Roosevelt's foreign policies and war programs had served to unite the party in later years, the coalition had asserted itself effectively on many domestic issues. There was also another discouraging prospect. The Democratic administration in Washington was confronted in the postwar period with the threat of rampant inflation rather than severe depression and deflation as in the 1930s. The politics of inflation, unlike the politics of depression, made it difficult to attract and retain the support of major interest groups.

Although the Republicans were themselves divided, they were united in their determination to recapture control of the national government, which they confidently expected to do by winning the midterm elections of 1946 and the presidential election two years later. The unanswered question was: How durable was the Roosevelt coalition?

Harry S. Truman: The Man of Independence

The symbol of the Democrats' declining fortunes in the aftermath of the war and the natural target of Republican attacks was Harry S. Truman, the thirty-third President of the United States. Succeeding to the presidency on April 12, 1945, Truman was immediately faced with a multitude of perplexing problems and momentous decisions, including the use of the atomic bomb, the establishment of the United Nations, and the question of how best to deal with the Soviet Union. As Louis W. Koenig has written, "For virtually eight years of as troublous a time as our country and our world have known, a President of the United States arose seven mornings a week to a frame of things in which most news from every front was foreordained to be bad news and in which the unwelcome surprise, the unforeseen setback, had become routine, chronic emergency a way of life, and the conquest of dismay a permanent and indispensable habit of mind."

Truman was born on May 8, 1884, in Lamar, Missouri, a small town in the western part of the state. The son of a farmer and horse trader, and the descendant of forebears from Virginia and Kentucky, young Truman grew up in and around Independence. After being graduated from high school in 1901 and failing because of poor eyesight to secure an appointment to West Point, he worked at a variety of jobs, including farming. His National Guard unit was sent to France in 1918, and he served as an artillery officer on the Alsatian front. After the war the Missourian married Elizabeth Virginia Wallace, a childhood sweetheart, and with an army friend started a retail men's clothing store in Kansas City. The postwar recession caused the business to fail in 1922.

After his business failed, Truman turned to politics. His friendship with the brother of Thomas J. Pendergast, a powerful Democratic politician in Kansas City, helped him win the position of county judge. In the late 1920s and early 1930s Truman served as the top administrative official of Jackson County. He proved to be a hard-working and conscientious county officer. In 1934 Judge Truman secured the endorsement of the Pendergast machine in a bid for a United States Senate seat, and he was elected in the Democratic sweep of that year. In the Senate he was sometimes referred to as the "Senator from Pendergast," but he was a consistent if rather undistinguished supporter of the New Deal.

After his reelection in 1940, Truman began to receive some national attention. His concern about the large amount of waste in defense programs and the neglect of small business in the awarding of war contracts led him to propose an inquiry into defense spending. He was given the responsibility of conducting this investigation, and during the years 1941–1944 the so-called Truman Committee gained a reputation as a guardian of the public interest. Truman also made an impression on Franklin D. Roosevelt and other party leaders, and they turned to him as a compromise candidate for the vice-presidency in 1944 when it became apparent that neither Vice President Henry A. Wallace nor Presidential assistant James F. Byrnes would prove acceptable to a majority of the delegates at the Democratic National Convention. Truman was a border-state senator, he had a liberal voting record, and he was on good terms with all segments of the party, including Southern congressmen.

Harry Truman seemed in many ways to be an ordinary man, a small-town, middle-class American. He was a friendly, direct, and down-to-earth man, unpretentious, sincere, and uncomplicated. Devoted to his family, he liked the simple things of life—a visit with friends, an occasional drink, and a little poker with the boys. He played the piano and liked to read history. Bespectacled and scholarly in appearance, he spoke in a voice that was flat and monotonous. As Truman himself once said, "I look just like any other fifty people you meet in the street." Truman could be petty and pugnacious, he sometimes acted impulsively, and he was not above name-calling in public. A fierce partisan, he tended to accept Democrats as he found them, and his unswerving loyalty to friends did not always serve him well. But he also possessed many excellent and unusual qualities. He worked hard and studied diligently. While some- what awed by the enormous responsibilities that confronted him in the White House, he never doubted his ability to handle them. He displayed courage and boldness in the presidency, and he soon demonstrated a capacity for making decisions. A sign on his desk read: "The buck stops here." Truman also had, in Koenig's words, "a gift of simplification, a knack of seeing issues divested of complication and irrelevancy and of stating them in plain, blunt terms."

Truman had limited preparation for the awesome responsibilities he faced as President, and that fact no doubt helps explain a certain confusion and vagueness as to direction in the first part of his administra- tion. Conservatives hoped that the new President's moderate views would bring him into their camp. But Truman did not commit himself to the conservatives' cause. In fact, he did just the opposite. In a comprehensive message to Congress on September 6, 1945, only three weeks after V-J Day, he revealed his progressive inclinations and expressed a determina- tion to add to the structure of New Deal reforms. He presented a twenty-one point reform program. Among his recommendations were the extension of economic controls in the postwar period, an increase in the minimum wage from 40 to 65 cents an hour, the extension of the Social Security System, a full-employment program, more slum clearance and public housing projects, a public works program, the regional develop- ment of "the natural resources of our great river valleys," the reorganiza- tion of the executive branch of the federal government, and the establish- ment of a permanent Fair Employment Practices Commission. Soon afterward, Truman recommended the national control of atomic energy, a national health insurance system, federal aid to education, and American approval of the St. Lawrence Seaway.

Although Truman had put himself on record as favoring a broad program of domestic reform, few of his recommendations were approved during the next two years, except for the Employment Act and the Atomic Energy Act of 1946. He seemed to desire a continuation of the New Deal but also the maintenance of harmonious relations with Congress, which was in a conservative mood and was determined to assert its independence of executive restraint. A series of labor crises and the losing struggle to control prices and maintain economic stability dominated the domestic scene in 1945 and 1946. The President also experienced a succession of personal difficulties with executive subordinates, leading to the resignation of such men as Harold L. Ickes and Henry A. Wallace, and helping to alienate many liberals from the administration. Then, in November 1946, the resurgent Republicans captured control of Congress.

Truman's administration in late 1946 seemed to have run aground after months of drift and vacillation. The President's leadership appeared to be designed to promote a politics of stalemate. Truman himself, Samuel Lubell remarks in *The Future of American Politics* (1952), was "a product of political deadlock." Lubell pictures Truman as "the man who bought time," as a leader whose role was "to raise all issues but to settle none." Although this harsh judgment contains a good deal of truth, it is not the whole truth. It does not adequately take into account the turbulent times, the bitter partisanship, and the conflicting pressures of the early postwar years.

The Eightieth Congress, 1947–1948

Republican leaders interpreted their thumping congressional victory in 1946 as a repudiation of Democratic reformism, and they turned with alacrity to the task of reducing taxes, passing legislation to control labor unions, and freeing business from governmental restraints. If Senator Arthur H. Vandenberg was the most influential Republican spokesman on foreign affairs, Senator Robert A. Taft of Ohio was the most powerful party leader in the domestic arena. The son of William Howard Taft, the younger Taft had come to the Senate in 1939, contended for his party's presidential nomination in 1940 and 1944, and in 1947 headed the Republican policy committee. A man of ability, integrity, and intelligence, the Ohio Senator was frequently referred to as "Mr. Republican." Although he was willing to support federal programs to develop public housing and to aid education, he was basically a conservative, a spokesman for economic conservatism. "We have got to break with the corrupting idea that we can legislate prosperity, legislate equality, legislate opportunity," he declared.

After the Republicans organized the new Congress, which convened in January 1947, they immediately moved to secure further relief from the high wartime taxes. Federal taxes had already been cut twice since the end of the war, and President Truman warned that additional reductions would only pour more fuel on the fiery inflation then raging. But Congress would not be deterred. In June it passed a tax bill that provided proportionately greater relief to those in high income brackets than to people with lower incomes. Truman vetoed this measure, asserting that it would bring about the "very recession we seek to avoid." A few weeks later the President vetoed a second tax reduction bill with provisions very much like the one passed in June. A third tax cut, providing for a $4.8 billion reduction, was finally passed over Truman's veto, becoming the Revenue Act of April 1948. Although the lawmakers approved an anti-inflation bill in the fall of 1947, they were unwilling to give the President any real power to enforce the new legislation.

The most important domestic statute enacted during the Eightieth Congress was the controversial Taft-Hartley Labor-Management Relations Act of 1947. The Republicans were determined to curb the power of organized labor, and under the circumstances it was probably inevitable that some kind of labor-control law would be passed. The Wagner Act of 1935, the basic labor policy statute, had long been criticized in some quarters as one-sided and unfair to employers. Wartime labor strife had led to the imposition of restrictions on labor unions by the Smith-Connally War Labor Disputes Act of 1943. The long series of strikes following the war, as well as John L. Lewis's contemptuous defiance of the government during the war and again in 1946, brought mounting public pressure for congressional action. Congress responded by passing the Case bill in 1946, only to have President Truman veto it on the ground that its various restraints were "punitive." When the Eightieth Congress convened, a large number of regulatory bills were introduced, including one with severe restraints presented by Fred L. Hartley, Jr., of New Jersey, the Chairman of the House Committee on Education and Labor. The Hartley bill was rushed through the lower house and passed on April 17 by a large majority. Action in the Senate was led by Taft, the Chairman of the Labor and Public Welfare Committee. Under his direction, a more carefully drafted and less vindictive labor bill was formulated and eventually adopted, after additional compromises, by both houses in June. The measure outlawed the closed shop; prohibited several "unfair" labor practices by unions, including jurisdictional strikes and secondary boycotts; forbade campaign contributions by labor unions; required loyalty oaths from union officers; and authorized the issuance of injunctions to halt strikes and a "cooling-off" period as long as eighty days in strikes that would create a national emergency.

The sponsors of the Taft-Hartley bill described it as "the first step toward an official discouragement" of a trend that had "permitted and encouraged" labor "to grow into a monster supergovernment." Truman responded with a sharp veto on June 20. He charged that the strike procedures provided in the bill were impractical, that the measure was biased against labor, and that it would "reverse the basic direction of our national labor policy." The Republicans, with notable help from Southern

Democrats, swiftly overrode the veto—by a vote of 331 to 83 in the House and 68 to 25 in the Senate. In practice the Taft-Hartley Act proved less harmful to labor's interests than its opponents had feared. Yet it hurt weak unions in some industries, made organizing more difficult, and encouraged many states to enact stronger "right to work" laws. Union leaders denounced Taft-Hartley as a "slave labor law," and with its passage they rallied their forces behind the Truman administration.

The President and his congressional opponents fought one battle after another in 1947 and 1948. Truman, with an eye on the election of 1948, repeatedly urged Congress to pass a broad range of social welfare measures. But Congress largely ignored the Chief Executive's recommendations for the extension of New Deal social welfare concepts in such fields as housing, education, medical care, and social security. It refused to enact strong price controls, forced the adoption of tax reductions that favored the rich, and reduced appropriations for agricultural programs and reclamation. General appropriations were constantly reduced from the administration's budget requests. "This Congress," observed T. R. B., the *New Republic* columnist, "brought back an atmosphere you had forgotten or never thought possible. . . . Victories fought and won years ago were suddenly in doubt. Everything was debatable again." Truman's vetoes appeared to confirm this point; he issued more than sixty in 1947 and 1948.

Truman renewed and sharpened his demands for domestic reforms in early 1948. But the administration got little from Congress. Rent controls were extended for another year, a severely limited housing program was approved, and an agricultural bill was passed providing for a continuation of price supports at 90 percent of parity through 1949 and thereafter on a flexible basis. Congress also extended the Reciprocal Trade Agreements Act, though for only one year rather than the three recommended by the President. In foreign policy legislation, of course, the Truman administration scored a series of impressive triumphs. Congress also authorized the creation of a commission on the reorganization of the executive branch of the government. Truman appointed former President Herbert Hoover to head this inquiry, and after an extensive study the Hoover Commission in 1949 issued eighteen comprehensive reports, recommending the consolidation and streamlining of numerous executive departments and agencies. Many of these recommendations were put into effect during Truman's second term.[1]

The Eightieth Congress followed Truman's recommendation in pass-

---

[1]The Reorganization Act of June 1949 authorized the President to submit plans of reorganization which would become automatically effective unless Congress specifically disapproved.

ing a new Presidential Succession Act, placing the Speaker of the House and the President pro tempore ahead of the members of the Cabinet in the line of presidential succession after the Vice President. And Congress adopted, in 1947, the Twenty-second Amendment to the Constitution, limiting the President's tenure to two terms. It was ratified by the requisite number of states in 1951.

The Election of 1948

As the presidential campaign of 1948 got under way, the Democratic party was badly split. Henry A. Wallace, around whom critics of the Truman administration's cold war policies were rallying, had announced his intention of running for President on an independent ticket. The President's strong advocacy of a civil rights program had spurred a group of Southern governors to begin laying plans for a regional opposition movement against the national Democratic party. Truman's popularity in all parts of the country had dropped to a low level. "People are restless, dissatisfied, fearful," one administration member explained. "They want someone who can 'take over' and solve everything." A new liberal organization known as the Americans for Democratic Action (ADA) wanted to dump Truman and nominate a more attractive standard-bearer in 1948.

Although Truman had earlier given some thought to the possibility of stepping aside in favor of the universally admired General Dwight D. Eisenhower, he had decided by the end of 1947 to run in his own right. He announced his decision publicly on March 8, 1948. Truman's various reform proposals during the early months of 1948 were designed to provide him with a coherent program and a tactical advantage over his Republican opponents in the forthcoming campaign. Moreover, Clark Clifford, the President's Special Counsel, and other administration officials had begun to develop a strategy for the next presidential campaign soon after the disastrous congressional elections of 1946. In a confidential memorandum to Truman on November 19, 1947, Clifford summed up the views that had been developed within the administration on "the Politics of 1948." He advised the President to stake out a liberal position in dealing with the next session of Congress, to exploit his conflicts with his congressional opponents, and to move forward in the field of civil rights.

The Republican National Convention was held in Philadelphia, beginning on June 21. The front-runner in the contest for the presidential nomination was Governor Dewey, who in late May had won an impressive primary victory in Oregon over former Governor Harold E. Stassen of Minnesota. Senator Taft was also an aspirant for the honor, and party regulars seemed to prefer him to Dewey; but the Senator's isolationist record, outspoken conservatism, and unexciting campaign style made him a less attractive possibility than the internationalist and progressive New York Governor. The delegates unanimously nominated Dewey on the third ballot and selected Governor Earl Warren of California as the vice-presidential nominee. The platform, to the chagrin of some extreme conservatives, was a moderate document which, by implication at least, accepted the main features of Roosevelt's New Deal and Truman's foreign policy.

Three weeks later the Democrats convened in Philadelphia to choose their national ticket. The convention was steeped in gloom. A movement by the ADA, labor leaders, and city bosses to draft General Eisenhower had failed shortly before the convention when Eisenhower unequivocally rejected the overtures made to him. Thus the nomination went to Truman almost by default, though Senator Richard B. Russell of Georgia received most of the Southern delegate votes. Senator Alben W. Barkley of Kentucky, whose old-fashioned keynote address had roused the convention out of its lethargy, was made the vice-presidential nominee. The platform praised the Truman administration's international policies and called for the enactment of most of the President's progressive recommendations. The forthright endorsement of civil rights was made only after a bitter floor fight in which the young mayor of Minneapolis, Hubert H. Humphrey, and other Northern liberals demanded that the rather vague plank proposed by the administration be strengthened. "I say the time has come to walk out of the shadow of states' rights and into the sunlight of human rights," declared Humphrey.

President Truman brought the Democratic delegates to life when he appeared before them at two o'clock in the morning to deliver his acceptance speech. "Senator Barkley and I will win this election," he cried. As the climax to his fighting address, Truman announced that he was calling the Eightieth Congress—the worst Congress in American history, he asserted—into special session on July 26, the day turnips are planted in Missouri. He wanted to give the Republicans a chance to carry out their campaign pledges immediately, explained the President, and thus enable the voters to "decide on the record." The Republicans accused Truman of resorting to petty politics. The "turnip Congress" remained in session for almost two weeks, but it accomplished nothing of importance, which was what Truman expected.

Meanwhile, however, the Democratic party seemed to be splitting apart as as a result of insurgency on the right and the left. A revolt by Southern Democrats, which had been brewing for months, was precipitated by the action of the party's national convention in Philadelphia and the dramatic walkout of the Mississippi and Alabama delegates. A conference of the Southern rebels met in Birmingham on July 17. The bolters proceeded to organize the States' Rights Democratic party, to nominate Governor J. Strom Thurmond of South Carolina for President and Governor Fielding L. Wright of Mississippi as his running mate, and to draft a platform that emphasized states' rights and opposition to the Democratic party's civil rights proposals. The Dixiecrats, as they were soon dubbed, conducted a vigorous campaign during the following months in an effort to unite the South against the regular Democratic ticket. Since they controlled the Democratic party machinery in several states, they were able to place their electors on the ballot as the regular Democrats. The States' Righters hoped to prevent either of the major parties from obtaining a majority in the electoral college, thus throwing the election into the House of Representatives where they might become the deciding factor.

In some respects the threat to the Democratic ticket from the left appeared even more ominous. At the end of 1947, Henry Wallace had announced his willingness to run for President on a third-party ticket sponsored by the Progressive Citizens of America. Many radicals and disgruntled liberals were expected to support Wallace in demanding a more conciliatory approach to the Russians and a domestic program described by the former Vice President as "progressive capitalism." Representatives of the Wallace movement met in Philadelphia on July 23 to launch their campaign. They organized the Progressive party, nominated Wallace and Senator Glen Taylor of Idaho as their standard-bearers, and drafted a platform that blamed the Truman administration for the cold war, condemned its containment policies, and urged a variety of domestic reforms, including the nationalization of basic industries and equal treatment of all minority groups. Although some old-time New Dealers and a wide assortment of radicals took part in organizing the new party, it was apparent that Communists were extremely active in its campaign. Even so, the Wallace movement seemed to pose a formidable challenge to the Democrats in the key Northern states.

President Truman's chances of winning the election looked hopeless. Many Democratic leaders had a defeatist attitude, and the party was disorganized and badly needed money. The Republicans, meanwhile, were conducting an efficient and well-financed campaign. Traveling in his "Victory Special" train, Governor Dewey toured the country, talking confidently and a bit smugly about efficiency and good government. He emphasized the need for an administration that would promote national unity and the cause of peace. Dewey's magisterial campaign, avoiding specifics somewhat in the manner of Franklin D. Roosevelt's approach in 1932, seemed calculated to ensure a Republican victory. But it made the GOP nominee appear rather remote to the voters—a machine with a cellophane cover, in the opinion of one contemporary. Near the end of the campaign, some of Dewey's advisers expressed concern over the damage Truman might do between election day and January 20, which prompted one reporter to ask ironically: "How long is Dewey going to tolerate Truman's interference in the government?"

Nevertheless, the Democrats under Truman's leadership breathed life into their own campaign. The President's decision to convene the "turnip Congress" revealed an important part of his campaign strategy. He would make the Eightieth Congress rather than the more progressive Dewey his principal target, blaming the Republican congressmen for the failure of his anti-inflation recommendations, his civil rights proposals, and such social welfare measures as additional public housing and an increase in the minimum wage. "I'm going to fight hard," Truman told Senator Barkley at the outset of the campaign. "I'm going to give them hell." And fight hard he did! Acting as if he expected to win, the President made one of the most strenuous campaigns in our modern history. He traveled an estimated 31,700 miles, mostly by train, spoke more than 350 times, and was heard directly by approximately 12 million Americans. Speaking extemporaneously at "whistle-stops" across the country, where his friendliness and warmth of personality came through, Truman hammered away at the record of what he called the "do-nothing, good-for nothing" Eightieth Congress, charging it with the responsibility for high prices and rents, for the housing shortage, and for cutting back on such programs as conservation and reclamation. The crowds that gathered to hear the President grew in size, and people increasingly voiced admiration for his plucky fight in the face of apparent defeat.

Figure 3 "Give-'em-hell Harry" *(National Park Service Photograph, Courtesy Harry S. Truman Library)*

In his homely but hard-hitting remarks, Truman pictured the Republicans as the party of "privilege, pride, and plunder," a party with little interest in the common people. Truman's attack on Republican Toryism was shrewdly intended to hold most of the old New Deal coalition together. Making an intense appeal to normally Democratic elements, he urged a resumption of the New Deal on a broad front and warned the various interest groups not to risk losing the benefits of the Democratic reforms of the past fifteen years.

Despite Truman's gallant fight, most informed observers agreed that he would lose the election. All of the leading polls, political analysts, and important newspapers predicted a Dewey victory. After checking with its correspondents, the *New York Times* concluded that Dewey would receive 305 electoral votes to Truman's 105. *Life* magazine carried Governor Dewey's picture on its cover the week before the election, describing him as the "next President."

The election results surprised almost everybody, and Truman's sensational victory has to be characterized as one of the most extraordinary in American history. The outcome revealed that the public opinion polls had failed to detect a swing to President Truman late in the campaign. The Democrats' success also suggested that the political experts had underestimated the extent to which the party of Roosevelt and Truman had become the normal majority party in the United States. In an election marked by a low voter turnout, Truman received 24,105,812 popular votes (49.5 percent) and 303 electoral votes to Dewey's 21,970,065 (45.1 percent) and 189. Thurmond received 1,169,063 popular votes and carried four Southern states (with 39 electoral votes), while Wallace had a popular vote of 1,157,172 and won no electoral votes. The Democrats recaptured both houses of Congress, gaining 75 seats in the House of Representatives and 9 in the Senate. They won 20 of the 32 gubernatorial contests. Governor Dewey carried 16 states, most of which were in New England, the Middle Atlantic region, and the Plains belt.

In the immediate aftermath of Truman's surprising victory, George Gallup, the well-known pollster, admitted, "I just don't know what happened." Senator Taft expressed the feeling of many Republicans when he exclaimed, "It defies all common sense." Basically, Truman's triumph resulted from his success in maintaining the old Democratic coalition. He ran well among labor voters, ethnic groups, and farmers. "In a sense," observes Eugene H. Roseboom, "Roosevelt won his greatest victory after his death." The country was at peace, the economy was doing well, and a consensus had emerged on national policy in the cold war. Ironically, the Progressive party and the Dixiecrat movement probably ensured Truman's election. The Wallace party, by attracting Communists and other radicals, removed the taint of their support from the Democrats. The States' Righters failed to bring about the defection of the entire South, and by undertaking a racist campaign against the Truman administration, persuaded Negro voters in the North to rally behind the President's banner. Another element in the Democratic success of 1948 was the fact that the party had a considerable number of strong local candidates, including Hubert H. Humphrey in Minnesota and Adlai E. Stevenson, who was elected Governor of Illinois. And President Truman's own role must not be overlooked, for he was doubtless his party's greatest campaign asset.

The Fair Deal, 1949–1952

In his annual State of the Union message on January 5, 1949, President Truman outlined what came to be called the Fair Deal. "Every segment of our population and every individual," he declared, "has a right to expect from our Government a *fair deal*." Truman recommended an increase in the minimum wage from 40 to 75 cents an hour, the broadening of the Social Security System, national health insurance, federal aid to education, low-cost housing and slum clearance, repeal of the Taft-Hartley Act, and an increase of $4 billion in federal taxes to help finance the new programs and reduce inflationary pressures. As the commentator Elmer Davis once said, "It was roses, roses all the way for Harry Truman when he rode in the bright sunshine to be inaugurated. But a good deal of the rest of the way . . . was poison ivy."

Although the Democrats controlled Congress throughout Truman's second administration, the President's legislative proposals were subjected to continual congressional assault and subterfuge. Congress refused to vote higher taxes or to authorize the price controls Truman had urged. It would not repeal the Taft-Hartley Act. It rejected the administration's new approach to the problem of agricultural subsidies and turned down its recommendations for the extension of the TVA concept to the Missouri River and other river valleys. The Eighty-first Congress defeated Truman's national health insurance plan, disapproved his proposal for the establishment of a new Department of Welfare with Cabinet rank, failed to pass legislation to provide federal aid to education, and filibustered to death a Federal Employment Practices Commission bill.

President Truman's legislative setbacks cannot be entirely attributed to the opposition of congressional conservatives, though they were a potent influence in the failure of many administration measures. Truman's reform efforts did not receive the impetus of the great public enthusiasm that had sustained the early New Deal. In fact, the Fair Deal precipitated a round of violent controversies and attacks in the press and on the platform, leading many contemporaries to conclude that Americans were too confused and divided to know what they wanted or needed. Truman

Figure 4 Dowling on the Fair Deal *(Harry S. Truman Library)*

himself was unable to stimulate broad public support for his reform
program. He usually thought it necessary to give priority to his administration's international objectives. The recession of 1949 caused many
congressmen to doubt the wisdom of a tax increase or other domestic
reforms. The growing obsession with the question of Communist subversion hurt the administration's Fair Deal programs, and the Korean war
consumed the attention and energy of the President and Congress after
June 1950.

As the Eighty-first Congress began its work in January 1949, Truman
had high hopes for the repeal of the Taft-Hartley Act. Senator Taft was
willing to make some concessions, and the administration might have
obtained a compromise measure correcting some provisions of the 1947
law. But the administration was not enthusiastic about such a compro-

mise, and one that got through the Senate bogged down in the House of Representatives. The administration's health insurance plan called for prepaid medical, dental, and hospital care to be financed by employee and employer contributions through a payroll tax and government subsidies. The American Medical Association conducted a frenzied lobbying and advertising campaign against the proposed legislation, which it condemned as "nationalized, bureaucratic, governmental or socialized medical care." Congress bowed before this onslaught. The President was no more fortunate with his recommendation for federal aid to education. Although the Senate passed a bill appropriating $300 million to the states for the support of education, this measure died in the House as a result of the Protestant-Catholic conflict over whether federal aid should go to private and parochial schools as well as to public institutions.

On the agricultural front, the administration in April 1949 presented the Brannan Plan, named for Secretary of Agriculture Charles F. Brannan. This proposal sought to maintain a "farm income standard" comparable to that of the previous decade, to hold food prices at reasonable levels, and to reduce the government's storage expenses if possible. The plan would have retained high fixed support prices for basic commodities. The novel feature of the scheme was the recommendation that the prices of perishable commodities be determined by the free market, with the government compensating the producers for the difference between the market price and a price considered fair by the Department of Agriculture. The Brannan Plan was vigorously opposed by all the major farm organizations except the Farmers' Union; the critics charged that the plan would cost too much and lead to the regimentation of American farmers. Congress would not pass the proposed legislation. Only the heavy demands for food and fiber at home and abroad—demands underwritten by the Marshall Plan and the Korean war—prevented an acute agricultural problem from emerging before the 1950s.

Truman's worst defeat came in his fight for civil rights legislation. During his second administration, Truman repeatedly tried to get Congress to establish a permanent Federal Employment Practices Commission (FEPC), to enact antilynching and anti-poll tax laws, and to give legislative sanction to the other recommendations contained in the 1947 report of his Commission on Civil Rights. Southern Democrats, with strong Republican assistance, stymied all these efforts. In 1949 a bipartisan group of congressional reformers had some success in weakening the House Rules Committee, which had long been a bottleneck for civil rights measures, but it failed to modify the cloture rule that permitted filibusters in the Senate. Two efforts to invoke cloture by civil rights advocates failed in 1950. A "voluntary" FEPC bill and a measure to grant suffrage and self-government to residents of the District of Columbia did pass the

House, only to be killed in the Senate. President Truman had to resort to executive action in order to make any immediate headway in the civil rights struggle. He issued Executive orders in 1948 seeking to end discrimination and segregation in the armed forces and in government departments. He established a special committee in 1951 to bar the awarding of defense contracts to companies practicing discrimination. He strengthened the Civil Rights Section of the Justice Department, named the first Negro to a federal judgeship, and appointed a black man as Governor of the Virgin Islands. Truman was the first President in modern times to proclaim the equality of blacks, to assail discrimination and violence against them, and to identify his office with the broad objectives of the civil rights movement.

The Eighty-second Congress, elected in 1950, proved even less cooperative than the Eighty-first in responding to Truman's legislative proposals. Although the Democrats retained nominal control of both houses, the conservative coalition was stronger in 1951 and 1952 than it had been in the previous Congress. Exploiting the fears and frustrations connected with the Korean war, internal subversion, and corruption in government, the Republicans made a good showing in the midterm elections; they gained twenty-eight House seats, five Senate seats, and seven governorships. Republican charges that corruption was rampant in the Truman administration served the interests of the President's opponents in other ways than the ballot box; they helped destroy any lingering hopes Truman had for his unfinished program of social reform. The "mess in Washington" never involved Truman personally, but there was enough evidence of "five percenters"—expediters who sold actual or pretended influence with government officials—and irregularities in various governmental agencies to lend some credence to the charges. The President's military aide, General Harry H. Vaughan, was shown to have been given a $520 deep freeze unit under somewhat cloudy circumstances, while the wife of a Reconstruction Finance Corporation official was the beneficiary, for practically nothing, of a $9,540 mink coat. Irregularities in the Internal Revenue Service forced the resignation of four collectors and a number of other officials.

It would be a mistake to say that the Fair Deal was a complete failure. In 1950 Congress increased the social security benefits by 77 percent and extended the system's coverage to an additional 10 million people. It raised the minimum wage to 75 cents an hour, extended rent controls, and gave the Chief Executive some powers to deal with the problem of inflation. The National Housing Act of 1949, passed with the help of Senator Taft, authorized the construction of 810,000 subsidized low-income housing units over the next six years, as well as grants for slum clearance and rural housing. Congress also increased the appropriations for power development and reclamation in the West, for the TVA, and for the Farmers' Home Administration, which was carrying on some of the work of the Farm Security Administration. While Congress rejected Truman's national health insurance plan, it did pass the Hill-Burton Act, which authorized matching federal and state grants for the construction of public and nonprofit hospitals and clinics. In 1950 it set up the National Science Foundation. And at Truman's insistence, Congress in the same year passed the Displaced Persons Act. This statute increased the number of such persons to be admitted to 415,000 over the next three years and remedied some of the defects Truman had complained about in earlier legislation.

The Fair Deal attempted to adapt American liberalism to the new postwar conditions. "The Truman Administration established no radically new programs," as Richard O. Davies points out, "but it performed remarkably well in updating and expanding existing programs and, especially, in serving to assimilate the New Deal into American life." Yet the politics of stalemate continued, reflecting the powerful conservative coalition in Congress, the internal conflict within the majority party, and the ambivalence of the public mood.

SUGGESTIONS FOR FURTHER READING

Samuel Lubell's classic book, *The Future of American Politics** (3d ed. rev., 1965), offers a provocative analysis of Franklin D. Roosevelt's political revolution, of the voting coalition he brought together, and of how, "after twenty years of victories, the coalition became deadlocked within itself." Especially important for an understanding of the Truman years is Alonzo L. Hamby's *Beyond the New Deal: Harry S. Truman and American Liberalism* (1973).

For two sympathetic biographies of Harry S. Truman, see Jonathan Daniels, *The Man of Independence* (1950), and Alfred Steinberg, *The Man from Missouri: The Life and Times of Harry S. Truman* (1962). Cabell Phillips, *The Truman Presidency: The History of a Triumphant Succession** (1966), is probably the best overall account of the administration. Bert Cochran, *Harry Truman and the Crisis Presidency* (1973), is a critical assessment. The most useful documentary works are Louis W. Koenig, *The Truman Administration: Its Principles and Practice* (1956), and Barton J. Bernstein and Allen J. Matusow (eds.), *The Truman Administration: A Documentary History** (1966). Alonzo L. Hamby has brought together a good collection of essays under the title *Harry S. Truman and the Fair Deal** (1974).

Susan M. Hartmann, *Truman and the 80th Congress* (1971), is an informative study. David B. Truman, *The Congressional Party: A Case Study* (1959), examines the workings of the Eighty-first Congress. James T. Patterson's *Mr. Republican: A Biography of Robert A. Taft* (1972) is an outstanding study of a key figure.

*Available in paperback edition.

Richard S. Kirkendall has written a fine essay, "Election of 1948," in Arthur M. Schlesinger, Jr., and Fred L. Israel (eds.), *History of American Presidential Elections, 1789–1968* (1971), vol. IV, pp. 3099–3210. This work, which contains valuable contemporary documents, is also useful for the national elections of 1952 through 1968. Other books on the 1948 election include Irwin Ross, *The Loneliest Campaign: The Truman Victory of 1948* (1968); Jules Abels, *Out of the Jaws of Victory* (1959); Alexander Heard, *A Two-Party South?* (1952); Norman D. Markowitz, *The Rise and Fall of the People's Century: Henry A. Wallace and American Liberalism, 1941–1948* (1973); and Allen Yarnell, *Democrats and Progressives: The 1948 Presidential Election as a Test of Postwar Liberalism* (1974).

Among the scholarly monographs dealing with the Fair Deal and other aspects of the Truman administration are Allen J. Matusow, *Farm Policies and Politics in the Truman Years** (1967); Richard O. Davies, *Housing Reform during the Truman Administration* (1966); R. Alton Lee, *Truman and Taft-Hartley: A Question of Mandate* (1966); and Richard M. Dalfiume, *Desegregation of the U.S. Armed Forces: Fighting on Two Fronts, 1939–1953* (1969). The best study of civil rights in the Truman era is Donald R. McCoy and Richard T. Ruetten, *Quest and Response: Minority Rights and the Truman Administration* (1973). For labor policy, see Harry Alvin Millis and Emily Clark Brown, *From the Wagner Act to Taft-Hartley: A Study of National Labor Policy and Labor Relations* (1950). Edward S. Flash, Jr., *Economic Advice and Presidential Leadership: The Council of Economic Advisers* (1965), is helpful on economic issues. Richard E. Neustadt, "Congress and the Fair Deal: A Legislative Balance Sheet," *Public Policy,* vol. 5 (1954), pp. 349–381, provides a guide to the political history of the Truman era.

Chapter 4

The Korean War and the Politics of Loyalty

In its early stages the cold war between the United States and the Soviet Union was centered in the eastern Mediterranean and Europe, and the American containment policy, while worldwide in its implication, was largely confined to Europe. But the conflict soon shifted to the Far East, and the outbreak of the Korean war in June 1950 precipitated a major change in American Far Eastern policy. The fall of Nationalist China and the beginning of the Korean war, moreover, unleashed a wave of anti-Communist hysteria within the United States. The stage was thus set for the extraordinary rise to power of Senator Joseph R. McCarthy, the frustration of the hapless Truman administration, and the election of Dwight D. Eisenhower as President in 1952.

American Dilemma in the Far East

World War II stimulated the growth of nationalist sentiment throughout Asia and encouraged anti-imperialist revolutions that brought about the rapid dismantling of the old British, French, and Dutch hegemonies. In China and Indochina these national movements were led by Communists.

The United States constructed one defense against the postwar revolution in East Asia by undertaking the destruction and reconstruction of the old Japan. Under General MacArthur's direction a new constitution was adopted, a parliamentary system introduced, agrarian reforms carried out, and a variety of other progressive changes completed. A reconstructed Japan could not dominate the Far East, however, and in no other part of the region was the United States in such a favorable position in the postwar years.

On the mainland of East Asia the key country was China, whose political independence and territorial integrity had been American objectives for almost half a century. During the war United States leaders helped persuade Stalin to sign a treaty of alliance and friendship with China, recognizing the Nationalist government rather than the Communist forces under Mao Tse-tung. But the fact was that China was deeply divided, and Chiang Kai-shek's Kuomintang party was too corrupt, inefficient, and dictatorial to unify the country. Hoping to head off a civil war and to effect a coalition government, President Truman dispatched General George C. Marshall to China in December 1945. Marshall secured a cease-fire and other tentative agreements, but neither side wanted to give up its major political objectives, and no settlement could be reached.

The Nationalists and the Communists were soon locked in an all-out military struggle. At first the Nationalists appeared to have the advantage, since they held the most territory, had the larger army, and were better equipped than their adversaries. But Chiang's government had alienated the great majority of the populace, including business people and intellectuals. When General Albert C. Wedemeyer visited China in the summer of 1947 to report on the situation for Secretary of State Marshall, he was dismayed at the political and military ineptitude of the Kuomintang. The Nationalist armies were soon in retreat everywhere, and by early 1949 Chiang had lost half of his troops and 80 percent of the equipment given him by the United States. Before the end of 1949, he fled with the remnants of his army to the island of Formosa. Meanwhile, in September 1949, Mao Tse-tung had announced the formation of the People's Republic of China, with its capital at Peking.

The impending breakdown of Nationalist control in 1949 confronted the Truman administration with the task of explaining the failure of its China policy. This was not an easy undertaking, for there had long been a group of "Asia-firsters" in the United States who believed that their government had neglected its interests and obligations in Asia, first by giving priority to the defeat of Hitler in the early 1940s, and later in concentrating its energies on the defense of Europe in the cold war. On August 5, 1949, with the collapse of Nationalist authority clearly imminent, the State Department issued a lengthy White Paper that sought to explain American policy in China. The United States had extended over $2 billion in grants and credits to the Kuomintang—representing far greater resources than those available to the Chinese Communists—and the Nationalists' failure, the document contended, was the result of a great internal change within China, a genuine revolution, over which the United States had no control. The United States could have attempted a "full-scale intervention" with troops, Secretary of State Dean Acheson remarked, but it "would have been resented by the mass of the Chinese people, would have diametrically reversed our historic policy, and would have been condemned by the American people."

During the winter of 1949–1950, the Truman administration's foreign policy received one blow after another. The loss of Nationalist China and a divisive debate over NATO had apparently destroyed bipartisanship. The Russians had exploded an atomic bomb, and early in 1950 a Sino-Soviet pact had been concluded between the two Communist powers. The United States had begun to negotiate a peace treaty with Japan, but there was mounting uneasiness and open hostility among the Japanese because of the American desire to retain military bases on the islands. At about this time the National Security Council was completing its reassessment of United States foreign and defense policies; NSC 68 forecast "an indefinite period of tension and danger" and urged the United States to undertake "a bold and massive program" to meet the Soviet challenge. A new challenge came in June 1950 when North Korean troops crossed the 38th parallel and began an invasion of the Republic of South Korea.

The Korean War, 1950–1952

Korea—the "Hermit Kingdom"—had been dominated by Japan during most of the twentieth century. At the Cairo conference in 1943 Allied leaders promised the Koreans their freedom "in due course." Russian troops moved into the northern part of the peninsula just before the Japanese surrender in August 1945, and a short time later American soldiers occupied South Korea. It was decided rather arbitrarily that the occupation zones would be divided at the 38th parallel, and it was assumed that an independent Korean government would eventually take over throughout the peninsula. But that was not to be, for with the beginning of the cold war, the division of Korea became permanent.

In late 1947 the United States took the Korean question to the United Nations Assembly, requesting that body to sponsor free elections throughout Korea. United Nations representatives were denied entry into North Korea, but elections were held under UN auspices in South Korea. The Russians proceeded to establish a Communist "people's government" and to train and equip a strong army in North Korea. The United

States did not create a large and well-equipped army in South Korea, fearing that President Syngman Rhee might resort to force in an effort to unify the north and south. Meanwhile, there were frequent border clashes between the two Koreas, neither of which recognized the legitimacy of the other's government.

Communist leaders probably thought there was a good chance that the United States would not come to South Korea's defense. American troops had been withdrawn, and the military forces of the United States were generally in a very weakened state. Nevertheless, North Korea's assault on June 25, 1950, brought a decisive response from the United States. President Truman, with the concurrence of his advisers, immediately instructed General MacArthur to furnish arms and supplies to the hard-pressed South Koreans. The Truman administration also moved swiftly to bring the matter before the United Nations. In an emergency session on the afternoon of June 25, the Security Council adopted a resolution by a vote of 9 to 0 condemning the invasion and demanding the withdrawal of North Korean troops from South Korea.[1]

The North Korean advance could not be halted by the South Koreans, and within three days the invaders had captured the capital city of Seoul. Truman began to send American air and naval forces into the fray. On June 27 the UN Security Council, with the Soviet delegate still absent, adopted by a vote of 7 to 1 an American-sponsored resolution calling on member nations to provide all necessary assistance to the Republic of Korea. Three days later Truman made the difficult decision to send two divisions of American ground troops from Japan to Korea. He also authorized a naval blockade of North Korea. Soon afterward the Security Council recognized the United States as the leader of the UN forces in Korea, and Truman named General MacArthur to head the defending army. While these developments took place, the nation rallied behind the President's decision to resist the North Korean aggression. Truman had acted "with a magnificent courage and terse decision," declared the *New York Herald Tribune* in a front-page editorial.

For a time the South Korean situation looked hopeless. The North Korean army advanced down the peninsula for almost six weeks, overrunning most of the south and pushing the Republic of Korea and U.S. 8th Army soldiers to a perimeter around the southern port of Pusan. There the defenders finally held their ground, their position strengthened by heavy reinforcements and crucial support from American air opera-

[1]Jacob Malik, the Russian delegate, was absent when the Security Council met on June 25. He was absent because the Russians had been boycotting the UN in protest against the failure of the international organization to admit the People's Republic of China earlier in the year. Had Malik been present on the 25th, he could have exercised the veto to prevent UN action in Korea.

tions. On September 15 MacArthur launched a brilliant amphibious operation with a successful landing at Inchon near the western end of the 38th parallel. At the same time the UN forces broke out of the Pusan encirclement and began a drive northward. A large number of North Korean soldiers were trapped, over half of them were soon captured or killed, and the rest were driven out of South Korea. Seoul was recaptured on September 26, and MacArthur's men were soon at the 38th parallel.

Having driven the Communist invaders out of South Korea, the UN forces had to make a tough decision: should they undertake an invasion of the North? Would such action bring the Chinese Communists into the war? President Truman first approved military operations north of the 38th degree of latitude on September 11, if, as he later wrote, "there was no indication or threat of entry of Soviet or Chinese Communist elements in force." The UN General Assembly also gave its approval.

Figure 5 The Korean War, 1950–1953 *(From A History of the American People by Norman A. Graebner, Gilbert C. Fite, and Philip L. White. Copyright © 1970 by McGraw-Hill, Inc.)*

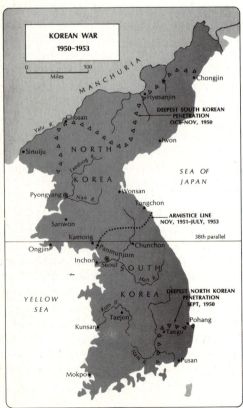

MacArthur's forces crossed the 38th parallel on October 7 and began a rapid advance up the peninsula. By the end of the month they were within fifty miles of the Yalu River, the boundary between North Korea and Manchuria. Although the Truman administration did not believe the Chinese would intervene in the Korean war, it wanted to make sure that air strikes were confined to the Korean peninsula. This concern was a major reason for Truman's famous conference in mid-October with General MacArthur on Wake Island. The General assured Truman repeatedly "that the Korean conflict was over and that there was little possibility of the Chinese coming in."

By the time Truman left Wake Island on his long flight back to Washington, the first military units of the Chinese "volunteers" were crossing the Yalu into Korea. Mao Tse-tung and his associates had evidently decided that a reunited Korea under American control would be intolerable—a powerful opponent at China's very doorstep. But the large-scale Chinese intervention did not come until after MacArthur had commenced his last great offensive. On November 26, thirty-three Chinese divisions hit the middle of the UN line. MacArthur's armies had advanced along two widely separated routes, which left the center wide open. The Communists exploited this mistake, forced the UN soldiers into a retreat, and within two weeks had isolated MacArthur's units into three bridgeheads. The Chinese and North Koreans quickly cleared most of the northern peninsula, sent MacArthur's forces reeling across the 38th parallel, and once more forced the abandonment of Seoul.

The month of December in 1950 was a grim time for Americans. United States and South Korean military units suffered a series of humiliating defeats. The UN soldiers during the cruel winter of 1950–1951 not only faced a ferocious enemy, equipped with Russian tanks and aircraft, but also had to cope with bitter cold, numerous storms, and an exceedingly rugged terrain. General MacArthur importuned Washington for permission to bomb "the privileged sanctuary of the adjacent Manchurian border." President Truman and his advisers considered MacArthur's proposals too risky. They were acutely aware of the Soviet Union's obligation to China under the mutual security pact of February 1950. They were afraid of getting trapped in a large land war in China and of precipitating a global war in the Far East.

In January 1951 the U.S. 8th Army, under the command of General Matthew B. Ridgway, finally halted the Communist advance in South Korea. The UN forces slowly resumed the offensive, and by March they had reoccupied Seoul and reached the 38th parallel once more. As MacArthur's men moved northward, the question of crossing the parallel was again raised. With the Republic of Korea largely cleared of Communist troops, President Truman and many United Nations spokesmen believed the time was ripe for a negotiated settlement. MacArthur was

Figure 6   American Forces Assault a Hill in Korea *(U.S. Army Photograph)*

informed by Washington on March 20 that Truman was about to seek a settlement of the war through diplomatic means. At this point the General openly challenged the President. On March 24 MacArthur defiantly threatened mainland China with an attack. In Truman's opinion, this threat killed any hope of an early truce. In a letter to Representative Joseph W. Martin, which the Congressman read in the House of Representatives on April 5, MacArthur expressed his views freely and vigorously. He wanted to reunify Korea, unleash Chiang for an attack on mainland China, and fight communism in Asia rather than in Europe.

Truman could no longer brook such insubordination, and on April 10 he relieved MacArthur of his command, replacing him with General Ridgway. The General's dismissal created a furor such as the country had not experienced since the controversy over Roosevelt's court reorganization bill in 1937. The White House received a flood of vituperative letters and telegrams—more than 27,000 within twelve days. Flags were flown at half-mast in Massachusetts and Ohio, Truman was burned in effigy in towns across the country, and several state legislatures condemned him for his "irresponsible and capricious action." Republican leaders in Washington urged a congressional investigation and talked of impeaching the President.

In a few days Douglas MacArthur flew into San Francisco and began a triumphal tour of the United States. He was accorded great ovations. In a moment of high drama he appeared before a joint session of Congress on April 19. "I address you," the General began, "with neither rancor nor bitterness in the fading twilight of my life, with but one purpose in mind: To serve my country." MacArthur described the frustration and humiliation he had suffered in trying to win a war in Korea under the restrictions imposed by his Washington superiors. He rejected the concept of limited war. His views were endorsed by such prominent Republicans as Robert A. Taft and Herbert Hoover, and the controversy that swirled around his dismissal whipped up the GOP assault on Truman and Acheson. But the reaction to the MacArthur affair went beyond politics. It revealed the dissatisfaction with containment as a strategic concept in the conduct of American foreign policy. For containment ran counter to the nation's historical approach to international conflict, to the American expectation of quick solutions and total victories in foreign disputes and wars.

A joint Senate committee under the chairmanship of Senator Richard B. Russell held extensive hearings on the MacArthur case between May 3 and June 25, 1951. MacArthur presented his case, but so did the Truman administration, whose position began to elicit more public understanding and backing as the hearings continued. Many Americans, probably a majority of them, came to agree with the administration's contention that Europe was the crucial theater in the cold war and that it would be a terrible mistake for the United States to become involved in a full-scale war with China in Asia. General MacArthur's challenge did not reverse American policy in the Far East, but it did cause the administration to adopt a more inflexible posture toward Peking—nonrecognition became

Figure 7 U.S. Marine Artillerymen in Central Korea *(Defense Department Photograph)*

an established policy—and to increase its aid to the Chinese Nationalists on Formosa.

By the spring of 1951, the Korean conflict had become deadlocked. In April and May the American forces and their UN allies repulsed two major Communist offensives, with the enemy suffering heavy losses. The United Nations had branded China as an aggressor in February 1951, and on May 18 the United States secured UN approval of an embargo against the shipment of munitions and critical war materials to China. Still, the military action had bogged down in the general vicinity of the 38th parallel. When the Soviet delegate to the UN suggested in June 1951 that an armistice be arranged, with mutual withdrawal of the two sides behind the 38th parallel, Washington welcomed the move. Leaders of the opposing forces began discussions looking toward an armistice on July 10, only to have them break down two days later. They were continued in an on-again, off-again fashion during the rest of the year. A truce was held up because of the disagreement over an exact boundary and the disposition of the prisoners of war.

The Korean war was the first war ever fought by a world peace organization with an international army. Technically, the war was "a police action by the United Nations." But its consequences—for Korea and for the United States—were profound. Sixteen nations eventually sent military units to Korea or provided other assistance to the UN forces there. The United States, however, bore the burden of the war, along with the South Koreans. The Americans provided half of the ground forces, 86 percent of the naval power, and 93 percent of the air power. The United States suffered 142,000 casualties in Korea. At home, the Korean intervention brought the passage of the Defense Production Act of August 1950 and new economic controls. Rigid price controls and rationing were not necessary, but taxes were increased and efforts were made to prevent price increases and large wage hikes. In December 1950, following the Chinese intervention in the war, President Truman declared a state of national emergency and outlined a vast new mobilization program.

The Korean war greatly stimulated American military preparedness, which had been kept at a low level by economically minded congressmen (and for a time by the Truman administration). By June 1952 almost $2\frac{1}{4}$ million men and women had been added to the U.S. armed forces, and the air force had been enormously expanded. NATO, which had been slow to get off the ground, was also given a vigorous boost.

Internal Security and the Politics of Fear

By the time the shooting war began in Korea in mid-1950, the American people had succumbed to an irrational fear of disloyalty and subversion within the United States, and this outbreak of distrust and hysteria was to last until about 1954. Many factors were involved in the development of America's second Red Scare[2]—the exigencies and setbacks of the cold war, the Truman administration's loyalty program, a series of sensational spy cases, the Korean war, the Republican party's desperate search for a viable issue to use against the Democrats, and the emergence of an extraordinary demagogic leader. During the late forties and early fifties suspicion destroyed habitual trust and guilt-by-association tactics damaged the lives and reputations of many men and women. In the quest for security, teachers were required to sign loyalty oaths, the courts and Congress assumed a harshly punitive attitude toward Communists, and liberals and reformers of every kind were criticized.

Following World War II the Federal Bureau of Investigation began the first comprehensive scrutiny of government workers, and the federal departments undertook their own loyalty checks. In November 1946 the President created a Temporary Commission on Employee Loyalty to study the whole question, and its major recommendations were embodied in Truman's Executive Order No. 9835 on March 21, 1947. This order instituted a thorough investigation of all federal civil servants. The administration's loyalty inquest, while thorough, was conducted with procedural safeguards and provision for nonjudicial review. By the time the loyalty checks were completed in April 1951, 3,225,611 workers had been cleared, 2,941 had resigned, and 304 had been dismissed on the basis of reasonable doubt.

In 1948 the Truman administration began the prosecution of the top Communist party leaders under the Smith Act of 1940. After the Supreme Court upheld the conviction of the Communist leaders, the government proceeded to prosecute dozens of lesser figures in the party. The administration's actions and rhetoric doubtless helped develop the framework for the extravagant anticommunism of later years.

The first public awareness of Russian wartime espionage came well before the introduction of Truman's loyalty program. Early in 1945 FBI agents discovered a large number of classified State Department documents when they raided the offices of *Amerasia,* a small Communist-sponsored magazine specializing in Far Eastern affairs. The following year, in February 1946, it was disclosed by a Canadian Royal Commission that several local spy rings had given the Russians military information and atomic secrets during the war. Meanwhile, the House Un-American Activities Committee was engaged in a search for subversives. Two of the

[2]The first Red Scare in 1919–1920 was characterized by an outbreak of intolerance and mob violence directed at bolshevism and ideological nonconformity.

witnesses who appeared before HUAC in the summer of 1948 provided information that led to one of the most bizarre and sensational cases in American history. Elizabeth Bentley and Whittaker Chambers—both former Communists—described the existence of two independent espionage rings operating in Washington for the Soviet Union in the 1930s.

Chambers, a senior editor of *Time* magazine, identified Alger Hiss, the highly respected president of the Carnegie Foundation for International Peace, as a member of a Communist cell in Washington during the thirties. Later in the fall of 1948 Chambers broadened his charges, asserting that Hiss had given him copies of State Department documents to be turned over to Soviet agents. To prove his charges, Chambers escorted government agents to his farm at Westminster, Maryland, where he removed microfilm copies from a hollowed-out pumpkin! He claimed that the documents had been given to him by Hiss in 1938. Hiss, appearing before a federal grand jury in New York, denied that he had ever given State Department documents to Chambers or to anyone else. But the grand jury indicted him on two counts of perjury; the statute of limitations prevented him from being tried for treason. The trial began in May 1949 and ended six weeks later in a hung jury. A second trial was concluded in late January 1950, with Hiss being found guilty and sentenced to five years in prison.

Many liberals felt that Alger Hiss was being persecuted by a vindictive congressional investigating committee, and some men in high places, like Dean Acheson, refused to turn their backs on him. For others the Hiss case confirmed their darkest fears and suspicions. Representative Richard M. Nixon of California, one of the most aggressive HUAC members in the whole affair, described the case as "the most treasonable conspiracy in American history." To many people who had long suspected the liberalism of Roosevelt and Truman, Hiss had become the symbol of all that had gone wrong in the United States and the world. And if Hiss was guilty of subversion, why not others like him?

The espionage in which Hiss was implicated occurred before the war, but other cases soon produced evidence of Communist infiltration in more recent years. In March 1949 a young New Yorker named Judith Coplon, a former political analyst in the Department of Justice, was arrested with her Russian lover on the charge of stealing classified documents for Soviet agents.[3] The case of Dr. Klaus Fuchs, revealed to the public in early February 1950, was much more important. Fuchs, a German-born scientist employed in the British nuclear energy establishment, had worked at Los Alamos, New Mexico, during the war on the development

---

[3]Miss Coplon was tried and convicted in two separate cases in 1949 and 1950, but she escaped imprisonment when her convictions were overturned on appeal because of technicalities. The government declined to prosecute her again.

of the first atomic bomb. When arrested by the British, he confessed to transmitting important atomic secrets to the Russians between 1942 and 1947. The story Fuchs told led to the arrest of Harry Gold, an accomplice in the United States, and four other Americans: Julius and Ethel Rosenberg, Morton Sobell, and David Greenglass. They were all charged with passing atomic secrets to the Russians during and after the war. They were tried and convicted in 1951. The Rosenbergs were sentenced to death and were executed in June 1953.

Hiss and Fuchs and the Rosenbergs seemed to explain many of the disappointments and setbacks the United States had suffered since the war. At a time when the President was asking Congress to vote billions of dollars to halt the Communist expansion in Europe and Asia, how else could one explain the fall of China, the loss of America's atomic monopoly, and the inability to win the war in Korea? Disloyalty, subversion, and trickery at home—by intellectuals, left-wingers, and one-world New Dealers—must be at the root of the nation's difficulties. As Senator Homer Capehart of Indiana exclaimed, "How much more are we going to have to take? Fuchs and Acheson and Hiss and hydrogen bombs threatening outside and New Dealers eating away the vitals of the nation. In the name of Heaven, is this the best America can do?"

Men like Capehart had earlier tried to cope with the threat of internal subversion by adopting stronger antisubversive legislation. They had been denied a new law in 1948, when President Truman successfully vetoed the Mundt-Nixon bill. But the shocking developments of 1949, the rising tide of anticommunism, and the sensational charges made by Republican congressmen smoothed the path for the McCarran Internal Security Act of September 1950, which was passed overwhelmingly over Truman's veto. The McCarran Act required Communist and Communist-front organizations to register with the Attorney General, made them publish periodic financial statements and other reports, and forbade Communists to work in defense plants or use American passports. The new law broadened the definition of espionage and sabotage, extended the statute of limitations for prosecution, and made it illegal to *conspire* to perform any act that would "substantially contribute" to the establishment of a totalitarian government in the United States. In the McCarran-Walter Act, which was passed over Truman's veto in 1952, Congress provided for the screening of undesirables seeking entry into the United States and struck at communism through various exclusion and registration clauses.[4]

One of the consequences of the heightened public concern over

[4]The McCarran-Walter Act was primarily designed to provide an up-to-date codification of the nation's immigration laws. It repealed the notorious clauses excluding Orientals from the United States but retained the quota system.

internal security in the United States was the Republican party's discovery and eventual exploitation of the issue. Many Republicans were predisposed to seize hold of this issue because of the long-time conservative hostility toward the New Deal. The Truman administration's containment policy, its comprehensive loyalty program, and the defection of Henry A. Wallace shielded the Democrats from a penetrating Republican attack invoking the Communist issue in the campaign of 1948. But the loss of that election left the Republicans frustrated and embittered, and the events of 1949 and 1950 brought them finally to the employment of anticommunism as a principal weapon in their political war against the Democrats.

The man most successful in demonstrating the political possibilities of the Communist issue was a first-term senator from Wisconsin named Joseph R. McCarthy. A lawyer and former circuit judge, McCarthy had narrowly defeated Senator Robert M. La Follette, Jr., in the Republican primary of 1946 and had gone on to defeat his Democratic opponent in the November election. The Wisconsin Senator violated the Senate's rules and customs from the beginning of his tenure, spouted extravagant assertions, and engaged in questionable dealings with lobbyists for certain vested interests. He had displeased powerful senators from both parties, lost his only major committee assignment, and was worried about his chances of reelection in 1952. At this point, while casting about for an issue—any issue—that would revive his political fortunes, he adopted the anti-Communist tactic.

McCarthy first came to the attention of the American public as a result of a speech he made to the Republican Women's Club of Wheeling, West Virginia, on February 9, 1950. Asserting that the United States had been the greatest power in the world on V-J Day, he explained that the country's strength had diminished "because of the traitorous actions of those who have been treated so well by this Nation." McCarthy's precise words on this occasion will probably never be known, but according to the radio and newspaper men who followed his rough draft, he held up a sheaf of papers and shouted: "I have here in my hand a list of 205—a list of names that were made known to the Secretary of State as being members of the Communist Party and who nevertheless are still working and shaping policy in the State Department." The Senator was hard to pin down, but his charges were swiftly carried by the mass media from one end of the country to the other.

Back in Washington the Democrats sought to deal with McCarthy by having a subcommittee of the Senate Foreign Relations Committee make a thorough investigation of his accusations. The subcommittee, under the chairmanship of Senator Millard E. Tydings of Maryland, began a series of extensive hearings on March 8, 1950. McCarthy soon stated that he would rest his case on his contention that Professor Owen Lattimore of Johns Hopkins University, a Far Eastern expert who had served as a consultant to the State Department on several occasions, was the "top Russian espionage agent" in the United States. Lattimore denied under oath that he was a Communist or a "follower of the communist line." When he was later indicted for perjury, his case was thrown out by the court. The Tydings committee reported in July 1950; its Democratic majority called the McCarthy charges "a fraud and a hoax" on the Senate and on the American people.

Most Republican congressmen defended McCarthy. McCarthyism, Robert Griffith remarks, "was shorthand for the issue of 'communism-in-government,' a preeminently Republican issue which served as the cutting edge of the party's drive for power." This was borne out in the congressional elections of 1950, when the Republicans invoked the subversive theme with a vengeance. In California, for example, Richard M. Nixon was elected to the Senate by exploiting McCarthyite issues. McCarthy became the most popular campaigner for the GOP and probably contributed to the defeat of Senator Tydings in Maryland and Governor Chester Bowles in Connecticut.

The Korean war also strengthened McCarthy by refueling anti-Communist extremism, and in the early fifties his influence increased spectacularly. He fought off all efforts in the Senate to restrain him, and throughout 1951 added his reckless voice to the China inquest and continually sought to discredit the Truman administration. His wild accusations and innuendos resulted in a long succession of charges and countercharges. Few public figures in American history have matched McCarthy's intemperate and vituperative attacks on his adversaries. He denounced all the "egg-sucking phony liberals" whose "pitiful squealing . . . would hold sacrosanct those Communists and queers" who had sold China into "atheistic slavery," and he committed himself to driving out the "prancing mimics of the Moscow party line in the State Department."

McCarthy was not the only practitioner of McCarthyism; he was joined by many Republican politicians and some powerful anti-Communist Democrats. But the Wisconsin Senator was the star of the show. He dominated the channels of mass communications. He intimidated government officials and private citizens, and while many Washington politicians deplored his methods, few of them would openly challenge him at the height of his power. By 1953 McCarthy was given credit for having won almost a dozen Republican Senate elections, and a "myth of political invincibility" had grown up about him. This estimate was exaggerated, but unquestionably McCarthy was an influential force in American politics.

"I Like Ike": The Election of 1952

The frustration and rancor that spread through American society during
the final years of Harry S. Truman's Presidency brightened Republican
prospects in the election of 1952. Truman's popularity ebbed sharply, and
in the public mind his administration was associated with a wide
assortment of national setbacks and threatening problems—the involvement in Korea, Chinese aggression, internal communism, corruption in
government, high taxes, and inflation. Republican leaders were determined not to let electoral success slip from their grasp as they had done in
1948, and that determination was one reason for the most vigorous
intraparty struggle the GOP had experienced in a generation.

The fight for the Republican nomination in 1952 reflected the sharp
division in the party that had existed for many years. The more conservative faction championed Senator Taft, who had announced his candidacy
in October 1951. Strongly supported by the regular party leaders and
business interests of the Midwest, the conservative wing urged a real
alternative to the Democrats. The liberal-internationalist wing of the
Republican party, which was strongest in the East and in the Far West,
viewed Taft's position on foreign and domestic questions with suspicion,
and men like Governor Dewey doubted that he could win if nominated.
Liberal Republicans pinned their hopes on General Dwight D. Eisenhower, then on leave from the presidency of Columbia University to serve as
Supreme Commander of the NATO forces in Europe. A draft Eisenhower
movement began to take shape by the late summer of 1951, and in January
1952 the General finally agreed to accept the nomination if it were offered
to him.

Eisenhower won the New Hampshire primary in March and later was
victorious in several other primaries. Meanwhile, Taft was campaigning
hard and obtaining a large number of delegate commitments, especially in
the Middle West and the South. As the preconvention campaign proceeded, Eisenhower's spokesmen charged that the Taft-controlled state
organizations in the Southern states were disqualifying pro-Eisenhower
delegates chosen by local and state conventions. By the time the
Republican National Convention opened in Chicago on July 7, Taft
probably had a slight lead over Eisenhower in the number of committed
delegates, though it was clear to most observers that the General was far
more popular than the Senator with rank-and-file Republicans.

When the convention began, the Eisenhower forces succeeded in
passing by a vote of 658 to 548 the so-called fair play amendment, which
provided that the contested delegates seated by the national committee
during the previous week could not vote on the credentials of other
delegates. This victory foreshadowed Eisenhower's nomination, for the
Eisenhower delegations challenging the regular slates in Texas, Georgia,

and Louisiana were later seated by convention vote, and the General was nominated on the first ballot. Senator Richard M. Nixon was selected for the vice-presidential nomination. The Republican platform was strongly critical of the Democratic administration, charging that in seven years it had "squandered the unprecedented power and prestige which were ours at the close of World War II" and that it had "lost the peace so dearly earned by World War II."

There were several aspirants for the Democratic nomination, but most of them were handicapped at first by uncertainty over President Truman's own possible candidacy. This was not true of Senator Estes Kefauver of Tennessee, who had won a Senate seat in 1948 by defeating the machine of Edward H. Crump of Memphis. Kefauver had attracted national attention as Chairman of the special Senate Subcommittee to Investigate Interstate Crime. But he was not popular with the big-city Democratic bosses because his investigations had disclosed links between organized crime and local politics. Nor was he acceptable to Truman, whose administration, he declared, should be doing more to clean up corruption in government. The Tennessee Senator entered the March 11 New Hampshire Democratic primary and to the surprise of the nation defeated the President in the preferential vote. This shocking development no doubt hastened Truman's announcement that he would not himself be a candidate for reelection, an announcement he made on March 29 at a Jefferson-Jackson Day dinner in Washington. In order to stop Kefauver, who went on to win a series of other primaries, Truman turned to Adlai E. Stevenson, who had made a fine record as Governor of Illinois. When Stevenson insisted that he had no interest in running for President, Truman and other party leaders endorsed seventy-four-year-old Alben W. Barkley, who eventually retired from the race because of opposition from several labor leaders.

At the Democratic National Convention, also held in Chicago that year, party leaders again sought to persuade Governor Stevenson to seek the nomination, and he reluctantly agreed. Although Kefauver led on the first two ballots, his brave fight was unavailing against the power and influence of the administration and other Democratic leaders. Stevenson was nominated on the third ballot, and Senator John J. Sparkman of Alabama, one of the architects of the compromise civil rights plank designed to prevent a Southern bolt, was chosen as his running mate. The platform committed the party to the repeal of the Taft-Hartley Act, maintenance of high price supports for agriculture, and continuation of the Fair Deal. Under the theme of "peace with honor," the assembled Democrats endorsed American intervention in Korea and praised the Truman administration's foreign policies. In accepting the presidential nomination, Stevenson warned that "sacrifice, patience, understanding and implacable purpose may be our lot for years to come. Let's face it. Let's talk sense to the American people."

The Republican campaign did not get off to a fast start, since General Eisenhower was rather fumbling and uninspiring in his early speeches. In September Eisenhower's "great crusade" began to pick up momentum. The GOP candidate began to stress the formula Senator Karl E. Mundt called K_1C_2—Korea, communism, and corruption in government. Eisenhower pledged his support to all Republican candidates, including extreme conservatives and such rabid anti-Communists as Senator McCarthy. He made a special effort to assuage the bitterness of the Taft faction, arranging a special conference with the Senator in New York City on September 12. As a result of that meeting the two Republican leaders reached an agreement on the importance of fiscal responsibility in the conduct of the national government, the need to reduce federal expenditures and balance the budget, and the necessity of defending "liberty against creeping socialism."

The Eisenhower campaign ran into real trouble only once—the dramatic episode of the secret Nixon fund. On September 18 it was disclosed that Richard M. Nixon, the GOP vice-presidential nominee, had benefited from a private fund of about $18,000 contributed by California businessmen. Eisenhower, who had said that his administration would be as "clean as a hound's tooth," was in a dilemma. Some of the General's advisers urged him to remove Nixon from the ticket, but Eisenhower hesitated. Meanwhile, Nixon fought back, presenting his case to the people in a national television broadcast on September 23. The speech was melodramatic but effective. The Senator emphasized his own relatively limited personal assets, noted that his wife Pat "doesn't have a mink coat," and referred to his cocker spaniel Checkers—a gift to his children—"regardless of what they say about it, we're going to keep it." The response was all that Nixon could have wished; nearly 200,000 telegrams poured into the party's national committee urging Nixon's retention on the ticket. Eisenhower himself accepted this verdict.

In the meantime, the Democrats had launched their campaign. Stevenson quickly emerged as something of a television personality—articulate, thoughtful, and witty. He had a special way with words. He assured his audiences that "if the Republicans will stop telling lies about us, we will stop telling the truth about them." It was clear to Stevenson that in some respects the Truman administration would be a liability to his campaign, and he sought to establish his independence of Truman. The Democratic nominee laid out his position in a series of extraordinary addresses during the campaign. Basically he continued the New Deal–Fair Deal line.

The Republicans had a popular candidate, they were united in supporting him, and their campaign was abundantly financed. Republican strategists made extensive use of television, which assumed importance for the first time in a presidential campaign, and they used the advertising and public relations techniques of Madison Avenue to give their candidates a good "image." Party campaigners, including McCarthy and Nixon, did not neglect the Communist issue. They spoke scornfully of the "egghead" support that Stevenson was receiving. As the campaign developed, Eisenhower began to emphasize the Korean war. He described the negotiations as a "swindle," a "Soviet trap" designed to enable the North Koreans to renew their strength. At Detroit on October 24 the General made a sensational announcement: "I shall go to Korea."

Both major parties waged vigorous and comprehensive campaigns. The Democrats, remembering the miracle of 1948, hoped the voters would respond to their campaign slogan that Americans had "never had it so good." But the election returns dashed their hopes. Eisenhower won 33,824,351 popular votes (55.4 percent) to Stevenson's 27,314,987 in the heaviest turnout (63.3 percent of the potential electorate) since 1908. The electoral vote was 442 to 89, with the Democratic ticket carrying only nine Southern and border states.

The defections from the Democratic coalition were numerous, including Southerners, Catholics, certain ethnic groups, and even low-income voters. In the South, where Governor James F. Byrnes of South Carolina and Governor Allan F. Shivers of Texas actively supported Eisenhower and Nixon, the Republican ticket obtained 48.9 percent of the popular vote and carried Virginia, Florida, Tennessee, Texas, and Oklahoma. Almost one-fourth of Eisenhower's total vote came from people who had voted for Truman in 1948, and many new voters cast their ballots for the Republicans. Negroes were the only group that gave Stevenson as high a percentage of its vote as for Truman four years earlier. Yet the election was preeminently a personal victory for Dwight D. Eisenhower, and only his immense popularity allowed the Republicans to win control of Congress. The Republicans gained 22 House seats—3 more than the 218 needed to give them control—and only 1 Senate seat, just enough to make it possible for them to organize that body. A majority of the voters still thought of themselves as Democrats. Still, after twenty years of Democratic control, the Republicans were moving back to 1600 Pennsylvania Avenue, and also to supremacy on Capitol Hill.

SUGGESTIONS FOR FURTHER READING

For the complex situation in China during and after World War II and the American effort to deal with it, see the outstanding work by Herbert Feis, *The China Tangle: The American Effort in China from Pearl Harbor to the Marshall*

*Available in paperback edition.

Mission* (1953); Tang Tsou, *America's Failure in China, 1941–1950* (1963); and Warren I. Cohen, *America's Response to China: An Interpretative History of Sino-American Relations** (1971).

Glenn D. Paige, *The Korean Decision** (1968), is a detailed account of decision making between June 24 and June 30, 1950. The best of several books on the Korean war is David Rees, *Korea: The Limited War** (1964). Allen S. Whiting's *China Crosses the Yalu: The Decision to Enter the Korean War** (1960) throws light on an important aspect of the war. John W. Spanier's *The Truman-MacArthur Controversy and the Korean War** (1959) is a scholarly treatment of that subject, stressing the concept of "limited war." For another account of the Truman-MacArthur conflict, see Richard H. Rovere and Arthur M. Schlesinger, Jr., *The MacArthur Controversy and American Foreign Policy* (rev. ed., 1965). A broader treatment of the impact of the Korean war on American politics can be found in Ronald J. Caridi, *The Korean War and American Politics: The Republican Party as a Case Study* (1968).

Several illuminating studies have been completed on the internal security problem and the anti-Communist hysteria at midcentury. Alan D. Harper, *The Politics of Loyalty: The White House and the Communist Issue, 1946–1952* (1969), is a balanced treatment of the Truman administration's loyalty program and its response to the anti-Communist issue. Much more critical of the Truman administration are Athan Theoharis, *Seeds of Repression: Harry S. Truman and the Origins of McCarthyism* (1971), and Richard M. Freeland, *The Truman Doctrine and the Origins of McCarthyism: Foreign Policy, Domestic Politics, and Internal Security, 1946–1948** (1972). Walter Goodman, *The Committee: The Extraordinary Career of the House Committee on Un-American Activities* (1968), is a solid study. Earl Latham's *The Communist Controversy in Washington: From the New Deal to McCarthy** (1966) provides a full discussion of the rising Communist issue, which is explained in terms of a conservative drive for power. Latham had edited a useful collection of essays entitled *The Meaning of McCarthyism** (1965). The most revealing appraisal of McCarthy's character is Richard H. Rovere's *Senator Joe McCarthy** (1959). The most thorough study to date of McCarthy's political career is Robert Griffith's prize-winning *The Politics of Fear: Joseph R. McCarthy and the Senate** (1970), which focuses on the senatorial stage upon which the Wisconsin Senator operated. Michael Paul Rogin, *The Intellectuals and McCarthy: The Radical Specter** (1967), is a brilliant work that emphasizes the role of political elites in the development of McCarthyism.

An excellent brief analysis of the election of 1952 by Barton J. Bernstein is contained in Schlesinger and Israel (eds.), *History of American Presidential Elections*, vol. IV. Also see Samuel Lubell, *The Revolt of the Moderates* (1956); Bert Cochran, *Adlai Stevenson: Patrician among the Politicians* (1969); and Joseph Bruce Gorman, *Kefauver: A Political Biography* (1971).

Chapter 5

Eisenhower
and the Politics
of Moderation

Dwight David Eisenhower, the nation's thirty-fourth President, suited the 1950s singularly well. Coming to office at a time of confusion, division, and bitterness, the immensely popular "Ike" rendered the decade's politics less acrimonious, eased the accumulated tensions of a generation of crisis, and helped to restore a sense of national unity. The new President's moderate Republicanism and restrained approach to government appealed to millions of Americans who had grown weary of great public enterprises and social conflict. The purposes and style of the Eisenhower administration blended comfortably into a national mood of complacency, well-being, and self-indulgence.

Eisenhower's two terms in the White House contained their full share of setbacks and unexpected difficulties, including two serious illnesses the President suffered in 1955 and 1956. Many of the General's early supporters were disappointed by the results of his executive leadership, in some cases because the administration did not challenge the New Deal, in others because it did not undertake fresh programs and a more venturesome course in domestic affairs. Yet there were some notable accomplishments during Eisenhower's Presidency, and there can be no doubt that he greatly influenced the course of our recent history. Richard Rovere has suggested that, in part because he was a Republican, Eisenhower was able to do "many of the things that needed doing and that could not have been done by a Democratic administration." Thus he liquidated the Korean war without being labeled an appeaser, and his administration helped to establish the New Deal as an enduring feature of our national government.

The New Republican Administration

Dwight D. Eisenhower's long years of military service gave him a unique background among twentieth-century Presidents. Born in 1890 at Denison, Texas, into an economically pressed family of Pennsylvania Dutch descent, he spent his boyhood in Abilene, Kansas, which was still something of a frontier town at the turn of the century. In some ways Ike never left home, for his world would always retain the traditional American values and virtues he had assimilated as a boy in Abilene. In other respects, however, his world soon broadened. He received an appointment to West Point and was graduated from the Military Academy in 1915. After serving as an officer in the tank training program at Camp Colt during World War I, he held a variety of assignments at army posts and service schools during the next two decades. He distinguished himself in army maneuvers held in Louisiana in 1941 and was subsequently assigned to the war plans division of the War Department. General Marshall soon recommended him to command American forces in Europe, and he served as Commander of the Allied invasion of North Africa, Sicily, and Italy. He was then selected as the Supreme Commander of the Allied forces in Europe, and in this role he directed the momentous invasion of France and the subsequent conquest of Germany. He emerged from the war as a five-star general and an authentic military hero.

The General had demonstrated a remarkable talent for leadership. His military success had come not as a result of genius as a strategist or brilliance as a field commander, but basically as a result of his unusual personal qualities and his capacity as a coordinator and conciliator. He knew how to direct large operations, was willing to shoulder vast responsibilities, and was familiar with the operation of modern bureaucracies. Eisenhower was also at home in the realm of international relations, and he was firmly committed to a policy of internationalism. In other ways he was ill-equipped for the task of presidential leadership. His civilian experience before 1952 was severely limited, he was not well acquainted with the way in which the political system worked in the United States, and he was unfamiliar with the problems and complexities of American society. His ideas, embodying such basic values as self-reliance and faith in free enterprise, while widely shared by his fellow Americans, tended to be cast in a simplistic and somewhat romantic mold of an earlier day. The new President was also a man of extraordinary personal warmth and charm. As Arthur Krock of the *New York Times* wrote in 1957:

> His manner is genial; his ways and reflexes are kindly. His bearing is soldierly, yet his well-tailored civilian clothes never seem out of character. His smile is attractively pensive, his frequent grin is infectious, his laughter ready and hearty. He fairly radiates "goodness," simple faith and the honorable, industrious background of his heritage.

Eisenhower's approach to the presidency differed sharply from that of his immediate predecessors. He had no taste for the ordinary ways of the politician: for the rough-and-tumble of active partisanship, for haggling over matters of patronage, for involvement in the details of government. This "least partisan President," as Rexford G. Tugwell has called him, seemed to stand above the political battles, to preside over his administration rather than to be actively involved in it. Especially at first, before Senator Taft's death in the summer of 1953, he approached Congress with great deference. He seemed to feel that the President should not initiate legislation or attempt to coerce Congress. He also relied heavily upon a carefully organized staff and departmental system. Former Governor Sherman Adams of New Hampshire became the "assistant to the President." His task was to direct a staff in serving as a clearinghouse on policy.

If Sherman Adams shielded Eisenhower from many troublesome details and as a trusted assistant supervised important governmental functions in the White House, the members of the Cabinet assumed larger roles in the operation of the executive branch. The most prominent Cabinet official was Secretary of State John Foster Dulles. The second most influential Cabinet member was Secretary of the Treasury George M. Humphrey, an Ohio industrialist and financier. "In cabinet meetings I always wait for George Humphrey to speak," Eisenhower once said, because "I know . . . he will say just what I am thinking." Another businessman, Charles E. Wilson, president of the General Motors Corporation, was appointed Secretary of Defense. Ezra Taft Benson of Utah, a farm marketing specialist and an apostle of the Mormon church, became Secretary of Agriculture. The other departments were also headed by businessmen or Republican politicians, except for Secretary of Labor Martin P. Durkin, a Democrat, a Catholic, and the president of the United Association of Journeyman Plumbers and Steamfitters. According to one wit, the new Cabinet contained "eight millionaires and a plumber."

Figure 8 President Eisenhower and Secretary of State Dulles *(National Park Service Photograph, Courtesy Dwight D. Eisenhower Library)*

Eisenhower was determined to balance the federal budget, remove as many economic controls as possible, and prevent the government from becoming further involved in business. He also hoped to heal the sharp division in the Republican party, to curb its strong isolationist tendencies, and to modernize it in certain other respects. It soon became apparent that one of the threats to the kind of Republican party Eisenhower envisaged—and indeed to the functioning and success of the administration itself—was the virulent anti-Communist movement led by Joseph R. McCarthy.

The Climax of McCarthyism

Many people assumed that the election of a Republican President would cause McCarthy and other vociferous anti-Communists to lose influence and fade from the headlines. But McCarthyism did not disappear. The administration was zealous in its own search for subversives in government, broadening the definition of "security risk" to include behavior quite unrelated to disloyalty. Almost 3,000 such "security risks" were dismissed from government positions in 1953 and 1954, although none of them were charged with subversion or were brought to trial in a court of law. The most publicized security case was that of J. Robert Oppenheimer, who had played a major role in the development of the atomic bomb during World War II. President Eisenhower, following the initiative of Chairman Lewis L. Strauss of the Atomic Energy Commission, directed in late 1953 that Oppenheimer be barred from access to classified documents. The FBI had prepared a report that detailed the scientist's prewar associations with Communists, and the President acted against him because of alleged "fundamental defects in his character." Oppenheimer was exonerated several years later.

It was soon evident that the administration's security program and anti-Communist activities did not satisfy Joe McCarthy. Senator Taft had hoped, in organizing the upper house in the Republican-controlled Eighty-third Congress, to sidetrack McCarthy by giving the chairmanship of the Senate Internal Security Committee to the colorless William E. Jenner. McCarthy was made Chairman of the Senate Government Operations Committee, and he also assumed the chairmanship of that committee's Permanent Subcommittee on Investigations. The Wisconsin Senator quickly asserted the subcommittee's claims to at least a share of the jurisdiction over communism in government. He loudly objected to Eisenhower's appointment of Charles E. Bohlen as Ambassador to the Soviet Union, charging that Bohlen, a career diplomat who had been at the Yalta Conference, was "Acheson's architect of disaster." In March 1953 McCarthy announced that he had "negotiated" an agreement with Greek shipowners to stop all trade with mainland China and North Korea. McCarthy's subcommittee carried out a search for Communists in the Voice of America program, demoralizing the staff of that agency in the process. Two of the Senator's assistants, chief counsel Roy M. Cohn and "consultant" G. David Schine, made a whirlwind trip to Western Europe in the spring of 1953, searching for "subversive" literature in the libraries of the American Information Service. The State Department also issued a new directive banning from American information activities all "books, music, paintings, and the like . . . of any Communists, fellow travelers, *et cetera.*" Throughout 1953 and the first part of 1954 McCarthy made one wild charge after another, dramatically announced numerous "disclosures" of Communist infiltration, and conducted a series of widely publicized investigations.

The administration avoided a confrontation with McCarthy and in many instances went out of its way to please him. Thus R. W. Scott McLeod, a McCarthyite, was made security officer for the State Department, and Secretary Dulles allowed McCarthy a strong voice in the department's personnel policy. Eisenhower was privately contemptuous of McCarthy, but he was quoted as saying, "I will not get in the gutter with that guy." In any case, Eisenhower thought the best way to deal with McCarthy was to ignore him.

The McCarthy committee's investigation of alleged subversion among scientists working for the Army Signal Corps center at Fort Monmouth, New Jersey, led the Senator, in February 1954, to launch a direct attack upon the Army. A New York dentist named Irving Peress, who had been inducted into military service in 1952, subsequently refused to sign an Army loyalty certificate. When called before the McCarthy committee, he had invoked the Fifth Amendment. The Army had then released Peress, giving him an honorable discharge. McCarthy was incensed. He brought General Ralph W. Zwicker before his committee to explain what had happened. Conceding that the Army had mishandled the case, Zwicker promised to see that it did not happen again. But under orders from his superiors, the General would not reveal the names of those persons who had processed Peress's release. McCarthy proceeded to browbeat and humiliate Zwicker, accusing him of being "ignorant," of "shielding Communist conspirators," and of being "a disgrace to the uniform." Secretary of the Army Robert T. Stevens, under strong pressure from the Pentagon, defended Zwicker and ordered him and other officers not to testify further before the McCarthy committee.

When a meeting between Stevens and McCarthy resulted in a "memorandum of agreement" between the two, it was widely regarded as an administration surrender to the high-riding Senator. But McCarthy had finally overreached himself. On March 11, 1954, the administration counterattacked. The Army charged that McCarthy and Cohn had persistently and flagrantly sought preferential treatment for Private G. David Schine after his induction into the armed forces. The Wisconsin Senator met this challenge by making forty-six charges against the Army. To investigate the charges and countercharges, the Permanent Subcommittee on Investigations voted to make its own inquest, with Senator Karl Mundt temporarily replacing McCarthy as Chairman.

The committee began its inquiry on April 22, and for the next five weeks its proceedings were followed as closely as a dramatic production by a nationwide television audience. McCarthy himself was the center of the hearings. He bullied and harangued Secretary Stevens for thirteen days. He was constantly interrupting witnesses, making insinuating comments and veiled threats, and shouting "point of order, Mr. Chairman." Some members of the committee, such as Senator Stuart Symington of Missouri, stood up to him, and Joseph N. Welch, the counsel for the Army, was more than a match for the Wisconsin Senator in most of their verbal encounters. The hearings revealed McCarthy to millions of Americans as uncouth, brutal, unscrupulous, and contemptuous of decent men. Technically, neither McCarthy nor the Army won in the committee

Figure 9 "The Grand Inquisitor" during the Army-McCarthy hearings *(United Press International Photo)*

hearings, but in reality the Senator lost; for the inquiry contributed greatly to his own self-destruction.

The Senate finally bestirred itself to deal with McCarthy. On June 11, 1954, Ralph Flanders, an elderly Republican from Vermont, introduced Senate Resolution 261, calling for McCarthy's removal from the chairmanship of the Committee on Government Operations and its Permanent Subcommittee on Investigations. Flanders later changed the resolution to one of censure. A struggle over the resolution followed, but eventually the senators agreed to have the matter considered by a select committee of six members headed by Arthur V. Watkins, a respected Republican from Utah.

The Watkins committee considered five general categories of charges against McCarthy. The Wisconsin Senator testified at length in his own behalf. In September the committee adopted a unanimous report which recommended that McCarthy be censured on two counts. The Senate slowly moved to consider the censure report in the fall of 1954, and after a good deal of debate and maneuvering the first vote was taken on December 1. All efforts to head off censure by McCarthy's defenders were defeated, and on March 2 the upper house voted by a margin of 67 to 22 to condemn the Wisconsin Senator on two counts—for contempt and abuse of the Subcommittee on Privileges and Elections in 1952, and for contempt and abuse of the Senate and its select committee in 1954.

McCarthy's decline was rapid in the wake of his censure. Long before he died in May 1957, at the age of forty-nine, he had become just another member of the Senate, a man of some lingering notoriety but no longer a figure of any real consequence.

In retrospect it is clear that Americans were regaining their sense of proportion and becoming less obsessed with anti-Communist apprehensions by the time the Senate voted to censure Joe McCarthy. Tensions began to ease with the signing of an armistice in the Korean war in July 1953. The Democratic victory in the midterm congressional races of 1954, which cost McCarthy and other Republican congressmen their chairmanships, may also have contributed to the decline of McCarthyism. By the mid-1950s the Supreme Court was moving in a more liberal direction in dealing with cases involving civil liberties and civil rights. The Court held in several cases that congressional investigating committees violated the constitutional rights of witnesses, it curtailed the scope of the administration's security program, it overturned the convictions of Communists, and it ruled that the State Department could not deny passports to citizens on arbitrary grounds. But even though McCarthyism had passed from the scene, the manifestations of intolerance, the suspicion of radicalism and unorthodoxy, and the coercive pressures for conformity were still much in evidence.

The Eisenhower Policies

Dwight Eisenhower's concept of a limited role for the federal government in the economic life of the nation, a concept he labeled "dynamic conservatism," was quickly put into effect by the new administration. The President and his advisers cut back on the recommended expenditures in the Truman budget for foreign aid and military equipment. Some 200,000 civilian workers were removed from the federal payroll during Eisenhower's first term. The administration ended most of the Korean war controls over rents, wages, and prices. The Reconstruction Finance Corporation was allowed to expire in 1953, and efforts were made to sell or close down government establishments that competed with private enterprise. Commissions were formed, conferences were held, and orders were issued to wipe out duplication, increase efficiency, and reduce expenditures throughout the government service.

The economic conservatism of the administration was manifested in other ways as well. Some of the President's appointments to the independent regulatory commissions, such as that of John C. Doefer, the new Chairman of the Federal Communications Commission, were actually opposed to public regulation of the industries they were supposed to supervise. Secretary of Commerce Sinclair E. Weeks, a Massachusetts manufacturer, had scarcely taken office before he fired Dr. Allen Astin as head of the Bureau of Standards for not being mindful of the "business point of view." The furor that resulted in this instance caused Weeks to restore Astin to his position. When a measure was introduced in Congress, in the spring of 1955, to have the government provide Dr. Jonas Salk's polio vaccine free to American children, Secretary of Health, Education, and Welfare Oveta Culp Hobby strongly opposed it on the ground that it would lead to "socialized medicine" by the "back door." Eisenhower himself took a firm stand against so-called socialized medicine proposals, and he spoke out against medical insurance amendments to social security bills.

Republican candidates had promised in 1952, as in earlier campaigns, to undo the "excesses" of the Roosevelt and Truman administrations: to balance the budget, reduce federal spending, cut taxes, check inflation, and restore an "unregulated" economy. Nevertheless, Eisenhower's proposed budget for the fiscal year 1953–1954 contained a deficit of $5.5 billion (a considerable improvement over the $9.9 billion projected by the Truman administration). This so shocked Senator Taft, when he learned of it in a conference with the President, that he exclaimed with great emotion: "You're taking us down the same road Truman traveled." The administration finally managed, with the ending of the Korean war, to pare the deficit down to $3.1 billion. But the next fiscal year ended with a deficit of over $4 billion, and Eisenhower was able to avoid deficits in only three of his eight years in office. By 1956 the administration's nondefense expenditures were higher than those under Truman, and Eisenhower's proposed budget of $71.8 billion for fiscal 1957–1958 set a peacetime record. The expenditures for national defense, foreign aid, and social welfare along with such recurring outlays as farm subsidies constituted a major portion of the budget and could not easily be reduced. When the economy experienced trouble, as it did in 1954 and 1958, it seemed wise to resort to the fiscal remedies provided by the New Deal and the Fair Deal.

The administration's agricultural policies provide a graphic illustration of this point. Eisenhower and Secretary of Agriculture Benson, a vigorous advocate of private enterprise on the farm, hoped to minimize the government's role in the agricultural economy and at the same time to contribute to the solution of the "farm problem," which involved huge annual surpluses, a continuing decline in total net agricultural income, and a steady drop in the farmer's share of the retail cost of his product. Benson was convinced that the rigid price support system caused farmers to overproduce, thus driving prices down and forcing the government to assume an increasingly heavy burden of subsidies. The administration managed, after a heated congressional struggle, to get the principle of flexible supports incorporated into the Agricultural Act of January 1954. This statute authorized price supports on basic farm commodities ranging from 82$\frac{1}{2}$ to 90 percent of parity for 1955 and from 75 to 90 percent for 1956 and subsequent years. But surpluses continued to pile up and government costs continued to mount.

The administration tried another approach. This was the "soil bank" scheme, for which Congress appropriated funds in 1956. Under this plan farmers who agreed to cut their acreage below their normal allotments or to commit a portion of their land to soil conservation rather than commercial use would receive government payments for participating in the acreage reserve and conservation reserve programs. Although more than 12 million acres were soon put into the soil bank, the farm problem remained as intractable as ever. Concentrating on their best land and employing scientific methods and the new chemical fertilizers, farmers were able to produce as much on fewer acres as they had in previous years. By 1958 the federal government was spending six times as much on its agricultural programs as in 1952.

The dimensions of Eisenhower's "dynamic conservatism" were fully revealed in the administration's proposals in the areas of natural resources and the production of electrical power. An early indication of Eisenhower's approach came in the disposition of the tidelands oil—the rich offshore oil deposits claimed by California and the Gulf states. President Truman had twice vetoed measures designed to turn these rights over to the claimant states, and the Supreme Court, in 1947 and 1950, had decided that the federal government had the "paramount rights" to the offshore lands. Eisenhower pledged his support to the states during the campaign of 1952, and as President he promoted the adoption of the Submerged Lands Act of May 1953. This law invalidated earlier arrangements and granted the states title to the coastal lands within their "historic" boundaries.

Near the end of his first administration, Eisenhower supported a congressional amendment to the Natural Gas Act of 1938 which would have exempted gas companies from regulation by the Federal Power Commission. Administration spokesmen argued that this action would stimulate gas production and the expansion of gas distribution facilities. Just before the bill was passed, Senator Francis P. Case of South Dakota learned that an oil company had contributed $2,500 to his campaign for reelection, evidently expecting him to vote for the exemption amendment. Case returned the money and voted against the bill, and in the wake of all the publicity that resulted the President decided to veto the measure.

Eisenhower regarded federal control of electrical power as a menace to private enterprise, as a danger to local autonomy, and as "a threat deadly to our liberties." In his first State of the Union message he advocated a natural resources program based on "a partnership of the states and local communities, private citizens and the Federal Government, all working together." In some cases, the administration conceded, the federal government had to take the major part in river development projects. Thus Eisenhower agreed to large federal expenditures for the construction of hydroelectric, irrigation, and other water supply facilities on the upper Colorado River. He also supported the St. Lawrence Seaway, signing a measure in 1954 that created a public corporation to finance, construct, and develop the American portion of the long waterway connecting the Atlantic and the Great Lakes.

In many other cases the Eisenhower administration worked hard to curtail federal involvement in stream development and power projects. Eisenhower cut the budget of several federal power projects and abandoned certain undertakings already approved by Congress. The administration strongly opposed a Democratic plan, carried over from the Truman period, for the federal construction of a high multipurpose dam and hydroelectric plant in Hell's Canyon along the Snake River. Eisenhower and Secretary of the Interior Douglas McKay endorsed the proposed construction of three smaller dams by private concerns, and the Federal Power Commission eventually granted the Idaho Power Company a license for this purpose. Republicans were then able to beat back a movement in Congress to authorize the building of a high dam by the federal government. Eisenhower also won some concessions for his partnership approach in the Atomic Energy Act of 1954, which authorized the operation of new atomic energy plants by private companies.

Although the President referred to the Tennessee Valley Authority as an example of "creeping socialism," he did not attack the TVA directly. Opposing the TVA's request for funds to build a new steam generating plant to serve the power needs of the Memphis area, Eisenhower and his advisers sponsored a proposal for the private construction of a steam generating plant in West Memphis, Arkansas, which would contract with the Atomic Energy Commission to feed its power into the TVA system, thus enabling the Authority to meet its obligations to the AEC and to serve the needs of Memphis. The new plant would be built and operated by a syndicate headed by Edgar H. Dixon of Middle South Utilities, Inc., and Eugene A. Yates of the Southern Company. Despite the opposition of the TVA board of directors and many political leaders in the Tennessee Valley, the AEC, following Eisenhower's wishes, signed a long-term contract with the Dixon-Yates combine on October 5, 1954. The terms were extremely generous to the private utilities.

Senator Albert Gore of Tennessee and some other senators sought unsuccessfully in 1954 to secure congressional action against the Dixon-Yates scheme, and the issue was used against the Republicans in the midterm elections of that year. But Dixon-Yates did not become vulnerable until Senator Lister D. Hill of Alabama charged, in February 1955, that a "conflict of interest" had been involved in the negotiation of the contract. It was eventually revealed that Adolphe H. Wenzell, an officer of a Boston investment firm scheduled to finance the Dixon-Yates project, had earlier served as a consultant to the Bureau of the Budget and had advised the government to sign the contract. This disclosure proved acutely embarrassing to Eisenhower, who decided to cancel the contract with the utilities in July 1955, after Memphis had conveniently announced its intention to build its own power plant.

The more liberal and moderate domestic legislation of the Eisenhower years owed a great deal to Democratic support, and in some ways the Republican President got along better with opposition congressmen than with members of his own party. A series of amendments broadened the Social Security System, including an act in 1954 that extended the System's coverage to 10 million workers and self-employed people. The minimum wage was raised in 1956 from 75 cents to a dollar an hour. The Refugee Relief Act of 1953 provided for the admission to the United States of more than 200,000 refugees and displaced persons. The administration supported the Federal-Aid Highway Act of 1956, under which a 41,000-mile interstate highway system was launched, largely at federal expense. Eisenhower also endorsed a modest proposal for federal aid to the states for public education.

Despite its businessman's orientation and its conservative rhetoric, the Eisenhower administration adopted most of the policies of its opposition; it supported the welfare state that had developed in America and used governmental power to manage the economy. Americans could no longer use "the governmental processes that were applicable in 1890," Eisenhower declared in April 1957. "We have got to adapt the great principles of the Constitution to the inescapable industrial and economic conditions of our time, and make certain that . . . our people participate in the progress of our economy."

Change and Continuity in National Politics

Dwight Eisenhower's venture into politics and the "crusade" he began in 1952 were inspired in part by his strong desire to unify and revitalize the Republican party, which would be the instrument for the adoption of new and badly needed national policies. Yet Eisenhower's "modern Republicanism" encountered hard going almost from the beginning, and his success as a party leader was limited. His vision of a new and more purposeful Republican party was never clearly elaborated. Many Republican congressmen and other influential party members who welcomed Ike's triumphs at the polls were strongly opposed to many of his foreign and domestic proposals. Eisenhower sought to demonstrate his effectiveness as a party leader by vigorously campaigning for the election of a new

Republican Congress in the midterm elections of 1954, but the results were disappointing.[1]

Even so, by the middle of 1955 Eisenhower could afford to be optimistic about the progress and prospects of his administration. The new Democratic Congress had proved surprisingly cooperative, the economy was once more booming, and the President had apparently achieved notable success at the summit conference held in Geneva during the summer. The administration's optimism was suddenly shattered on September 24, 1955, when the President suffered a heart attack while vacationing in Denver. The nation held its breath as Eisenhower's doctors, including the eminent Boston cardiologist Paul Dudley White, attended him at the Lowry Air Force Base's Fitzsimons Hospital. Press secretary James C. Hagerty kept the news media fully informed of the President's medical condition during the next several weeks. There were no complications, however, and in mid-November he was moved to his Gettysburg farm, where he assumed an increasing portion of his normal executive duties. During earlier weeks Vice President Nixon had presided over meetings of the Cabinet, and the efficient White House staff had continued to function smoothly.

Although Eisenhower had not, prior to his illness, indicated whether or not he would run for a second term, he came under mounting pressure to do so as his convalescence progressed. The President was cautious, however, postponing a final decision and talking often about his desire to retire to a quieter life at his Gettysburg farm. Meanwhile, his message to Congress in January 1956 hardly sounded like that of a leader contemplating early retirement; it was a comprehensive and generally progressive set of recommendations for the building of "an ever-stronger, ever-better America." In mid-February 1956 Eisenhower's doctors reported, after a thorough examination of the President, that he would be able to "carry on an active life for another five to ten years" in view of his "good recovery." Two weeks later Ike announced, in a nationwide television address, that he would accept renomination.

Eisenhower's renomination was now only a formality to be completed by the party's national convention, which was held in San Francisco in August 1956. But before that meeting there was another moment of shock and dismay involving the President's health. He underwent a serious operation on June 9 for ileitis (an intestinal obstruction), but his recovery was rapid, and any doubts about his ability to campaign in 1956 were soon removed. He was quickly renominated when the Republican delegates convened in San Francisco. Richard M. Nixon was renominated for Vice

[1]The Democrats recaptured control of Congress by a margin of one vote in the Senate and twenty-nine in the House.

President, although Eisenhower had been somewhat slow in endorsing him for the position. A "stop Nixon" movement launched on July 25 by Harold E. Stassen, Eisenhower's adviser on disarmament, finally suffered an ignominious collapse.

In the meantime, the Democrats had held their convention in Chicago in early August, following a long and hard-fought struggle between Adlai Stevenson and Estes Kefauver for a nomination that appeared, for a time following Eisenhower's heart attack, to be worth a good deal more than it had in 1952. The Tennessee Senator, employing a folksy campaign style and prodigious energy, made a fast start early in the year by winning the New Hampshire and Minnesota primaries. Stevenson also conducted a strenuous campaign, attracting broad support from party regulars and capturing important Democratic primaries in Oregon, Florida, and California. Stevenson's lead was so great by summer that Kefauver withdrew on July 16, endorsing the former Illinois Governor for the nomination. This left Governor W. Averell Harriman of New York as Stevenson's only challenger, and despite former President Truman's last-minute endorsement of Harriman, Stevenson was easily nominated on the first ballot at the convention in Chicago. In a surprise move, Stevenson asked the delegates themselves to select the party's vice-presidential nominee. A spirited contest resulted between Senator Kefauver and Senator John F. Kennedy of Massachusetts, with the Tennessean winning a narrow victory on the second ballot.

The presidential campaign of 1956 was a dull and uninspiring affair. The Democrats found it difficult to combat Republican boasts of having brought peace, prosperity, and unity at home. The Republican party, the President asserted in his acceptance speech, "is again the rallying point for Americans of all callings, ages, races and incomes," and the millions of "I Like Ike" buttons seemed to bear him out. Unlike 1952, Eisenhower spoke mainly in lofty terms ("leave the yelling to the opposition," he advised).

Stevenson tried hard to develop a distinctive program that would build on his party's liberal heritage. But he seemed less convincing, less buoyant, less sparkling than he had in the campaign of 1952. Nothing seemed to work for the Democrats. Stevenson accused Eisenhower of being "a part-time leader," thereby referring indirectly to his health, only to have Ike's doctors report late in the campaign that the President was in "excellent health." Eisenhower easily countered Stevenson's pledge to end the military draft and create a volunteer defense corps. When the Democratic presidential nominee talked about the dangers of radioactive fallout and promised to stop all United States testing of nuclear weapons, Republican leaders contended that such a course would be impractical and that it would endanger national defense. The Hungarian uprising and

Figure 10   Campaigning in 1956 *(National Park Service Photograph, Courtesy Dwight D. Eisenhower Library)*

the Suez crisis, occurring just before the election, appeared to enhance the experienced Eisenhower's advantage in the minds of many Americans. Although the administration seemed somewhat vulnerable on such issues as the farm question, the high cost of living, and its handling of natural resources, the President showed signs of adding support in many new quarters, including Negro voters.

Eisenhower won by a landslide. His plurality was more than 9 million votes (out of 62 million cast), and he received 457 electoral votes to Stevenson's 73. The Democratic ticket carried only seven states— Missouri and six Southern states. Eisenhower did well everywhere, even in the South, and he captured such Democratic strongholds as Chicago and Jersey City. Yet Eisenhower's victory was an anomalous one. The

Democrats won Congress—49 to 47 in the Senate and 234 to 201 in the House—making Eisenhower the first President since Zachary Taylor in 1849 to begin a term with both houses of Congress in the hands of the opposing party.

Republican congressional fortunes dropped even further in the midterm elections of 1958. Eisenhower was still held in the public's affection, but talk of a "lack of leadership" was heard more often as his second administration unfolded. New problems and perplexities began to confront Eisenhower early in his second term, including a scandal involving Presidential assistant Sherman Adams.[2] Although a White House manifesto contended that if a new Democratic Congress were elected, "we are certain to go down the left lane which leads inseparably to socialism," the voters paid little heed to such warnings: they gave the Democrats their most thoroughgoing triumph since the election of 1936. The Democrats would control the next Congress by margins of 64 to 34 in the Senate and 282 to 154 in the House. The election of 1958 brought many new faces to Washington, including quite a number of young and progressive congressmen, but the Eighty-sixth Congress did not venture far from the middle-of-the-road programs recommended by the administration.

Dwight D. Eisenhower dominated the national political scene in the 1950s. He shattered the Democratic majority in presidential elections. He appealed to the new white-collar elements, to the residents of the mushrooming suburbs, to the growing number of independent voters. He was able to exploit the vast economic and social changes taking place in the Southern states, whose political solidarity his candidacy disrupted in 1952 and 1956. Nevertheless, Eisenhower proved unable to transfer his own popularity to other Republican candidates; that is, he was unable to create a new majority coalition to replace the one he had broken up.

Second Term: Problems and Portents

The second Eisenhower term was far more troubled and in some ways considerably less successful than the first. A series of controversies over administration budget requests, school desegregation, national defense, and welfare policies, in addition to new international crises, marked

---

[2]A House of Representatives committee discovered, during the summer of 1958, that Adams had apparently sought to influence the Securities and Exchange Commission and the Federal Trade Commission in the interest of Bernard Goldfine, a wealthy Boston textile producer and long-time friend of the Presidential assistant. Adams had accepted several gifts from Goldfine, including an expensive vicuña overcoat. Adams denied any wrongdoing, though he conceded that he might have made mistakes in "judgment." Eisenhower defended Adams' "personal and official integrity," but the latter soon resigned. As for Goldfine, he was eventually tried and convicted for income tax irregularities.

Eisenhower's final years in the White House. The economy went into a sharp recession in the latter part of 1957 and continued weak during most of 1958, and a long steel strike in the summer and fall of 1959 helped disrupt the recovery that began in late 1958. Eisenhower's principal advisers changed in his second term: Humphrey and Wilson left the Cabinet in 1957, Adams resigned in September 1958, and Dulles had to retire because of illness in the spring of 1959. The President experienced another serious illness himself when he suffered a stroke on November 25, 1957. Although he was pronounced "completely recovered" on March 1, 1958, his leadership appeared to become irresolute and spasmodic. In the late 1950s, as the pressure mounted for greater federal activities in such areas as education, public works, and civil rights, Eisenhower's domestic policies seemed increasingly inadequate.

One of the issues that came to the fore early in Eisenhower's second administration was the enforcement of the federal courts' desegregation

Figure 11   The Little Rock School Crisis *(United Press International Photo)*

orders. A series of cases initiated by the National Association for the Advancement of Colored People culminated in the historic decision of *Brown v. Board of Education of Topeka* (1954), in which a unanimous Supreme Court struck down the "separate but equal" doctrine in public facilities enunciated in 1896 in *Plessy v. Ferguson.* Resistance soon developed in the Southern states, and in September 1957 Governor Orval E. Faubus of Arkansas confronted the President with a constitutional crisis by ordering the National Guard to prevent Negro students from attending a Little Rock high school. After a federal court had decreed the removal of the National Guardsmen and angry demonstrators made it impossible for the Negro children to attend the school, Eisenhower ordered federal troops sent into Little Rock to enforce the court's order. "Mob rule," the President said when he dispatched the troops to Little Rock, "cannot be allowed to override the decisions of our courts." Eisenhower, however, had done little to encourage compliance with the federal courts' desegregation decrees or to help make Americans sensitive to their legal and moral implications. He did lend his support to the modest civil rights legislation of 1957 and 1960.

The record of the Eighty-fifth Congress (1957–1958) was one of moderate achievement—a compromise between the "mildly conservative" President and the "mildly liberal" congressional leadership of Lyndon B. Johnson and Sam Rayburn. Several issues relating to national defense received attention during the second session of this Congress. The President worked hard and successfully to secure the passage of a military reorganization bill in 1958, and Congress established a civilian-controlled National Aeronautics and Space Administration. Although the administration gave greater priority to the development of new, complex defense systems than to the development of space technology, a succession of space probes was carried out following the firing of the first successful American satellite, *Explorer I,* from Cape Canaveral on January 31, 1958.

The administration's major accomplishment in the field of education in 1958 was the National Defense Education Act, which included a provision for $295 million in loans to needy college students. The second session also passed the Alaskan statehood bill; emergency housing and highway construction legislation to help combat the recession; the Transportation Act of 1958, designed to resuscitate the failing railroads; a low-support farm bill with few controls and generally in line with administration recommendations; and an unprecedented four-year extension of the Chief Executive's power to negotiate reciprocal trade agreements.

Eisenhower seemed to become more active and occasionally more aggressive in seeking the realization of his objectives during his last two years in office. Following the Democratic congressional victory of 1958, he set himself to prevent the large appropriations for domestic programs urged by liberal Democrats. He made greater use of the veto and, employing press conferences and public appeals, tried to dramatize the issue of "lavish spending." Thus the President was able, with the powerful assistance of the conservative coalition in Congress, to frustrate such Democratic proposals as a comprehensive program of aid for school construction and teachers' salaries, a giant area redevelopment program, and increased minimum wage and medical care for the aged under social security. But during 1960 liberals discovered in the need for a rapid rate of growth in the national economy a new issue on which to base their demands for more extensive social welfare legislation. Meanwhile, there was mounting evidence of partisan divisions between the executive and legislative branches. A $750 million pay increase for federal employees was passed over the President's veto, and the Democrats, anticipating success in the approaching elections, refused to approve a measure creating a large number of severely needed new federal judgeships.

The Eisenhower administration was identified with the enactment of some significant legislation in the Eighty-sixth Congress (1959–1960). Perhaps the best example on the domestic side was the relatively conservative revision of the Taft-Hartley Act completed in 1959. Hearings held in 1957 by the Senate Select Committee on Improper Activities in the Labor or Management Field revealed widespread racketeering and corruption in the International Brotherhood of Teamsters and other unions. In 1958 the Senate passed a mild anticorruption bill sponsored by Senator John F. Kennedy, but it died in the House of Representatives. During the closing days of the 1959 session, Congress passed a stronger measure, which became the Landrum-Griffin Act. The law contained a number of anticorruption features, and it broadened the boycott and picketing provisions of the Taft-Hartley Act. In another act of 1959, Congress established the Labor Pension Reporting Service to compel unions to publish an accounting of the pension and welfare funds under their control.

Eisenhower's most important contributions as President came in his first administration. In his second term he seemed to become more irritable; to grow more resistant to change; to be increasingly unaffected by the intellectual ferment, the technological breakthroughs, and the movements for equality in American society. Nevertheless, the Eisenhower years brought a period of relative calm to American politics. Eisenhower's leadership moved the Republican party to a more moderate position on international questions, weakened the reactionary elements in determining its domestic policies, and narrowed its differences with the Democrats.

SUGGESTIONS FOR FURTHER READING

The best place to begin a study of the Eisenhower administration is Herbert S. Parmet, *Eisenhower and the American Crusades* (1972), the first scholarly assessment. Also valuable are Charles C. Alexander, *Holding the Line: The Eisenhower Era, 1952–1961* (1975); Robert L. Branyan and Lawrence H. Larsen (eds.), *The Eisenhower Administration, 1953–1961: A Documentary History* (2 vols., 1971); and Eisenhower's own comprehensive narrative of events, *The White House Years** (2 vols., 1963–1965). The best biography of Eisenhower is Peter Lyon's *Eisenhower: Portrait of the Hero* (1974). Merlo J. Pusey, *Eisenhower the President* (1956), is an admiring account, while Marquis Childs, *Eisenhower, Captive Hero: A Critical Study of the General and the President* (1958), focuses on the Eisenhower myth and public image. Dean Albertson (ed.), *Eisenhower as President** (1963), is a useful collection of contemporary appraisals.

Several of Eisenhower's advisers have written personal accounts. Among the best of these are Arthur Larson, *Eisenhower: The President Nobody Knew** (1968), a favorable but perceptive interpretation; Emmet John Hughes, *The Ordeal of Power: A Political Memoir of the Eisenhower Years** (1963), by a man who gradually became disillusioned with the administration; and Sherman Adams, *Firsthand Report: The Story of the Eisenhower Administration** (1961), a straightforward account.

There are only a handful of scholarly books devoted to the Eisenhower policies. Gary W. Reichard's *The Reaffirmation of Republicanism: Eisenhower and the Eighty-third Congress* (1975) is a valuable treatment of Eisenhower's relations with his first Congress. Aaron B. Wildavsky deals with the first of the Eisenhower administration's "scandals" in *Dixon-Yates: A Study in Power Politics** (1962). Other conflicts of interest are discussed in David A. Frier, *Conflict of Interest in the Eisenhower Administration** (1969). Two other matters are treated in Ernest R. Bartley, *The Tidelands Oil Controversy: A Legal and Historical Analysis* (1953), and William R. Willoughby, *The St. Lawrence Waterway: A Study in Politics and Diplomacy* (1961).

Several studies analyze Eisenhower's Presidential leadership, including Richard E. Neustadt, *Presidential Power: The Politics of Leadership** (1960); Walter Johnson, *1600 Pennsylvania Avenue: Presidents and the People, 1929–1959** (1960); and Elmer E. Cornwell, Jr., *Presidential Leadership of Public Opinion* (1965). James L. Sundquist, *Dynamics of the Party System: Alignment and Realignment of Political Parties in the United States** (1973), throws light on national politics since 1945. Sundquist's *Politics and Policy: The Eisenhower, Kennedy, and Johnson Years** (1968) analyzes domestic legislation. V. O. Key, Jr., with the assistance of Milton C. Cummings, Jr., *The Responsible Electorate: Rationality in Presidential Voting, 1936–1960* (1966), follows the shifting pattern of voting behavior among socioeconomic groups.

*Available in paperback edition.

Chapter 6

International Relations in a Nuclear Age, 1953–1960

The major theme in world affairs during the 1950s continued to be the cold war and the wide-ranging efforts of the Soviet Union and the United States to counter each other's moves and to win the support of other nations. By the time the new Republican administration took over the national government in Washington, the Russians had achieved a rough parity with the United States in atomic weapons. They had also developed long-range aircraft capable of delivering nuclear weapons to targets in the Western Hemisphere. This meant that the two superpowers had established what one contemporary aptly described as a "nuclear balance of terror."

Many Americans expected President Eisenhower to adopt a bold new approach that would turn back the advances of international communism, and they were encouraged in their expectations by the brave rhetoric of Republican spokesmen. Eisenhower, like his Secretary of State, believed in "personal" diplomacy, and the next eight years were to witness many summit meetings and other high-level international conferences. But administration leaders, while continuing to advertise new departures in foreign relations, soon discovered their freedom of action circumscribed by a variety of stubborn realities. In practice they continued the policies of the Truman years, relying on collective security, regional alliances, foreign aid, and support of the United Nations.

The "New Look" in Foreign Policy and Defense

John Foster Dulles was the dominant figure in the conduct of the Eisenhower diplomacy. A prominent Presbyterian layman, Dulles had almost a sense of predestination about his role as Secretary of State; his family background, long experience in foreign affairs, abundant energy, and supreme confidence surely encouraged such a feeling. While Dulles shared Eisenhower's broad internationalist outlook, he was even more passionately committed to the reform of United States foreign policies than the new Chief Executive. He believed that Americans were losing the cold war because their policies were static and materialistic. The nation needed to reassert its traditional moral mission and identify itself with the universal longing for peace. Eisenhower and Dulles were sensitive to the deep division in the Republican party on international issues, and their espousal of the "reform" movement in foreign policy was no doubt intended in part as a means of reassuring the Taft coalition.

The Eisenhower administration proclaimed a "new look" in foreign policy, and for a time there was an appearance of novel approaches and techniques. Administration leaders wanted to revamp national defense policy in order to get a "bigger bang for the buck"—cutting expenditures for conventional warfare and relying on air power and nuclear weapons. In December 1953 Secretary Dulles threatened France and other laggard members of the European Defense Community with an "agonizing reappraisal" of the United States commitment in Europe. A few weeks later, in a speech on January 12, 1954, Dulles announced "the deterrent of massive retaliatory power." According to the Secretary, it would "depend primarily upon a great capacity to retaliate, instantly, by means and at places of our own choosing." Dulles's most notorious policy was what he called "brinkmanship." In an interview published in *Life* magazine on January 16, 1956. Dulles spoke of his approach to foreign affairs:

> The ability to get to the verge of war without getting into the war is the necessary art. If you cannot master it, you inevitably get into wars. If you try to run away from it, if you are scared to go to the brink, you are lost. We've had to look it square in the face—on the question of enlarging the Korean War, on the question of getting into the Indo-China war, on the question of Formosa. We walked to the brink and we looked it in the face.

On January 7, 1953, two weeks before Eisenhower entered the White House, Senator John W. Bricker, a Republican from Ohio, introduced a resolution proposing a constitutional amendment which would render the provisions of treaties conflicting with the Constitution null and void, require that a treaty "shall become effective as internal law in the United States only through legislation which would be valid in the absence of a treaty," and empower Congress "to regulate all executive and other agreements with any foreign power or international organization." The Bricker amendment had powerful support from such organizations as the American Bar Association. Eisenhower and Dulles tried for almost a year to work out a compromise. This proved impossible, and Eisenhower eventually declared that he was "unalterably" opposed to the Bricker resolution in its existing form. By curtailing executive autonomy in the area of foreign relations, Eisenhower argued, Bricker's proposal would take away the maneuvering room the President must have in foreign affairs. The amendment was finally defeated on February 26, 1954, but it came within a single vote of securing the necessary two-thirds majority.

One aspect of the administration's new design in foreign relations was its plan to carry out extensive reforms in the military establishment. President Eisenhower and Secretary Wilson rejected the premise of NSC 68 that the United States could spend up to 20 percent of its gross national product on arms. Defense expenditures were reduced in both fiscal 1954 and 1955. The ground forces were diminished by one-third between 1953 and 1955, and the size of the Army was cut from about 1,500,000 in 1953 to 873,000 in 1960. The Navy also suffered some reductions in this period.

Eisenhower gave a good deal of time to the task of modernizing the military establishment. The Defense Reorganization Acts of 1953 and 1958 were intended to coordinate and centralize the vast enterprises of the Department of Defense. The administration sought to replace an obsolescent military apparatus with "highly mobile naval, air, and amphibious units" in combat readiness, prepared to strike quickly, and in some cases equipped with tactical atomic weapons. But the new defense policies resulted in reliance on strategic air power and nuclear weapons, for this course seemed to promise maximum destruction at minimum cost. The whole approach was epitomized by the doctrine of "massive retaliation" enunciated by Dulles in January 1954.

Another powerful influence in shaping the Eisenhower administration's foreign policies was developments abroad, particularly within the Communist bloc. After the death of Stalin, Russian leaders soon began to make peaceful overtures to the United States. In 1955 they agreed to a definite peace treaty for Austria and took part in a widely acclaimed summit meeting in Geneva. They began to talk about the desirability of "peaceful coexistence." By the mid-1950s the Soviet system in Eastern Europe was becoming less monolithic; first Poland and then other Russian satellites won a degree of control over their own affairs.

The European Focus

Despite the spread of the cold war to all parts of the globe, the most important theater for American policy makers continued to be Europe. By 1953 the North Atlantic Treaty Organization had provided an integrated command system for Western Europe, and the United States had contributed large stockpiles of weapons and equipment for the alliance's military needs. But NATO's troop strength was far below the projected levels, and the European members of the organization appeared reluctant to undertake large-scale rearmament when the United States was concentrating its energies on the Korean war. Then, in the spring of 1952, France, Italy, the Benelux countries, and West Germany signed treaties for the establishment of the European Defense Community (EDC).

The European Defense Community quickly encountered opposition, especially from the French, who began to have second thoughts about the proposed rearmament of Germany and were disturbed by the specter of foreign control over France's internal affairs. While the French delayed, Secretary Dulles did his best to bring them into line, threatening in late 1953 an "agonizing reappraisal" of American policy toward Europe. The problem of strengthening NATO, however, was more fundamental than French recalcitrance. The Soviet peace offensive encouraged a more relaxed atmosphere in Western Europe, while the growing fear of a thermonuclear holocaust simultaneously raised doubts among Europeans about the real benefits of NATO. In August 1954 the French Assembly finally acted, decisively defeating a resolution to ratify the EDC.

American leaders were stunned and keenly disappointed. But it was Britain and not the United States that rescued the situation. Prime Minister Anthony Eden took the leadership during the following weeks in arranging a compromise that was formally approved in Paris in October 1954. Using the Brussels Pact of 1948, Eden and other Western European leaders created an alliance to be called the Western European Union (WEU). The arrangement ended the Allies' military occupation of West Germany except for a small garrison in West Berlin, restored sovereignty to the Federal Republic of Germany, and provided for Western Germany's admission to NATO in 1955. The Russian response to these developments was the Warsaw Pact of May 1955, which bound the East European satellites to the U.S.S.R. in a tight military alliance.

Meanwhile, however, other developments were encouraging new approaches in the relations between the two superpowers. The truce in Korea and a compromise peace in Vietnam in 1954 contributed to the relaxation of international tensions. The American allies in Western Europe, fearing atomic devastation in case of war between the United States and the Soviet Union, welcomed the prospect of a détente between the rival powers. Eisenhower and many other Republicans were eager to cut back federal expenditures and to balance the budget. In mid-May 1955 the Foreign Ministers Conference was finally able, after years of controversy and delay, to agree upon an Austrian peace treaty. The treaty signed in Vienna ended the four-power occupation of Austria and created an independent, neutral state.

Plans for a summit meeting were worked out in the spring of 1955, and the top leaders of the Soviet Union, the United States, Great Britain, and France opened the conference in Geneva on July 18. Eisenhower quickly sounded a note of hope and goodwill by urging a new approach to the problem of German unification, free communication between East and West, peaceful use of atomic power, and some practical contributions to disarmament. The warmth of Eisenhower's personality made a tremendous impact on the conference. At one point the President turned to Premier Nikolai Bulganin and declared: "The United States will never take part in an aggressive war." To which Bulganin responded: "Mr. President, we believe that statement." It was this atmosphere that produced a "spirit of Geneva."

But when it came to more concrete matters, the summit meeting made little or no progress. In the case of Germany, the United States demanded free elections and suggested that a reunited Germany be given the right to join NATO. Russia advocated a general European security pact which would include the withdrawal of all foreign troops from Germany. Neither side would retreat from its basic position. As Walter LaFeber has written, "The United States had successfully armed and tied West Germany to the Western alliance, while at the same time pushing on the Soviets the blame for blocking reunification through free elections." The Americans did present a new disarmament scheme at Geneva—an "open-skies" plan calling for the exchange of information on each nation's military facilities and allowing planes to photograph each nation's territory to prevent any possible surprise attacks. The Soviet leaders rejected the plan on the ground that it would infringe Russia's territorial sovereignty.

Still, the early optimism of the Geneva meeting did not disappear completely. Certain developments within the Soviet Union helped sustain the thaw in the cold war. For one thing, the new Soviet leaders accelerated their de-Stalinization campaign. At the Twentieth Communist Party Congress, held in Moscow in February 1956, Nikita S. Khrushchev denounced Stalin and his use of terror. While still critical of capitalist states, he declared that "war is not a fatalistic inevitability."

Later developments in 1956, however, provided little comfort to those people who hoped for an American-Russian rapprochement. In October, after Polish Communists had succeeded in easing the grip of Soviet control somewhat, Hungarians staged an uprising against Russian domination. But 200,000 Soviet soldiers and hundreds of tanks soon swept into Hungary, and the revolt was ruthlessly put down. While these spectacular events were taking place, President Eisenhower made no move to intervene; the people of the Western nations could only look on in resignation and despair.

The Progress of Containment in the Far East

The Eisenhower administration's Far Eastern diplomacy was in considerable part an inheritance from, and a natural outgrowth of, the Truman period, as was evident in such policies as the nonrecognition of the People's Republic of China, the support of Nationalist China, the strong commitment to the defense of South Korea, and the aid given to the French in Indochina. The determination by Eisenhower and Dulles to go beyond the Truman-Acheson policies in Asia was also a corollary of their broader indictment of the Truman administration's handling of foreign affairs and a concession to the extreme nationalist, Asia-oriented right wing of the Republican party. Thus when Eisenhower announced, soon after entering the White House, that the U.S. Seventh Fleet would "no longer be employed to shield Communist China," he was suggesting that the doctrine of "liberation" might be applied in the Far East.

The administration's first diplomatic problem in the Far East was the ending of the Korean war. In mid-December 1952, after returning from Korea, Eisenhower had warned that unless the war could be brought to an end quickly, the United States might retaliate "under circumstances of our own choosing." During its first months in office the Eisenhower administration not only "unleashed" Chiang Kai-shek, but also hinted that if the war continued, the United States would bomb Chinese bases, blockade the mainland of China, and use tactical atomic weapons. For whatever reason, the Communists indicated their willingness to resume the Korean truce talks in the early spring of 1953, and on July 27 of that year an armistice was finally signed. It provided for a cease-fire, for a demilitarized zone that coincided with the military line and generally followed the 38th parallel, and for a possible conference within three months to consider the withdrawal of all foreign forces from the peninsula and "the peaceful settlement of the Korean question." The Korean war was finally over, but a permanent settlement failed to emerge in the aftermath of the armistice. Instead, Korea was divided, like Germany, into Communist and non-Communist states.

By the early months of 1954, the focus of the American containment policy in Asia had shifted to Indochina, where French colonialism had encountered mounting resistance following World War II. A strong nationalist movement had developed in Vietnam, led by Ho Chi Minh, a longtime Communist and professional revolutionary. War in Vietnam dragged on for years, with the resistance forces employing Mao Tse-tung's doctrines of peasant guerrilla warfare. The Chinese Communists, having overcome Chiang's forces, recognized Ho's Vietminh early in 1950 and began to send it arms. The United States, shocked over the "loss" of China and increasingly obsessed with a determination to contain the Communists in the Far East, began to provide the French in Indochina with military and economic supplies in the spring of 1950. The war went badly for the French, however, and by 1954 they were on the verge of military collapse. Thousands of their best troops were surrounded in a military garrison at Dien Bien Phu, an ill-advised defensive site near the Laotian and Chinese borders. On March 20, 1954, the French Chief of Staff arrived in Washington to request American intervention.

Eisenhower and his advisers were fully aware of the implications of a French defeat in the Indochinese war. As the President warned in early April, "You have a row of dominoes set up, you knock over the first one, and what will happen to the last one is that it will go over very quickly. So you have the beginning of a disintegration that would have the most profound influence." Dulles felt strongly that the United States could not permit the loss of Vietnam to the Communists, and he joined Admiral Arthur W. Radford, Chairman of the Joint Chiefs of Staff, in urging that Congress be requested to pass a resolution authorizing an air strike to save Dien Bien Phu. Other leaders, however, suggested a more cautious approach. Public opinion also proved to be critical of such a venture, and British leaders, in spite of American appeals, would not endorse any kind of joint support of the French. In the end Eisenhower decided against intervention. Although the doctrine of massive retaliation logically called for an attack on mainland China, the United States had followed a course the London *Economist* described as "vociferous inaction."

Dien Bien Phu fell on May 7, and the French, facing the prospect of further military losses in other parts of Indochina and domestic disenchantment with the war, gave up the struggle and accepted a compromise, which was signed at Geneva on July 20 and 21, 1954. The Geneva Armistice and Agreements provided for a cease-fire in Vietnam, recognized the independence of Laos and Cambodia, and divided Vietnam along the 17th parallel, with the Communists under Ho Chi Minh in control in the north and the French puppet emperor Bao Dai and his new Prime Minister, Ngo Dinh Diem, dominant in the south. One provision stipulated that internationally supervised elections to determine the reunification of Vietnam would be held in 1956. Although the major powers, including mainland China, worked out the Geneva Agreements, the United States was not a formal party to the arrangement. Yet when South Vietnam refused to take part in the general elections called for in the Geneva Agreements, the United States supported the Saigon regime.

The United States moved to strengthen its Far Eastern position in other ways. Secretary Dulles took the lead in creating the Southeast Asia Collective Defense Treaty, which was signed in Manila on September 8, 1954, by representatives of the United States, Britain, France, Australia, New Zealand, Pakistan, Thailand, and the Philippines. The Southeast Asia Treaty Organization (SEATO) would, if any of its members were threatened with armed aggression, "meet in order to agree on the measures which should be taken for common defense." In a separate protocol the SEATO allies later agreed to defend the independence of South Vietnam, Laos, and Cambodia. Dulles praised SEATO as a vital part of the American defense system in the Far East—an Asian counterpart of NATO—but the two alliances were not very analogous. SEATO had no armed forces of its own and possessed no permanent command structure or standing military organization.

Another area in which the United States policy of containment in the Far East collided with the aims of mainland China was Formosa (Taiwan). The question of the two Chinas persisted from the beginning to the end of the Eisenhower administration. The malignant character of the Chinese Communists became an *idée fixe* in American thought. The immediate area of confrontation between the United States and mainland China was not Formosa and the nearby Pescadores Islands but the small offshore islands of Quemoy, Matsu, and the Tachens, which were also occupied by Nationalist forces. In September 1954 the Chinese Communists began to bombard Quemoy and Matsu, apparently as a prelude to assaulting them. Near the end of 1954 the United States signed a mutual defense treaty with the Nationalist government, pledging itself to defend Formosa and the Pescadores and to station American land, naval, and air forces "in and about" the area. The Communists soon began to move into the Tachen Islands, causing the evacuation of the Nationalist forces with American assistance. On January 24, 1955, Eisenhower went before Congress to request authority for the use of United States forces in protecting the Nationalists. Congress responded swiftly by passing a joint resolution on January 28, authorizing the President to use whatever means he considered appropriate to defend Formosa and the Pescadores, as well as "such related positions and territories" as he found necessary. A war scare followed, but the crisis gradually eased when the attackers relented in their bombardment of the islands.

In August 1958 the Communists resumed their heavy shelling of the offshore islands, and the United States was faced with another crisis in the Far East. Secretary Dulles declared that the joint congressional resolution of 1955 might apply to Quemoy and Matsu, and he implied that the United States would defend the islands if they were invaded. Meanwhile, a powerful American striking force was assembled in the Formosa area, and United States naval units escorted supply carriers to the beleaguered Nationalist outposts. It was a time of enormous tension, when many observers fearfully anticipated the outbreak of Sino-American hostilities. The administration then appeared to adopt a more moderate position, and Dulles hinted that the offshore islands might be demilitarized and even abandoned by Chiang if the Communist attacks were ended. The bombardment was eased, and the acute crisis slowly passed, though the status of Quemoy and Matsu remained uncertain through the remainder of the Eisenhower Presidency.

The Eisenhower administration decided soon after the signing of the Geneva Agreements in the summer of 1954 to supply aid to the anti-Communist government of South Vietnam. Although American leaders suggested the desirability of introducing certain domestic reforms in South Vietnam, Prime Minister Ngo Dinh Diem followed his own course. He eliminated Bao Dai in 1955 and made himself President. He refused to permit the general elections scheduled for 1956, and his government became increasingly repressive. Diem's Communist opponents occasionally resorted to terrorism, but North Vietnam did not publicly announce a war of liberation against the south until 1960. At the end of that year the National Liberation Front of South Vietnam (NLF) was established, and within a short time men and supplies were being sent from North Vietnam to the Vietcong, as the NLF was called.

The American position in the Far East was little if any better at the end of the decade than it had been in 1953. To be sure, the Eisenhower administration had ended the Korean war, and a settlement of sorts had been brought to that troubled peninsula, But the focus of the containment policy had shifted to Indochina, where, in spite of large amounts of United States aid, prospects for the non-Communist states were perilous and uncertain. The Chinese Nationalists still survived on Formosa— thanks to American power—but the illusions surrounding their reconquest of the mainland had long since disappeared. While SEATO gave the United States a defensive alliance in Asia, it was little more than a paper organization. At the same time, Americans were increasingly identified as imperialists in the minds of anticolonialists in the Far East.

The Middle East, Latin America, and the Third World

The cold war was altered in several respects during the years after 1953 but in none more dramatically than the growing involvement of the underdeveloped countries of the world in the struggle. By the mid-1950s the cold war had moved from Europe and the Far East to the Middle East, a vast and strategic area embracing some twelve countries and stretching from the Dardanelles to the Caspian Sea and from Egypt to the Gulf of Oman. Long dominated by Western colonialism, this "bridge of three continents" contained the richest oil resources in the world along with masses of desperately poor people, a feudalistic society, and backward and unstable governments. An upsurge of nationalism and independence movements had swept over the Middle East following World War II, and by midcentury the populations of the various states were infused with an ardent Arab nationalism, a strong hatred of colonialism, and a fierce hostility toward the Jewish state of Israel.

The emergence of Egypt as the leader of the Arab nations and the eager champion of Arab nationalism complicated Western diplomacy in the Middle East. A revolution led by young, nationalistic army officers had deposed the inefficient and corrupt regime of King Farouk in 1953 and resulted in the establishment of an Egyptian republic. General Abdel Gamal Nasser soon became the head of the revolution and the Premier of the new republic. Nasser set about improving the internal conditions of his country and uniting the Arab nations. In October 1954 he completed an agreement with Britain providing for the withdrawal of British troops from the Suez Canal within twenty months. Nasser secured economic aid from the United States and the Soviet Union. He formed a close military alliance with Syria, Yemen, and Saudi Arabia. He proposed the construction of a huge dam at Aswan, on the upper Nile River, to increase the nation's arable land and encourage its industrialization and economic growth.

In 1955 American leaders indicated their willingness to provide Nasser with a substantial part of the funds needed to construct the Aswan dam. The United States also moved to create the equivalent of NATO and SEATO in the Middle East. In February 1955 Secretary Dulles was instrumental in bringing Turkey and Iraq into a defensive alliance, which was soon broadened to include Great Britain, Iran, and Pakistan. In effect, the NATO line had been extended from Turkey to India. This Baghdad Pact was very upsetting to Nasser, who viewed it as an effort to split the Muslim world in two and as a means of enhancing the influence of Iraq as a rival of Egypt for Arab leadership in the Middle East.

Meanwhile, the recurrent truce violations and border clashes between Egypt and Israel finally resulted in a large-scale Israeli raid in February 1955 on the Egyptian territory of Gaza. This Israeli success spurred Nasser's determination to strengthen Egypt's armed forces, and after the signing of the Baghdad Pact he found Russian leaders quite willing to supply him with arms. The Egyptian leader also intimated that the Soviet Union might finance the building of the Aswan dam on more favorable terms than the Western powers. In the spring of 1956 Egypt withdrew its diplomatic recognition of Nationalist China and extended recognition to the People's Republic of China. These actions no doubt influenced Dulles's abrupt announcement, in July 1956, that the United States had decided not to advance funds for the Aswan dam.

Nasser responded to this rebuff within a week by nationalizing the Suez Canal on July 26, 1956. The British and French protested Nasser's seizure of the canal, but a compromise resolution in the United Nations that would have satisfied the European allies was blocked in the Security Council by a Russian veto. Israel, provoked by the repeated conflicts along its border with Egypt, convinced of the desirability of a preventive war against the Egyptians, and probably secretly encouraged by the British and French, suddenly attacked Egypt. The Israeli forces drove swiftly across the Sinai Peninsula, scattering a much larger Egyptian army and approaching the canal within a few days. Meanwhile, the British and French, after issuing an ultimatum to the two sides to stop the fighting on the ground that the conflict endangered the operation of the canal, moved against the Egyptians themselves on October 31. Egyptian forces managed to obstruct the canal with sunken ships, however, and Syrian saboteurs succeeded in cutting British oil pipelines from Iraq, thus making the Western nations dependent on the United States for petroleum.

The Anglo-French intervention came as a surprise to the Eisenhower administration, which was preoccupied with the approaching national elections. Angry and embarrassed over their allies' action, the Americans strongly endorsed the cease-fire resolution overwhelmingly passed by the UN General Assembly on November 2. Three days later the UN agreed to create an international emergency force to "secure and supervise the cessation of hostilities." The speedy arrival of the UN Emergency Force permitted the invaders to withdraw with a modicum of dignity, but no one could doubt the extent of the Anglo-French setback. The Suez crisis had separated and almost shattered the Western alliance.

On January 5, 1957, President Eisenhower asked Congress for authority to counter the threat of Communist infiltration in the Middle East. Two months later Congress passed a joint resolution approving the extension of economic and military aid to any nation in the area "requesting assistance against armed aggression from any country controlled by international communism." The success of this Eisenhower Doctrine in halting Soviet penetration of the region was limited.

In April 1957, when King Hussein of Jordan was confronted by an anti-Western revolt, Eisenhower sent the Sixth Fleet to the eastern Mediterranean and provided Hussein with $10 million in American aid. The pro-Western government in Jordan managed to survive the crisis.

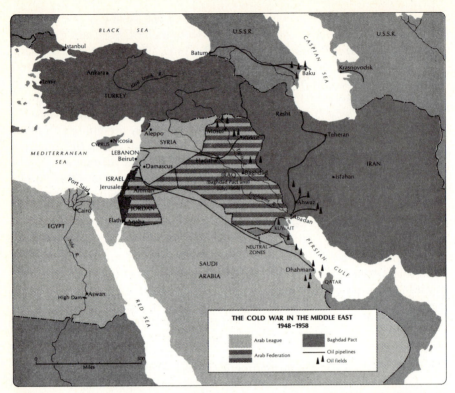

Figure 12 The Cold War in the Middle East *(From A History of the American People by Norman A. Graebner, Gilbert C. Fite, and Philip L. White. Copyright © 1970 by McGraw-Hill Inc.)*

More severe crises developed as Nasser's influence and intrigue spread throughout the Middle East. In the late spring of 1958 the pro-Western government of Lebanon came under strong pressure from Nasser supporters, and when Lebanese leaders were unable to obtain help from the United Nations and the Arab League, they turned to the United States. Eisenhower was reluctant to intervene with force, fearing the Russian and Arab reaction, but when the pro-Western government of Iraq was overturned by a Nasserite revolt in mid-July, he decided to act. He ordered the Sixth Fleet into the eastern Mediterranean and the landing of 9,000 troops in Lebanon. Meanwhile, the British moved about 3,000 troops into Jordan in response to King Hussein's plea for support.

Despite the protests and warnings from Egypt and the Soviet Union, the situation in the Middle East gradually improved. The United States recognized the new regime in Iraq, thus easing Arab fears considerably. Dag Hammerskjold, the Secretary General of the United Nations, helped work out arrangements that led to the withdrawal of American and British troops from Lebanon and Jordan in November 1958. The prospects for long-range stability, however, were not bright.

As the cold war extended to the Middle East in the 1950s, it also began to move into Latin America. The region was extremely vulnerable to such conflict. In 1953 and 1954 the radical regime of President Jacobo Arbenz of Guatemala, encouraged by Communist elements in that country, began to expropriate foreign holdings and to promote subversive movements in neighboring states. This threatened to give the Communists their first foothold in the Western Hemisphere. Secretary Dulles sought to deal with this threat through diplomatic channels, persuading the Tenth Inter-American Conference, meeting in Caracas in March 1954, to condemn "any dominion or control of the political institutions of any American state by the international Communist movement." This did not stop Guatemalan leaders, who obtained a shipment of military equipment from Czechoslovakia in May and in early June proclaimed martial law, claiming that a foreign plot sought to overturn the government. The United States had supplied weapons to Honduras and Nicaragua, and the Central Intelligence Agency engineered a successful invasion of the country by Guatemalan exiles. Arbenz appealed to the United Nations, where Russia sparked a bitter debate, and a call for an end to hostilities was approved by the Security Council. But the Council deferred action. Arbenz soon fled to Czechoslovakia, and a strong anti-Communist government came to power in Guatemala.

Evidence of deteriorating United States–Latin American relations was dramatically revealed in the spring of 1958 when Vice President Nixon and his wife undertook an eighteen-day goodwill tour of leading South American countries. They were met with popular demonstrations and mobs, evidently organized by Communists and other enemies of "Yankee imperialism." Some changes in American policies had been made by this time, and others were gradually initiated. In 1955 the United States agreed to a liberalization of its treaty with Panama. United States leaders promoted regional free trade agreements in Latin America and backed an international program to stabilize the price of coffee. They agreed in the late fifties to supply almost half the capital for a new billion dollar Inter-American Bank to make development loans.

Near the end of the Eisenhower period, a perplexing situation developed in Cuba. When the repressive regime of Fulgencio Batista was overthrown and a new government headed by Fidel Castro took control on January 1, 1959, public opinion in the United States was highly favorable toward the change. It soon became evident, however, that Prime Minister Castro was no ordinary liberal. He undertook an extensive program of agrarian reform and began to confiscate foreign assets, including over 1 billion dollars of American holdings. In February 1960 Castro signed a five-year trading agreement with the Soviet Union, and he soon extended diplomatic recognition to the People's Republic of China.

The United States had tried unsuccessfully in the late summer of 1959 to isolate and restrain Cuba with diplomatic pressure exerted through the inter-American foreign ministers. In May 1960 Washington ended all economic aid to Cuba, and in July of that year the President, on the recommendation of Congress, virtually ended the import of Cuban sugar. When Cuba complained of American action to the UN Security Council, Khrushchev could not refrain from a shrill denunciation of the United States, warning that "Soviet artillerymen can support Cuba with rocket fire" if the United States attacked the island. In the fall of 1960 the United States imposed an embargo on all exports to Cuba except food and medicine and began a naval patrol in the Caribbean to stop any possible invasion of Nicaragua and Guatemala by Castro's forces.

It became apparent in the 1950s that there were three large groups of nations in the world: the Western bloc, the Communist bloc, and a growing number of neutral states. The Bandung Conference of 1955 was an indication of the increasing importance of the Third World of the nonaligned nations. While that conference mounted a sharp attack on colonialism, its most significant action was its formulation of the doctrine of "neutralism," an affirmation that much of Asia and Africa would not ally itself with either side in the cold war and that its major goal was to liberate the underdeveloped nations of the world from dependence upon the economically advanced powers.

Neutralism spread from Asia to the Middle East and Africa. Although the superpowers' struggle for the support of the newly independent states of sub-Saharan Africa soon brought the cold war to that vast region, the first major international crisis did not come until 1960, when a confusing and chaotic upheaval began in the Congo. The trouble started after the Congo became independent of Belgium. The complex developments that followed included the return of Belgian military units, the outbreak of civil war, the involvement of the Soviet Union and other Communist nations in the struggle, American support of an anti-Communist faction, and eventually United Nations intervention in the form of an international peace force.

New Controversies and New Directions in Europe

The thaw in the cold war that was manifest during much of Eisenhower's first term in the White House had clearly succumbed to a new freeze well before the President's second inauguration. The "spirit of Geneva" had disappeared in the face of the integration of West Germany into the North

Atlantic Treaty Organization, the failure to reach agreement on the German problem, and the inability of the superpowers to work out a mutually acceptable formula for the limitation and control of armaments. United States–Russian rivalry for the allegiance of the emerging nations of Asia and Africa also indicated the resurgence of East-West friction.

The comfortable assumption most Americans held about United States military superiority over the Soviet Union was suddenly upset in the late summer and fall of 1957. The Russians announced in August that they had successfully tested an intercontinental ballistic missile. On October 4 they launched the first man-made earth satellite—*Sputnik* ("traveling companion" in Russian), a 184-pound vehicle. A month later they launched *Sputnik II,* six times heavier than *Sputnik I* and carrying aboard a live dog. During the next few years the Russians made other spectacular ventures into space. The Soviet Union possessed the most powerful army in the world, it was developing a navy second only to that of the United States, and its submarine fleet was unexcelled by any other nation's.

News of Russia's sensational accomplishments in the development of long-range missiles and the launching of powerful satellites into space coincided with the U.S.S.R.'s diplomatic gains in the Middle East and its growing intransigence in the on-again, off-again disarmament negotiations. Many United States military spokesmen and political leaders urged a concentrated effort to overtake the Russians, but the Eisenhower administration did not immediately surrender to the advocates of a huge increase in military spending. Nor was the public altogether prepared to undertake yet another forward leap in the arms race. A *New Yorker* cartoon in September 1957 showed a middle-aged, middle-class woman saying to her husband: "It's a great week for everybody. The Russians have the intercontinental ballistic missile, and we have the Edsel."

Torn between its commitment to economy and the pressure for greater military preparedness, the administration followed a middle course in the years after 1957. Military expenditures for missiles and other new devices were increased, although not as much as many critics wanted. The United States fired its first ICBM (the Atlas) in the fall of 1958, and by 1960 each branch of the armed forces had designed and put into operation a wide variety of missiles.

The threat of a terrible nuclear conflict haunted the minds of men everywhere. The Joint Congressional Committee on Atomic Energy reported in August 1959 that an attack on this country might well kill 50 million people and seriously injure an additional 20 million, while destroying or making uninhabitable half of all the nation's dwellings. By 1958 disarmament talks had begun to focus on the possibility of formulating an agreement to halt the testing of nuclear weapons, a proposal Prime

Minister Jawaharlal Nehru of India had urged as early as 1954. Recognizing an opportunity for a propaganda coup, Soviet leaders announced in March 1958 a unilateral suspension of nuclear testing. The United States countered with a proposal for joint technical studies of feasible means to detect violations of such a test ban, and in August Washington and London suggested a one-year moratorium on testing. Negotiations for a more permanent disarmament settlement were resumed in Geneva at the end of October, but in spite of the hundreds of sessions held during the next two years, no agreement could be reached. Meanwhile, however, the three nuclear powers voluntarily adhered to the cessation of tests begun in 1958.[1]

The unresolved problem of Germany continued to be an incendiary issue. The United States had followed the twofold policy of urging the reunification of the two Germanies through free elections and the rearmament of West Germany. The Russians had urged German reunification under various guises but had adamantly opposed free elections, while linking the settlement of the German question with a general European security arrangement, including the withdrawal of American forces. Soviet leaders were especially concerned about the status of West Berlin, which not only provided the Western Powers with a ready source of intelligence concerning the Communist world, but also served as an avenue of escape for some three million East Germans who had fled to the West since 1945.

In November 1958 Khrushchev suddenly announced a six-month deadline for a settlement of the West Berlin question; if an agreement was not reached by May 27, 1959, he threatened to sign a separate peace treaty with East Germany and relinquish to it the control of Berlin. Another nerve-tingling crisis now enveloped the cold war antagonists. But the Western Allies took a firm stand in the face of this Russian harassment. The Berlin crisis subsided during the early months of 1959, and the Russians began to reveal their interest in another summit meeting. In September 1959 the ebullient Khrushchev made a two-week tour of the United States that culminated in a visit with President Eisenhower at his Camp David retreat in Maryland. During the meeting the Soviet Premier canceled his Berlin ultimatum, while Eisenhower conceded that the troublesome question of West Berlin should be resolved in the near future. Late in the year at a meeting in Paris, Eisenhower and other Western leaders agreed to invite Khrushchev to a top-level conference in May 1960.

[1]Great Britain was the third nation to develop a nuclear bomb, having exploded a hydrogen bomb in 1957. France began to develop such a bomb in the late 1950s and successfully tested it in 1960.

Figure 13 Eisenhower and Khrushchev at Camp David, September 1959 *(U.S. Navy Photograph, Courtesy Dwight D. Eisenhower Library)*

A few days before the summit meeting convened in Paris, the Soviet Union announced that an American plane had been shot down over Russia on May 1. The United States indicated that the aircraft was a weather plane that had wandered off course. Soviet leaders then revealed that the American plane had been downed 1,200 miles inside Russia, that the aircraft was a high-level photoreconnaissance plane (it was later learned that the airplane was flying from Pakistan to Norway), and that the pilot had conceded the "spy" character of his mission. Khrushchev bitterly attacked the United States for its "aggressive acts," denounced Eisenhower, demanded an apology for the invasion of Soviet territorial sovereignty, and threatened to destroy those "accomplices" in Europe that provided bases for the U-2 flights. Acutely embarrassed, President Eisenhower now admitted the validity of Khrushchev's accusations; he described the U-2 flights, which had been going on since 1956, as "a distasteful but vital necessity."[2]

It is clear that Khrushchev used the U-2 incident as a pretext to destroy a meeting that he no longer wanted. He was under pressure in the Kremlin, and his caustic public statements on the Berlin situation during

---

[2]The pilot of the U-2 plane, Francis Gary Powers, was subsequently tried by the Russians and convicted of espionage. He served almost two years in a Russian prison before being exchanged in February 1962 for Colonel Rudolf Abel, a Russian who had been convicted of espionage in the United States in 1957.

the weeks before the summit meeting suggested the difficulties that would have attended the Paris negotiations. American prestige did suffer as a result of the episode. Khrushchev announced that Eisenhower's scheduled visit to the U.S.S.R. later in the year must be canceled, and he soon made it clear that no serious negotiations would be undertaken with the United States until the advent of a new presidential administration.

Not all American problems in Europe during the second Eisenhower administration were the result of Soviet opposition and diplomatic initiatives. The American decision to provide West Germany with tactical nuclear weapons disturbed some members of NATO, and as the missile rivalry increased there were sharp differences between the United States and other Western powers. Meanwhile, General Charles de Gaulle, who came to power in France in 1958, proposed a radically new approach to the control of NATO—a three-power directorate of the United States, Britain, and France.

President Eisenhower did his best as his administration neared its end to achieve the elusive peace he so passionately desired. He made three goodwill trips between December 1959 and the summer of 1960—to India, the Middle East, and southern Europe; to Latin America; and to the Far East. "Our basic aspiration," he declared on one of these tours, "is to search out methods by which peace in the world can be assured with justice for everybody." Ironically, the last six months of Eisenhower's administration were among the most trying of his eight years in the White House: the Paris summit meeting was a fiasco, the long-continued disarmament negotiations at Geneva soon broke up, the President's trip to Japan had to be canceled, a new crisis developed in the Congo, and the Communists appeared to have found in Cuba an ally only a few miles from United States soil.

Still, Dwight Eisenhower pursued a moderate course in military and diplomatic matters, and he kept the United States from involvement in another war. In a farewell address delivered on the eve of his retirement from the White House, Eisenhower warned against the military-industrial complex—against the "conjunction of an immense military establishment and a large arms industry." It was a prescient warning, in view of the swollen defense budgets of the postwar period, the close ties that linked the nation's industrial society and the military, and the enormous power concentrated in the Pentagon and the giant corporations that dominated the business of defense procurement.

SUGGESTIONS FOR FURTHER READING

In addition to the books cited in earlier chapters by Ambrose, LaFeber, Parmet, and Spanier, Louis L. Gerson, *John Foster Dulles* (1967), and Townsend Hoopes,

The Devil and John Foster Dulles (1973), are useful for United States international involvement during the Eisenhower years. The foreign policies of Eisenhower's first administration are critically examined by Norman A. Graebner in *The New Isolationism: A Study in Politics and Foreign Policy since 1950* (1956). Robert E. Osgood and others, *America and the World: From the Truman Doctrine to Vietnam** (1970), is a series of thoughtful articles reappraising United States foreign policy after two decades of cold war. For the Eisenhower military policy, see Samuel P. Huntington, *The Common Defense: Strategic Programs in National Politics** (1961). Seymour Melman, *Pentagon Capitalism: The Political Economy of War* (1970), throws light on the military-industrial complex. Valuable information is contained in the annual volumes of *The United States in World Affairs,** written for the Council on Foreign Relations.

For a good treatment of the remilitarization of West Germany, consult James L. Richardson, *Germany and the Atlantic Alliance: The Interaction of Strategy and Politics* (1966). John Mander analyzes the crisis over West Berlin in *Berlin, Hostage for the West** (1962). Davis Wise and Thomas B. Ross have written a revealing journalistic account entitled *The U-2 Affair** (1962). Among the many books on United States involvement in the Far East during the 1950s are Fred Greene, *U.S. Policy and the Security of Asia** (1968); Melvin Gurtov, *The First Vietnam Crisis: Chinese Communist Strategy and United States Involvement, 1953–1954** (1967); and George M. Kahin and John W. Lewis, *The United States in Vietnam** (rev. ed., 1969). The Middle East crisis of 1956 is dealt with in Herman Finer, *Dulles over Suez: The Theory and Practice of His Diplomacy* (1964), which is severely critical of Dulles's role. For the United States and Cuba, see Theodore Draper, *Castro's Revolution: Myths and Realities** (1962).

*Available in paperback edition.

Chapter 7

The Perils
of a Triumphant
Capitalism

Emerging from the depression that racked the nation in the pre-World War II years, the United States entered the greatest and most sustained period of prosperity in its history. Although the passage from war to peace proved difficult, the economy did not revert to the hard times of the 1930s. Instead, Americans enjoyed an almost uninterrupted boom which raised production figures, incomes, and standards of living to heights thought incredible a short time earlier. Despite several recessions, the gross national product, in constant dollars, increased more than twice the rate of the population growth. By 1960 the GNP had reached $500 billion, and within little more than another decade it had climbed to the trillion dollar level. "It became clear to all the world," the economist Harold G. Vatter has written, "that the United States economy after mid-century was capable of producing enough to provide every man, woman, and child with a minimum-comfort level of living."

Economic Trends and the Distribution of Abundance

The economy came through the rocky shoals of the immediate postwar period in surprisingly good condition. The sharp cutbacks in federal spending—from an annual rate of $91 billion during the first quarter of 1945 to a rate of $26 billion a year later—were only moderately depressing in their effect on the national economy. Inflation became a serious problem in 1946 and 1947, complicated in part by the failure of Congress and the President to impose adequate controls. But citizens and public officials alike seemed to have confidence in the capacity of the "built-in stabilizers" and discretionary action by government to counter downward economic movements. The economy did lose its buoyancy in the fall of 1948, by which time the heavy postwar consumer demand had largely been satisfied and inventories had been built up. Unemployment eventually rose to 7.6 percent of the total labor force.

Recovery from the 1949 recession was well under way when the outbreak of the Korean war triggered a new boom, which reached its peak in the second quarter of 1953. A substantial reduction in military spending, accompanying President Eisenhower's ending of the war in Korea, and a slowdown in retail sales were factors in bringing on another recession, in the fall of 1953. The Eisenhower administration, having abandoned most of the emergency controls surviving from the Truman government, also contributed to the economic stringency by resorting to a tight money policy in trying to contain inflation. Nevertheless, the new administration's faith in the ability of the economy to right itself seemed to be justified when a brisk recovery from the recession began in the autumn of 1954. The upturn was encouraged by a tax cut in 1954.

Economic life flourished during the mid-fifties. Demand slackened in 1956 but not enough to halt overall business expansion. The economy weakened during the latter part of 1957, however, and the country entered the worst recession it had experienced since World War II. The slump resulted from a substantial decrease in business investment in plant and equipment as well as cutbacks in defense spending and a drop in net exports. The 1957–1958 recession differed from its two predecessors in that prices continued to rise while production dropped, employment fell off, and consumer spending remained static. Production moved upward in the fall of 1958, though unemployment hovered around 6 percent at the end of the year. The economic stabilizers helped to cushion the impact of the downturn, and the easy credit policy adopted by the Federal Reserve Board encouraged better times.

Early in 1960 the economy faltered again, and the situation worsened during the rest of the year. Eisenhower's fiscal and monetary policies played a part in what has been called the "year of the hidden recession," while consumer credit and bank loans shrank in the face of high interest rates and a reduced money supply. By the beginning of 1961, factory output had declined, unemployment stood at almost 7 percent, and steel mills operated at only 50 percent of capacity. The recession "bottomed out" in February 1961, and during the administration of John F. Kennedy the economy improved under the stimulus of expansionary fiscal and monetary policies. But joblessness continued to mar the recovery. Kennedy proposed various solutions—including an $11 billion tax reduction bill—to solve the problems of an inadequate growth rate and too much unemployment.

The economic expansion that began early in Kennedy's term increased during the administration of Lyndon B. Johnson and continued month after month. The prosperous years between 1961 and 1969 represented the longest unbroken peacetime economic growth in American history. The real rate of economic growth during the 1960s was around 5 percent a year, and the level of inflation was held to about 1 percent annually during the first half of the decade. The tax cut of 1964, a liberal monetary policy, the Johnson administration's large domestic expenditures, and the increasing costs of the Vietnam war all contributed to the economic dynamism of the mid-1960s. But President Johnson and his advisers made the mistake of assuming that the administration's expensive social reform programs and the increasing appropriations for the war in Southeast Asia could be financed without additional taxes. The result was mounting inflation and growing concern about the economy.

Richard M. Nixon, who became President in January 1969, was determined to slow the inflation. He wanted to restrict the government's intervention in the economy, to reduce the federal budget, and to have the Federal Reserve System tighten the money supply. Efforts to achieve these objectives helped precipitate a recession. The real gross national product declined in 1970 for the first time since 1958, the stock market dropped over 300 points by mid-1970, and unemployment reached 6 percent by the end of the year. Yet prices kept climbing. Nixon then abruptly shifted from a restrictive to an expansionary fiscal strategy, calling for massive deficit spending to restore full production and employment. The economy continued to be sluggish in 1971, while unemployment remained high and prices kept going up. The administration eventually resorted to more stringent controls, but after some recovery in 1972, economic conditions worsened. Inflation moved to spectacular heights, and by 1974 the erratic behavior of the economy threatened to produce a severe recession.

Despite the economy's instability and its uneven distribution of earnings and profits, Americans enjoyed an era of extraordinary affluence during the three decades after 1945. The civilian labor force grew from 54 million workers in 1945 to 78 million in 1970. Whereas unemployment during the 1930s ranged between 15 and 25 percent of all workers, the average unemployment rate during the 1950s was 4.6 percent. Corporate profits rose from $33 billion in 1963 to $51 billion in 1968. Per capita income, in constant dollars, went up from $1,350 in 1945 to $1,824 in 1960 to over $2,000 in 1970. By 1971 more than half the families in the country received annual incomes of $10,000 or more.

All levels of American society have increased their incomes since the 1930s, but the relative positions of the various income segments have changed little. The top 5 percent of the recipients received a little over one-fifth of the national income in 1970, as compared to about one-third in 1929. On the other hand, the 20 percent of the population receiving the least income consistently obtained about 5 percent of the national income during the postwar years. Indeed, prosperity was far from being universal in America, social mobility was limited, and for a goodly number of people opportunity was nonexistent.

The Miracle of Production

So expansive was the American economy that the output of goods and services doubled and then redoubled during the twenty-five years after 1945. World War II revivified the nation's industrial and business system, created a huge backlog of consumer demand and purchasing power, and left the United States as the dominant economic power in the world. Prosperity in the years that followed was also promoted by the growth of population, the vital role government had come to assume in the nation's economic life, and the increase in production resulting from technological innovations. The federal government's enormous military budgets (they reached $50 billion a year in the early 1960s), its foreign aid programs, and its far-reaching social welfare programs constituted a profoundly important element in the national economy. The expenditures of federal, state, and local governments after the mid-1950s made up about one-fifth of all purchases in the private sector, dwarfing those of any other "industry." Federal support for research and development (R&D) spurted ahead in

Share of Aggregate Income before Taxes Received by Each Fifth of Families, 1947–1972
(Percent)

Income rank	1947	1950	1960	1966	1972
Total families	100.0	100.0	100.0	100.0	100.0
Lowest fifth	5.1	4.5	4.8	5.6	5.4
Second fifth	11.8	11.9	12.2	12.4	11.9
Third fifth	16.7	17.4	17.8	17.8	17.5
Fourth fifth	23.2	23.6	24.0	23.8	23.9
Highest fifth	43.3	42.7	41.3	40.5	41.4
Top 5 percent	17.5	17.3	15.9	15.6	15.9

Source: Economic Report of the President, 1974 (Washington, 1974), p. 140.

the late fifties, following *Sputnik*, and by the mid-sixties had reached $15 billion a year—two-thirds of the total national expenditures for R&D. Increasing horsepower per worker, use of the mass production system, application of the principles of scientific management, and growing reliance on scientific and technological research all contributed to the increase in productivity.

The talisman of the new productivity was automation, the great contribution of the 1950s. Simply put, automation involved the use of machines to operate other machines. It meant "the introduction of self-regulating devices into the industrial sequence through the feedback principle whereby electronic sensing devices automatically pass information back to earlier parts of the processing machine, correcting for tool wear or other items of control."[1] The perfection of computer systems was a vital part of the trend toward automation. The result was increased production and output per employee-hour, improved quality and uniformity of products, and more efficient management and greater speed in decision making. Automation not only affected industrial work in factories but also rapidly transformed many jobs in office, administrative, and service occupations.

Some old industries, including coal, textiles, and public transportation, declined in the postwar period and became less important in the overall configuration of American business. Other mature industries expanded after 1945—sometimes in spectacular fashion, as in the case of automobiles, sometimes at a slow but steady rate, as was true of steel. One of the traditional industries that played an important part in the peacetime prosperity was housing, which usually represented at least 20 percent of all private investment. Construction of all kind boomed in the postwar years, but the growth of residential housing, held back for a decade and a half by depression and war (the value of all United States housing was less in 1945 than in 1929), enjoyed a phenomenal advance in the new era. Government support, through G.I. loans, the Federal Housing Administration, and public housing appropriations, augmented the large investments from private sources to create a great housing boom in the 1950s. During some years over a million new units were constructed.

Automobiles, another mature industry, continued to be crucially important to the well-being of the national economy. The industry went through a temporary period of rebuilding immediately after the war, but it soon entered a flush period that surpassed even the 1920s. Factory sales of cars and trucks averaged almost 7 million a year in the fifties, and in the

[1]Harold G. Vatter, *The U.S. Economy in the 1950's: An Economic History* (New York, 1963), p. 11.

peak year of 1955 over 9 million cars, trucks, and buses were sold. Dominated by General Motors, Ford, and Chrysler, the industry made use of a type of product innovation known as "dynamic obsolescence" or "planned obsolescence," in which new models featuring ever-more powerful engines and an endless array of frills were emphasized. The advent of the small car—the so-called compact—from abroad in the mid-1950s brought a sharp jump in the importation of Volkswagens and other foreign brands, and American producers belatedly introduced their own compacts. The auto industry sustained a vast network of enterprises: automobile dealerships, garages, filling stations, a giant highway system, and the manufacture of tires and other accessories, in addition to a multitude of services catering to the motoring public such as motels and drive-in restaurants.

Chemicals became the "premier industry" in the United States after World War II. Du Pont, Monsanto, Dow, and other large corporations produced a large number of synthetic industries, plastics, synthetic rubber, synthetic fibers, drugs, and detergents. Profits were enormous. The industrial chemicals market grew at an annual rate of 10 percent between 1947 and 1960.

The extraordinary increase in the consumption of electrical power in the United States in the 1940s and 1950s both reflected and contributed to the growth of three industrial giants: the electrical power utilities and the related electrical machinery and equipment industry, the electrical appliance industry, and electronics. Growing at a rate of 15 percent a year, electronics had become the nation's fifth largest industry by 1960, exceeded only by automobiles, steel, aircraft, and chemicals. One major category of the industry included such products as computers, testing and measuring equipment, industrial control equipment, microwave communications systems, television sets, radios, phonographs, tape recorders, and high fidelity components.

The aircraft and air transport industries represented relatively new arrivals as major components of the United States economy. The shift to jet propulsion in commercial aviation boosted the industry in the 1950s, while the development and production of missiles in the late fifties and early sixties resulted in some retrenchment in the manufacture of aircraft. A related area that grew spectacularly in the 1960s was the space industry. Metals like aluminum developed rapidly in the postwar era, as did such fuel industries as natural gas.

The productivity of agriculture was even greater than that of industry. A technological explosion on the nation's farms resulted in the annual production of huge surpluses in the post-World War II period. Agricultural production per employee-hour in 1958 was more than three times the average level of the 1930s. By 1960 the government had 1.4

billion bushels of wheat in storage, as well as vast amounts of other price-supported commodities. Technological innovations and scientific advances enabled a relatively few large farmers to supply the greater part of the market demand. Farming had become agribusiness. The celebrated family farm clearly faced extinction, even though millions of poor rural inhabitants continued to hang on to the only economic livelihood most of them had ever known.

One of the notable features of the economic scene during the three decades after 1945 was the way in which the new industrial and business developments contributed to the transformation of several regions. The expansive forces that promoted these regional changes varied. The aircraft industry, for instance, spurred the rapid development of the Pacific Coast economy during the 1940s and 1950s. Government expenditures for defense and space programs played an important role in the economic growth of such states as California, Texas, Massachusetts, and Ohio. The South benefited in the contest for new industry because of its abundant land and water, its supplies of electrical power and other fuels, and its favorable tax policies. Moderate climate was also an asset of the Southern states.

The most dramatic economic growth in the postwar period took place in the Pacific Coast states and particularly in California, where a distinctive style of life furnished one of the incentives for westward migration. By 1963 California had passed New York as the wealthiest and most populous state in the Union; it was first in both industrial and agricultural production. The most spectacular Southern development occurred in Texas, where a giant petrochemical industry grew up in a complex of Gulf Coast cities. The rapid growth of Florida was scarcely less impressive, and that state's economic life flourished on the basis of tourism, citrus fruits, and the space industry. The Great Lakes and Middle West regions, long the country's agricultural and industrial heartland, basically held their position in the national economy—no mean feat in itself. Some other leading industrial and business centers, such as Pennsylvania, faced serious stagnation in certain industrial lines. Much of New England fought a rearguard action to prevent a lag in economic growth as compared with other parts of the country. Large depressed areas such as Appalachia, as well as numerous centers of declining industries and hundreds of depopulated counties and small towns throughout the country, failed to participate directly in the economic expansion.

Structure and Competition

No aspect of the American economy was more prominent than the continuing trend toward large-scale corporate enterprise. The growing concentration of economic power in the United States went far beyond the combination movement at the turn of the century and the widespread holding companies and business consolidations that marked the 1920s. By the 1950s and 1960s giant corporations dominated almost every area of the nation's business, and a few hundred large concerns exerted a preponderate influence on the economy as a whole. In 1960, 600 corporations had annual earnings of over $10 million. These 600 companies made up only $1/2$ of 1 percent of all United States corporations, but they accounted for 53 percent of total corporate income. The emerging supercorporations were national and even international in operation, bureaucratic in organization, and increasingly diversified in the range of their products and services. Small business enterprise did not disappear, but its role grew less significant in the economy. In 1958 there were some 5 million individually owned businesses outside of farming, mining, and fishing in the United States, but 85 percent of all employed persons were working for someone else—as compared with 36 percent in 1900.

Oligopoly, or the dominance of an industry or business by a few large firms, became the rule. Three automobile companies produced 95 percent of the new cars manufactured in the United States, three aluminum companies produced 90 percent of all the aluminum, and three radio and television networks monopolized the nation's airwaves. Bank deposits increased fourfold between 1940 and 1960, but the number of banks declined by over a thousand during the two decades, and branch banking became increasingly common. In the aircraft industry in the mid-fifties ten firms employed 94 percent of the total labor force; in petroleum fifteen firms employed 86 percent; in steel thirteen corporations hired 85 percent; in office machinery four concerns employed 71 percent; and in electrical machinery six employed 50 percent of all workers.

The trend toward bigness in the United States economy was encouraged by hundreds of mergers every year. Holding company pyramids came into vogue again, and a new form of consolidated firm emerged in the conglomerate, which brought together under one financially powerful management several companies frequently producing products that were quite unrelated to each other. Mergers and acquisitions were a widely chosen alternative to the creation of new capacity and additional output, which might have been attended by price reductions. Acquisitions were also accelerated by tax deductions afforded profitable acquiring companies. The new technology contributed to the further growth of industrial concentration, since the costs of research, retooling, and development in an age of faster-than-sound transport, atomic power, and intercontinental missiles were simply prohibitive for smaller firms.

Ownership and management in the large corporation were now almost completely separate, and a new professional managerial class, possessing enormous power, directed the great business units. Since most of the new capital for the operation of the supercorporations was generated internally from profits and depreciation accounts, the large concerns no longer were very dependent upon banks, insurance companies, and individual investors. At the same time, these large bureaucracies were sensitive to the conditions and morale of their employees. Because most of them competed in a broad consumers' market, they were increasingly concerned about their "public image" and very attentive to the requirements of public relations. They sought long-run security in a variety of ways, including diversification through product innovation or merger. After the war, Alfred D. Chandler wrote, "nearly all the major oil and rubber companies began producing petrochemicals, rubber chemicals, plastics, and many sorts of synthetics; and the automobile companies began turning out tractors, farm equipment, marine engines, and other non-automotive products." With the strategy of diversification came a new decentralized structure in large-scale business.

Economic concentration clearly led to a decline in traditional competition, increased the incidence of so-called administered prices, and made for instability in the economy. Nevertheless, a good deal of competition continued to exist in some sectors of the nation's economy, including construction, mining, services, and trades, where a large number of producers or service units prevailed. Some authorities pointed out, moreover, that competition was widely evident in quality, product design, and advertising. John Kenneth Galbraith, in *American Capitalism: The Concept of Countervailing Power* (1952), argued that the long trend toward concentration of industrial enterprise in the hands of a few firms had created "not only strong sellers . . . but also strong buyers." In this system of countervailing power, according to Galbraith, "one large bloc is offset by the growth of another group in an effort to prevent its own exploitation."

The record of the federal government's antitrust suits since 1945 reveals its recurrent attempts to halt the trend toward ever-greater economic concentration. In a case against the Aluminum Company of America, decided in 1945, the government secured the dissolution of the corporation. The following year, in a suit against three giant tobacco companies for conspiring to control the price of leaf tobacco and cigarettes, the government won another important decision. Significantly, the Supreme Court in this case declared that monopoly consisted as much in possession of power to suppress competition and raise prices as in the commission of unlawful acts. The Celler-Kefauver Act of 1950, an amendment to the Clayton Antitrust Act of 1914, made it illegal for a corporation to acquire in whole or part the assets of another corporation if the effect would be to lessen competition. The Justice Department, under this authority, initiated a number of successful suits to prevent mergers or acquisitions in the milk, steel, paper, and sugar industries. In one of the most famous court actions of the postwar period, Du Pont was forced to divest itself of its 23 percent stock interest in General Motors.

The nation was shocked in 1960 when twenty-nine leading electrical equipment companies and forty-four of their officers were brought to trial for conspiring to rig bids and fix prices on $1.75 billion worth of equipment sold between 1955 and 1959. The government won the case, and the guilty firms were fined a total of $1.9 million. In a series of decisions during the immediate postwar years, the Supreme Court invalidated the notorious basing-point pricing system, which had long been used in such industries as steel and cement to avoid price competition.[2] The courts in other decisions opened patents to more liberal licensing arrangements, prohibited tying contracts, required the sale rather than the mere leasing of equipment, and in general assured greater access to technological knowledge.

Critics of the big corporations seemed more concerned with the social implications of corporate power than with its economic consequences. Thus William H. Whyte's widely read book, *The Organization Man* (1956), emphasized the malign effects of big business bureaucracy. He lamented the way in which it smothered individuality and caused the new businessman to abandon the "Protestant ethic" and assume the "social ethic."

There was still much talk in America about "free enterprise," and Washington lawmakers were not unresponsive to the precarious position of many small businessmen. The House of Representatives set up a Small Business Committee as early as 1941, and the Senate created its own Select Committee on Small Business in 1950. The Small Business Administration was established in the fifties to absorb the remaining functions of the Reconstruction Finance Corporation and the Small Defense Plants Administration and to render aid "to small business concerns, including financial, procurement and technical assistance."

If the power of the federal government was used in some instances to protect the small businessman, it was exercised in many cases actually to foster the growth of oligopoly. World War II encouraged this development, for it ushered in a new era of government-business cooperation, and it allowed the great corporations to fortify themselves in preparation

---

[2]The "Pittsburgh-plus" system illustrates the way in which the basing-point price arrangement operated. Under this scheme of administered prices, buyers of steel in Atlanta had to pay the equivalent of freight charges on steel from Pittsburgh to Atlanta, even though the steel was produced in Birmingham, a relatively short distance away.

for peacetime operation. Congress strengthened the monopolistic principle of resale price maintenance in the McGuire Act of 1952.[3] The Reed-Bulwinkle Act, also passed in 1952, exempted railroads from public approval of agreements relating to "rates, fares, classifications, divisions, allowances or charges." The government gave its approval in 1968 to a merger of the Pennsylvania and New York Central Railroads.

The link between government and business was most conspicuously manifested in the defense and space programs. A community of interest developed between the Pentagon and the giant corporations that received the bulk of the procurement funds, and the defense contractors were frequently able to avoid competition or to secure payments for billion dollar cost overruns, as in the case of Lockheed's C-5 transport plane. Early in 1969 some 2,072 retired military officers of high rank were employed by 100 of the major defense contractors. In 1966 a single firm—General Dynamics—received government contracts totaling $2.2 billion. Lockheed, the recipient of $2 billion in defense contracts in 1968, faced bankruptcy in 1971. But Congress came to its aid, authorizing a $250 million loan to rescue the company.

Patterns of Trade and Distribution

The domestic commerce and foreign trade of the United States in the postwar years revealed the extent to which the economy had shifted to a mass consumption base at home and how dominant it had become in the international sphere as the world's industrial and financial center. The domestic market seemed to be almost insatiable, and it was sustained year in and year out by accumulated savings and rising incomes, large annual crops of new babies, a vast network of credit, new technology, huge government expenditures, and enormous advertising outlays. The country's preeminent position in the world economy reflected its importance as a market for goods and as a source of goods and savings.

In the new "affluent society" the business world was drawn as if by a magnet to the needs and desires of the consumer. He was, as George E. Mowry puts it, "daily cajoled by advertising, frequently consulted as to his wishes by market surveys, and his future inclinations to buy or not to buy [were] intently studied by research organizations." A marginal decline in the consumer's purchasing expectations, Mowry noted, "was often enough to curtail inventories and cause the stock market to waver." The consumer orientation was evident in the growing importance of the service industries and trades. By the late 1950s more workers were

[3]This legislation, an amendment to the Federal Trade Commission Act, authorized the continued exemption from antitrust prosecution of resale price maintenance; it permitted individual firms to enforce fair trade contracts against nonsigners and to fix stipulated as well as minimum resale prices.

employed in services than in the production of goods. Expenditures for services had risen by 1963 to 41.3 percent of all consumer spending (the figure for 1950 was 36.9 percent), as compared with 13.7 percent for durable and 44.8 percent for nondurable goods.

The consumer market not only spread into all manner of personal services but also came to encompass an endless array of durable goods: television sets, stereos, tape recorders, dishwashers, home freezers, boats, sporting goods, and so on, not to mention new houses and new automobiles. The "youth market" developed rapidly in the 1960s, with a host of its own special products. Americans spent increasing amounts of money for entertainment, recreation, and travel. This far-flung consumer culture spawned a variety of new institutions, such as gourmet food stores, art centers, record stores, and pet shops. At the same time, the older trend toward larger retail stores continued in the form of chain stores, department stores, and mail-order houses. The most impressive new type of store in the retail area was the supermarket, whose spacious and glistening rows of well-displayed merchandise included virtually any item the customer might fancy.

Economic prosperity had become dependent in considerable degree upon the creation of what John Kenneth Galbraith called a "synthesis of desire," in which advertising played an indispensable part. Advertising in such traditional media as newspapers and periodicals enjoyed a substantial increase, but the most spectacular new medium for this purpose was television. One development in this field was the popularization of depth psychology and the use of motivational research in an effort to discover what would have a favorable effect on the consumer's ego and libido. The public relations expert became a prominent figure in the postwar business world, and every corporation of any size had its own public relations department, where such schemes as "press junkets" and newsworthy activities were conceived. Frederic Wakeman's popular novel, *The Hucksters,* drew public attention to the existence and influence of the advertising business—"Madison Avenue"—and alerted many readers to the cynicism of some advertising methods.

The flourishing business involving consumer goods and services was stimulated by the ready availability of credit. Total private debts in the United States increased from $73 billion to $196 billion during the 1950s. Credit was available for nearly every kind of purchase, and consumer buying was facilitated by checking accounts, credit cards, home mortgages, auto loans, installment buying, and finance companies. The credit card, often valid throughout the world, became a symbol of United States affluence and consumerism.

While a large number of Americans customarily spent more than they earned, many others were able to save money. Personal savings contributed directly to the impressive growth after 1945 of life insurance companies, savings and loan associations, mutual savings banks, investment companies, and credit companies, in addition to commercial banks. An enormous increase took place in private pension funds—from a total of $11 billion in 1950 to $44 billion in 1959. The stock market also reflected the mounting volume of savings and investments in the United States. There were at least 20 million individual stockholders in 1965, in contrast to only 6^1/$_2$ million in 1952. Some so-called growth stocks, such as IBM, doubled their assets every four or five years beginning in the late 1940s and were traded at 60 to 70 times their earnings in the 1960s.

American leaders worked to reduce international economic barriers during and after the war. They pursued a liberal tariff policy, especially during the years 1946–1950, entering into the General Agreement on Tariffs and Trade in 1947 and extending the reciprocal trade program every few years. The United States also contributed to the internationalization of foreign lending. It took the lead in 1944 in creating the International Monetary Fund, to avoid drastic fluctuations in exchange rates and competitive currency devaluations following the war, and the International Bank for Reconstruction and Development to provide long-term investment funds to Europe and less developed countries.

The United States was a leading supplier of goods and services, accounting in 1961 for nearly one-fourth of the total world exports of manufactures and for almost one-third of the world exports of capital goods. It also exported large amounts of military equipment and many agricultural goods, especially cotton, wheat, tobacco, soybeans, and poultry. The Marshall Plan and other foreign aid programs were obviously designed to support American economic interests overseas. Foreign trade and investment were likewise promoted through liberal tax policies and such agencies as the International Cooperation Administration, established in 1948.

American corporations and citizens in the postwar era made large investments abroad. These investments totaled more than $12 billion in Europe alone by the mid-1960s. By 1963 United States firms controlled over half of the British automobile industry, 40 percent of the German petroleum industry, and 40 percent of the French telegraph, telephone, electronics, and statistical equipment business. One estimate fixed the gross value of products manufactured by American companies abroad in 1967 at over $100 billion.

Reversing a longtime trend, the United States after 1945 became a major importer of industrial and consumer goods. Americans were increasingly attracted to the efficient, low-priced cars, cameras, stereo equipment, and other products from countries like Germany and Japan. The United States had also become more dependent on foreign raw materials such as iron ore, bauxite, and crude oil. In addition to payments for imports, the United States had spent almost $100 billion in economic and military aid to other countries by the late 1960s. Large private investments outside the United States also affected the balance of payments adversely, as did American travel abroad, interest on foreign investments in the United States, foreign transportation, and the like. As the deficits mounted in America's balance of payments, the position of the United States in the world economy began to be affected. The gold drain from the United States became a chronic problem after 1958, and the possibility of a dollar crisis grew steadily larger. The crisis came in 1971, forcing the Nixon administration to devaluate the dollar.

The Worker's World

One manifestation of the sustained prosperity in postwar America was the general security enjoyed by most workers. The civilian labor force expanded enormously, from 57.5 million workers in 1946 to 82.6 million in mid-1972. Labor's share of the national income rose appreciably. Total nonagricultural weekly earnings increased from $45.58 in 1947 to almost $120.00 in 1970; real weekly earnings of factory workers went up 50 percent between 1945 and 1970. Organized labor, having grown to maturity, assumed a place of great power in the economy. American workers increasingly took on a bourgeois appearance.

The composition of the working force underwent great change during the three decades following the war. The number of farmers declined steadily and by 1960 made up only 8.5 percent of the nation's workers. At some point in the fifties the number of persons engaged in goods-producing activities dropped below 50 percent of all civilian labor, and in 1960 the blue-collar percentage of all workers had fallen to 45, as compared to 59 in 1929. The great increase in employment occurred in the ranks of white-collar workers, including business and personal services, finance, distribution, education, and government.

The growing dominance of the white-collar worker in the world of labor was manifested in part by the accelerated movement of women into positions of gainful employment. Between 1940 and 1960, approximately 9.4 million women joined the labor force as against only 7.5 million men. During the same years the percentage of married women working outside the home doubled, and by 1960 about one-third of all married women were gainfully employed. In the 1960s two out of every three clerical workers were women (only one out of four had been in 1900). Women began for the first time to enter such fields as finance and public relations.

Organized labor, moving ahead on the basis of the great expansion of the New Deal years and World War II, made impressive progress, particularly during the first postwar decade. The number of union members in the United States climbed from 14.7 million in 1945 to 18.1 million in 1960 and 20.7 million ten years later. Organized labor's share of the total labor force began to decline slightly in the fifties, moving from a peak of 28 percent in 1953 to 26.2 percent in 1960. Even so, by the late fifties two-thirds of the production force in manufactures was unionized. While experiencing some decline in the sixties, organized labor began to make gains among new groups of workers, including retail clerks, teachers, and government employees.

Labor-management relations became far less antagonistic and much more stable than they had been in the 1930s. The 116-day steel strike of 1959 demonstrated how disruptive national strikes in vital industries could be, but in general the relationship between labor and management had become peaceful and stable. A key factor in labor's cooperative attitude was the fact that workers won so many benefits in the new era. Having secured legal safeguards to ensure its right to organize and bargain collectively, labor enjoyed great success in gaining its specific economic objectives at the bargaining table. The scope of its negotiations with management came to include a wide range of "fringe benefits," among which were pension plans, paid vacations and holidays, sickness and hospitalization benefits, and supplementary unemployment insurance.

An important new characteristic of the corporate environment was the long-term labor contract, which became common in most of the large industries. The practice of "pattern settlements" also spread, whereby wage agreements in certain big industries like automobiles and electrical manufacturing were followed in other industries. General Motors and the United Automobile Workers agreed as early as 1948 to an "escalator clause" in a new contract, tying wages to the cost of living, and similar arrangements were soon included in most leading contracts. Growing use was made of what was termed the "annual improvement factor," through which a portion of the gains from improved productivity was transferred to the wage earner each year. Another innovation was the "package settlement" that combined a cost-of-living adjustment with so many cents per hour for fringe benefits, to which was frequently added a separate productivity increment. In the early fifties the Congress of Industrial Organizations and many members of the American Federation of Labor began to demand a guaranteed annual income, and soon afterward some labor representatives introduced the notion of a salary status for production workers rather than hourly wages.

Another example of labor progress was the merger, in December 1955, of the AFL and CIO into one great federation. Although the differences and the rivalry between the two national organizations had been acute in the thirties and forties, the situation changed considerably during the first decade after the war. The Taft-Hartley Act of 1947 tended to unify labor against the common enemy, and the old industrial versus craft distinction was no longer a significant source of friction. The new AFL-CIO brought the great majority of American unionists into one organization, with George Meany of the AFL as president and the dynamic Walter P. Reuther of the CIO as senior vice-president. But it soon became evident that the merger had not solved the problem of jurisdictional rivalry and internal friction.

Nor did the AFL-CIO show much initiative in trying to bring in unorganized workers. While union bureaucracy increased and organized labor became more centralized, the movement lost its old militancy. Trade unionism in the 1950s seemed to be hardening. As David Brody has written, "Its ideas lacked freshness, its policies popular appeal. Age crept up even on those new style leaders like Walter Reuther, who were raised in the great upheaval of the thirties."

Organized labor's loss of vitality in the 1950s and 1960s was also related to the changing structure of employment. Increasingly after midcentury, new jobs in the labor market were being created in such tertiary areas as government and services rather than manufacturing, where some older industries were declining and automation was taking its toll of workers. The white-collar group was difficult to organize, having a traditional aversion to unionization. Labor organizations also faced a variety of other difficulties, including powerful opposition from many employers, the hostility of local authorities in the South and other rural areas, and a number of strong political barriers. The Taft-Hartley Act, with its list of "unfair labor practices," reduced union power in several respects. A wave of restrictive state laws was enacted at about the same time, striking at the union shop and tending to favor nonunion workers.

Behind the legislatures and the courts was a public that had become more and more critical of organized labor's "excesses." Many people disliked the union encouragement of "featherbedding"—the retention of useless positions—and public support was also alienated because of mounting evidence of labor racketeering. Basically, however, a large number of Americans, perhaps even a majority, had begun to feel that big labor had grown too powerful and irresponsible. This attitude was broadened and reinforced by congressional revelations in the late 1950s. Early in 1957 a special Senate committee under the chairmanship of John L. McClellan of Arkansas launched an extensive investigation of corruption and other "improper activities" in the labor and management fields. The McClellan committee found evidence of widespread bribery, graft, misuse of union funds and expense accounts by labor leaders, racketeering, corrupt practices, and undemocratic internal politics in many unions. The publicity resulting from this inquest led to the passage of the

Landrum-Griffin Act of 1959[4] and spurred the more responsible labor leaders to set about putting their own house in order.

Few developments in the postwar era were more disturbing to labor than the rapid progress of automation. The continuing mechanization of industries such as coal mining, steel, longshoring, and certain of the mass production lines drastically reduced the employment in those areas. Automation alone eliminated an estimated 1.5 million blue-collar workers between 1953 and 1959. When new machinery and technological advances forced middle-aged and older workers out of jobs, it was frequently impossible for them to find substitute employment or to secure the training and expertise necessary for more sophisticated work. School dropouts and young people from disadvantaged groups were doubly handicapped, for many of them were financially unable or insufficiently motivated to acquire much education and training, and without such preparation they stood no chance in the competition for good jobs.

One industry that clearly had a surplus of labor was agriculture, in which production increased as the number of workers declined. The total number of farm workers dropped from 10.3 million in 1946 to fewer than 5 million in 1970. The federal government's expensive price support system principally aided large commercial farmers. According to the *Economic Report of the President* in 1959, "More than 2.5 million farmers—whose annual sales are less than $2,500 and who produce each year only about 9 percent of our marketed farm products—receive only very small supplements, or none at all, to their incomes from Government expenditures for price support." Even more discouraging was the tragic plight of about 200,000 migrant farm workers, who provided much of the seasonal labor for the orchards and truck farms of California and other areas specializing in the production of fruits and vegetables. The low wages, inadequate housing, and social deprivations suffered by these workers and their families represented a status little better than peasantry.

A great majority of postwar Americans were more fortunate. They had jobs and, equally important, opportunities for new jobs and occupational advancement. They had shared in the postwar prosperity. Millions of men and women, moreover, had used their jobs and professions as escalators not only to a higher standard of living but also to a social status within the great American middle class.

SUGGESTIONS FOR FURTHER READING

There is no adequate economic history of the postwar period, but Harold G. Vatter's *The U.S. Economy in the 1950's: An Economic History** (1963) provides

[4]This measure sought to provide greater protection for individual union members and closer government supervision of union activities.
*Available in paperback edition.

an authoritative treatment of one decade. Various other aspects of the United States economy are dealt with in Michael Gort, *Diversification and Integration in American Industry* (1962); Robert T. Averitt, *The Dual Economy: The Dynamics of American Industry Structure** (1968); John B. Rae, *Climb to Greatness: The American Aircraft Industry, 1920–1960* (1968); and Lawrence J. White, *The Automobile Industry since 1945* (1971). The distribution of income in the years after 1945 is analyzed by Robert J. Lampman, *The Share of Top Wealth-Holders in National Wealth, 1922–1956* (1962), and Gabriel Kolko, *Wealth and Power in America: An Analysis of Social Class and Income Distribution** (1962). On the economic transformation of the South, see Thomas D. Clark, *The Emerging South** (2nd ed., 1968), and James G. Maddox and associates, *The Advancing South: Manpower Prospects and Problems* (1967).

Thomas C. Cochran's *American Business in the Twentieth Century* (1972) is a thoughtful synthesis of modern United States business history. See also Morton S. Baratz, *The American Business System in Transition** (1970). The role of the corporation is treated in Richard J. Barber, *The American Corporation: Its Power, Its Money, Its Politics** (1970); Willard F. Mueller, *A Primer on Monopoly and Competition* (1970); Robert Sobel, *The Age of Giant Corporations: A Microeconomic History of American Business, 1914–1970** (1972); and Morton Mintz and Jerry S. Cohen, *America, Inc.: Who Owns and Operates the United States** (1971). A small volume that identifies some of the newer tendencies in the American economy is Adolf A. Berle, *Power without Property: A New Development in American Political Economy** (1959). Three of John Kenneth Galbraith's books are important for an understanding of recent United States economic developments: *American Capitalism: The Concept of Countervailing Power** (1952); *The Affluent Society** (1958); and *The New Industrial State** (1967).

Herbert Stein's *The Fiscal Revolution in America** (1969) provides a first-rate account of the historical development of the "new economics" and a good study of the various postwar administrations' fiscal policies. Robert Lekachman's *The Age of Keynes** (1966) is illuminating in this connection, as is A. E. Holmans' *United States Fiscal Policy, 1945–1959: Its Contribution to Economic Stability* (1961). Jim F. Heath's *John F. Kennedy and the Business Community* (1969) is basically an economic history of the New Frontier. An important aspect of the relationship between government and business is critically explored in Walter Adams and Horace M. Gray, *Monopoly in America: The Government as Promoter* (1955). Bernard D. Nossiter explodes several myths concerning the economy in *The Mythmakers: An Essay on Power and Wealth** (1964).

For the economic implications of research and technology, see Leonard S. Silk, *The Research Revolution* (1960), and Walter Breckingham, *Automation: Its Impact on Business and People** (1963). The postwar labor situation is examined in Joel Seidman, *American Labor from Defense to Reconversion* (1953); Frank Cormier and William J. Eaton, *Reuther* (1970); and John Hutchinson, *The Imperfect Union: A History of Corruption in American Trade Unions** (1970).

Chapter 8

The Emergence
of a New
Social Order

The social order in recent America has experienced profound change, despite the fact that many traditional social patterns have continued to hold sway. The enormous growth of the economy and the pervasive influence of technology accelerated the pace of social change in the postwar years. In certain respects American society became more homogeneous, more stable, more conservative, and less divided by geography and national origin. Yet it was also being redefined by such factors as class, age, and ethnicity.

Postwar Demographic Trends

If American society continued to be mobile and dynamic in the postwar era, it was also extraordinarily expansive. The population increased from 139.9 million in 1945 to 151.3 million in 1950. During the 1950s total population grew by more than 24 million people, a remarkable growth rate of 18.5 percent in that decade. The 200 million mark was passed in 1967, and the total number of Americans had increased to 211 million by 1974. An important factor in this growth was a reversal of the declining birthrate of the prewar period. The birthrate, which stood at 19.4 per thousand in 1940, rose to 23.3 in 1946, to 25.8 in 1947, and to 25 or above during the years 1951–1957. The rate began to drop in the late fifties, and it fell still further in later years as Americans became more concerned about environmental problems at home and soaring population in much of the rest of the world.

The marrying age for men and women dropped at the end of the war, as millions of G.I.'s came home and as Rosie the riveter left the war plants. The "nesting" phase of the postwar period had begun, and from 1947 to about 1960 the United States enjoyed the greatest "baby boom" in its modern history. In 1947 there were 3.5 million births, a jump of 800,000 in one year, and the number of new babies increased with every change of the calendar, reaching 4.3 million in 1960. The baby boom of the forties and fifties had a telling effect upon the age distribution of the American people. In 1970 there were twice as many fourteen-year-olds as there were people forty years of age.

The population was growing older as well as younger. The death rate declined from 10.8 per thousand in 1940 to about 9.4 per thousand in 1970. Almost 11 percent of all Americans were sixty-five or older in 1970, as compared with about 8 percent in 1945 and only 4.1 percent in 1900. While the total population has doubled since 1920, the *older* population has quadrupled! As longevity continued to rise, the male-female ratio among older adults also widened. At birth there are about 104 males to every 100 females, but by age nineteen the ratio is about even. By age sixty-five, however, there are only about 75 men to every 100 women.

By the early 1970s life expectancy at birth in the United States had risen to more than seventy-one years—an increase of over six years for males and of more than eleven years for females since 1940. Better diets made possible by the higher standard of living in the postwar period contributed to this improvement in the health of the American people. But the most important factor was the spectacular progress in medical science. Many dreaded diseases, including diphtheria, typhoid fever, and poliomyelitis, were virtually eliminated. Syphilis and tuberculosis in the early 1960s caused only one-tenth as many deaths per hundred thousand people as in 1939. Infection-fighting drugs made possible tremendous advances against bacteria and virus disease: penicillin during World War II; streptomycin in 1945; and in the following years aureomycin, terromycin, izoniazid, the Salk and Sabin vaccines, cortisone, oral antidiabetic drugs, and an array of tranquilizing agents. Great advances were also made in the field of heart surgery, in the techniques of organ transplants, and in the development of psychiatry. The mounting evidence that death and certain serious diseases were associated with the heavy use of

Selected Statistics, 1945–1970

	1945	1950	1960	1970
Population	140,468,000	152,271,000	180,671,000	204,879,000
Percentage urban	58.6	64.0	69.9	73.5
Percentage rural	41.4	36.0	30.1	26.5
Percentage nonwhite	10.0	10.5	11.0	11.1
Birthrate (per 1,000				
population)	20.4	24.1	23.7	18.2
Life expectancy				
White	66.8	69.1	70.6	71.7
Nonwhite	57.7	60.8	63.6	64.6
High school graduates				
(as percentage of all				
persons over 16 years old)	47.9*	59.0	65.1	78.0
Labor union				
membership	14,796,000	15,000,000	18,117,000	20,752,000
Gross national product				
(billions of dollars)	211.9	284.8	503.7	977.1
Motor vehicle				
registrations	31,035,420	49,200,000	73,900,000	108,400,000
Advertising expendi-				
tures (millions				
of dollars)	2,874	5,710	11,932	19,600
Military personnel on				
active duty	12,123,455	2,357,000	2,494,000	2,874,000

*Figure for 1946.

Sources: *Historical Statistics of the United States, Colonial Times to 1957*; *Statistical Abstract of the United States, 1973*; and *Digest of Educational Statistics, 1970.*

tobacco encouraged nearly 8 million Americans to quit smoking between 1965 and 1970, during which time the incidence of cigarette smoking declined from 41.6 to 36.7 percent. As people lived longer, the ravages of heart disease, cancer, and mental illness increased. Death on the highway also took a mounting toll; almost 55,000 died in automobile accidents in 1971 alone.

Although American society became more homogeneous with the ending of large-scale immigration in the 1920s, the nation retained much of its ethnic and "racial" heterogeneity. The nonwhite component of the population, which had been slowly declining in the prewar decades, increased somewhat after the war, rising from about 10.5 percent in 1945 to over 12 percent in 1970. The great majority of the nonwhites were Negroes, who numbered about 22.5 million in 1970 (about 11 percent of the total population). There were also some 790,000 Indians, 590,000 Japanese, 435,000 Chinese, and 343,000 Filipinos in the population. The proportion of foreign born in the population continued to decline, falling from about 7 percent in 1950 to 4.7 percent (about 9.6 million) in 1970. Immigration after the war was around 300,000 a year, including thousands of "war brides" from Germany, Japan, and other occupied countries and several hundred thousand "displaced persons" admitted by special act of Congress. A great many Puerto Ricans, who were not technically immigrants, also poured into New York's Spanish Harlem and other urban ghettos. By 1970 Puerto Ricans and other Spanish-Americans in the United States numbered over 9 million, or about 5 percent of the total population.

Americans had always been characterized as a people on the move, and in the postwar years the open road beckoned them as never before. In the age of the automobile, the jet airliner, and the expense account, people traveled constantly for business and pleasure. One out of every five Americans changed his place of residence each year. Among the more notable aspects of this geographic mobility was the continued movement of people from the farm to the city. Over two-fifths of the counties in the United States lost population during the 1960s, and a net out-migration was the experience of about 70 percent of all counties during that decade. As the rural population declined, the nation became increasingly urbanized: 58.9 percent in 1945, 69.9 percent in 1960, and 74 percent in 1972.

The regional redistribution of population since the early 1940s is also noteworthy. The rapid movement of blacks out of the South, a phenomenon that began during World War I, was accelerated during and after World War II. The number of Negroes living outside of the Southern states increased from 3 million in 1940 to over 7 million in 1960, and today almost half of all American blacks live in non-Southern states. Some regions grew much more rapidly than others in the postwar period. The population of the Pacific Coast, for example, increased 40.2 percent in the 1950s and that of the mountain states 35.1 percent in the same decade. During the 1960s the population of the Northeast, by contrast, increased only 9.7 percent and that of the North Central region 9.6 percent, while the percentage gain in the South was 14.2 and that of the West 24.1.

The massive redistribution of population in the period following World War II blurred the old regional identities in the United States; yet regionalism persisted and in some respects found new expression as a result of demographic trends and economic developments. The growing importance of the service sector of the economy and the emergence of new "footloose" industries in search of locations with climatic, visual, and recreational advantages contributed to the regional pattern of growth. The rapid influx of people into these areas and the dynamic quality of their economies combined with a distinctive life-style to give some of them a peculiar kind of regional character. At the same time, the most clearly identified section in modern America—the South—lost some of its homogeneity and apartness following the war.

Urbanization

If regionalism became less important as a distinguishing feature of American life, urbanization became a much more powerful force in the nation's social order. The most spectacular example of metropolitan growth was the supercity, or "megalopolis"—great concentrations or clusters of cities so closely situated as to constitute one enormous urban area. The region from Boston to Washington formed one of these "conurbations," but by the 1970s there were ten or twelve others, such as the area stretching from San Francisco and Oakland south to San Jose. It was truly the age of the Metro-American.

Most large American cities after World War II were hard hit by the separation between the central city and the mushrooming suburbs that surrounded them. A mighty exodus from the inner cities to the peripheral areas was soon under way, with the middle class leading the way. Of 13 million dwelling units erected in nonfarm areas between 1946 and 1958, 85 percent were constructed outside the central cities. The suburban trend reflected the great increase that was simultaneously taking place in social mobility. Much of the young, active, and better-educated population left the old parts of the metropolis for the new suburbia. The development of suburbia involved not only the attraction of open and unsettled country, where badly needed homes could be bought or built at reasonable cost, but also a flight from the encroachment of blacks and other newcomers in the old city. Still other factors encouraged the growth of the postwar suburbs: the role of housing developers and speculators, the mortgage policies of federal agencies like the FHA, the use of the automobile as a major means of transportation, the construction of new highways and freeways, the use of assembly-line construction with standardized materials.

Some of the suburban developments were mushroom communities that were built almost overnight. One of the best-known builders and merchandisers of new homes in bulk was William Levitt, whose firm built and sold 17,500 homes in Levittown, Long Island, in the postwar years, using mass production methods. The Levitts developed another Levittown in Bucks County, Pennsylvania, during the early 1950s. The first batch of 16,000 houses on 1,100 streets "cut through acreage where but a few months ago local farmers raised only spinach." Penn Kimball described the new Levittown in the *New York Times Magazine*:

> Starting from scratch, the Levitts will have converted eight square miles of open farm country into a densely populated community of 70,000. Paved

streets, sewer lines, school sites, baseball diamonds, shopping center, parking lots, new railroad station, factory sidings, churches, trunk arteries, newspapers, garden clubs, swimming pools, doctors, dentists and town hall—all conceived in advance, all previously planned in one of the most colossal acts ever of mortal creation.

As a rule the rapidly growing suburbs were neither planned nor controlled. They sprang up randomly in the outlying areas, often unlovely settlements comprising rows of identical houses in the middle of small lots. The suburban sprawl scattered residential developments over large areas, since single-family houses took up much more room than multiple-family dwellings. People usually drove to work—alone or in car pools—and housewives were forced to drive wherever they went and were constantly chauffeuring their children from one activity to another. During the 1950s several sociologists and novelists criticized the life-styles and attitudes of the suburbanites, citing their bourgeois smugness and conformity, the pressures on the commuting father, the child-centered and mother-dominated homes, the aesthetic unattractiveness of the suburbs, and their social shortcomings.

Whatever one thought of the new suburbia, the flight from the inner city continued and the urbanization of the outlying areas went on apace. Suburban institutions such as schools, churches, civic organizations, shopping centers, and organized "culture" groups flourished. In time, moreover, some of the defects of unattractive suburbs were remedied. Trees and shrubs were planted, houses were repaired and enlarged, and even the tract housing usually escaped the fate of becoming new slums. No matter how ordinary their houses or how stultifying their lives may have seemed, most suburban dwellers did have more room, better living accommodations, more fresh air, and more independence than they would have had in the old parts of the metropolis. The suburbs themselves varied, of course, and while they tended to be internally homogeneous, they were typically differentiated along social and economic lines—a circumstance that would create serious obstacles to the development of areawide governments or planning authorities.

The decay and disorganization in the great cities grew progressively worse as the middle class continued to move out, as the cost of social services mounted, as the tax base shrank, and as crime grew worse. In the early 1970s many cities were reporting the abandonment of houses, despite a housing shortage. In a typical case a speculator would purchase an old house, make a few repairs, and sell it to a low-income family at an inflated price under a mortgage guaranteed by the FHA. Shortly after moving in, the family would find the property in need of extensive repair. Since the new owners were often unable to make such repairs and since they had only a small equity in the property, they would move out, with the house going to the FHA at a substantial loss to the government.

The growth of the suburbs tended to lock nonwhite and other poor people into the urban ghettos and in effect to create two cultures. On the other hand, the report of the Advisory Commission on Intergovernmental Relations in the mid-1960s concluded that "in the small and medium sized metropolitan areas outside the Northeast some elements of both high and low socioeconomic status tend to be equally important in both central cities and suburbs, while other low status characteristics predominate in the suburbs and some high status characteristics are more important in the central city." Some big cities became "black" cities. Washington, D.C., was 60 percent black by the early seventies, while Newark, Gary, and Richmond had a Negro population of about 50 percent by that time. The terrible conditions in the ghettos and the ethnic concentrations in the nation's large cities were of central importance in the great riots in Watts, Detroit, Newark, and other places in the 1960s. Most metropolitan authorities tried to deal with the urban blight by bulldozing the slums away and building huge high-rise apartments.

Notable efforts were made to arrest the decay of the inner city and to rejuvenate the metropolis. Urban renewal was usually the focus of these efforts, and in city after city new skylines arose comprising office buildings, apartment complexes, public housing, and downtown shopping centers. Some attempts were made to retain and restore old buildings that were still basically sound, although the new functional but uninspiring buildings too often replaced the old elegant structures. In an effort to eliminate the perennial traffic problem, most cities constructed huge freeways and hundreds of parking lots. A few cities, including San Francisco and Atlanta, laid plans in the 1960s for elaborate new rapid transit systems. There was also some evidence of a cultural revival in many American cities. A new breed of mayors appeared, better educated, more sophisticated, and more dedicated to improving the city than the average prewar mayor. In some cases cities made genuine progress. Pittsburgh, for instance, achieved marked success under the leadership of Mayor David Lawrence and an urban reform coalition. The city's central business district was revitalized, and its accomplishments in such activities as housing renewal and pollution control were impressive. Other cities, including Miami, Florida, and Nashville, Tennessee, combined overlapping county and municipal governments by creating new metropolitan systems.

In an environment of "urban catacombs and suburban cellblocks," some bold spirits dreamed of constructing entirely new cities. A scattering of "new towns," somewhat reminiscent of the Greenbelt towns of the New Deal period, appeared in the 1960s. Perhaps the best-known of these communities was Reston, Virginia, near Washington, D. C. Reston, which was officially opened in December 1965, was an imaginative arrangement of several neighborhoods of clustered "town houses," situated on plazas that were grouped around an artificial lake and opening on acres of wooded and terraced land. The houses were reached by walkways inaccessible to automobiles, and the shops and other community facilities were all within easy walking distance.

The small town has not disappeared from the contemporary scene. The census of 1970 identifies almost 21,000 different incorporated and unincorporated places, only some 7,000 of which are classified as urban. More than half of the country's nonmetropolitan municipalities grew during each of the last three decades. The President's Commission on Population and the American Future recently reported that, when asked where they would prefer to live, Americans show pronounced preferences for small towns and rural areas. Still, the traditional community based on local attachments, a particular place, and a web of personal relationships has declined.

Class and Status in Contemporary America

The long period of prosperity that began in the early 1940s enabled most Americans to make steady advances in occupational status, income, and standard of living. They appeared to be achieving the "new goals of human happiness and well-being" Franklin D. Roosevelt had spoken of in his Economic Bill of Rights message of 1944. Many observers echoed former TVA director David E. Lilienthal's statement in the early 1950s that "one finds the physical benefits of our society distributed widely, to almost everyone, with scant regard to status, class, or origin of the individual." In the piping good times of the postwar era, Americans began to feel an exhilarating sense of new possibilities—for better jobs, higher incomes, business ventures, opportunities to enter college or professional school, and changes in social status. The new affluence, it seemed, was boosting occupational and social mobility, stimulating movement up the ladder of wealth and status, and thus reordering the nation's social classes. Many social commentators concluded that income in the United States was becoming better distributed and that the hardening of class distinctions during the previous half-century was being reversed.

Although the benefits of prosperity were widely shared in American society after 1945, a decided concentration of wealth at the top continued, though at a slightly reduced level. Studies of stratification in postwar America showed the presence of marked differentials in wealth and income and in social participation, authority and power, education, health, safety, and legal protection. While lacking an established aristocracy, the United States possessed a discernible upper class, set apart not only by income and wealth but also by position, elegant life-style, membership in exclusive clubs, patronage of private schools, extensive travel, and, in some older regions, connection with old locally prominent families.

The extent to which political and economic power was monopolized in the postwar period has been a matter of considerable disagreement among social commentators and scholars. It was argued by many political scientists and other social analysts that a "pluralist" system had emerged in the United States, despite the trend toward economic concentration, bureaucracy, and centralized administration. Power in this system was dispersed among numerous voluntary associations or "veto groups," which balanced each other in a rough equilibrium. Other analysts contended that power was concentrated in the hands of economic and social elites. The sociologist C. Wright Mills asserted in *The Power Elite* (1956) that most people in the American political system were powerless and that a complex elite of political, business, and military leaders ruled the country. Mills stressed elite domination rather than class conflict, but in the 1960s several other writers began to emphasize class differentials and tensions in explaining the concentration of wealth and power in the United States.

While there was substantial working-class social mobility in this period, the most impressive economic and social leveling was the broadening of the middle class. The steady increase in per capita income, the vast changes in the structure of employment, and the great expansion in the number of college graduates all helped swell the ranks of the middle class.

If the middle register of the American social order was expanding, it also appeared to be increasingly homogenized. Americans, especially the white-collar employee and the suburban dweller, seemed to conform not only in dress, food, and housing, but even in their ideas. Novels such as Sloan Wilson's *The Man in the Gray Flannel Suit* (1956) and sociological studies like C. Wright Mills's *White Collar: The American Middle Classes* (1951) called attention to the loss of individualism, the stuffiness, and the mindless materialism that characterized contemporary middle-class living. The psychologist Erich Fromm, for instance, wrote of the prevalence of individuals with a "marketing orientation," who wanted to avoid having to make choices and eagerly accepted values imposed by the group. David Riesman noted how the consumer-oriented economy reinforced the old American tendency to conform to the tastes and attitudes of one's neighbors. Riesman suggested, in *The Lonely Crowd: A Study of the Changing American Character* (1950), that the American character had changed from an "inner-directed" type, responding to a sort of internal gyroscope, to an "other-directed" personality, basically attuned to the mass values of his neighbors.

The greatest split within the middle class was that between its white-collar and blue-collar components. Millions of industrial workers had become, by any objective measure, members of the middle class, and many skilled workers now earned more than office workers, schoolteachers, and people in the service trades. Yet the entry of skilled and semiskilled workers into the economic middle class did not lead to wholesale adoption of middle-class manners and tastes—of values and attitudes, social life, methods of rearing children, social roles, and the like. Reporting in 1964 on the results of a study of working-class married couples, the sociologist Mirra Komarovsky wrote: "From all appearances, the working-class style of life—its values, attitudes, institutions—remains in many respects quite distinct from the dominant . . . patterns of contemporary American society."

In the late 1950s social critics began to point out the persistence of poverty in the United States. But poverty was not "discovered" in the postwar era until the early 1960s. One of the writers who publicized its existence was Michael Harrington, whose popular *The Other America: Poverty in the United States* was published in 1962. Harrington argued that too much had been made of the country's affluence, since, by his count, something like one-fourth of all Americans were living in poverty (which the federal government defined as a family income below $3,000 a year). As Harrington said, poverty in America "is a culture, an institution, a way of life."

The government's definition of poverty was extremely narrow, and in many respects it was a highly arbitrary and unrealistic means of dividing the poor and the nonpoor. A great many people remained barely above the poverty level, although they were frequently somewhat better off than they had been a generation earlier. The economist Leon Keyserling called such people the "deprived Americans." They stood above the poverty line but fell short of the minimum requirements for "a modestly comfortable level of living." In 1964 Keyserling estimated the number of such deprived persons (those with family incomes between $3,500 and $4,500 a year) at 77 million. They included manual laborers, laundry workers, clerks, and many similar low-paid people. While lacking income, moreover, they were expected to provide their families with the amenities that advertising, television, and national folklore had long proclaimed to be middle-class custom.

The absence of militant class consciousness on the part of Americans is striking. At least three-fourths of United States adults label themselves as middle class. There is some evidence to support such a generous characterization. Education during the last three decades has been a powerful vehicle of social equality. The treatment of minority and ethnic groups has improved. Some old vestiges of social inequality, such as high society and the servant class, have disappeared. The nation's consumer culture has become pervasive. Americans look, dress, and act more alike than ever before.

Ethnicity and Equal Rights

The concept of the melting pot has long appealed to the American imagination. The idea of America as a refuge for downtrodden people from other lands and the conviction that such newcomers could be quickly and harmoniously assimilated into the national culture were embodied in the metaphor. "We Americans are children of the crucible," Theodore Roosevelt had declared. Following the war many people with immigrant backgrounds moved up the occupational ladder, entering white-collar employment and the professions, taking advantage of educational opportunities, and steadily improving their economic and social status. These elements were rapidly assimilated, and fewer and fewer of their number thought of themselves as having any national identification other than American, although a considerable number of people associated their religious faith with the national origins of their fathers and grand-fathers. Anti-Semitism, which seemed to increase during the war, de-clined sharply in the years that followed.

The situation for black Americans in the mid-1940s was far less encouraging than for other minority groups. The elaborate structure of Jim Crow proscription was intact throughout the South, and Negroes in all parts of the country were the daily victims of social prejudice and discriminatory treatment in employment, housing, and education. Never-theless, World War II had a notable effect upon American blacks, giving them new experiences, new skills, and new confidence in themselves. The ideological conflict between the United States and the Communist powers caused American policy makers to become more sensitive to the status of Negroes and other minority groups at home. At the same time, the emergence of new nations from colonialism in Asia and Africa, under the direction of nonwhite leaders, had a profound influence upon American blacks. Things were changing—even in the South. Following the Supreme Court's invalidation of the white primary in 1944, Negroes began to take part in that crucially important part of the electoral process in the one-party South. Another kind of change occurred in New York in 1947 when a talented baseball player named Jackie Robinson joined the Brooklyn Dodgers and thus became the first Negro to play in the major leagues.

The major manifestations of these new currents came in the arena of national politics and were dramatized in the civil rights program spon-sored by the Truman administration. In the 1950s the Supreme Court became the main instrument for reform in race relations, and its decisions sparked the civil rights movement during that decade. The momentous school desegregation decision, *Brown et al. v. Board of Education of Topeka,* was handed down on May 17, 1954. Speaking for a unanimous court, Chief Justice Earl Warren declared that "in the field of public education the doctrine of 'separate but equal' has no place." It would be hard to exaggerate the influence of the *Brown* decision as a dynamic factor in the development of the modern civil rights movement.

Although the progress of school desegregation in the Southern region was slow in the late fifties, the civil rights movement entered a new phase during the second half of the decade, in response both to the Supreme Court's decision in the *Brown* case and to the development of new leaders, new organizations, and new tactics that went beyond the NAACP approach. The starting point of this black protest was the simple, unpremeditated act of a forty-three year-old Negro seamstress in Montgomery, Alabama, named Rosa Parks. Tired after a hard day's work, Mrs. Parks on December 1, 1955, suddenly decided that she would not surrender her bus seat to a white person. She was promptly arrested. The response of the black community could scarcely have been predicted. Under the leadership of the Montgomery Improvement Association, the city's Negroes rallied overwhelmingly to support a crippling boycott of the local bus system. The boycott was maintained for almost a year and ended in an impressive victory for the blacks after the federal courts invalidated the Alabama segregation laws. The Montgomery bus boycott was a portent of things to come. Its church meetings, singing of old religious hymns, frequent reference to American ideals, nonviolent tactics, and black unity and discipline would be characteristic of the "movement" during the years ahead.

The leader of the Montgomery Improvement Association was an eloquent young Baptist minister named Martin Luther King, Jr. The son of a successful Atlanta preacher and a doctoral graduate of Boston University in theology, King developed during the long months of the Montgomery struggle a program of nonviolent resistance. It was based on the evangelical Christianity in which he had been nurtured and on Mahatma Gandhi's Satyagraha philosophy, to which King had been attracted for some time. King would use "nonviolent direct action" to provoke crisis and "creative tension," which would force the white community to confront its racism. "If we are arrested every day, if we are exploited every day, if we are trampled over every day," the young minister declared at one of the Montgomery mass meetings, "don't ever let anyone pull you so low as to hate them. We must use the weapon of love. We must have compassion and understanding for those who hate us." In 1957 King organized the Southern Christian Leadership Conference, with headquarters in Atlanta, and the influence of his leadership soon spread throughout the South.

The black protest movement took still another turn on February 1,

1960, when four students from North Carolina Agricultural and Technical College, an all-Negro institution in Greensboro, took seats at a Woolworth lunch counter and refused to move when they were denied service. This new tactic, based on King's nonviolent ethic, quickly caught on; the result was a wave of sit-ins at lunch counters and restaurants, "kneel-ins" at churches, and other challenges to segregated facilities in the South. The sit-ins also produced a new civil rights group, the Student Nonviolent Coordinating Committee (SNCC), and during the next year over 50,000 people were involved in demonstrations in about 100 cities. SNCC, according to its historian, Howard Zinn, "became the militant arm of the civil-rights movement for the next four years." In the spring of 1961 the Congress of Racial Equality (CORE) sponsored some so-called "freedom rides" through the South to challenge the continued segregation of interstate buses and terminals.

By the summer of 1963 the equal rights movement had almost reached flood tide. School desegregation had, to some degree at least, breached the defenses even of Mississippi and Alabama. Protests and demonstrations, often accompanied by white retaliatory beatings and bombings, flickered over the South like heat lightning. In April 1963 Martin Luther King led a giant demonstration in Birmingham to protest the city's segregated businesses and institutions. Millions of Americans sw what happened on their television screens when the Birmingham police, under the notorious segregationist T. Eugene "Bull" Connor, turned on the black demonstrators with clubs, police dogs, and high-pressure water hoses. A different kind of demonstration took place in Washington, D.C., on August 28, 1963, when over 200,000 black and white marchers gathered before the Lincoln Memorial in a dramatic gesture of protest against the federal government's long indifference to the Negro's plight in America. Dr. King's eloquent address—his great dream of racial equality and brotherhood some day—was a fitting climax to this stirring demonstration. Meanwhile, the work at the grass-roots level continued. SNCC, for example, initiated voters' registration drives in Mississippi in 1962 and 1963, and joined other equal rights organizations in planning a great "Mississippi Summer" in 1964.

Ironically, the legal and political progress of the early 1960s served to heighten black expectations that all too often were not realized, leading to greater frustration within the black community. Nothing revealed the growing mood of frustration, bitterness, and anger in the black community more dramatically than the explosion of ghetto riots between 1964 and 1967. These uprisings were largely unplanned, unorganized, and unscheduled, but much of the violence that attended them was directed at such symbols of white power as the police and white-owned businesses. The four-year period of ghetto rebellions began in New York's Harlem in July

1964, with an outburst of arson, looting, and attacks on whites. But it was the following summer's riot in Watts, a black community in Los Angeles, that first aroused the country to the danger of large-scale ghetto violence. Watts erupted five days after President Johnson signed the Voting Rights Act of 1965, and it resulted in the deaths of 34 people, in the arrest of almost 4,000 persons, and in an estimated $35 million in property losses. In the midst of the riot there were cries of "burn, baby, burn" and "kill whitey." The climax came in 1967, when forty-one major outbreaks occurred, including terrible riots in Newark and Detroit. Joseph Boskin, a historian who has studied the revolt of the urban ghettos, concludes that "the revolts of the mid-1960's—more than the nonviolent movement of Dr. Martin Luther King and the extraordinarily powerful civil rights movement of the early 1960's—directed attention to the anguished plights of millions of Negroes, Puerto Ricans, and Mexican-Americans living in the urban centers of the country."

The ghetto riots were also related to an accelerating shift in the direction and control of the equal rights movement—from interracial collaboration to black domination. The white liberal response to racism seemed to many young blacks to be inadequate, paternalistic, and even hypocritical. "White liberal," as August Meier and Elliott M. Rudwick observe, thus joined "Black Bourgeoisie" and "Uncle Tom" as "an epithet of opprobrium in the vocabulary of many Negro militants." As the radicalization of the civil rights movement proceeded, as its more militant spokesmen began to emphasize the economic, housing, and educational inequalities oppressing the masses, the demands for "Freedom Now!" became more strident. Dr. King, the most charismatic leader of the civil rights crusade during its nonviolent phase, faced a growing challenge from more militant black leaders. It was this challenge, in part at least, that caused King to become steadily more critical of the American war in Vietnam, which was infused with racial implications, and to plan a mighty "poor people's" march on Washington in the spring of 1968.[1] The minister was killed in Memphis before he could lead the Washington march, and his death as much as any other single event of the late 1960s symbolized the end of a reform movement that had already lost its direction, its unity, and much of its momentum.

One expression of the new black militancy was the slogan "black power," which seems to have been used first by Stokely Carmichael in 1966. Carmichael, the chairman of SNCC, asserted that the black masses suffered from both class exploitation and white racism. He and his successor, H. Rap Brown, rapidly became more radical, more hostile toward whites, and more committed to the concept of black power. Some

[1]See p. 241.

of the more moderate separatists advocated "black capitalism," the creation of industries and retail businesses operated by Negroes. Others, like Carmichael, urged the establishment of separate political parties. A more revolutionary group known as the Black Panther party was organized in Oakland, California, in 1966 by Huey P. Newton and Bobby Seale. Many of the Black Panthers and black ideologues among college students praised revolutionaries like Ernesto ("Che") Guevara, subscribed to a Marxist or Maoist theory of class struggle, and supported the alignment of American blacks with Third World peoples. The Black Muslims represented still another of the black nationalist groups. The most magnetic leader of the Black Muslims was Malcolm X, whose influence grew in the sixties despite his break with Elijah Muhammad in 1963 and his assassination in 1965.

The black power movement nourished the growth of racial consciousness among Negroes, promoted the development of black pride and black culture (including Afro hair styles, soul food, and Afro-American history), and helped complete a revolution in the thinking of black Americans. But it also did much to fragment the movement for racial reform. Most of the older, established civil rights organizations and Negro leaders, including Martin Luther King and Roy Wilkins, opposed the separatism of the black power program and continued to use nonviolent methods, integration, and political and economic reforms. The new black militancy also encouraged the "white backlash" and frightened many white liberals, who interpreted black power to mean black supremacy, reverse racism, and another form of *apartheid*.

The black revolution sparked a broader ethnic crisis that involved demands by other submerged groups for entrance into the major institutions of American society. Many of these groups assumed a more militant position in the 1960s, manifested renewed interest in cultural nationalism, and began to advocate brown or yellow or red power. This was the case with the Mexican-Americans, who constituted the nation's second largest minority. While composing only 2.3 percent of the national population in 1960, they numbered almost $3^{1}/_{2}$ million and made up 12 percent of the population in Texas, New Mexico, Arizona, Colorado, and California. The postwar period witnessed continued migration from Mexico to the United States, increasing self-awareness and recognition among Chicanos of the cultural values of the Mexican heritage, some improvement in the social conditions of *la raza*,[2] and eventually the development of movements by Mexican-Americans for a greater share in the American way of life through an insistence on equality of economic opportunity, education, and full civil rights.

---

[2] A term connoting ethnic solidarity and a sense of common destiny.

The programs and organizations that sprang up in the 1960s were known collectively as the Chicano movement. It was given direction by a number of new leaders, ranging from moderate advocates of nonviolence to fiery militants. The first Chicano to achieve national recognition was César Chávez of California. Chávez organized the National Farm Workers' Association in 1963, and led a successful strike and boycott of the grape growers in Delano, California, two years later. The "Huelgo" drive and other strikes of the *obreros* led by Chávez in the vineyards and vegetable fields symbolized and helped mobilize the Chicano revolt. Meanwhile, Reies López Tijerina of New Mexico organized the separatist and millennial *Alianza Federal de Mercedes* (Federal Alliance of Land Grants); Rodolfo ("Corky") Gonzales led the Crusade for Justice in Colorado; and in Texas José Angel Gutierrez established a new political party known as *La Renza Unida*. A cultural separatist wing of *La Causa* also emerged, demanding bilingual education in the public schools, Chicano courses, and the like.

The plight of the oldest of all Americans, the Indians, constituted a tragic and poignant national wrong. In the early 1970s over 300,000 "urban" Indians had left the reservations and were living in the nation's cities, often in wretched poverty. Approximately 477,000 Indians remained on the reservations, occupying a kind of no-man's-land between the status of a "dependent nation," subject to the guardianship of the Bureau of Indian Affairs, and exclusion from many rights held by other Americans. During the late 1960s and early 1970s Indian protests over the problem of alienated lands and the policies of the BIA mounted, to the accompaniment of renewed interest in an Indian culture and heritage. The seizure of Alcatraz Island, the capture of Wounded Knee, South Dakota, and the occupation of the BIA offices in Washington, D.C., by Indian militants provided dramatic evidence of yet another minority's rebellion.

The Search for Community

"Around one's home and the places where one shops and the corridors through which one travels," Richard A. Lamanna has written, "there is for each of us a public sphere wherein our sense of security, self-esteem, and propriety is either reassured or jeopardized by the people and events we encounter." Lamanna also observed that at the very time people were drawing physically closer together and becoming increasingly dependent upon one another, they were "drifting toward an extreme form of individualism and privatization of social behavior which undermines the foundations of communal life." The great challenge before American society in the 1970s was to strike "the right balance between freedom and community that will do justice to individual and subgroup differences yet remain compatible with the requirements of a technologically advanced society."

One of the things that has tended to cast Americans adrift is the growing instability of the family. Not only has the extended family with deep roots in a particular locality become a victim of modern mobility, but the nuclear family itself has been subjected to heightened strain and has undergone considerable change. On the surface, at least, the late forties and the fifties seemed to be a time of well-being for the American family. Indeed, the interest many people displayed in their homes, gardens, and the "do-it-yourself" vogue suggested an extreme preoccupation with the cares and rewards of private life. Nevertheless, the mood of "togetherness" in the 1950s did not altogether conceal a broad uneasiness about the disintegration of the family as an organic and healthy institution.

This vague anxiety was related to a number of significant social forces, including the massive uprooting of Americans during World War II; the accelerating mobility that characterized United States life; the increasing size, complexity, and bureaucratization in almost every aspect of economic and social endeavor; and the growth of secularism and the weakening of religious sanctions. Families became decentralized, and the nation's affluence itself encouraged a phenomenon demographers called "uncoupling." Young people and older folk set up separate one-person households in increasing numbers. Relations between parents and children became less and less certain as the youth developed their own values in a rapidly changing society. Juvenile delinquency increased. The training of children was increasingly left to the schools and other outside agencies. The economic system made husband and wife much more independent of each other than was true in earlier periods.

Marriage and the traditional role of housewife became steadily less fulfilling to American women, a tendency that millions of men found difficult to comprehend. All through the 1950s, John Brooks wrote in 1966, "the girls seem to have been sneaking away from diapers and pacifiers to nice, calm, stimulating offices, even though the popular books and magazines of the time did everything possible to make them feel guilty about it." The process picked up speed in the sixties and seventies. Women—and men—are increasingly less willing to tolerate an unhappy marriage. The combination of more education for women, a greater percentage of women in the labor force, freer attitudes toward sex, and the current dominance of the youth culture is likely to alter still further attitudes toward marriage and childbearing in the United States.

Meanwhile, the voluntary group has become more than ever before the primary institution for maintaining American society or reforming it. The ordinary citizen is likely to belong to voluntary associations of several types, and in a sense the family, the community, and the church have been reduced to virtual subspecies of such organizations. These associational establishments perform substantial cultural, social, civic, and economic functions. There are hundreds of thousands of these private groups—trade associations and chambers of commerce; agricultural and horticultural federations; labor unions; professional societies; associations of scholars, scientists, engineers, civil servants, and military officers; groups involved in public health and social welfare; athletic associations; leagues of lobbyists; and so forth. Service clubs flourished in the postwar decades as the older fraternal societies and secret orders declined. All of these associations, Rowland Berthoff suggests, "indulged in rituals that were merely symbolic of the social integrity of the group, but more than ever such private organizations carried the weight of the cultural, philanthropic, and even spiritual concerns of American society—of nearly everything that was neither narrowly economic nor technically governmental."

The ethnic protest movements of the 1960s, the insurgence of students and of women, and the development of a counterculture all demonstrated, in one way or another, the search for new forms of community in a swiftly changing society. The search took many different directions. Some people worked hard to revitalize and adapt established institutions like the church. Others launched campaigns to renew their neighborhood, and the antipoverty programs of the sixties were commu-

Figure 14   Exodus from a Rock Music Festival, White Lake, N.Y., August 1969 *(United Press International Photo)*

nity-centered endeavors calling for neighborhood participation. The "hippies" who were attracted by the thousands in the mid-1960s to the Haight-Ashbury district of San Francisco and to places like the East Village in New York City were searching for alternative ways of living. The students who attacked established institutions and the military-industrial complex in the late sixties were rebelling against the anonymity of contemporary society and the impersonality and bureaucracy of the huge multiversities. Encounter and sensitivity groups, institutes like Esalen, and rock concerts were widely regarded as new forms of communion.

The emergence of the communal movement in recent years provides another example of the revolt against modern urban-industrial society and traditional ideas about community life. The *New York Times,* reporting the results of a survey it had made, estimated in December 1970 that there were at least 2,000 communes in the United States. During the early seventies there were perhaps as many as 3,000 scattered over the country, with possibly 150,000 people involved. Strange and wonderful visitors descended on areas like the mountains of New Mexico in search of "community." The communes were of many types—rural, urban, working, cooperative, and so on—and they varied in population from about 10 to 100 or more members. Although they frequently rejected modern technology and creature comforts, discarded the nuclear family, and displayed a good deal of anti-intellectualism, they also emphasized many traditional American values such as individualism, local autonomy, self-sufficiency, open space, and nature.

The postwar period has had more than its share of social tensions and dislocations. Social conflict growing out of racial prejudice, ethnic and minority discrimination, extensive poverty, and the disappearance of older forms of community has left its scars. But there is reason to think that support has grown for a social order based on cultural diversity and mutual respect among many distinctive social groups.

SUGGESTIONS FOR FURTHER READING

As yet there is no adequate social history of the United States since 1945. Rowland Berthoff's *An Unsettled People: Social Order and Disorder in American History** (1971) provides a perceptive and illuminating background to the postwar era. Max Lerner's *America as a Civilization: Life and Thought in the United States Today* (1957) is a broad-ranging social commentary especially useful for the first postwar decade. Social trends continuing into the 1960s are discussed in John Brooks, *The Great Leap: The Past Twenty-five Years in America** (1966), while

*Available in paperback edition.

informative descriptions of American society at particular points in recent years are provided by Ben J. Wattenberg, *This U.S.A.: An Unexpected Family Portrait of 194,067,296 Americans Drawn from the Census* (1965), and E. J. Kahn, Jr., *The American People: The Findings of the 1970 Census* (1974).

The persistence of regionalism as manifested in the contemporary American South is shown in John C. McKinney and Edgar T. Thompson (eds.), *The South in Continuity and Change* (1965), and John Shelton Reed, *The Enduring South: Subcultural Persistence in Mass Society* (1972).

A good place to begin the study of postwar urbanization and metropolitan life is Zane L. Miller's *The Urbanization of Modern America: A Brief History** (1973), Blake McKelvey's *The Emergence of Metropolitan America, 1915–1966* (1968), and Sam Bass Warner's *The Urban Wilderness: A History of the American City** (1972). *The Emerging City: Myth and Reality* (1962), by Scott A. Greer, deals with the leadership, governance, and distribution of power in contemporary American cities. Among the most instructive of the many books on the urban crisis and efforts to revitalize the modern city are Scott A. Greer, *Urban Renewal and American Cities: The Dilemma of Democratic Intervention** (1966); Jeanne R. Lowe, *Cities in a Race with Time: Progress and Poverty in America's Renewing Cities* (1967); and Daniel Patrick Moynihan (ed.), *Toward a National Urban Policy* (1970). Jane Jacobs offers a sharp critique of modern urban culture and the work of urban planners in *The Death and Life of Great American Cities** (1961). Different historical approaches are revealed in Roy Lubove, *Twentieth-Century Pittsburgh: Government, Business, and Environmental Change** (1969), and Stephan Thernstrom, *The Other Bostonians: Poverty and Progress in the American Metropolis, 1880–1970* (1973).

For the rapid growth of suburbs following World War II, see Robert C. Wood, *Suburbia: Its People and Their Politics** (1958); William M. Dobriner, *Class in Suburbia** (1963); Herbert J. Gans, *The Levittowners: Ways of Life and Politics in a New Suburban Community** (1967); and Scott Donaldson, *The Suburban Myth** (1969). Auguste C. Spectorsky, *The Exurbanites* (1955), contains a wry description of some inhabitants of the belt just beyond suburbia. Excellent in showing the impact of mass society on village life is Arthur J. Vidich and Joseph Bensman, *Small Town in Mass Society: Class, Power, and Religion in a Rural Community** (1960). Maurice R. Stein, *The Eclipse of Community: An Interpretation of American Studies** (1960), is a revealing treatment of several well-known community studies. For the recent commune movement, see Ron E. Roberts, *The New Communes: Coming Together in America** (1971), and Laurence R. Veysey, *The Communal Experience: Anarchist and Mystical Counter Cultures in America* (1973).

Several of the dimensions of class and status in contemporary America are revealed in Peter M. Blau and Otis Dudley Duncan, *The American Occupational Structure* (1967); Ferdinand Lundberg, *The Rich and the Super-Rich: A Study in the Power of Money Today** (1968); Richard Parker, *The Myth of the Middle Class: Notes on Affluence and Equality* (1972); Michael Harrington, *The Other America: Poverty in the United States** (1962); and Herman P. Miller, *Rich Man, Poor Man** (1971).

The literature on the civil rights movement and black protest is extensive. Among the most illuminating general works are C. Vann Woodward, *The Strange Career of Jim Crow** (3d rev. ed., 1974); Louis Lomax, *The Negro Revolt** (1963); Charles E. Silberman, *Crisis in Black and White** (1964); Benjamin Muse, *The American Negro Revolution: From Nonviolence to Black Power, 1963–1967* (1968); and Anthony Lewis, *Portrait of a Decade: The Second American Revolution** (1964). The reaction of the South in the 1950s is analyzed in Numan V. Bartley, *The Rise of Massive Resistance: Race and Politics in the South during the 1950's* (1969); Neil R. McMillen, *The Citizens' Council: Organized Resistance to the Second Reconstruction, 1954–64* (1971); and Donald R. Matthews and James W. Prothro, *Negroes and the New Southern Politics** (1966).

For Martin Luther King, Jr., see the useful volume by David L. Lewis, *King: A Critical Biography** (1970), and King's two books: *Strike toward Freedom: The Montgomery Story* (1958) and *Why We Can't Wait** (1964). Howard Zinn, *SNCC: The New Abolitionists* (1964), and August Meier and Elliott M. Rudwick, *CORE: A Study in the Civil Rights Movement, 1942–1968* (1973), are good for those organizations. Black militancy and black nationalism are dealt with in Eldridge Cleaver, *Soul on Ice** (1967); Malcolm Little, with the assistance of Alex Haley, *The Autobiography of Malcolm X** (1965); C. Eric Lincoln, *The Black Muslims in America** (1961); and E. U. Essien-Udom, *Black Nationalism: A Search for an Identity in America** (1962).

The following volumes provide helpful introductions to some of the other minority groups in contemporary America: Stan Steiner, *The New Indians** (1968) and *La Raza: The Mexican-Americans** (1970); Matt S. Meier and Feliciano Rivera, *The Chicanos: A History of Mexican Americans** (1972); Peter Matthiessen, *Sal Si Puedes: Cesar Chavez and the New American Revolution** (1973); and Nathan Glazer and Daniel Patrick Moynihan, *Beyond the Melting Pot: The Negroes, Puerto Ricans, Jews, Italians, and Irish of New York City** (1963). For the so-called white ethnics, see Arthur B. Shostak, *Blue-Collar Life** (1969), and Michael Novak, *The Rise of the Unmeltable Ethnics: Politics and Culture in the Seventies** (1972). Milton M. Gordon's *Assimilation in American Life: The Role of Race, Religion, and National Origins* (1964) is a valuable study of ethnic group relations.

The Cultural Dimensions of Affluence and Anxiety

American culture was profoundly influenced by the long-sustained prosperity of the postwar period and by the awareness of living under the shadow of a global holocaust. Many traditional values persisted in the new era, while long-time trends like secularization continued and were frequently accelerated. But there were also powerful new forces that affected the nation's culture, including the development of the mass media, particularly television. In the 1960s a much-publicized counterculture began to emerge that savagely attacked established cultural patterns and sought alternative life-styles and values. Meanwhile, the literary scene changed drastically in the quarter-century following the war, reflecting not so much the realities of the evolving American society as the subtle shifts in fundamental assumptions, outlook, and values.

Education and Science: Expansion and Crisis

The postwar educational expansion rested on the traditional American belief in the social utility of as much education as possible for everyone, a widely shared view that was almost a public creed. There were also more tangible factors in the growth of the schools: continuing prosperity, the broadening middle class, the baby boom, the G.I. Bill of Rights, and the demands of an increasingly complex society in a technological era.

Almost every year witnessed more people in attendance at every level of education. The number of children attending public schools increased from 25 million in 1945 to 40 million in 1970. Expenditures for public schools rose during the 1950s from $6 billion to $15 billion a year, and the proportion of the gross national product devoted to education steadily increased. Teachers' salaries enjoyed marked improvement, the average expenditure per pupil went up substantially, the school term lengthened, and facilities gradually improved. College and professional school enrollments boomed. By 1970 almost 59 million students were attending schools in the United States, and public expenditures for education totaled more than $35 billion annually.

This expansion was attended by constant pressure on the local school authorities and an unending series of problems. Perhaps the most difficult of all problems was the question of adequate financial support, especially in the poorer states and more disadvantaged areas. In the absence of broad federal support there was no effective means of equalizing educational funds, and thousands of small, poorly equipped schools continued to exist in many rural areas. The high school dropout rate in poor localities was notoriously high, and even when disadvantaged youths remained in school, the curriculum was ill-adapted for their future occupational and social needs.

During the 1950s the public schools became the subject of widening criticism, much of it by educators. The criticism centered on the charge that the educational system lacked intellectual vitality and discipline, that it emphasized mediocrity at the expense of excellence, and that it promoted athletics and social activities rather than basic academic work. A spate of books and articles challenged the rationale of a "child-centered" school system and pointed out the essential mindlessness of the "life adjustment" doctrine associated with "progressive education." Such books as Albert Lynd's *Quackery in the Public Schools* (1953) and Arthur E. Bestor's *Educational Wastelands* (1953) proclaimed their themes in their titles. Later in the decade James B. Conant, former president of Harvard University, wrote a widely read volume, *The American High School Today* (1959). Conant found fault with the current educational methodology for slighting the teaching of English grammar and composition, for neglecting foreign languages, and for failing to meet the needs of either the brightest or the dullest students.

Russia's spectacular success in launching the two *Sputnik* satellites in the autumn of 1957 had a galvanizing effect upon American thinking about the school system, for it dramatized the apparent superiority of Soviet scientists, highlighted the fact that the U.S.S.R. spent a larger percentage of its income on education than did the United States, and increased the influence of the critics of the educational system at home. *Sputnik* undoubtedly contributed to the passage of the National Defense Education Act (NDEA) of 1958. This legislation provided loan funds for college students as well as fellowships for advanced study in new and expanded programs. It also sought to strengthen the instruction in mathematics, the sciences, and foreign languages at the elementary and secondary school levels. Federal aid, as well as the grants made by such private foundations as the Fund for the Advancement of Education, encouraged reforms in teacher training methods; better facilities; and new courses in the natural sciences, foreign languages, and other fields. Innovators like Jerome S. Bruner demonstrated novel approaches to learning, and the school curriculum soon began to include the "new math," the "new biology," and so forth.

Although federal aid to education became an established fact in the 1960s, it was still far too small to solve the financial problems of the schools. In the late sixties and early seventies, city after city rejected bond issues designed to finance the schools, and the courts in California and several other states struck down the heavy reliance on property taxes in educational expenditures. Yet the performance of the average public school continued to leave much to be desired. The writer Charles E. Silberman, in conducting a three-year investigation of the schools in the late 1960s, found overwhelming evidence of repressive and arbitrary rules, the dehumanizing of learning, and what he called the "killing of dreams and the mutilation of spirits." He was dismayed to discover "what grim, joyless places most American schools are, how oppressive and petty are the rules by which they are governed, how intellectually sterile and aesthetically barren the atmosphere, what an appalling lack of civility obtains on the part of teachers and principals, what contempt they unconsciously display for children as children."

The development of higher education after 1945 in the United States was nothing less than spectacular. College and university enrollment more than doubled between 1940 and 1960, climbing to over $3^{1}/_{2}$ million by the latter year. The college population almost doubled again during the decade of the sixties. The growth of community and junior colleges, once scorned as "high schools with ashtrays," was especially notable in the 1960s, and by 1972 approximately $2^{1}/_{2}$ million students were attending institutions of this type. The inundation of the campuses in the postwar years created enormous problems, including the need for more classrooms, dormitories, library facilities, and laboratory equipment. But the needs were somehow met, and state and private support of higher education became steadily more impressive. The federal government also contributed indispensable assistance, first in the form of the G.I. Bill and various foreign exchange programs and later through the NDEA legislation and the educational measures of the sixties.

The democratization of higher education, paralleling the growth of the middle class, went a long way to end the old exclusiveness of the nation's colleges. University professors after midcentury were increasingly drawn from new-stock Americans and other new additions to the middle class. With the expansion of higher education, a college degree became a prerequisite for a growing number of occupations. One study found, for example, that almost 60 percent of the big business leaders of 1952 were college graduates, as compared with 30 percent a generation earlier. Meanwhile, the universities became more intimately involved in the larger community: in the social application of their scientific and social science investigations, in their cultural programs, and in big-time football and other athletic events.

Many educational institutions became huge "multiversities"— impersonal, mechanical in approach, bureaucratic. Student demonstrations at the University of California, Berkeley, in 1964 and on many other campuses in later years were, in part at least, protests against enormous classes, a routinized approach to learning, a sterile lecture system, and the neglect of individual student development. The ferment of the 1960s, including the Vietnam war, had a pronounced impact upon colleges and universities. Students seemed to become more socially conscious, and they began to demand a greater voice in the operation of the universities. A student rebellion swept the country during the late 1960s. This movement resulted in greater student involvement in academic decision making, the relaxing of *in loco parentis* rules, the introduction of new courses, and increased enrollment from minority groups. Still, the student movement did not radically transform American institutions of higher education. As the campus upheavals subsided after 1970, there was mounting concern over the "new depression in higher education," a consequence of the leveling off in the rate of growth of the college-age population and of the economic recession of the Nixon and Ford years.

No aspect of contemporary intellectual progress can compare with the dramatic emergence of science in American life. By 1965 a million Americans held scientific degrees, and the annual output of new science Ph.D.'s was about 8,000. Whereas the federal government was spending a paltry $50 million for scientific research and development in 1939, it was allocating approximately $15 billion for such work by the mid-1960s. An incredible proliferation of scientific literature resulted from the publication of hundreds of thousands of scientific papers every year. Employment opportunities continually increased for engineers, scientists, and technicians.

The great accumulation of significant new scientific knowledge involved basic research, the application of scientific findings to new processes and products, and the commercial development of new technology. Among the more notable developments by American scientists were the advances in nuclear physics, the progress of medical science, the perfection of the electronic computer and its application to the automation of factories, the rise of jet air transportation, and the spectacular successes in exploring outer space. Americans won more than their share of the prestigious Nobel Prizes in science and medicine. Scientists in the postwar era were increasingly called upon by government, business, and private organizations for their expertise and assistance in solving problems and formulating policies. Universities became heavily involved in governmental and commercial enterprises. These trends reflected what has been called the "dialogue between science and American society." Although the long-range social implications of this fabulous development are far from clear, Americans may find it difficult to assimilate the new scientific culture without jeopardizing many of their long-time cultural traditions and cherished humanistic values.

The Changing Shape of American Religion

Religion prospered in the post-World War II era. Church membership increased from 64.5 million (49 percent of the total population) in 1940 to 118 million (64 percent) in 1963 and to 131 million (64 percent) in 1970. Almost all religious bodies added to their membership during this period, the Pentecostal groups, Southern Baptists, and Roman Catholics being especially notable for their rates of growth. By 1972 the membership of the Roman Catholic Church stood at 48.2 million. The various Baptist churches counted 27 million members, the Methodists 13 million, and the Lutherans 8.8 million. Jewish congregations comprised 5.6 million members. Most Americans were prepared, in response to an inquiry of the mid-fifties, to identify themselves in religious terms: 68 percent as Protestants, 23 percent as Catholics, and 4 percent as Jews. Gallup polls taken in 1968 indicated that on Sundays 43 percent of the nation's adult population went to church, that 98 percent of those questioned claimed to believe in God, and that 65 percent believed in hell and 60 percent in the devil.

Among the more noteworthy aspects of the religious landscape in the early postwar years was the vogue of a "peace-of-mind" religion which seemed to result, in some measure, from the shadow of the bomb, the frustrations of the cold war, and the search for relief from social ills. The "cult of reassurance" was reflected in a rash of inspirational books such as Fulton J. Sheen's *Peace of Soul* (1949) and Norman Vincent Peale's *The Power of Positive Thinking* (1952), in spectacular films like "The Ten

Commandments," and in religious songs like "I Believe" and "The Man Upstairs." Even theologians seemed to foster the idea that the church's role was, as one scholar has said, "to translate the Gospel into the pieties of contemporary culture." Closely related to these developments was a new interest in revivalism and the extraordinary phenomenon of Billy Graham's mass conversions. Graham, a clean-cut and eloquent young Baptist minister, spoke with passionate sincerity and powerful effect, reasserting fundamentalist doctrine in a modern idiom. Graham led one great crusade after another for Christ, speaking for example to 60,000 people at one time in New York's Yankee Stadium.

Religion in America clearly reflected and was part of the popular culture. It was also boosted by politicians, including top leaders in Washington, which led William Lee Miller to speak of "piety on the Potomac" in describing the 1950s. President-elect Eisenhower declared in late 1952, for instance, that "our government makes no sense unless it is founded on a deeply felt religious faith—and I don't care what it is!" In 1954 Congress lent its support to the new piety, adding the phrase "under God" to the pledge of allegiance and during the next year making it mandatory that all United States currency bear the inscription "In God We Trust." Some contemporaries lamented the fact that all creeds seemed to be submerged in a kind of "civil religion," which might be called the "American Way of Life."

Will Herberg has noted that, fundamentally, one's "ultimate, over-all way of life is one's religion." In *Protestant—Catholic—Jew,* an influential book published in 1955, Herberg suggested that the impressive growth of religion following World War II was part of a search for identity, especially by third-generation Americans in a rapidly changing social order where ethnic and other distinctions seemed to be disappearing. Thus, while the church enabled Americans to maintain some nominal distinctions, it also contributed to the homogenizing of the society. Much of the church growth took place in the suburbs, and to a considerable extent the new institutional strength of the churches was a product of suburbia. The expansion of the middle class was particularly significant for American Catholics, whose rapid economic and social advancement ended the class disparity that had previously set them apart from the mainstream Protestantism.

At a more fundamental level the return to religion in contemporary America mirrored an alteration in outlook—a decline of optimism, of faith in progress, of confidence in man's ability to play a constructive role in the world. American theologians like Reinhold Niebuhr and Paul Tillich, while not denying the desirability of social reform, pointed to the inadequacies of the progressive "social gospel." No longer optimistic about the perfectibility of man, they sought to develop modern versions of Calvinism and other old orthodoxies. Their impact in the United States was considerable, and for a while at midcentury neo-orthodoxy became the vogue in certain religious quarters.

More significant in the long run, however, was the new vitality demonstrated by the ecumenical movement in America. One manifestation of this movement was the merger of several important Protestant denominations, including two branches of the Society of Friends in 1955, the Congregational Christian Churches and the Evangelical and Reformed Church in 1957, and two large Presbyterian bodies in 1958. The National Council of the Churches of Christ, the main vehicle for interdenominational cooperation, grew rapidly after its reorganization in 1950. American religious groups also took an active part in the World Council of Churches, which was organized in 1948 and held its Second Assembly in Evanston, Illinois, in 1954. The movement received support from the Vatican as well as from most American Protestant and Jewish leaders.

In spite of these trends, religious division and conflict had by no means disappeared from the American scene. Catholics might be more fully assimilated into the national culture than ever before, but they were still resented and distrusted by many Americans. Organizations like the Protestants and Other Americans United for Separation of Church and State focused their attention on Roman Catholics, as did Paul Blanshard in such books as *American Freedom and Catholic Power* (1949) and *Communism, Democracy, and Catholic Power* (1952). The issue of federal aid to education and the possible support of parochial schools became a bitterly divisive issue among United States churches, with both sides sometimes resorting to name-calling.

No development of the postwar period provoked such a storm of protest and anguished condemnation as did the United States Supreme Court decision in *Engel v. Vitale* (1962), which held that compulsory prayer in public schools was unconstitutional. The House of Representatives Committee on the Judiciary held hearings on the matter, many bills were introduced in Congress to restore prayer in the schools, and one congressman presented Emanuel Celler, the chairman of the committee, with a petition containing 170,000 signatures asking that God be returned to his rightful place in the classroom. The court's ruling was frequently disregarded, and many schools carried on with prayers as usual, seldom receiving any interference from local officials. In the meantime, another series of Supreme Court decisions, those involving school desegregation and civil rights, resulted in much controversy in religious circles, particularly in the South where rank-and-file church people tended to divide along racial lines in debating the Court's decrees.

The social gospel was not abandoned by American churches in the postwar years, despite the peace-of-mind emphasis and the somber views of the neo-orthodox. Most churches continued to perform good works in society, but a broader and stronger social reform impulse began to course through United States churches in the late 1950s and early 1960s. One example of this involvement of religious bodies in social meliorism was the role of the black church in the equal rights movement and especially the extraordinary leadership of Martin Luther King, Jr., in making the Negro church a powerful lever in the fight for racial justice and equality. White ministers and lay leaders, most notably outside of the South, soon began to take an active part in the struggle for civil rights, integration, and social justice in other areas.

The 1960s brought new controversies and new developments to American churches. The churches, in part no doubt because of their participation in the social reform movements of the time, seemed to be increasingly inadequate, to be in a state of crisis. This sense of crisis contributed to the emergence of the so-called "New Theology," which owed a good deal to the work of Dietrich Bonhoeffer, a German theologian martyred by the Nazis, and John A. T. Robinson, an English bishop. The New Theology emphasized the concept of "immanence," the idea that God dwells in man, as opposed to "transcendence," or the otherness of God. Those who came to be called the "God Is Dead" theologians embodied this distinction in their thinking. The New Theology implied that many of the traditional moral assumptions of Christianity had been destroyed by the evils of modern life. Harvey Cox's widely read *The Secular City* (1965) argued in favor of the new "secularity" with its pragmatic and technological style. Theology, Cox declared, must make religion relevant and responsive to the new forces in society.

The religious revolution of the 1960s was particularly evident among the young, some of whom now believed that mysticism or astrology or magic were more helpful guides to ultimate truth than either science or religion. Yet the dissent of American youth and their counterculture contained a strong appeal to faith. The new supernaturalism was apparent in the antiwar movement, and many of the peace demonstrations in 1969 were filled with religious symbolism. Some of it was absorbed by the established churches in the form of happenings, rock masses, light shows, and readings from Eastern mystics. Pentecostalism also exerted a strong appeal to young Americans, as evidenced by the so-called "Jesus Freaks," who were Bible-oriented but employed the language of the counterculture.

In some ways the nation's Catholics experienced an even more profound upheaval. This eruption was to some extent a consequence of the extraordinary influence of Pope John XXIII, who died in mid-1963. Although this much-loved Pope reigned for less than five years, he took the first real steps toward reconciliation with other Christian churches, and he convened the first Vatican Council in several centuries. The Vatican Council (1962–1965) brought a more democratic spirit involving the substitution of modern languages for Latin in the liturgy and greater Catholic participation in ecumenical activities. It recommended the creation of a synod of bishops to consult with the Pope in managing the church, adopted a flexible position on birth control, attacked anti-Semitism, condemned nuclear arms, and proposed numerous changes in doctrine and practice.

If the reforms associated with Pope John proved upsetting to many conservative Catholics in the United States, the more traditional policies of his successor, Paul VI, aroused the opposition of numerous liberals and moderates in the American Catholic Church. Thus Pope Paul's long-awaited encyclical on birth control, *Humanae Vitae* (*Of Human Life*), reaffirming the church's ban on artificial contraception, was widely challenged and was opposed by a majority of the younger priests. The revolution in the American Catholic Church released the energies of individuals and groups for the support of other movements. Priests and nuns took a leading part in the civil rights movement. Father James Groppi's open-housing marches in Milwaukee attracted national attention. Catholic radicals, led by the Fathers Berrigan, were in the vanguard of the peace movement. Well might the *National Review* burst out in the spring of 1965, "What, in the name of God, is going on in the Catholic Church?"

Popular Culture

Any realistic characterization of the consumer culture in the United States must stress the sheer volume and variety of items purchased by Americans in their supermarkets, department stores, specialty shops, and shopping malls. An incredible array of products was consumed which an earlier generation, more circumscribed by the need to buy basic necessities, would have considered unattainable luxuries—art objects, stereo sets, jewelry, exotic foods, wine, camping and boating equipment, swimming pools, outdoor cooking facilities, power tools, and sporting goods, not to mention houses, appliances, and automobiles. Vacation travel became almost universal, and the motel became as ubiquitous as the automobile. Teenagers in the affluent society following World War II comprised an important part of the new consumerism, with their patronage of television, movies, records and phonograph equipment, and distinctive youth clothes.

The Golden Age of Television! Nothing was more central to mass culture than the small, glittering screen that soon made its way into virtually every American house and apartment. "The most striking thing about the arrival of television on the American scene," John Brooks wrote, "was certainly the almost apocalyptic suddenness with which it became a fully established part of our national life, complete with a huge audience and an established minority opposition, affecting not only all our other communications media and the whole world of our popular arts but also our manners, morals, habits, ways of thinking." Television was almost unknown at the end of the war, and only a few thousand sets had been sold by 1947. By 1960 there were approximately 45 million sets in operation, and a decade later 96 percent of the country's households had at least one TV set, a growing number of them being equipped to receive transmission in color.

Almost everyone quickly accepted the idea that television was the *new* medium. Three national networks, dominating the field of mass entertainment, presented numerous programs designed to attract a mass audience. Most of this fare, including the soap operas, westerns, quiz programs, and variety shows, was incredibly vapid and uninspiring. The live coverage of athletic events soon became a TV staple, and by the 1960s television audiences for professional and college football, basketball, and baseball were enormous. There were some holdouts among academics and urban intellectuals, who complained about the superficiality of most programs and the tyranny TV exercised over children, but their reservations did nothing to stem the tidal wave of enthusiasm for the new medium. Still, the low level and trivial character of many of the network programs did provoke criticism, and the revelation of rigged quiz shows, highlighted by the dramatic case of Charles Van Doren in 1959, increased the adverse opinion of TV's performance.[1]

Few people doubted the tremendous potential of television. It seemed to offer great hope, for example, as a means of easing the loneliness and brightening the lives of older people, of slum dwellers, of rural households. No other communications medium could compare with television in its capacity to dramatize individual events, to etch them indelibly into the viewer's mind. Thus it seemed that the whole nation focused its attention on the Kefauver crime hearings, on the quadrennial political conventions beginning with 1952, on the Army-McCarthy hearings, on the events following the assassination of John F. Kennedy, and on the urban riots and peace marches of the 1960s. Daniel J. Boorstin has suggested that "just as the printing press democratized learning, so the television set has democratized experience."

---

[1]Van Doren, an assistant professor at Columbia University and member of a well-known literary family, had been a highly successful and widely admired contestant on NBC's program "Twenty-One" in 1956 and 1957. He later admitted that he had been carefully coached, provided with the correct answers to questions, and eventually told to lose to another contestant. Early in 1962 Van Doren was convicted of perjury before a grand jury investigating the case in 1959 and given a suspended sentence.

The attack of the critics had some effect, for the networks cautiously began to introduce greater variety into their programming. Some high caliber classical music, ballet, and drama programs were presented, as well as some excellent documentaries, public affairs forums, and news commentaries. Education television eventually made a place for itself, and National Educational Television became a real force in the early 1970s, stimulated by a $150 million contribution from the Ford Foundation. There are now well over 200 noncommercial television stations operating in the United States.

Television greatly restricted the role of radio, limiting it largely to news and music. Yet, while losing the central place it had enjoyed in the entertainment field during the 1930s and 1940s, radio remained an indispensable medium of popular culture. Radio had two huge constituencies: the millions of Americans on the highway at any given time and the millions of teenagers who listened to it as a source of current popular music. The wisecracking disc jockey became a cultural hero to the younger generation. FM stations, of which there were more than 2,000 in the early 1970s, frequently played classical music and presented cultural programs.

With the spectacular growth of television, the movies ceased to dominate the popular culture as they had in the prewar years, and Hollywood's voice became less powerful. Average weekly movie attendance dropped by about half between 1948 and 1958, and many movie theaters were forced out of business. One response by the moviemakers to the box office decline was the production of high-priced extravaganzas like "The Ten Commandments," "Exodus," and "Cleopatra"—the last a colossal flop. Some Hollywood pictures such as "Dial M for Murder" and "Born Yesterday" achieved a high level of technical excellence, and others, especially such popular musicals as "The Music Man," "My Fair Lady," and "The Sound of Music," proved to be smashing box office attractions. But great numbers of inferior pictures were made during the fifties. Toward the end of that decade, Hollywood capitulated to television by making available for showing on the home screen most of its huge library of films.

The 1960s brought new vitality to American movies, including the growing importance of small independent companies. Another factor was the importation of creative foreign films and their influence on American producers. Some noteworthy movies resulted, among them being "The Graduate," "Patton," "Mash," "Dr. Strangelove," "Easy Rider," "Midnight Cowboy," and "Z." The star system declined, meanwhile, although celebrated performers like Ronald Colman, Clark Gable, Bette Davis, Gary Cooper, Spencer Tracy, and Humphrey Bogart, as well as such newer stars as Elizabeth Taylor, Marlon Brando, Grace Kelly,

Figure 15 The Showgirl and the Playwright—Marilyn Monroe and Her Husband Arthur Miller *(United Press International Photo)*

William Holden, Gregory Peck, Paul Newman, Richard Burton, Marilyn Monroe, and George C. Scott, continued to attract large followings. With the liberalization of obscenity laws, X-rated films became common. Movies became sexier than ever in the mid-1960s.

Popular music, a major component of contemporary mass culture in the United States, attracted the largest audiences in history through the media of radio, television, recordings, and tapes. Although the more conventional music forms represented by such varied performers as Guy Lombardo, Duke Ellington, Count Basie, and Louis Armstrong remained popular, a new style known as bebop or modern jazz emerged in the mid-1940s. Looser in rhythm and more advanced in harmony than earlier jazz, it was played by small ensembles mainly for listening rather than dancing. It was best exemplified in the music of the alto saxophonist Charlie Parker and the trumpeter Dizzy Gillespie and in the "smooth jazz" of the Dave Brubeck Quartet.

"Rock 'n roll" was a reaction against the prevailing popular music in America. A rhythm and blues variant with overtones of country and white gospel music, it erupted in 1954 with Bill Haley's recording of "Rock around the Clock," which eventually sold 16 million copies. Singers like

Chuck Berry, Fats Domino, and Carl Perkins prepared the way for rock 'n roll's tremendous success, but its most popular exemplar proved to be Elvis Presley, a young white truck driver from Tupelo, Mississippi, with a wild vocal style. Presley's succession of hit recordings included "Hound Dog," "I Got A Woman," "Long Tall Sally," and "Gonna Sit Right Down and Cry." Folk music also grew in popularity, especially after it became identified closely with the equal rights movement in the early 1960s. Pete Seeger, Bob Dylan, and Joan Baez attracted large audiences wherever they performed. The rise of country music was nothing less than phenomenal. "Country" was a generic term applied to such musical varieties as "hillbilly," "mountain," "cowboy," "western," and "rockabilly." Nashville, with its Grand Ole Opry, became known as the music capital of the United States.

Rock music, which owed a good deal to black music and the new dances, came to dominance in the sixties. Introduced in England by the Beatles, the Rolling Stones, and other groups, the new rock music was based on the older rock 'n roll, employing a system of intensely amplified electrical guitars and other instruments. The Beatles appeared on Ed Sullivan's Sunday evening TV show in 1964, and thereafter their music quickly became the rage in the United States. During the years that followed, innovators such as Bob Dylan, John Sebastian, the Procol Harum, Paul Butterfield, Janis Joplin, and Frank Zappa elaborated the new music into folk-rock, country-rock, classical motif-rock, blues-rock, and jazz-based rock. Groups like the Who, the Yardbirds, and Led Zeppelin revealed the range of hard-rock sounds. Rock also stimulated new ideas and new forms in other kinds of music. It was an important element in the musicals *Hair* and *Jesus Christ Superstar.*

The consumer culture in America was nourished by old as well as new media. Newspapers were still widely read, although the daily papers were hard hit by rising costs, labor strikes, and increasing competition from radio and television. Newspaper publishing, more than ever, had become a species of big business, and the trend toward consolidation went forward steadily. The quality of the newspapers was not very high, except for a few first-rate papers like the *New York Times,* the *Washington Post,* and the *Los Angeles Times.* Most papers had a more or less standardized assortment of features and departments—sports, home furnishings, food, comics, finance, editorial, and the like—and the great emphasis was on the highest possible display of advertising. One interesting new trend noticeable in the 1960s was the rapid growth of small-town and suburban newspapers.

The mass media magazines were also threatened by the emergence of national television in the 1950s, but many of them enjoyed immense circulations during the first two postwar decades. Henry Luce's *Time* claimed almost 14 million readers in the mid-1960s, while *McCall's* was read by nearly 14 million adult women and *Ladies Home Journal* by almost 12 million. The *Reader's Digest* was even more successful. Nevertheless, ruinous competition for circulation, chronic management upheavals, and unequal editorial quality contributed to the demise of many famous magazines, among them *Collier's, The Saturday Evening Post, Look,* and *Life.* The pulp magazines, including the "romance" periodicals, the comic magazines, and pornographic journals, continued to prosper. Aside from the pulps, the magazines that seemed to fare best were usually those aimed at special audiences, periodicals as varied as the *National Geographic, Psychology Today, Ebony, Playboy, Esquire, The New Yorker,* and numerous hobby and sports publications.

The popular book, in a variety of forms, was another agent of mass culture in the United States. By 1966, at least 38,000 titles were available in paperback editions, many of them serious works and even classics. Books that reached a huge market, however, were often ephemeral, popular fiction like westerns, sexual novels, and detective stories, much of which appealed to the romanticism and nostalgia in the American mind. Thus Harold Robbins's series of sexual novels, beginning with *The Dream Merchants* (1949), enjoyed tremendous success, as did Grace Metalious's sexual epic of a small New England town, *Peyton Place* (1956), and Jacqueline Susann's stories of sexual conquest and ennui among the jet set, *Valley of the Dolls* (1966) and *The Love Machine* (1969). Even more remarkable was the popularity of Mickey Spillane's books, which had sold over 50 million copies by 1969. The spy novel, a detective variant, was widely read by Americans. Ian Fleming's James Bond (Secret Agent 007) adventures proved especially popular in the 1950s and 1960s, and resulted in a series of lucrative movies. The popular book also included comic books, of which 650 titles, with a combined circulation of 100 million a month, were in print in 1953–1954.

The possible consequences of America's fantastic consumer culture—its penchant for the cheap and sensational, its homogenizing tendencies, its vulgarization of the older, established culture, and its threat to rigorous standards—evoked stringent criticism from guardians of "high" culture. The offensive was led by a group of New York intellectuals associated with the *Partisan Review* and other magazines; they argued that the more culture spreads, the more it tends to become corrupted and commercialized. Mass culture did not lack for defenders, however. Most of its advocates, including the spokesmen for the great foundations, maintained that the spread of culture was inherently good for the country and would eventually overcome the deleterious effects of such cultural democratization. Marshall McLuhan contended that the old intellectual and aesthetic standards had been made anachronistic by technological innovation, particularly in the electronic media, and that society was being reordered. Content was far less important than the experience of seeing and hearing, according to McLuhan. Others suggested that popularity and validity are not mutually exclusive, and that there have been accomplishments of genuine merit in the popular arts.

Art and American Life

The cultural boom that developed in the United States by midcentury extended to the fine arts as well as the popular culture. Not only were more and more Americans financially able to patronize artistic endeavors, but the number of well-educated people with an interest in the arts had reached substantial proportions. Cultural centers, arts councils, and local art museums multiplied. The number of symphony orchestras in the United States more than doubled between 1950 and 1965, and virtually no American city with as many as 50,000 inhabitants was without such an orchestra. Innumerable chamber music groups, "art" cinema houses, FM radio stations, and community theaters made their appearance.

In spite of the public's heightened interest in the arts and increasing private support of artists, the continuing need for more adequate economic backing eventually resulted in greater governmental involvement at all levels in the promotion of art and culture. Thus in the 1960s New York City completed its Lincoln Center for the Performing Arts, an impressive complex for concerts, opera, ballet, and drama. In 1964 Los Angeles inaugurated its huge music center pavilion, and in 1971 the John F. Kennedy Center for the Performing Arts in Washington, D.C., was opened. Congress passed the National Arts and Humanities Act which provided, among other things, for federal grants-in-aid to groups and individuals concerned with creative and performing arts.

The American response to operatic and other forms of classical music was most noteworthy in its enthusiasm for performing artists. But there were some outstanding American composers of "serious" music, including Kurt Weill, Vittorio Giannini, Roger Sessions, Elliott Carter, George Crumb, and Hugo Weisgall. The most successful was Gian Carlo Menotti, who in the early 1950s wrote the opera *Amahl and the Night Visitors* specifically for television. His most famous work was *The Saint of Bleecker Street* (1954). Many universities attracted composers such as Walter Piston and Douglas Moore as permanent residents. The versatile Leonard Bernstein, conductor of the New York Philharmonic Orchestra, produced operas, symphonies, chamber music, and musical comedies. Summer music festivals continued to flourish.

Ballet also enjoyed considerable support in the United States, not only in the widespread interest in famous foreign groups but also in the support of numerous local organizations. Among American companies the most important were the New York City Ballet (established in the new Lincoln Center), the American Ballet Theater, and the Robert Joffrey group, which first went on tour in 1956.

Frank Lloyd Wright, a prewar giant in the architectural field, lived until 1959. He and several other well-known architects continued an older, more romantic tradition—the experimental search for the unique design. Just before his death Wright completed one of his most impressive works, the Guggenheim Museum in New York City. Built in the form of a huge white cylinder, it featured a spiraling ramp from top to bottom from which paintings and other artistic works could be viewed.

Perhaps the most conspicuous evidence of "modern" architecture in the years following the war was the growing popularity of the so-called international style, which was exemplified in the work of men like Ludwig Mies van der Rohe and in such structures as the Lever Building and the UN Secretariat in New York City. Employing new building materials such as stainless steel, aluminum, and enormous quantities of glass, the international style had the great virtue of simplicity and of sweeping, geometric lines. But all too often the new public and commercial buildings designed in this style were simply glass-walled rectilinear structures. A number of modernist designers eventually altered the Miesian style. Eero Saarinen made some radical changes in roof design, exemplified in the TWA Terminal at New York's Kennedy Airport. Edward Stone introduced novel uses of decoration, employing filigree work, tiles, and hanging plants in such buildings as the American embassy in New Delhi. Minoru Yamasaki, a Japanese-American, combined Saarinen's experimentation with roof design with Stone's interest in horizontal shape and decoration in notable buildings like the St. Louis Airport Terminal. Meanwhile, in private home design the so-called ranch and split-level buildings became universally popular.

The greatest artistic renaissance in post-World War II America occurred in the field of painting. American painters moved away from the realism and socially conscious themes and mood of the 1930s—from regionalism in painting, folk art, and the WPA artists' projects—toward abstraction, surrealism, and new art forms. Even the realistically oriented Andrew Wyeth, the single most popular American painter of modern times, considered himself an abstractionist. Like some other realists, his pictures projected a haunting quality of fantasy and dreaminess.

The movement that dominated American art in the postwar period was called "abstract expressionism." Rejecting representational art and traditional symbols of visual communication, the expressionists sought, whatever their particular emphasis, to create a mood or feeling, not a figure as it actually existed. These painters were unconcerned with perspective or objects except as they might be used to symbolize powerful life forces. They seemed to paint without plan or precision—with great splashes of color, crude shapes, and gobs of paint slapped or dripped on huge canvases. Much of this work could be characterized as "action painting." As Harold Rosenberg wrote in an essay on the expressionist movement:

> At a certain moment the canvas began to appear to one American painter after another as an arena in which to act—rather than as a space in which to reproduce, re-design, analyze or "express" an object, actual or imagined. What was to go on canvas was not a picture but an event. . . . What matters always is the revelation contained in the act. . . . the way the artist organizes his emotional and intellectual energy as if he were in a living situation.

Traditionalists were frequently shocked and offended by the new art, while those without artistic knowledge often found it uninteresting, unintelligible, and chaotic. Yet abstract expressionism mirrored contemporary American society surprisingly well.

The most famous of the abstract expressionists was Jackson Pollock (1912–1956). He laid his huge canvases on the floor, working from four sides, walking around on the canvas, literally in the painting. Pollock produced a number of extraordinary works, such as his *Blue Poles,* notable for its use of brilliant color. Among the other well-known expressionists was Mark Rothko, who painted great pools or vaguely defined planes of color. Franz Kline's paintings consisted of wide black strokes at seemingly random angles on a white background, conveying a generalized sense of modern tension. Great, gaudy slashes of paint characterized the work of Willem de Kooning, who was most famous for "The Women," a series of paintings completed in the early 1950s.

One of the new directions taken by American painters was "pop art," whose antecedents included abstract expressionism, the dadaists, and such works of Picasso as *Plate with Wafers* (1914). "Pop" artists, painters of the popular and commercial image, seemed to be satirizing the nation's consumer-oriented, mass-production–consumption society. Their work contained an element of social realism and a statement about the deteriorating human environment. Robert Rauschenberg, one of the new mode's originators, created a successful object work in 1955 which he entitled simply *Bed.* It consisted of a real quilt and pillow on a stretcher, with other designs and objects being added. Jasper Johns produced a celebrated work he called *Painted Bronze* (1960), a casting of two Ballantine Ale cans with the labels painted on. Andy Warhol and other free spirits made Pop art the vogue during the following few years.

"Op" art also gained popularity. Using long-known techniques to achieve optical illusion, a group of Op artists sought to arrange line,

Figure 16 Jackson Pollock's *Echo*, 1951 *(Oil on canvas, 7'7⁷⁄₈" × 7'2". Collection, The Museum of Modern Art, New York. Acquired through the Lillie P. Bliss Bequest and the Mr. and Mrs. David Rockefeller Fund)*

shape, and color in such a way as to create movement on the canvas or the illusion of great depth in the midst of a plane. A good example was Benjamin Cunningham's *Equivocation* (1964). Whether or not Pop and Op art were authentic art forms was much debated. Although the genre produced some talented practitioners such as Claes Oldenburg, it also resulted in the production of much that was superficial, banal, crudely sensational, and fraudulent.

The Literary Imagination

Unlike the aftermath of World War I, the years following World War II failed to produce a notable literary renaissance in America. Several of the major literary figures of the interwar period continued to be productive in the 1940s and 1950s, including Ernest Hemingway, John Dos Passos, Eugene O'Neill, John Steinbeck, and William Faulkner. Few of these writers, however, added to their earlier reputations, and none was closely identified with any important new development in creative writing. Hemingway produced only two major works after the war, and one of these, *Across the River and into the Trees* (1950), proved a great disappointment. The other was a short novel entitled *The Old Man and the Sea* (1952), a compelling story of individual heroism in the face of relentless adversity. Faulkner, who wrote steadily until his death in 1962, was perhaps the most talented of all modern American writers. He turned out a succession of novels in the postwar period, among them being *Intruder in the Dust* (1948), a Pulitzer Prize winner concerned with race relations. *The Town* (1957) and *The Mansion* (1959) completed his trilogy on the Snopes clan. The human drama that Faulkner unfolded had a Southern setting, but his artistic genius transcended regionalism and at its best achieved a powerful universality in its depiction of the contingency and precariousness of the human condition.

A series of war novels published between 1945 and 1952 bridged the country's transition from war to peace. The most widely acclaimed of these novels was Norman Mailer's *The Naked and the Dead* (1948), a work obviously influenced by the examples of Hemingway and Dos Passos. It described the adventures of a combat platoon in the Pacific theater. Many of the war novels focused on the relationship between the individual and the impersonal military machine.

Postwar realism was illustrated in the work of such writers as John O'Hara and John Gould Cozzens, who ably portrayed small-town well-to-do groups; but this literature became steadily less characteristic of the literary scene. The social tragicomedies of John Marquand, usually set against the relatively fixed society of New England, began to seem more parochial. Life seemed to have become too threatening, tenuous, and ambiguous to give social comment in fiction the fixed moral background that traditional storytelling requires. Saul Bellow's character in *Henderson the Rain King* summed up the mood: "Nobody truly occupies a station in life any more. There are displaced persons everywhere."

Novelists and poets turned to the isolated individual experience. Their writings reflected a deep-seated anxiety that the emerging technological society was threatening to destroy the individual entirely. So strong was this sense of alienation—of the feeling that people are strangers even to themselves—that the writers found it almost impossible to create order in their imaginary world. Heroes and heroines disappeared from modern fiction, or they assumed absurd dimensions like Yossarian in Joseph Heller's *Catch-22* (1961), or they were simply anti-heroes. The compelling focus became the individual's search for his or her own identity.

Many of the new writers departed radically from the conventional format of the American novel. The "beatnik school," including such novelists and poets as Jack Kerouac and Allen Ginsberg, drew a picture of violence, perversion, and madness in their work. Vladimir Nabokov, a Russian emigré writer, produced one of the best fictional portrayals of contemporary America: the novel *Lolita* (1955), the story of an automobile tour of the United States taken by a seedy and depraved refugee scholar and a rudderless and sexy American adolescent. The book is funny and sad, and its evocation of the physical and moral aspects of postwar America is curiously unforgettable. J. D. Salinger, a favorite of high school and college students in the 1950s, was concerned in *Catcher in the Rye* (1951) with the inner rebellion of Holden Caulfield and his search for identification and self-awareness. He explores the same theme in *Franny and Zooey* (1961). Another gifted young writer, John Updike, illustrated the use of unconventional form in *The Centaur* (1963), while revealing the modern concern with individual character and the anti-hero in such novels as *Poorhouse Fair* (1959) and *Rabbit, Run* (1960).

One of the noteworthy features of the American literary scene since World War II has been the emergence of a new group of talented writers from the South. Perhaps the most brilliant of these authors were William Styron of Virginia and Flannery O'Connor of Georgia. Styron's major books included *Lie Down in Darkness* (1951), *Set This House on Fire* (1960), and *The Confessions of Nat Turner* (1967). The first is a powerful depiction of the deteriorating relationship between a girl and her father in the stifling atmosphere of a small Southern town. The last is a moving re-creation of the life of the famous slave insurrectionary. O'Connor, who died at an early age in 1964, provides an illustration of Southern gothic at its best. Her novels and short stories—*Wise Blood* (1952), *A Good Man Is Hard to Find* (1955), and *The Violent Bear It Away* (1960)—were tragicomic allegories on humanity's fall, redemption, and faith, written from the perspective of a devout Catholic. These writers had, as Louis Rubin has observed, a strong awareness of the "inroads of time," a special feeling for landscape and place, a "relish for rhetoric," and an "uninhibited commitment to the full resources of the language both spoken and written."

Some Southern writers were black, and the black experience provided the focus for another significant group of postwar novelists and poets. In a sense these authors perpetuated the socially conscious literature of the prewar years, since they were intent upon showing what it was like for a Negro to live in white America. Yet even they were forced to resort to symbols, and Ralph Ellison, in *The Invisible Man* (1952), the most celebrated Negro novel of the period, adopted an oblique approach in order to suggest how it felt to be a sophisticated and sensitive black man in a white-dominated society. In his book, Ellison uses the metaphor of "invisibility" to show that the black person in America has lived in the midst of a society which has refused to recognize his humanity. The best-known black writer of the 1950s and 1960s was James Baldwin, whose first novel, *Go Tell It on the Mountain* (1953), was about the great Negro migration from the South to the urban slums of the North. As the Negro revolt intensified, Baldwin spoke out eloquently and sometimes bitterly in support of the drive for racial equality. *The Fire Next Time* (1963), a work of nonfiction, was an anguished and deeply moving indictment of white racism in the United States.

In 1967 Norman Podhoretz, the editor of the Jewish journal *Commentary*, expressed the opinion that Jews were replacing Southern writers as "the leading school of novelists." There was unquestionably an outburst of creativity among Jewish writers in the United States in the postwar era. Saul Bellow, Bernard Malamud, Philip Roth, and several other young writers produced novels that dealt with American-Jewish life. Bellow, perhaps the most impressive of the group, in *The Adventures of Augie March* (1953), *Herzog* (1965), and other works not only provided a brilliant commentary on the confusion and sordidness of modern life, but also helped transform the novel from a story to pure expression. It is not clear whether this literature signaled the reawakening of Jewish consciousness or the literary climax of assimilation and the end of Jewish consciousness.

Although Norman Mailer is Jewish, he was not primarily concerned with ethnic and religious consciousness, and his literary imagination transcended that theme. Beginning with *Advertisements for Myself* (1959), Mailer gave evidence of having developed a literary genre peculiar to himself. His book included essays, doggerel verse, fictional experimentation, and a great deal of self-exposure. In the late 1960s Mailer turned to reporting, a shift evident in the work of such other writers as Truman Capote, and in a series of nonfictional books he dealt with events like the Democratic national convention of 1968 and the moon landing of 1969. As Richard Poirier has recently written, "More than anyone else of his time, Mailer is implicated, in every sense of that word, in the way we live now."

American poetry also entered into new directions and showed evidence of considerable vitality in the postwar period. A number of established poets from earlier years such as Robert Frost, Carl Sandburg, Archibald McLeish, W. H. Auden, Conrad Aiken, E. E. Cummings, Marianne Moore, and William Carlos Williams continued to be productive. Frost, the grand old man of American poetry, became more abstract in his old age. Another of the older poets, Ezra Pound, was declared insane and committed to a hospital in 1946. He continued to write, however, and ironically his *Pisan Cantos,* based on his experiences in an army prison camp in Pisa, won the Library of Congress's Bollingen Award in 1948. The newer poets were preoccupied with psychological and mythological themes, with humanity's alienation, and with its quest for self-identification. Robert Lowell's *Lord Weary's Castle* (1946), for instance, was the exploration of a ruined world. Many of these younger poets demonstrated great technical ability, new and intricate styles, and philosophical subtlety. Among the more impressive of these writers were Randall Jarrell, Karl Shapiro, Theodore Roethke, Richard Wilbur, Phyllis McGinley, William Meredith, and Louis O. Coxe.

When they thought of the theater, most Americans thought of Broadway and of such famous musicals as *Oklahoma, South Pacific,* and *My Fair Lady.* (The last, based on Bernard Shaw's *Pygmalion,* ran on Broadway for over five years.) But there were more serious dramas produced in the post-World War II period. Eugene O'Neill, the most famous American playwright, while demonstrating less vitality and originality than in earlier years, wrote four plays after 1945, including *The Iceman Cometh* (1946) and *Long Day's Journey into Night* (1956). Of the newer dramatists, the most prolific was Tennessee Williams, who produced a long series of plays. The best of these—such works as *The Glass Menagerie* (1945), *A Streetcar Named Desire* (1947), and *Cat on a Hot Tin Roof* (1955)—were powerful plays, with great psychological penetration. Arthur Miller, in dramas like *Death of a Salesman* (1948), *The Crucible* (1953), and *A View from the Bridge* (1955), protested against the materialism and conformity of midcentury life, while demonstrating his belief that tragedy was still possible in the modern theater and that its proper hero is the common person. Other talented playwrights included William Inge, Lillian Hellman, and Edward Albee. In *Who's Afraid of Virginia Woolf?* (1960), Albee exposed the illusions that people use to get along in modern life.

Critics and other informed observers could scarcely deny the fact that American culture was wonderfully dynamic and full of life in the years following 1945. The rest of the world could no longer ignore the cultural dimensions of the Western colossus—such of its manifestations as the expressionism of Jackson Pollock, the literature of Faulkner and Mailer, the scientific achievements of United States Nobel Prize winners, and the continuing American efforts to develop a workable system of universal education. In that sense, at least, American culture had achieved its independence.

SUGGESTIONS FOR FURTHER READING

Important trends in education are discussed in Martin Mayer's *The Schools**
(1961); Jonathan Kozol's *Death at an Early Age: The Destruction of the Hearts
and Minds of Negro Children in the Boston Public Schools** (1967); and Charles E.
Silberman's *Crisis in the Classroom: The Remaking of American Education**
(1970). On changes in the colleges and universities, see Clark Kerr, *The Uses of
the University** (1963), and David Riesman and Christopher Jencks, *The Academic
Revolution** (1968). H. L. Nieburg, *In the Name of Science* (1966), throws light on
the governmental role in scientific research and development.

The main contours of American religious history are outlined in Sidney
Mead's *The Lively Experiment: The Shaping of Christianity in America* (1963).
Important works on a variety of key religious themes in the recent period are dealt
with in Will Herberg, *Protestant—Catholic—Jew: An Essay in American Reli-
gious Sociology** (1955); Murray S. Stedman, Jr., *Religion and Politics in
America** (1964); Philip Gleason (ed.), *Contemporary Catholicism in the United
States* (1968); William G. McLaughlin and Robert N. Bellah (eds.), *Religion in
America** (1968); and David Edwin Harrell, Jr., *White Sects and Black Men in the
Recent South* (1971).

Russel B. Nye has written a sprightly history of popular culture entitled *The
Unembarrassed Muse: The Popular Arts in America** (1970). For other illuminat-
ing treatments of mass culture, see Reuel Denney, *The Astonished Muse: Popular
Culture in America** (1964); Russell Lynes, *The Tastemakers** (1954); Alvin
Toffler, *The Culture Consumers: A Study of Art and Affluence in America** (1964);
and Philip Olson (ed.), *America as a Mass Society: Changing Community and
Identity* (1963). The following books are valuable for particular aspects of popular
culture: Richard Griffith and Arthur Mayer, *The Movies* (rev. ed., 1970); Erik
Barnouw, *The Image Empire: A History of Broadcasting in the United States*
(1970); Bill C. Malone, *Country Music U.S.A.: A Fifty-Year History* (1968);
Charlie Gillett, *The Sound of the City: The Rise of Rock and Roll** (1970); Eileen
Southern, *The Music of Black Americans: A History** (1971); and Les Daniels and
John Peck, *COMIX: A History of Comic Books in America* (1971). Provocative
evaluations of the mass media and mass culture are provided by Dwight
Macdonald in *Against the American Grain** (1962); Marshall McLuhan in
Understanding Media: The Extensions of Man* (1964); and Daniel J. Boorstin in
The Image: A Guide to Pseudo-Events in America* (1964).

An excellent historical introduction to the arts in the United States is
provided in Oliver W. Larkin's *Art and Life in America* (1949). Architecture is
discussed in James M. Fitch, *American Building** (2d ed., 1966), and Ian
McCallum, *Architecture U.S.A.* (1959). For midcentury developments in American painting, see Sam Hunter, *Modern American Painting and Sculpture** (1959);
Frank O'Hara, *Jackson Pollock* (1959); and Harriet Janis and Rudi Blesh, *De
Kooning* (1960).

The broad expanse of American literature since World War II is surveyed in

*Available in paperback edition.

Ihab Hassan, *Radical Innocence: The Contemporary American Novel** (1961); Leslie Fiedler, *Waiting for the End: The American Literary Scene From Hemingway to Baldwin** (1964); Raymond M. Olderman, *Beyond the Waste Land: A Study of the American Novel in the Nineteen-sixties** (1973); and Alfred Kazin, *Bright Book of Life: American Novelists and Storytellers from Hemingway to Mailer* (1973). For Southern writers see John M. Bradbury, *Renaissance in the South: A Critical History of the Literature, 1920–1960* (1963). The work of recent black writers is assessed by Robert Bone in *The Negro Novel in America** (rev. ed., 1965). Allen Guttmann's *The Jewish Writer in America: Assimilation and the Crisis of Identity* (1971) is especially important for its historical and sociological perspectives.

Chapter 10

John F. Kennedy
and the Hazards of
International Leadership

By 1960 the postwar world appeared to have achieved a kind of fragile stability, and in the United States there were indications that the next decade would bring some major shifts in the nation's politics. John F. Kennedy, the youngest man ever to be elected to the presidency, succeeded the elderly Eisenhower, making himself the spokesman for "a new generation of Americans." Many people were hopeful that, under Kennedy's leadership, the United States would not only undertake a more aggressive foreign policy but would turn resolutely to the solution of the great social problems which had been neglected or postponed in the 1950s.

The Election of a New President, 1960

There was a spirited contest for the Democratic nomination in 1960. Four United States Senators became active candidates: Lyndon B. Johnson of Texas, Hubert H. Humphrey of Minnesota, Stuart Symington of Missouri, and John F. Kennedy of Massachusetts. Adlai E. Stevenson still had strong support and seemed to be waiting in the wings for a possible third call. Johnson, who was strong in the South, saw his best chance in the gratitude and loyalty he had won from virtually all Democratic senators in his skillful role of majority leader. Kennedy had launched a well-organized drive for the nomination immediately after the election of 1956, when he had first come to national attention as a surprisingly strong contender for his party's vice-presidential nomination. He was challenged by Humphrey in a series of primary contests early in 1960. The two key primaries turned out to be those in Wisconsin and West Virginia. Most observers thought that Humphrey had an advantage in Wisconsin, which adjoined his home state and seemed to reflect his brand of Midwestern liberalism, but Kennedy won a surprising victory there on April 5. The struggle then shifted to West Virginia, where the Massachusetts Senator's Catholicism became a major though largely silent issue in a strongly Protestant state. The outcome was a stunning victory for Kennedy by a 61–39 percent margin.

When the Democratic national convention met in Los Angeles in July, Kennedy was nominated on the first ballot, receiving 806 votes to 409 for Johnson and 86 for Symington. Having secured the nomination, the Massachusetts Senator moved at once to strengthen the ticket by persuading Senator Johnson to accept the vice-presidential nomination.

Meanwhile, the Republican party managed to avoid the kind of divisive and heated nomination fight the Democrats had gone through. The principal reason for this situation was the powerful position Vice President Richard M. Nixon had established by the late 1950s. The Vice President encountered only one significant challenger along the road to his presidential nomination. The challenge came from Nelson A. Rockefeller, who was elected Governor of New York in 1958 in a sweeping victory over Averell Harriman. Handsome, hard-driving, and enormously wealthy, the ambitious Rockefeller sought to attract moderate and liberal Republican support as a fresh, exciting alternative to Nixon. But Nixon had far more political experience and know-how than the Governor, and he was identified with the popular Ike's Presidency and was strongly preferred by most party leaders. In December 1959 Rockefeller withdrew from the hopeless contest.

Nevertheless, in June 1960 Governor Rockefeller challenged the GOP and its platform committee, then at work in Chicago, in effect to repudiate the Eisenhower administration on a long list of national security, civil rights, and social welfare issues. Determined to avoid a bitter platform fight and to hold the party together for the November election, Nixon flew to New York for a secret meeting with Rockefeller. The two men agreed upon a detailed program which reflected the Governor's views on domestic and foreign policy. The "Compact of Fifth Avenue" infuriated conservatives like Senator Barry Goldwater, who characterized the agreement as the "Munich of the Republican Party." The Nixon forces managed to effect an acceptance of the main features of the agreement in the national convention, and the Vice President was easily nominated on the first ballot. Nixon selected Henry Cabot Lodge, Jr., ambassador to the United Nations, for the vice-presidential nomination.

Although Nixon and Kennedy had convincingly demonstrated mastery over their respective parties, both leaders suffered from potentially telling weaknesses. No one in public life was more patently ambitious than Nixon, who seemed to be a plastic man, without any genuine convictions, constantly manipulating himself in order to appear to better advantage. Kennedy, for all of his attractiveness, was regarded with suspicion in many quarters. He had failed to take a strong position on the issue of McCarthyism; his father, Joseph P. Kennedy, had a mean reputation as a conservative isolationist; and, most important, the Senator was a member of the Roman Catholic Church.

Kennedy, being in effect the challenger, took the initiative in developing campaign issues. He emphasized the need for positive leadership, public sacrifice, and vigorous action to "get America moving again." He frequently referred to an alleged "missile gap" between the United States and the Soviet Union, challenged the American commitment to defend certain offshore islands in the Formosa Strait, and criticized the administration for its handling of Castro's Cuba. Concentrating on the large industrial states, Kennedy also hammered away at unemployment, the worsening economic slump, and the need to stimulate economic growth.

Nixon stressed the compelling need for continued experienced leadership. "The major test to which the people of the country are putting the candidates," he declared, "is which by experience, by background, by judgment, by record . . . can best continue the leadership of Dwight D. Eisenhower and keep the peace without surrender for America and extend freedom throughout the world." A Gallup poll taken immediately after the two conventions gave Nixon a 50 to 44 lead over Kennedy, with only 6 percent of those questioned being undecided.

The "Catholic issue" reminded worried Democrats of Al Smith's disastrous campaign in 1928, and it was soon evident that, despite Nixon's refusal to invoke the question, the matter of Kennedy's religion had become the subject of widespread uneasiness as well as scurrilous attacks. In early September a highly publicized Washington convocation of conservative Protestant clergymen accused the Catholic church of openly intervening in political affairs, and they ascribed this and other evils to candidate Kennedy. The Democratic leader decided, as he had done in the West Virginia primary, that he must meet the issue directly.

He did so in a bold and dramatic appearance on September 12 before a group of 300 Protestant ministers in Houston. In his frank discussion of his religion he declared:

> I believe in an America where the separation of Church and State is absolute—where no Catholic prelate would tell the President (should he be a Catholic) how to act, and no Protestant minister would tell his parishioners for whom to vote—where no church or church school is granted any public funds or political preference—and where no man is denied public office merely because his religion differs from the President who might appoint him or the people who might elect him.

Kennedy's speech in Houston did not silence anti-Catholic bigots, but it offered reassuring answers to many reasonable questions on the subject.

A series of four television "debates" between the two major candidates gave Kennedy an opportunity to demolish the notion of his youthful inexperience and to force Nixon into the role of defending a passive administration. An estimated 70 million adult Americans viewed the first of the hour-long confrontations on September 26. Most people thought Kennedy appeared to best advantage during the initial encounter. According to a Roper poll, of 4 million voters who were decisively influenced by the debates, 3 million voted for Kennedy.

Nixon's relationship with President Eisenhower was both a source of strength and a continuing problem for the GOP nominee. Although Nixon privately disagreed with the administration's position on a number of issues, he found it necessary to endorse the Eisenhower policies as a whole. Eisenhower's own entry into the campaign was somewhat delayed, but he delivered several hard-hitting speeches in the closing weeks of the contest, attracting great crowds and enthusiastic responses wherever he appeared. Meanwhile, Nixon crammed into those weeks an extraordinarily full traveling and speaking schedule. The Republicans also launched a massive television effort in the final days of the campaign.

In an election that set a record for voter participation (over 10 percent greater than 1956), Kennedy had a popular margin of 119,450 votes out of 68.8 million cast, although his electoral advantage was 303 to 219.[1] Kennedy carried twelve states by margins of less than 2 percent of the two-party votes, and if 4,500 more voters in Illinois and 28,000 more in Texas had gone against him, he would have lost the election by 2 electoral votes. The Democrats carried Congress handily, however, winning a 65 to 35 majority in the Senate and a 262 to 174 superiority in the House.

---

[1]Senator Harry Flood Byrd of Virginia received 15 electoral votes: 8 from Mississippi, 6 from Alabama, and 1 from Oklahoma.

The Massachusetts Senator's strong showing in the industrial states of the East and Midwest was obviously an indispensable factor in his success, as was the powerful influence of Senator Johnson in the Democratic victories in Texas and several other Southern states. The business recession in the fall undoubtedly hurt the Republicans. Blacks had not initially responded with much enthusiasm to Kennedy's candidacy, but his emphasis on social reform coupled with Nixon's calculated efforts to attract Southern whites made the Democratic ticket more appealing to American Negroes. Then, near the end of the campaign, Kennedy and his brother Robert made a dramatic gesture that had a decided impact on black thinking: when Martin Luther King, Jr., was sent to a Georgia prison on a technicality, John Kennedy called Mrs. King to express his concern, while his brother managed soon afterward to secure the black leader's release on bail.

Kennedy's religious faith brought him some votes from Catholics who had supported Eisenhower, but it hurt him badly in the South and Midwest. An estimated 4.5 million Protestant Democrats who had voted for Stevenson switched to Nixon in 1960. Still, large numbers of Protestants who had supported Eisenhower voted for Kennedy in 1960.

The Kennedy Approach to Foreign Policy

The new President devoted most of his moving inaugural address on January 20, 1961, to the challenges that confronted American preemi-

Figure 17 John F. Kennedy Takes Command *(Army Signal Corps, Courtesy John F. Kennedy Library)*

nence in the world. He called upon his fellow citizens to join him in
developing new frontiers to achieve greatness. "Let the word go forth
from this time and place, to friend and foe alike," he declared, "that the
torch has been passed to a new generation of Americans—born in this
century, tempered by war, disciplined by a hard and bitter peace, proud
of our ancient heritage—and unwilling to witness or permit the slow un-
doing of those human rights to which this nation has always been committed, and to which we are committed today at home and around the
world."

John F. Kennedy had come to maturity during the years of Franklin
D. Roosevelt's burgeoning internationalism and wartime diplomacy. Born
on May 29, 1917, in Brookline, Massachusetts, Kennedy was part of an
Irish Catholic family that was rapidly moving up in the world as he
himself grew up. Someone has described him as "the first of the Irish
Brahmins." He was educated in private schools and was graduated with
honors from Harvard College in 1940. During the war he served in the
Navy and was seriously injured in 1943 when the PT boat he commanded
was sunk by a Japanese destroyer off the Solomon Islands. He was
elected to the House of Representatives in 1946 and was twice returned to
his seat before moving up to the Senate in 1952.

There was a bit of the scholar and the writer in the politician. His
senior thesis at Harvard, an examination of the reasons for Britain's
refusal to oppose Hitler's challenge in the 1930s, had been published as
Why England Slept (1940). He wrote a second book during his early
Senate tenure while convalescing from a serious operation on his injured
back. This work, *Profiles in Courage* (1956), surveyed the careers of
several courageous senators who, in times of crisis, stood against the
prevailing sentiment of their colleagues and the public. It won the young
Senator a Pulitzer Prize. Kennedy's intellectual qualities and personal
attributes were, in fact, quite extraordinary. His mind was practical,
ironic, skeptical, and inexhaustibly curious. He tended toward under-
statement. When asked on one occasion how he became a wartime hero,
Kennedy replied, "It was involuntary. They sank my boat." Kennedy was
convinced, as Aida DiPace Donald has written, "that one man in motion
could make a difference." He believed that the American presidency
required "a vigorous proponent of the national interest," that the White
House should be "the vital center of action," and that the President "must
be prepared to exercise the fullest powers of his office—all that are
specified and some that are not."

In the beginning Kennedy made few changes in the fundamental
American approach to the containment of communism. He bypassed such
frequently mentioned possibilities as Adlai E. Stevenson and Senator J.

William Fulbright in selecting a Secretary of State.[2] Instead, Kennedy chose Dean Rusk, a soft-spoken and urbane Southerner who had served as Assistant Secretary of State for Far Eastern Affairs in the Truman administration and since 1952 as president of the Rockefeller Foundation. Robert S. McNamara took over as Kennedy's Secretary of Defense. McNamara, who had been president of the Ford Motor Company, was an expert in applying statistical analysis to management problems. Distrusting professional diplomats, Kennedy surrounded himself in the White House with a group of bright young advisers. Several of these aides were academic intellectuals, such as McGeorge Bundy, special assistant for national security affairs, and Arthur M. Schlesinger, Jr., an adviser on Latin American affairs.

Assuming that United States and Russian thermonuclear power was so awesome as to constitute a "balance of terror" or a "mutual deterrent," Kennedy and McNamara adopted a strategy of "flexible response" in place of the Eisenhower-Dulles doctrine of "massive retaliation." Searching for a wider range of options and greater flexibility in meeting aggression, the new administration emphasized a balanced and diversified defense establishment, one that would include not only strategic and tactical nuclear weapons, but also conventional arms and guerrilla forces. The emphasis on a more sophisticated and diversified defense was accompanied by an increase in military expenditures. The defense budget rose by $7 billion during the first year of Kennedy's tenure. The airborne alert capacity of the Strategic Air Command was extended. The submarine-launched Polaris missile program was accelerated, as were the intercontinental Minutemen (which were launched from underground sites). The Army's combat divisions were increased from eleven to sixteen and modernized in various ways. The tactical wings of the Air Force were expanded from sixteen to twenty-one. The Marine Corps was enlarged. McNamara wanted to build up NATO's ground forces to the long-sought thirty divisions, and while this goal was never reached, about 400,000 American troops were stationed in Europe by 1963.

The strategy of "controlled and flexible response" was conceived as a means of preventing Communist subversion in the Third World and bolstering the American capacity to deter or resist local aggression. Identifying the most dangerous form of Communist expansionism as "wars of national liberation," the Kennedy administration created special forces to help put down aggression by guerrillas and concentrated on developing techniques of counterinsurgency. While expanding and diversifying the defense establishment, the Kennedy team sought to control

[2]Stevenson was appointed Ambassador to the United Nations.

nuclear forces more closely and thus reduce the chances of accidental war. McNamara opposed the proliferation of nuclear arsenals within the NATO alliance, and the administration canceled plans to provide Britain with a nuclear air-to-ground missile called Skybolt. France's Charles de Gaulle interpreted this decision as further evidence that the United States would not allow its European allies to use nuclear weapons in some future crisis.

Although President Kennedy fully subscribed to the containment policy and shared the conventional American view of communism as a monolithic force, he also realized that the key to world peace was improved relations between the United States and the Soviet Union. He hoped to relax cold war tensions. While his own public statements were not devoid of militant rhetoric, he abandoned most of the clichés of the cold war, especially in references to the Third World, where he claimed to be willing to accept neutralism and even socialism. In writing his inaugural address, he decided to use the word "adversary" rather than "enemy"—and he continued to make this distinction in later statements. "Let us never negotiate out of fear," he had declared on that January day in 1961, "but let us never fear to negotiate." By taking the lead in strategic weapons and building mobile strike units to suppress wars of national liberation, America would bargain with Russia from strength.

Kennedy thought that important changes should be made in our Latin American policy, and his administration expanded and reorganized foreign aid. The most successful of the Kennedy foreign aid programs was the Peace Corps, an idea JFK borrowed from others but pledged himself to during the campaign of 1960. The President announced the formation of the Peace Corps by Executive order on March 1, 1961. Congress passed legislation in September 1961 putting the program on a permanent basis and appropriating $30 million for its operation during the first year. During the next few years Peace Corpsmen served two-year stints in scores of underdeveloped countries, making significant contributions in such fields as education, sanitation, irrigation, and agriculture. The Peace Corps proved to be immensely popular in the United States, and it brought an overwhelmingly favorable response from other parts of the world.

The first two years of Kennedy's foreign policy were ambiguous. Kennedy brought renewed vigor and innovation to the handling of international relations, and he appealed successfully to the idealism and sacrifice of his fellow citizens, especially of young people. Yet the globalism of earlier years continued to hold sway, manifesting itself in the dangerous tendency to react indiscriminately to every international crisis without regard to national capability. Twice during the first twenty months of its tenure the Kennedy government was confronted with a crisis that threatened to plunge the world into nuclear war.

A Troubled Beginning: From the Bay of Pigs to the Berlin Wall

One of the problems Kennedy inherited from Eisenhower was Fidel Castro's revolution in Cuba. As President-elect, Kennedy first learned of a secret plan, approved by Eisenhower in the spring of 1960, for the invasion of Cuba by anti-Castro refugees. Kennedy's military advisers endorsed the scheme, and the Central Intelligence Agency assured him that the attack would succeed. Although Senator J. William Fulbright and a few others opposed the undertaking and JFK himself had some qualms about it, the President acquiesced in the foolhardy venture. Not only was Kennedy basically hostile to a Cuban revolutionary government like Castro's, but he had criticized the Eisenhower administration during the campaign of 1960 for not being tough enough with Castro.

The invasion took place on Cuba's southern coast at *Bahía de Cochinos* (Bay of Pigs) on April 17, 1961. The invading forces included fewer than 1,500 troops who were never able to establish a defensible beachhead along the swampy terrain selected for the operation. Lacking naval and air support, they were quickly pinned down by Castro's military forces. There was no popular uprising, and the invasion was completely crushed within three days.

The whole affair was an appalling and humiliating disaster for the United States and the Kennedy administration. The overconfident CIA had grossly misjudged the situation. The project was poorly planned, the size of the invading force totally inadequate, and the operation filled with tactical blunders and miscalculations. Kennedy was badly shaken by this early mishap in foreign policy.[3] The Bay of Pigs adventure brought an increase in Castro's domestic support and strengthened his ties with Russia. It gave Nikita Khrushchev a pretext to bluster and threaten. It outraged many Latin Americans, revived fears of Yankee imperialism in the Southern Hemisphere, and set back Kennedy's promising attempts to identify the United States with anticolonialism. It was a clear violation of American treaty agreements and obligations, not to mention domestic statutes outlawing such activities.

The Bay of Pigs setback encouraged President Kennedy to agree to a meeting with Premier Khrushchev and to test the Russian's mettle.

---

[3]To secure the return of some 1,100 invaders imprisoned in Cuba, the administration subsequently encouraged private American citizens to raise the $53 million in ransom money demanded by Castro and to negotiate the release of the prisoners.

Kennedy and Khrushchev held a series of private meetings in Vienna on June 3 and 4, 1961. They did not get along well. The two leaders did agree to stop the growing conflict in Laos (see page 187), but there was little harmony in their other discussions. Kennedy's position was that efforts to impose communism by force of arms in any country would threaten the balance of power all around the globe. Khrushchev would not agree to stop supporting what he termed "wars of liberation." He was even more militant about Berlin, renewing his demand of the late fifties for an "immediate" peace treaty with Germany and an end to the current four-power occupation of Berlin.

At Vienna Kennedy emphasized the American determination to defend West Berlin, but Khrushchev seemed to take these warnings lightly, and he insisted throughout the following summer that the problem of Berlin would have to be resolved before the end of 1961. If the West would not sign a treaty turning Berlin into a "free city," the Soviet Union would sign a separate peace treaty with East Germany, thereby automatically abrogating the right of the Western Powers to be in Berlin. The Russians wanted a satisfactory settlement in Germany before the effects of Kennedy's military buildup could be felt. But they were also concerned over another matter—the enormous success of West Berlin as a "showcase of democracy" behind the Iron Curtain. In the late spring of 1961 a thousand refugees a day, including many technicians, skilled workers, and young people, were flocking into West Berlin. The very economic survival of the East German state, not to mention its prestige, was involved in this swelling exodus. Fearful of appearing weak, Kennedy was resolved to make the Berlin crisis not only a question of West Berlin's rights, but, in Theodore Sorensen's words, "a question of direct Soviet-American confrontation over a shift in the balance of power."

During the weeks that followed the Vienna conference, Khrushchev heightened the tension over Berlin by increasing his demands for concessions from the Western Powers and by strengthening his military posture. Kennedy, bolstered by advice from such stout cold warriors as Dean Acheson, was prepared to engage in a "conflict of wills" with his Russian adversary. By July a war of words and of nerves had developed. On July 25 Kennedy announced that he was speeding up draft calls, extending enlistments, and mobilizing some reserve and National Guard units; he eventually increased the size of the armed forces by 300,000 men. At the same time he requested an additional defense appropriation of $3¼ billion. Congress voted Kennedy's new defense budget by overwhelming majorities. Encouraged in part by a presidential recommendation, a frenzy of fallout-shelter building momentarily swept the country. Then, suddenly, the climax came in Berlin.

Before dawn on August 13, 1961, the East German government

closed the border between East and West Berlin, and during the next few days the Communists began constructing an elaborate wall of concrete and barbed wire throughout the city, a barrier that was ultimately extended along the entire western border of East German. The Western Powers protested sternly but did not use force against the barricade. President Kennedy dispatched a battle force of United States troops down the 100-mile autobahn from West Germany through the Communist zone into Berlin as a gesture of defiance and as a test of Soviet intentions. The Communists did not halt this convoy. Kennedy also sent Vice President Johnson and General Lucius D. Clay (the Commander of the American forces in Germany during the Berlin blockade of 1948–1949) to West Berlin as evidence of continuing American support of the Allied position.

The Berlin crisis finally dissipated in the fall and winter. Khrushchev's wall was a brilliant and dramatic stroke, and it removed a running sore on the Russians' western flank. But the wall was also a confession of Communist frustration and bankruptcy.

Confrontation and Détente: The Cuban Missile Crisis and the Test Ban Treaty

The most crucial event of the Kennedy years and the most dangerous of all cold war confrontations was the Cuban missile crisis of October 1962. After the Bay of Pigs, Fidel Castro's hostility toward the United States understandably grew. He built up a large Cuban army, renewed a trade pact with the Soviet Union early in 1962, and boasted of his Communist ideology. In the summer of 1962 Khrushchev decided to deploy intermediate-range missiles on the island, the first such commitment of nuclear weapons outside of Russia. This Soviet effort was altogether a very large undertaking, involving many months of planning, 175 ships, 6,000 men, and a cost of about three quarters of a billion dollars. The success of this strategem would make the Russian strategic force more credible, weaken the United States in the eyes of its NATO allies, possibly enable Khrushchev to reopen the Berlin negotiations, and undermine the United States position in the Americas.

Unfortunately for Khrushchev, he was unable to achieve strategic surprise. United States officials were well aware of the heavy movement of Russian military equipment and personnel into Cuba, although they assumed that the U.S.S.R. was simply ensuring Castro's regime against external attack. When Kennedy learned of the clandestine construction of missile launching sites in Cuba, he began a series of secret meetings with close advisers in an atmosphere of utmost tension. Quick action was imperative since additional missiles were on the high seas and the missile sites would become operational within a matter of days. During the lengthy sessions of these top aides and officials, a variety of alternatives were explored, but gradually two possible courses of action came to the fore. One group, including the military spokesmen and Dean Acheson, argued vigorously for an air strike against the missile bases, even though such an attack would probably kill Soviet technicians working on the sites. A second group of the President's advisers supported Under Secretary of State George Ball's recommendation that some kind of blockade be instituted against Cuba. This would represent a flexible arrangement that would give the Russians the maximum opportunity to back down without humiliation. Ball's position won the support of Secretary of Defense McNamara and Attorney General Robert F. Kennedy, who became a key figure in the formulation of the American response.

It was the President, however, who dominated the secret meetings and made the ultimate decision. The discovery of the missiles put the administration in a difficult position. A "war party" had already begun to develop in the United States as rumors of Soviet military penetration of Cuba spread. The midterm congressional elections were less than three weeks away, and Republicans could be expected to make the most of any administration weakness in responding to new cold war challenges. Kennedy was determined to act, but he chose the more moderate course of imposing a blockade instead of an immediate attack on Cuba. At the same time, he decided upon a public confrontation in order to dramatize and reverse Khrushchev's cold war offensive. Having made these crucial

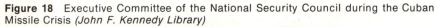

Figure 18 Executive Committee of the National Security Council during the Cuban Missile Crisis *(John F. Kennedy Library)*

decisions, Kennedy acted swiftly to put the plan into effect. On October 22, he briefed the Cabinet and congressional leaders, informed the other NATO nations of the situation, and called a meeting of the Organization of American States for the next day. At 7 P.M. he delivered a nationwide television address to the American people.

Kennedy described what had happened and told the country what to expect. The Russian tactic in Cuba, he declared, was "a deliberately provocative and unjustified change in the status quo which cannot be accepted by this country, if our courage and our commitments are ever again to be trusted by either friend or foe." He proclaimed a "strict quarantine"—actually a blockade—on "all offensive military equipment under shipment to Cuba." Even as the President spoke, the Strategic Air Command was beginning a "massive airborne" alert, 156 intercontinental ballistic missiles were in combat readiness, a fleet of Polaris submarines was on guard at sea, the Navy was establishing a 2,100-mile ring around Cuba (eventually employing 180 ships), and hundreds of thousands of men were placed in combat readiness.

The world shuddered as the two great powers confronted each other at the brink. Would Soviet missiles "fly" in defense of Cuba, as Khrushchev had previously warned? What would happen when the Russian missile-carrying freighters were intercepted by the American blockading units? The Soviet Union's immediate reaction was to denounce the American blockade as illegal. But finally, after two of the most anxious days in modern times, the crisis began to ease. A dozen Soviet vessels headed for Cuba suddenly reversed course or were diverted, prompting Secretary Rusk to remark: "We're eyeball to eyeball and I think the other fellow just blinked." Conditions remained dangerous and uncertain, but for once Khrushchev had overplayed his hand.

On October 26 a solution began to emerge. First through an unofficial emissary and then in a long, emotional letter, Khrushchev started backing off. The letter seemed to imply that Russia would remove the missile bases if the United States would end its blockade and promise not to invade Cuba. Before the United States could respond to this offer, a second Soviet message reached Washington on October 27, offering to dismantle the missile sites in Cuba if the United States would withdraw its missile bases from Turkey. Faced with this perplexing situation, American leaders adopted Robert Kennedy's suggestion that they respond to the first message and ignore the second. This ingenious expedient worked. The United States promised not to invade Cuba if the missiles were quickly withdrawn and if a number of Russian medium-range bombers were returned to the U.S.S.R. The United States also made an oral promise, delivered by Attorney General Kennedy to Soviet Ambassador Anatoly Dobrynin, that the American missiles in Turkey would be removed.[4] Khrushchev agreed to this arrangement, and the crisis ended.

The crisis over the Cuban missiles in the autumn of 1962 turned out better than Kennedy and his advisers had dared to hope. Kennedy, gaining new confidence, was at last persuaded that his will and courage were no longer in doubt. He became more moderate and less strident, at least in dealing with the U.S.S.R., and he understood that the missile withdrawal suggested no universal formula for dealing successfully with the Russians. As for Khrushchev, the missile crisis tarnished his image in many neutral countries and contributed to his decline within the Soviet bloc.

The missile crisis set the stage for a gradual improvement in Russo-American relations. The most notable evidence of this relaxation of tensions during the Kennedy administration was the agreement reached in the summer of 1963 to restrict the testing of nuclear weapons. The pressures and concerns that led to this so-called test ban were numerous and diverse. They included Kennedy's new confidence and the more moderate approach he began to employ toward the Soviet Union. There was also Khrushchev's desperate need to ease the military pressure on his slumping economy, the possibility that a diplomatic coup would restore his fading reputation, and the widening rift between Russia and the People's Republic of China. Both China and France coveted nuclear weapons, and the U.S.S.R. and the United States were by no means happy over the prospect of such nuclear dispersion. Still another consideration was the growing concern over the large amounts of radioactive materials being released into the atmosphere as a result of nuclear testing, which the U.S.S.R. had resumed in the fall of 1961 and the United States in the spring of the following year.

Disarmament talks had dragged on fruitlessly for years when Kennedy made the decision, in the spring of 1963, that the United States would not be the first nation to make further atmospheric tests. In a conciliatory address at American University on June 10, 1963, the President disclosed that representatives of Britain, Russia, and the United States would soon meet in Moscow to discuss the question of a nuclear test ban treaty. If the United States and its adversaries could not now end all differences, he declared, "at least we can help make the world safe for diversity. For, in the final analysis, our most basic common link is that we all inhabit this small planet. We all breathe the same air. We all cherish our children's future. And we are all mortal."

To emphasize the importance the administration attached to the Moscow deliberations, Kennedy selected W. Averell Harriman, perhaps the most experienced and formidable American who had dealt with the

[4]Actually, the decision had already been made to remove these missiles, which were regarded as obsolescent and no longer of strategic value.

Russians, to represent the United States. Harriman proved to be a skillful negotiator, and he had a large part in fashioning the treaty concluded by the three powers on July 25. Although the agreement did not provide for on-site inspection or ban underground testing, it did prohibit all nuclear tests in the atmosphere, in outer space, on land, and under water. The Nuclear Test Ban Treaty was quickly signed by about a hundred other nations, although neither the People's Republic of China nor France ratified it. While the treaty encountered some opposition in the United States, including that of a few scientists like Dr. Edward Teller who were concerned about the maintenance of the American nuclear deterrence, the Senate ratified the agreement, under strong administration pressure, on September 24 by a vote of 80 to 19.

The test ban treaty was one of Kennedy's most positive diplomatic achievements. The agreement had a profound impact upon world opinion, it reduced the pollution of the earth's atmosphere by radioactive fallout, and it offered renewed hope for the negotiated settlement of international conflicts. Yet, ironically, the underground testing clause provided a loophole through which the nuclear arms race was continued and new weapons were later perfected. "The eventual achievement of the atmospheric test ban in 1963," Robert E. Osgood has noted, "was more significant as a symbolic initiative toward détente than as a restriction of arms."

A few weeks after the treaty was signed, Kennedy proposed a joint Soviet-American expedition to the moon. He also approved the sale of $250 million worth of surplus wheat to Russia, which was suffering from a grain shortage. Washington and Moscow soon agreed to the installation of a "hot line" between the White House and the Kremlin. A mild thaw in the cold war had clearly begun, although there was little evidence of progress in the resolution of fundamental differences between the two superpowers.

Global Connections and Third World Policies

John F. Kennedy's foreign policies reflected his country's mounting interest during the late fifties and early sixties in the underdeveloped nations or the so-called Third World. Kennedy's concern over these emerging nations, many of which had only recently won their independence and were as yet aligned with neither side in the cold war, stemmed both from his desire to halt the spread of international communism and his belief that these countries constituted the real arena of competition between the United States and the Soviet Union. The American President understood that the underdeveloped countries desperately needed economic and technical assistance, and he appreciated the desirability of encouraging internal change and social reform in much of the Third World.

Although the United States generally remained aloof from the conflict between the new nations of Africa and their erstwhile European colonizers, it was impossible not to take some part in the Congo, which was plunged into civil war almost as soon as it received its independence from Belgium in 1960. Hoping to avoid a confrontation with the Soviet Union in the Congo, Kennedy supported the military efforts of the United Nations to suppress the Katanga secession movement led by Moishe Tshombe. The President persuaded Congress to purchase $100 million worth of UN bonds as a means of strengthening United Nations operations, which finally managed to reunite the country by early 1963. One of the tragedies of the conflict was the death of UN Secretary General Dag Hammarskjold, who died in a plane crash while trying to arrange a settlement in the Congo. His death precipitated a struggle in which the Soviet bloc tried to change the nature of the Secretariat into a "troika," or three-horsed harness arrangement, composed of Communist, Western, and neutralist representatives, each to have a veto. This scheme, which would have rendered the UN utterly powerless, was defeated in November 1961, with strong American help, and U Thant of Burma was chosen as Acting Secretary General.

Meanwhile, the Kennedy administration was taking a keen interest in Latin America, a region that had long felt neglected by the United States. While Kennedy's Latin American diplomacy was designed to counter Castroism and to win the support of the nations to the south in the cold war, the young Chief Executive seemed to sense the pressure for social change and the urge for a better life in this vast underdeveloped area. In mid-March 1961, Kennedy urged that a partnership be undertaken between the United States and the several Latin American nations in order "to satisfy the basic needs of the American peoples for homes, work and land, health and schools." The idea was received with enthusiasm in Latin America, and in August 1961 representatives of the OAS meeting in Punta del Este, Uruguay, formulated a blueprint for an Alliance for Progress.

The Act of Punta del Este called for a massive developmental program during the next decade, with the United States agreeing to provide over half of the $20 billion to be obtained outside of Latin America. In return the Latin American nations would make an enormous investment of their own, while committing themselves to important land and tax reforms. Although Congress appropriated funds to help inaugurate the new program and every American republic except Cuba joined it, the *Alianza* got off to a poor start. The Alliance seemed to lose some of its urgency following the missile crisis of 1962 and the discovery that Castro's revolution could not be easily exported. Increasing military costs in the United States and, during the next few years, the mounting American involvement in Vietnam also undermined United States support of the undertaking. Looking toward liberal and voluntary reforms, the Alliance was unable to reallocate to any significant degree the power and privileges of the wealthy oligarchies that controlled the region. Furthermore, the major revenue-producing properties in Latin America remained in the hands of United States corporations, and one of the strings attached to Alliance loans was that such money should be spent on relatively expensive American-made goods.

President Kennedy never questioned the need to support American commitments to contain communism in the Far East. One trouble spot was Laos, an isolated mountain country that bordered the People's Republic of China on the north and stretched southward roughly parallel to the divided Vietnam. The pro-Western Laotian government was weak and unstable, and by the beginning of the 1960s it was under increasing attack from the Pathet Lao, a revolutionary movement modeled on the Vietminh. By early 1961 the Communist-assisted Pathet Lao had captured the strategic Plain of Jars and was pushing south along the Vietnam border. In March Kennedy warned Moscow, Peking, and Hanoi that the United States would not tolerate a Communist takeover in Laos. The President decided against large-scale American intervention, however, and at the urging of Averell Harriman, sought a diplomatic solution that would preclude a Pathet Lao victory, avoid an armed confrontation with the Soviet Union, and establish a "neutral and independent Laos."

A neutralization formula was finally agreed to on July 21, 1962. Although the agreement prevented a superpower confrontation in Laos, the civil war was soon resumed by the Pathet Lao, which received military support from North Vietnam so that the Ho Chi Minh trail could be kept open as a means of supplying the National Liberation Front in South Vietnam. In May 1962 the United States sent troops into Thailand, which borders Laos on the west, in order to counter gains made by the Pathet Lao. Thailand, disturbed over the pending neutralization of Laos, had signed a treaty with the United States in March 1962, permitting the American government to come to the Thais' rescue, even if other SEATO members should object (thereby transforming the multilateral nature of the original SEATO pact). The neutralist government of Prince Souvanna Phouma was still trying to govern Laos at the end of 1963, with the United States continuing its grudging support.

The neutralization of Laos was related to the Kennedy administration's decision to base American defense of Southeast Asia on South Vietnam, whose independence Kennedy supported no less than did Eisenhower. Having accepted defeat at the Bay of Pigs and compromise in Laos, Kennedy was not inclined to give any ground in Vietnam. Yet the influence of North Vietnam was spreading among the South Vietnamese, and the National Liberation Front, or Vietcong, was increasing its attacks on the regime of Ngo Din Diem. A Vietcong victory, in the President's view, would lead to Communist control of all Vietnam, prepare the way for Communist success in Cambodia and Laos, and make the situation for the United States and its allies precarious in Thailand, Burma, and other East Asian countries.

Kennedy set about strengthening the Diem regime. At the suggestion of American experts, for example, Diem instituted a strategic hamlet program as a means of securing the countryside and protecting friendly peasants. In the spring of 1961 Kennedy sent Lyndon B. Johnson to investigate conditions in South Vietnam, and the Vice President brought back some ominous impressions. Johnson recommended an increase in American assistance to Diem, whom he jejunely characterized as the "Winston Churchill of Asia." In the fall JFK sent another mission to Saigon, headed by General Maxwell D. Taylor and presidential aide Walt Whitman Rostow. They reported that South Vietnam had enough vitality to justify a major United States effort, and their recommendations pointed toward greater reliance on a military solution. In a later report the Defense Department and the Joint Chiefs of Staff urged the desirability of using American troops if necessary to preserve the Diem government. They estimated the force needed would not exceed six divisions.

Vietnam seemed to offer the kind of situation in which the new Kennedy-McNamara flexible defense program could be employed successfully. Special forces like the Green Berets, the Americans assumed, relying heavily on technology and guerrilla warfare, would be able to put down insurrections or revolutions. The Cuban missile crisis probably accelerated the United States intervention in Vietnam. In any event, Kennedy steadily expanded the American training program in South Vietnam. By early 1962 there were over 4,000 military "advisers" in the country, compared to about 650 when Eisenhower left office.

Ultimately, American success in Vietnam rested upon the effectiveness of the Saigon government in resisting the challenge of the National Liberation Front. Although the United States made spasmodic efforts to persuade Diem to carry out land reform and other needed domestic changes, the South Vietnam leader showed little interest in such programs. The ruling Catholic minority encountered mounting dissent from the large Buddhist population, and in May 1963 a series of Buddhist protests were brutally suppressed by Diem. Such blatant repression not only played into the hands of the Vietcong but provoked outcries in the United States and eventually undermined the Kennedy administration's confidence in Diem. On November 1, 1963, a military conspiracy, with the knowledge if not the approval of Washington, overthrew the Diem regime and assassinated the President and his brother. Unfortunately, however, the new leaders came from the same conservative elements that had produced Diem.

Kennedy and his advisers insisted that the area south of the 17th parallel was vital to United States interests and that American success there would contribute to the isolation of the People's Republic of China and halt the Communist expansion in East Asia. By the end of Kennedy's thousand days, there were 16,000 American military men in South Vietnam, and they were more and more involved in the actual fighting there. Kennedy failed to give sufficient weight to the fact that the struggle in Vietnam was in large part a civil war and that the opponents of the pro-Western government in Saigon reflected nationalist sentiment as well as communist ideology.

Kennedy's international objectives also included a stronger trans-Atlantic partnership. Through a Grand Design for Europe, JFK hoped to strengthen the unity and effectiveness of the Western alliance. He envisioned a Western Europe united in the Common Market and moving toward political federation, cooperating with the United States and Britain in freer trade agreements which would promote the economic growth of non-Communist countries everywhere. To lend American support to this development, Kennedy persuaded Congress to pass the Trade Expansion Act of 1962, empowering the Chief Executive to lower tariff barriers in return for trade concessions. On the military front, the Kennedy administration opposed de Gaulle's plan to build an independent French nuclear deterrent. Kennedy wanted to broaden NATO's defense options, but his renewed emphasis on conventional weapons met with little favor from his European allies.

The easing of cold war tensions that followed the Cuban missile crisis encouraged European leaders to think seriously about revising their relationships with the United States. Thus General de Gaulle prepared a Franco-German treaty of friendship, worked to improve relations with the Warsaw Pact nations, and stepped up the pace of French nuclear development. He withdrew his country's naval forces from NATO and made a bold bid for European independence from American international domination. Early in 1963, in characteristically dramatic fashion, de Gaule rejected Britain's request for membership in the Common Market, repudiated the United States-sponsored multinational nuclear force (MNF), and declared that France would provide itself with the necessary nuclear defenses. Kennedy soon abandoned the MNF plan, and while he and other American spokesmen continued to talk about a stronger and more unified Europe, it had become clear that many of the NATO countries were no longer willing to follow American leadership unquestioningly.

Perhaps the most distinctive characteristic of Kennedy's foreign policy was its ambiguity. Thus he neutralized Laos but was drawn into ever-greater involvement in Vietnam. If, as McGeorge Bundy has said,

Kennedy "rejected the stale rhetoric of the cold war" and if he shifted its direction with the test ban agreement, he remained adamant in his conviction that the United States must meet the Communist challenge all over the world. Even so, Kennedy's record in foreign affairs was promising in some respects, and had he lived and served a second term in the presidency, there is at least a chance that contemporary American history would have been considerably different.

SUGGESTIONS FOR FURTHER READING

The Presidency of John F. Kennedy has been the subject of several books by White House "insiders." Three of the most important are Arthur M. Schlesinger, Jr., *A Thousand Days: John F. Kennedy in the White House* * (1965); Theodore C. Sorensen, *Kennedy* * (1965); and Roger Hilsman, *To Move a Nation: The Politics of Foreign Policy in the Administration of John F. Kennedy* (1964). Aida DiPace Donald (ed.), *John F. Kennedy and the New Frontier* * (1966), is a valuable collection of articles and essays on JFK and his administration. For the campaign and election of 1960, see the absorbing and informative popular account by Theodore H. White, *The Making of the President, 1960* * (1961), and the scholarly work edited by Paul T. David, *The Presidential Election and Transition, 1960–1961* (1961). William L. O'Neill's *Coming Apart: An Informal History of America in the 1960's* (1971) provides a critical perspective on the sixties.

The works cited in earlier chapters by Ambrose, LaFeber, and Spanier are useful for Kennedy's foreign policies. Robert E. Osgood and others, *America and the World: From the Truman Doctrine to Vietnam* * (1970), puts the Kennedy policies in the broad perspective of the 1950s and 1960s. For more critical appraisals see Louise FitzSimons, *The Kennedy Doctrine* (1972), and Richard J. Walton, *Cold War and Counterrevolution: The Foreign Policy of John F. Kennedy* * (1972).

David Green's *The Containment of Latin America: A History of the Myths and Realities of the Good Neighbor Policy* (1971) throws light on United States policies in Latin America. Among the numerous studies dealing with aspects of the Cuban problem are Theodore Draper, *Castroism, Theory and Practice* (1965); Mario Lazo, *Dagger in the Heart: American Policy Failures in Cuba* * (1968); Ramon Eduardo Ruiz, *Cuba: The Making of a Revolution* * (1968); Elie Abel, *The Missile Crisis* (1966); and Robert F. Kennedy, *Thirteen Days: A Memoir of the Cuban Missile Crisis* (1969). The Alliance for Progress is the subject of William D. Rogers, *The Twilight Struggle: The Alliance for Progress and the Politics of Development in Latin America* (1967), and Jerome Levinson and Juan de Onis, *The Alliance That Lost Its Way: A Critical Report on the Alliance for Progress* * (1970).

David Halberstam, *The Making of a Quagmire* (1965), and George M. Kahin and John W. Lewis, *The United States in Vietnam* * (rev. ed., 1969), are illuminating on the early phases of American involvement in Vietnam.

*Available in paperback edition.

Chapter 11

New Frontiers
and the Politics
of Reform

When he accepted his party's presidential nomination in July 1960, John F. Kennedy declared that the New Frontier "is here whether we seek it or not . . . [in the form of] uncharted areas of science and space, unsolved problems of peace and war, unconquered pockets of ignorance and prejudice, unanswered questions of poverty and surplus." During the campaign the young Democratic leader had promised to "get America moving again," at home as well as abroad, and in domestic affairs he was generally comfortable in the mantle of New Deal–Fair Deal reformism. He urged Congress to enact a broad array of proposals ranging from aid to depressed areas and expanded health insurance to larger defense appropriations and foreign assistance. But the record of the Eighty-seventh Congress (1961–1962) was not especially impressive, although a few notable measures were enacted. During the third year of his tenure, Kennedy showed definite signs of becoming a bolder and more advanced reformer, and when he left for Dallas in November 1963, he was already planning an ambitious reform program on which to run for reelection in 1964.

JFK and Economic Progress

The fourth postwar recession in the United States had not yet ended when Kennedy entered the White House, and during February and March of that winter more men and women were out of work than at any previous time in the postwar period. Kennedy's State of the Union message drew a bleak picture. "We take office," the new President said, "in the wake of seven months of recession, three and one-half years of slack, seven years of diminished economic growth, and nine years of falling farm income." Kennedy declared that his administration did not intend "to stand helplessly by." Among his recommendations to the first session of the Eighty-seventh Congress were measures designed to promote economic recovery and expansion, health care for the elderly, federal aid to schools, conservation and use of natural resources, highway construction, housing and community development, and the strengthening of national defense and foreign aid.

Kennedy's reform proposals did not fare well in 1961; of twenty-three proposed laws he sent to the House of Representatives that year, sixteen were defeated. Nevertheless, the administration could point to some accomplishments by the autumn of 1961 in its efforts to end the recession. The President expanded government expenditures in a variety of ways, tried to stimulate residential construction by lowering interest rates, and dealt adroitly with the balance-of-payments problem. Congress liberalized social security benefits, raised the minimum wage to $1.15 an hour (and authorized a further increase to $1.25 two years later), passed legislation enabling the states temporarily to extend unemployment benefits for an additional thirteen weeks, approved an expanded public works program, and passed a $4.88 billion omnibus housing bill. The most controversial measure adopted was the Area Redevelopment Act, a bill strongly supported by Kennedy and twice vetoed by Eisenhower. By the end of 1961 the Secretary of Labor had designated some 675 areas as "distressed" and thus eligible for federal aid under the law. Meanwhile, the recession had tapered off, in part because of the sharp increase in federal spending, and substantial economic recovery had occurred by late 1961.

The administration's major congressional triumph in 1962 was the Trade Expansion Act, which Kennedy hailed as the most significant advance in United States foreign policy "since the passing of the Marshall Plan." Designed to stimulate American competition and trade with the nations of the European Common Market, the act included the largest tariff-cutting power ever granted a President. Congress also enacted the administration's Manpower Retraining bill, which appropriated $435 million over the following three years, if the states would provide a like amount, for the training of the unemployed in new skills. Yet few of Kennedy's proposals came through the Eighty-seventh Congress without limiting amendments. Thus the accelerated Public Works Act of 1962 appropriated $900 million for projects in areas of high unemployment but failed to include the President's request for standby authority to initiate a $2 billion public works program.

Kennedy's "new approach" to the agricultural problem in the form of tighter production controls was rejected. The President and his Secretary of Agriculture, Orville L. Freeman, urged the adoption of the "supply management" technique, which was intended to prevent farm products from becoming surplus storage inventories while keeping farm income up and helping to preserve small farmers. The proposed legislation encountered strong opposition in Congress, particularly from Southern Democrats and Midwestern Republicans, some of whom cited the notorious case of Billie Sol Estes to buttress their arguments.[1]

Another of the administration's proposals to the second session of the Eighty-seventh Congress turned out better. This was the President's request for authority to establish a privately owned and financed corporation to administer a communications satellite system capable of relaying telegraph and telephone messages and television programs throughout the world. Despite the spirited attack on the measure in the Senate led by Paul H. Douglas of Illinois and Estes Kefauver of Tennessee, who labeled the bill a giveaway to the communications industry and urged that the system be owned and controlled by the government, the Communications Satellite Act was approved in 1962. The "Telstar" bill reflected Kennedy's enthusiastic commitment to the United States space program. On May 6, 1961, soon after the Russian cosmonaut Yuri Gagarin had circled the earth in a space vehicle, Commander Alan B. Shepard, Jr., made a 300-mile suborbital flight from Cape Canaveral. During the same month Kennedy urged Congress to commit the United States "to achieving the goal, before this decade is out, of landing a man on the moon and returning him safely to the earth." Congress responded by doubling NASA appropriations in 1962 and again in 1963. Project Apollo soon began to pay off. On February 20, 1962, Lieutenant Colonel John H. Glenn flew around the earth three times in his Mercury space capsule, *Friendship 7,* and landed in the Caribbean on the same afternoon.

One of Kennedy's mounting concerns, as the recession lifted in the

---

[1]Estes was an amazingly successful Texas promoter who made a fortune in a complicated series of business deals such as obtaining loans on fictitious liquid fertilizer tanks, bribing farmers to acquire false cotton acreage allotments, and receiving government storage fees for surplus grain that was often nonexistent. Estes was eventually prosecuted and sent to prison. The case provided a spectacular example of the possibilities of fraud and mismanagement in the nation's costly and bureaucratic farm subsidy system.

second part of 1961, was the danger of inflation. Kennedy and Secretary of Labor Arthur J. Goldberg worked closely in March 1962 with management and labor in the steel industry to avoid a strike and to negotiate a noninflationary labor contract. It was tacitly understood that the steel manufacturers would not raise their prices, but ten days later, on April 10, Roger M. Blough of the United States Steel Corporation informed the President that his company was increasing its prices by about $6 a ton. Five other large firms announced identical increases on the following day. Kennedy, feeling betrayed, denounced the steel companies' action as "a wholly unjustifiable and irresponsible defiance of the public interest." He quickly mobilized the power of the federal government against the offending firms. The Defense Department announced that it would award new contracts only to those companies that refrained from raising prices. The steel executives capitulated within seventy-two hours!

This incident served to increase business distrust of the Kennedy administration, which many businessmen regarded as "antibusiness." When the stock market, on May 28, 1962, experienced its most precipitous drop since the crash of 1929, the setback was attributed in business circles to "lack of confidence" in Kennedy's leadership. It is true that Kennedy was provoked into attacking the steel companies in 1962. He also fostered Justice Department suits against Chrysler Corporation executives for conflict of interest activities and against General Electric and Westinghouse officials for price-fixing conspiracies. On the other hand, there were many indications of Kennedy's economic conservatism, including his backing of AT&T on the Telstar bill, his successful efforts to obtain the Trade Expansion Act, his refusal to move against the oil depletion allowance, and his approval of the merger of Standard Oil of Kentucky and Standard Oil of California. He appointed such businessmen and financiers as C. Douglas Dillon, Luther H. Hodges, and Robert S. McNamara to his Cabinet.

Although the economy had improved, it was still hindered by certain basic underlying problems. Unemployment remained at a disappointing 5.5 percent. The annual increase in the gross national product for the period 1960–1962 was only about 3.6 percent, as compared with a growth rate in Western Europe of from 4 to 6 percent. These trends eventually helped persuade the President to follow the recommendations of Walter W. Heller, Chairman of the Council of Economic Advisers, and other liberal economists who were urging a substantial reduction of taxes even in a time of relative prosperity as a means of stimulating growth. Kennedy thus combined the conservatives' desire for a reduction in taxes with the Keynesian faith in the power of fiscal policy.

When the new Congress convened in January 1963, Kennedy presented a comprehensive proposal that would result in a reduction in taxes of over $10 billion dollars during a three-year period. While Kennedy set out to win the support of sophisticated businessmen for his tax-cut plan and to educate Americans generally as to the advantages of the "new economics," his proposal encountered criticism from many different directions. Congress was extremely slow in responding to the administration's request, and the House did not pass the bill until late September. In the Senate Harry Flood Byrd and other conservatives prevented a vote on the measure during the first session of the Eighty-eighth Congress.

Social Reform—and Losing Battles

John F. Kennedy came to the presidency by taking advantage of the vague discontents that had begun to spread through American society and by identifying himself with the growing desire for a renewed sense of national purpose, for the restoration of United States prestige in the world, and for a more dynamic administration in Washington. Although Kennedy persuaded Congress to enact several of his domestic reform bills, the administration's struggle to win approval for its major social welfare plans often proved to be a matter of losing battles.

At the outset the administration moved to eliminate a bottleneck in the House of Representatives by seizing control of the vitally important Rules Committee, where the Republican–Southern Democratic coalition was strongest. This committee, under Chairman Howard W. Smith of Virginia, had the power to clear or block the legislative path of all important measures considered in the House. The administration used all of its resources in obtaining the adoption of Speaker Sam Rayburn's resolution to enlarge the committee membership from twelve to fifteen. The liberalization of the Rules Committee made it easier to secure congressional action on such legislation as raising the minimum wage, area redevelopment, housing reform, and unemployment compensation.

But there were other discouraging aspects of the congressional scene for the President and his supporters, one of which was a shift in the party's leadership. In the Senate Lyndon Johnson's brilliant leadership was assumed by the mild-mannered Mike Mansfield of Montana, and when "Mr. Sam" died in November 1961, after serving seventeen years as Speaker, he was replaced by the less effective John W. McCormack of Massachusetts. Kennedy himself seemed curiously restrained in his relations with Congress, even when the large Democratic majorities repeatedly failed to enact the administration's principal bills. Always cognizant of his own slender electoral margin in 1960 and with his sights on a more impressive mandate in 1964, Kennedy was still constrained by the absence of a resounding call for social change among the American people.

The President's patience was not inexhaustible, however, and after two years of foot-dragging by a Democratic Congress, he decided to bring his legislative program more directly to the voters. Thus he involved himself actively in the midterm congressional elections of 1962, making many appearances in support of pro-administration Democratic candidates. The results were encouraging for the administration and the Democratic party, which avoided the normal midterm losses, gaining four Senate seats and suffering only nominal losses in the House.

One of the Kennedy administration's disappointing setbacks during the Eighty-seventh Congress was the fate of its ambitious education program. The administration's proposed legislation in 1961 provided for a federal grant of $2.3 billion over a three-year period for school construction and teachers' salaries, plus another $3.3 billion for the support of higher education over a five-year period. After passing the Senate in May, the measure was killed in the House. Catholic leaders insisted that parochial schools should share in the federal aid program, a demand the administration opposed, and the resulting controversy played into the hands of the opponents of the proposal. Many Southern congressmen were suspicious of federal aid because they viewed it as an instrument, in the hands of aggressive blacks like Representative Adam Clayton Powell, for the advancement of school desegregation. Kennedy's education assistance legislation, which had been broadened to include provisions for combating adult illiteracy and training handicapped children, fared no better in 1962.

The administration was also dealt another significant reversal in 1962 when Congress rejected its proposal for the creation of a Cabinet-level Department of Urban and Housing Affairs. The lawmakers also refused to act on the President's recommendation for a federally assisted mass transportation program, and such administration measures as the liberalization of the immigration law, youth employment legislation, federal aid to medical schools and medical students, and a bill to assist migrant workers all bogged down in Congress.

Kennedy was no more successful in his fight for the so-called Medicare program. He had cosponsored a federal medical assistance bill while in the Senate, but it had been sidetracked in favor of the Kerr-Mills Act of 1960.[2] As President, JFK presented his recommendations in a special message to Congress in February 1962, and the plan was incorporated into the King-Anderson bill. Medicare would have provided medical insurance under the Social Security Act for retired workers over sixty-

[2]A congressional report in 1963 revealed that less than 1 percent of the nation's elderly citizens were receiving benefits under the Kerr-Mills Act, and most of them were concentrated in five states. Those who received medical care through this federal program, moreover, were required to sign what some critics described as virtually a "pauper's oath."

five. As in the case of other retirement benefits, the insurance would be financed by payroll deductions.

The American Medical Association led a strong attack on the health insurance bill, characterizing it as "socialized medicine." The various health insurance firms also lobbied against the proposed law. Most Republicans and many Southern Democrats in Congress contended that Medicare would be too expensive, that it would exclude millions of people not covered by social security, and that the Kerr-Mills Act was adequate for the nation's needs. The administration marshaled all of its forces for the battle in 1962, and the President spoke out against the critics of the bill, on one occasion addressing a rally of senior citizens in Madison Square Garden. With the measure mired in the House Ways and Means Committee and facing the implacable opposition of Harry F. Byrd in the Senate Finance Committee, Kennedy persuaded the Democratic leadership in the upper house to attach a slightly amended form of the legislation to a depressed area appropriation bill, hoping by this strategem to bypass Byrd's committee, secure Senate passage, and force the House to act. But a motion to table the Medicare rider carried by a vote of 52 to 48.

Although defeated on Medicare, the Kennedy administration could point to some modest legislative accomplishments in the medical field. The administration urged the enactment of stronger drug control legislation, in part because of the revelations growing out of an investigation of the drug industry in 1959 by Senator Kefauver's Antitrust and Monopoly Subcommittee. The regulatory bill made little congressional headway in 1961, but during the following year it suddenly began to receive greater support as a result of national concern over the thalidomide scandal. It was shown that thalidomide, a European-manufactured tranquilizer, when taken by pregnant women, caused many babies to be born with deformities. The Drug Industry Act of October 1962 gave more powers to the Food and Drug Administration, while establishing additional safeguards in the manufacture, marketing, and prescribing of drugs. In 1963 Congress approved, in response to Kennedy's recommendation, a $329 million fund to be expended over the next four years for research and treatment of mental illness and mental retardation.

Most of the thirty-fifth President's domestic reforms—federal aid to housing, liberalization of social security, expanded public works, a higher minimum wage, increased federal aid to education—represented extensions of the New Deal and the Fair Deal. Still, Kennedy grew as a social reformer during his three years in the Presidency, and under his leadership critical beginnings were made in such fields as area redevelopment, manpower training, and ways of dealing with water and air pollution.

During his last year in office Kennedy began to call for an "unconditional war on poverty in America."

Kennedy and the Civil Rights Movement

Although the Democratic platform of 1960 contained the most far-reaching civil rights pledges that had yet been made by a major political party in the United States, the Kennedy administration demonstrated great reluctance in sponsoring a broad civil rights program in Congress. The reason was not hard to find: Kennedy feared that administration pressure for such legislation would jeopardize the enactment of other important New Frontier measures, especially among powerful Southern Democrats. The administration did exert its influence to help secure a two-year extension of the Civil Rights Commission in 1961, and during the following year it endorsed two voting rights proposals. One of these measures, a constitutional amendment outlawing the poll tax as a prerequisite for voting in federal elections, was approved by Congress.[3]

In sharp contrast to its relative inactivity in the legislative field, the Kennedy administration proved to be vigorous in its use of executive action to promote greater equality in such areas as voting rights, employment, transportation, and education. The Kennedy government expanded the appointment opportunities for blacks; Carl Rowan became Ambassador to Finland, Andrew Hatcher served as White House associate press secretary, and five black Americans were appointed to federal judgeships. The President gave strong support to the civil rights division in the Department of Justice, which emerged under Robert F. Kennedy's leadership as the strategic center of the administration's early efforts to advance the cause of Negro rights. The younger Kennedy was perhaps more deeply committed to the civil rights movement than any other top administration leader, and he brought into his department a remarkable group of talented and dedicated young people to work on the civil rights frontier.

One of the administration's most spectacular achievements through the use of its executive prerogatives was its effective desegregation of interstate transportation, including terminal facilities. Following the freedom rides in the spring of 1961, the Justice Department obtained from the Interstate Commerce Commission a self-enforcing order integrating interstate buses and railroads and the terminals they used. The department also moved against discrimination in airport facilities, securing voluntary desegregation in most cases and in a few instances resorting to

[3]Antipoll tax bills had been passed by the House of Representatives no less than five times during the 1940s, only to die in the Senate. The Twenty-fourth Amendment was ratified by the required majority of the states in 1964. Its only real effect was in the five states that still retained a poll tax: Alabama, Arkansas, Mississippi, Texas, and Virginia.

litigation to effect changes. The President conferred at the White House with delegations of Southern businessmen, theater owners, and newspaper editors in the interest of voluntary desegregation, and administration members like Secretary of Commerce Hodges of North Carolina worked to persuade Southern leaders to cooperate with the administration.

The government also moved against racial discrimination in employment and housing. Soon after assuming office, Kennedy established the President's Committee on Equal Employment Opportunity to combat racial discrimination in the employment policies of government agencies and private firms holding government contracts. Under the chairmanship of Vice President Johnson, the committee won agreements from several large government contractors. Although Kennedy had criticized Eisenhower during the campaign of 1960 for failing to eliminate racial discrimination in housing, he waited almost two years before issuing an Executive order on the matter. The order he finally signed on November 20, 1962, banned discrimination in federally owned and federally financed housing. But unfortunately certain types of housing were exempted from the antidiscrimination requirement, and in practice the order covered only about one-fifth of the new houses constructed in the United States.

Administration officials did their best through private conversations and behind-the-scenes work to smooth the way for school desegregation in Southern cities such as Memphis and New Orleans. In Virginia the Justice Department cast itself as the plaintiff in requesting the federal courts to compel the reopening of schools in Prince Edward County, which had been closed to forestall desegregation. Abraham A. Ribicoff, Secretary of Health, Education, and Welfare, announced in the spring of 1962 that only integrated schools would qualify for federal aid in "impacted" school districts,[4] and that the government was making plans to establish on-base schools where there were no desegregated public institutions in the vicinity of military bases.

The administration's greatest stress and its major success in the civil rights struggle was voting reform. The right to vote was basic, Robert F. Kennedy declared, "and from it all other rights flow." Whereas the Eisenhower administration had filed only six voting suits, the Justice Department under Kennedy brought thirty-two in less than two years. The Democratic administration emphasized the ballot in part because it seemed to offer a safer alternative to the more volatile direct action campaigns being waged by such organizations as CORE and SNCC. Although the Justice Department sent several hundred federal marshals

[4]Impacted school districts were those with large numbers of pupils resulting from the location of federal installations in an area. Congress had long provided federal aid for such districts.

to protect the beleaguered freedom riders in Montgomery in May 1961, such intervention troubled the President and his aides, who redoubled their efforts to effect change through administrative measures.

As the pressure for changes in racial practices mounted, the White House was eventually drawn into a dramatic confrontation with intransigent white supremacists in the Deep South. The spirit of defiance in Mississippi, the citadel of white supremacy, came to a climax in the early fall of 1962, with the threatened desegregation of the state university. The federal courts had ordered the admission of James H. Meredith, a black Mississippian who had served eight years in the Air Force. Governor Ross Barnett, who had been elected with strong Citizens' Council support, aroused the state with demagogic rhetoric and talk of nullification. The Governor defied the court orders and denied Meredith's enrollment in the University of Mississippi. The Kennedy administration tried persuasion at this point, but Barnett proved to be a devious adversary, and he secretly encouraged the gathering mob to attack Meredith and his escort of federal marshals when they appeared on the Ole Miss campus.

With a crisis at hand, the President addressed the nation over television, urging the students and people of Mississippi to comply with the court ruling. "The eyes of the nation and all the world are upon you and upon all of us," Kennedy said, "and the honor of your university and state are in the balance." Such pleas were to no avail. Meredith's appearance was greeted by an outbreak of violence, and only after a night of terror and a pitched battle involving thousands of students and segregationist sympathizers, on the one hand, and 400 federal marshals and a contingent of army troops, on the other, was the lone Negro enrolled. Kennedy moved to quell the riot by sending in regular troops and federalizing the state's National Guard. Two people were killed and 375 were injured in the melee. Meredith was registered under federal bayonets, and some of the troops remained on the campus until the university's first black student was finally graduated.

The force of events in the South, the rising tide of discontent in the Negro community, and mounting sympathy for the equal rights crusade among white Americans combined to bring about a decided alteration in President Kennedy's position. Among the developments that influenced the administration was a series of demonstrations beginning in early April 1963 against the segregated institutions and business places of Birmingham, Alabama. The demonstrations were led by Dr. King and the Reverend Fred Shuttlesworth. When the Birmingham police, under the leadership of the notorious segregationist T. Eugene "Bull" Connor, met the peaceful demonstrators with clubs, fire hoses, guns, and police dogs, vivid pictures of the brutal repression were seen in the news media and on television screens all over the country. The President eventually sent federal troops to restore order in the city. In June 1963, when Governor George C. Wallace threatened to "bar the entrance" of two black students whom the federal courts had ordered admitted to the University of Alabama, Kennedy federalized part of the state's National Guard in order to guarantee the enrollment of the students.

In an eloquent television address immediately after the Alabama episode, on June 11, Kennedy declared that America was confronted "primarily with a moral issue." Continuing, he warned that "the fires of frustration and discord are burning in every city, North and South, where legal remedies are not at hand."

> One hundred years of delay have passed since President Lincoln freed the slaves, yet their heirs, their grandsons, are not fully free. They are not yet freed from social and economic oppression. And this nation, for all its hopes and all its boasts, will not be fully free until all its citizens are free.

On the night of the same day the President spoke, Medgar Evers, the field secretary of the NAACP in Mississippi, was killed from ambush as he entered his home in Jackson.

On June 19 Kennedy sent Congress a comprehensive civil rights bill. Since a focal point of recent equal rights demonstrations had been the exclusion of blacks from lunch counters, restaurants, theaters, and the like, a public accommodations provision was said to be the "symbolic heart" of the administration's bill. Kennedy proposed a limited ban on discrimination in public places, requested power to enable the Justice Department to sue for school desegregation when an aggrieved citizen asked its help, and urged a broad provision authorizing the government to withhold funds for federal assistance programs in cases of discrimination.

The movement for Negro rights now seemed to be moving inexorably toward enactment of a broad civil rights law. The Birmingham demonstrations in the spring had sparked one black protest after another, and by the end of the year demonstrations, involving growing numbers of whites, had taken place in more than 800 cities and towns. The culmination came when 200,000 blacks and whites staged a great March on Washington on August 28, which the President praised for its "deep fervor and quiet dignity." When Martin Luther King delivered his powerful address on that occasion, he warned of the "whirlwind of revolt" that would sweep over the country if the rights of Negroes were delayed any longer. But it was soon apparent that Congress would be in no hurry to pass the civil rights bill. The Senate Judiciary Committee, under the chairmanship of Mississippi's James O. Eastland, held hearings on the proposed legislation but took no further action during the session. The most significant action was taken in the House, where the critical groundwork was laid for ultimate success as a result of intensive negotiations between administration spokesmen and congressional leaders of both parties.

The Kennedy administration became a full-fledged supporter of the equal rights movement only hesitantly and under considerable pressure. Nevertheless, no previous President had made more vigorous efforts to enforce the Constitution with regard to blacks. Kennedy's administration contributed substantially to the advancement of the nonviolent phase of the equal rights revolution. Despite the likelihood of losing several Southern states in 1964 and signs of the so-called "white backlash" in Northern suburbs, Kennedy continued until his death to fight for civil rights legislation.

The Death of a President and the Making of a Legend

In the fall of 1963 the President and his advisers were devoting more attention than usual to politics. In September Kennedy made a tour of eleven Western states, and he later made a number of appearances throughout the East. Democratic prospects in the South were a particular cause of concern to administration leaders, and Texas was especially critical because of a widening cleavage between a Democratic faction identified with Senator Ralph W. Yarborough and a more conservative element associated with Governor John B. Connally. Following a visit to Florida in mid-November, Kennedy flew to Texas for appearances in several cities, an inspection of space installations, and an effort to patch up differences between the feuding factions in the state's Democratic party.

Having been met by cheering crowds in San Antonio, Houston, and Fort Worth, President Kennedy and his wife, accompanied by Vice President Johnson, arrived in Dallas on November 22. Kennedy and the other dignitaries then set out this sunny Friday morning in a motorcade from Love Field for the Dallas Trade Mart, where the President was to make a luncheon address. The people of Dallas, a dynamic city of modern commerce but also the center of a virulent form of right-wing fanaticism, greeted JFK warmly, despite some recent rhetorical outbursts by local critics of the administration and several displays of violence by the radical right during the past few weeks. As the President's open car moved through the cheering crowds in downtown Dallas, three shots were fired from an upper window of the Texas School Book Depository. Kennedy was hit in the neck and the head, and Governor Connally, sitting in front of the President, was also wounded, though not fatally. Kennedy's car sped to nearby Parkland Memorial Hospital, but efforts to save the Chief Executive proved futile, and he died half an hour later, at 1 P.M. Shortly afterward, Lyndon B. Johnson took the oath of office as President; the oath was administered on board *Air Force One,* as the jet plane prepared to take the body of the fallen leader back to Washington.

Within an hour of Kennedy's death, an employee of the Texas School Book Depository named Lee Harvey Oswald was arrested, after having allegedly shot a Dallas policeman, and charged with the assassination. Oswald, a twenty-four year-old former Marine, was a self-styled Marxist who had lived for a while in the Soviet Union and married a Russian girl. Unstable and frustrated, probably psychotic, the young Texan was at one time a member of the Fair Play for Cuba Committee. He maintained his innocence through several hours of questioning, and then in a bizarre sequel two days after the President's assassination, Oswald was himself shot and killed while being moved to another jail. His assailant was a Dallas nightclub operator named Jack Ruby.[5]

News of John F. Kennedy's sudden and tragic death stunned and saddened the American people as had no other public happening since 1945. When the word reached Washington, crowds gathered in front of the White House, gazing silently and sadly through the iron fence at the deserted mansion. A grief-stricken nation paused to watch the solemn funeral rites, which culminated with the mass conducted by Richard Cardinal Cushing in St. Matthew's Cathedral and interment in the Arlington National Cemetery. Television made the whole event indescribably poignant. As William L. O'Neill has vividly written:

> To sit before the screen day after day exposed Americans to such images as no people had ever been. Films of the President's life punctuated the chronicle of somber events. The terrible moments were shown again and again, so were the great ones, and the most touching of all, the merely happy. Shots of his lovely wife Jacqueline, radiant at some public event, alternated with the ghastly pictures of her stricken face and bloodstained clothes. John F. Kennedy was alive and vigorous on some film clip in one instant, and lying in state the next. The drums rolled, the bells tolled, the heads of state marched in grim procession, and all the while his familiar voice filled the air.[6]

One of President Johnson's first official acts was to appoint a special seven-man commission under Chief Justice Earl Warren to investigate the assassination. The commission presented a report and a twenty-six-volume supplement on September 27, 1964. The report concluded that Lee Harvey Oswald, "acting alone and without advice or assistance," had shot President Kennedy. Unfortunately, the Warren Commission's

[5]Despite his plea of insanity, Ruby was convicted in March 1964 of "murder with malice" and sentenced to life imprisonment. He died of cancer before the courts had completed a consideration of his appeal.

[6]William L. O'Neill, *Coming Apart: An Informal History of America in the 1960's,* Quadrangle Books, Chicago, 1971, pp. 90–91.

findings, which were meant to reassure the public and put to rest the many rumors and suspicions surrounding the President's murder, left a good deal to be desired. Despite its bulk, the report was not a thorough and careful piece of research. Critics of the Warren Commission soon challenged its lone-assassin and "one-bullet" theories. A variety of hypotheses about the assassination were given currency in scores of articles and books, including one that pictured Oswald as only a decoy set up by the real assassin and another that attributed the murder to some United States agency like the CIA.

"What was killed in Dallas," James Reston wrote, "was not only the President but the promise. The death of youth and the hope of youth, of the beauty and grace and the touch of magic." Americans found it difficult to comprehend such tragedy; only the province of mythology seemed capable of lending meaning to an act so shocking and irrational. Out of this need was born the legend of Camelot, whose gallant young prince gave the nation a moment of glory before dying for its sins, but who also opened the way for change and reformation.

The slain President's admirers spoke of the glowing prospects his leadership had kindled and of the great progress that would have come in 1964 and later years had he lived. In *A Thousand Days* Arthur M. Schlesinger, Jr., wrote movingly of how Kennedy had "re-established the republic as the first generation of our leaders saw it—young, brave,

Figure 19 Caroline and John Dance in the Oval Office *(John F. Kennedy Library)*

civilized, rational, gay, tough, questing, exultant in the excitement and potentiality in history." Kennedy's youth, vitality, and modernity made him, in Adlai Stevenson's phrase, the "contemporary man." He understood better than most Americans the challenge of change, and he had a feeling for the way the world was going. Yet, in spite of its outward brilliance, the Kennedy administration did not bring extensive changes. Even so, the impact of John F. Kennedy's example and of his "style" was quite remarkable. No public figure since Franklin D. Roosevelt did as much as Kennedy to stimulate the idealism and sacrifice of young Americans. At the time of his death he seemed on the verge of capturing the imagination of the American people as had few of his predecessors. And his dreams, while largely unfulfilled, were prophetic.

A New President and a Democratic Landslide

"Let us continue" was the advice the new President gave to Congress in his first address on November 27, 1963. Lyndon Johnson took over the Oval Office of the White House confidently and with a firm hand. He conducted himself well, moving through the difficult days of his predecessor's funeral and memorialization with dignity and tact. Taking advantage of a more sober and supportive mood in Congress and throughout the country, Johnson adroitly maneuvered to break the long congressional deadlock. During the first hundred days of his administration the legislative logjam began to break up; the foreign aid bill was approved, the Higher Education Facilities Act was passed, the tax reduction bill was enacted, and the Kennedy civil rights legislation was passed by the House of Representatives. In 1964 during the second session of the Eighty-eighth Congress, Johnson's legislative accomplishments were still more impressive. Johnson also succeeded, in the spring of 1964, in arranging a labor-management agreement for the nation's railroads, thereby preventing a serious national strike and the possible resort to compulsory arbitration.[7]

While Lyndon Johnson was consolidating his national leadership, the two major political parties were making preparations for the presidential election of 1964. The Republicans, racked by internal conflict and

[7]The railroad dispute had been developing for many years and came to a head in August 1963 when management demanded the elimination of some 30,000 firemen on diesel locomotives and 19,000 train crewmen on the grounds that they were no longer needed and amounted to featherbedding. The railroad unions argued that maintenance of the jobs was necessary for railway safety. With a strike imminent in the summer of 1963, Congress passed the first peacetime compulsory arbitration act to deal with the problem, but the life of the arbitration act was only six months, and thus a new crisis developed the following spring. The President, with the help of Secretary of Labor W. Willard Wirtz, brought the two sides together at the White House for intensive negotiations, which resulted in an agreement signed in April 1964.

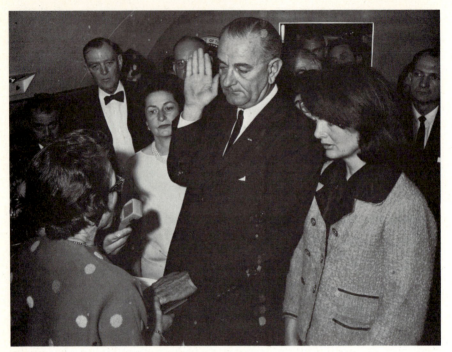

Figure 20 A New President Assumes Office aboard *Air Force One*, Dallas, Texas, November 22, 1963 *(Lyndon B. Johnson Library)*

frustrated by the resurgence of Democratic strength in the late fifties and early sixties, turned abruptly from the moderate course followed by their presidential nominees since 1940 and launched a militantly conservative campaign for control of Washington. A variety of right-wing organizations had sprung up, among them the John Birch Society, the Christian Anti-Communist Crusade, the Citizens' Council, and the Minutemen. In general they stressed economic freedom; opposition to governmental intervention, social democracy, and heavier taxes; and unrelenting hostility toward international communism, which they interpreted as a pervasive and subversive threat within the United States.

The radical right found a political figure to rally around in Senator Barry M. Goldwater of Arizona. Goldwater, a millionaire department store owner who was first elected to the Senate in 1952, had been a staunch supporter of Senator Joseph R. McCarthy. By 1960, when he made a powerful impression on conservatives at the Republican national convention, he had become an aggressive spokesman for right-wing elements. Goldwater summed up the tenets of his conservative Republicanism in *The Conscience of a Conservative,* a book he published in 1960.

He urged a sharp cutback in federal power and spending; a reassertion of state powers, including those involving school desegregation decisions; an end to farm subsidies and the restoration of agriculture to free market conditions; and a restriction of big labor power. He believed that America's objective in foreign policy should be "total victory" over "the all-embracing determination of Communism to capture the world and destroy the United States."

The conservative revival during the early 1960s was an important factor in the emergence of Barry Goldwater as a national figure, but it was a group of little-known Republicans that converted the movement into an effective political organization. Beginning in 1961, such GOP organization men as Clifton F. White of New York (head of the Young Republicans), Peter O'Donnell of Texas, and John Grenier of Alabama began the task of capturing the party machinery for the Senator from Arizona. The leaders of the Goldwater movement aimed both at securing the Republican nomination for the Senator in 1964 and at remaking the GOP as a vehicle of militant conservatism. Goldwater himself was tireless in his campaigning.

Meanwhile, the moderate wing of the Republican party was in disarray. Eisenhower was reluctant to take an active part in the drive for a moderate candidate; Nixon had retired after losing his bid for the governorship of California in 1962; and Rockefeller, while a proven vote-getter in New York, had been badly hurt by his recent divorce and remarriage to a divorcée whose former husband had gained custody of her children. The New York Governor continued to seek the GOP nomination, however, and while he defeated Goldwater in the Oregon presidential primary, he lost the crucial California primary to the Arizona Senator on June 2. Governor William W. Scranton of Pennsylvania made an energetic campaign in the few remaining weeks before the Republican national convention. But it was too late. Goldwater had won too many delegates in the selection process that reached from the local precincts to the state conventions.

At the Republican convention in San Francisco, July 13–16, the conservatives completed their long-awaited conquest of the Grand Old Party. Tightly controlled by Goldwater partisans, the convention rejected moderate, international Republicanism and revenged itself with verbal abuse of Governor Rockefeller and others who advanced antiextremist positions. Goldwater was easily nominated on the first ballot, and William E. Miller, a staunchly conservative congressman from upstate New York and Chairman of the GOP National Committee, was selected as the vice-presidential nominee. The platform was forthright in its conservatism.

The situation in the Democratic party was far simpler than that of the

Republican. While Republican factionalism was threatening to destroy the GOP, President Johnson was preparing the way for the greatest Democratic victory since the days of Franklin D. Roosevelt. Johnson, as William S. White has observed, was a "compulsive competitor," and he set out to win the presidency in his own right—and to win big. His remarkable success with Congress made him all the more formidable, and public opinion polls in the preconvention period showed him far in front of any Republican candidate. There were few surprises and not much drama in the Democratic national convention, which met in Atlantic City, New Jersey, August 24–27. Johnson was nominated by acclamation. His running mate, whose identity the President revealed only at the last minute, was Senator Hubert H. Humphrey of Minnesota. The convention's placidity had earlier been disturbed briefly by a fight over the seating of the all-white Mississippi delegation and the subsequent walkout of most of the Mississippi and Alabama delegates.[8] But otherwise the convention seemed to be united behind the President and his program.

In spite of the ideological contrast between the candidates and platforms, the presidential campaign of 1964 was a dull contest, filled with strenuous campaigning and a plethora of platitudes. A major theme of Goldwater's campaign was that "something basic and dangerous is eating away at the morality, dignity and respect of our citizens." The Republican standard-bearer continued to urge the need for a more militant foreign policy and to assert that the United States was pursuing "no win" policies abroad. In one campaign speech he declared: "I charge that this Administration is soft on Communism . . . I charge that this Administration has a foreign policy of drift, deception, and defeat."

Goldwater's campaign gave Johnson the great advantage of running as a social reform candidate and still seeming less "radical" than his opponent. At the same time, Senator Humphrey's selection for the vice-presidential nomination reassured many people as to Johnson's commitment to liberalism. When Goldwater tried to associate violence in the streets with civil rights demonstrations, the Democrats accused him of bidding for a white backlash, anti-Negro vote. When the GOP nominee said he wanted to strengthen social security, the Democrats recalled his earlier statements about making the system "voluntary." Over and over Goldwater demanded, "What kind of country do we want to have?" To which Johnson replied, "The kind we've made it," and then proceeded to talk about prosperity, progress in education, and the goals of the Great

[8]The regular Mississippi delegation had been challenged by the insurgent, largely black Mississippi Freedom Democratic party. The convention sought to allay this potentially explosive conflict by adopting a compromise permitting the regular delegates to take their seats if they would sign a party loyalty pledge. The compromise resolution also gave two convention seats to the challenging group and established an antidiscrimination requirement in the selection of delegates to future party conventions.

Society. Charging that Goldwater was "trigger-happy" and would endanger world peace if elected, the Democrats reminded the voters that he had
earlier recommended that NATO commanders be given control of tactical
nuclear weapons and that he had once said, "I'd drop a low-yield atomic
bomb on the Chinese supply lines in North Vietnam or maybe shell 'em
with the Seventh Fleet."

The election returns on November 3 confirmed the opinion polls'
forecast of a Democratic landslide. The Johnson-Humphrey ticket received a total of 43.1 million popular votes (61.4 percent) to 27.1 million
for Goldwater and Miller. The Democrats carried forty-four states and
the District of Columbia, with 486 electoral votes, while the Republicans
won only five Deep South states and Goldwater's home state of Arizona,
with 52 electoral votes. Only an unusual amount of ticket splitting saved
the Republicans from total destruction in the congressional races, in
which the Democrats added to their existing majorities by gaining
thirty-eight seats in the House and two in the Senate. Republican
candidates in state legislative races experienced numerous defeats, with
the GOP losing over 500 seats it had previously held. Since almost all state
legislatures were faced with the compulsory reapportionment of their
own bodies and with congressional redistricting as a result of *Baker v.
Carr* (1962) and *Wesberry v. Sanders* (1964), the Democrats were in a good
position to draw the new lines to their own long-range advantage.[9]

The sweeping Democratic victory at the polls in 1964 was based in
considerable part on Johnson's record of accomplishment as President
and on his emergence as a national leader. But it also mirrored the split in
the Republican party and the alarm many moderates and conservatives
felt over Goldwater's call for radical changes at home and abroad. The
times favored the Democratic administration. The economy was booming, and the tensions of the cold war had steadily eased since 1963. The
President used the power of his incumbency with telling effect, and he
attracted support from every segment of the population (receiving over 90
percent of the black vote!). Lyndon Johnson intended to discredit
thoroughly Goldwater's brand of conservatism and also to help elect a
congressional majority large enough to build his Great Society. He
appeared to have achieved both objectives.

SUGGESTIONS FOR FURTHER READING

The previously cited books by Sorensen, Schlesinger, Donald, and O'Neill are
useful in providing an introduction to the Kennedy administration and the politics

---

[9]The federal courts, in a series of landmark decisions beginning with *Baker v. Carr*,
stipulated that congressional and state legislative districting and apportionment should be
that, "as nearly as practicable, one man's vote . . . is to be worth as much as another's."
    *Available in paperback edition.

of the early 1960s. In this connection also see James T. Crown, *The Kennedy Literature: A Bibliographical Essay on John F. Kennedy* (1968); Jim F. Heath, *Decade of Disillusionment: The Kennedy-Johnson Years* (1975); and Richard E. Neustadt, *Presidential Power: The Politics of Leadership** (rev. ed., 1969). Tom Wicker's *JFK and LBJ: The Influence of Personality upon Politics** (1968) is a perceptive interpretation. Henry Fairlie, *The Kennedy Promise: The Politics of Expectation* (1973), is a critical assessment. For a useful specialized study, see Lawrence H. Fuchs, *John F. Kennedy and American Catholicism* (1967).

Economic trends and economic reforms during the early 1960s are treated in Jim F. Heath, *John F. Kennedy and the Business Community* (1969); Hobart Rowen, *The Free Enterprisers: Kennedy, Johnson and the Business Establishment** (1964); and Herbert Stein, *The Fiscal Revolution in America** (1969). The steel crisis of 1962 is described by Grant McConnell in *Steel and the Presidency— 1962** (1963). James L. Sundquist's *Politics and Policy: The Eisenhower, Kennedy, and Johnson Years** (1968) is indispensable for an understanding of the economic and social reforms of the Kennedy administration. Richard Harris, *The Real Voice* (1964), is a critical evaluation of the Kennedy administration's role in the passage of the drug legislation of 1962. On another controversial issue, see Max J. Skidmore, *Medicare and the American Rhetoric of Reconciliation* (1970).

The books by Lomax, Lewis, Silberman, and Muse, cited in Chapter 8, are valuable for the Kennedy administration and the equal rights movement of the early sixties. Alexander M. Bickel's *Politics and the Warren Court* (1965) is helpful in understanding national policy in the early 1960s. For a compelling account of the federal intervention at Ole Miss in 1962 and its background, see James W. Silver, *Mississippi: The Closed Society** (1964).

An absorbing though controversial account of John F. Kennedy's assassination is contained in William R. Manchester's *The Death of a President, November 20–November 26, 1963** (1967). Jim Bishop, *The Day Kennedy Was Shot** (1968), is another popular treatment. Perhaps the best of several books on the Warren Commission's report is Edward Jay Epstein, *Inquest: The Warren Commission and the Establishment of Truth** (1966). Michael Amrine has written a popular account of the presidential succession in 1963: *This Awesome Challenge: The Hundred Days of Lyndon Johnson* (1964).

A good beginning place for study of the presidential election of 1964 is Theodore H. White, *The Making of the President, 1964** (1965). For a more scholarly work, see Milton C. Cummings (ed.), *The National Election of 1964* (1966). Barry Goldwater and the Republican campaign are dealt with in Goldwater, *The Conscience of a Conservative** (1960); Bernard Cosman and Robert J. Huckshorn, *Republican Politics: The 1964 Campaign and Its Aftermath for the Party* (1968); Bernard Cosman, *Five States for Goldwater: Continuity and Change in Southern Presidential Voting Patterns* (1966); and Robert D. Novak, *The Agony of the G.O.P., 1964* (1965). The revival of the extreme right in American life is discussed in Arnold Forster and Benjamin R. Epstein, *Danger on the Right** (1964), and Seymour Martin Lipset and Earl Raab, *The Politics of Unreason: Right-Wing Extremism in America, 1790–1970** (1970).

Chapter 12

Toward the Great Society

Lyndon B. Johnson moved easily into the role of domestic reformer, working with skill, energy, and resourcefulness to advance first the Kennedy program and then his own more ambitious legislation. Johnson wanted desperately to be "President of all the people," and during his first years in the White House he seemed to have succeeded in creating a "national consensus." The new President hoped to improve the quality of American life and thus achieve a Great Society, which he described as "a place where the city of man serves not only the needs of the body and the demands of commerce but the desire for beauty and the hunger for community."

There was irony—indeed, tragedy—in the Presidency of Lyndon Johnson. For in spite of his impressive record of domestic reforms and the overwhelming mandate of 1964, Johnson soon began to lose the support of the public and to have a serious "credibility" problem. The Great Society lost its momentum, and, as we shall see in the next chapter, the administration virtually collapsed before LBJ left office.

Lyndon B. Johnson and the Politics of Consensus

Lyndon Baines Johnson's ascent to the pinnacle of national politics was quite as remarkable, in its own way, as that of Harry S. Truman or Dwight D. Eisenhower. Born near Stonewall, Texas, on August 27, 1908, Johnson grew up in the bleak Texas hill country surrounding Johnson City, which his grandfather had founded. The Johnsons, sturdy and self-reliant, were influential in the local community, and both Lyndon Johnson's father and grandfather had served in the state legislature. But the rural economy was depressed and times were hard as Lyndon grew up, and in order to complete Southwest Texas State Teachers' College at nearby San Marcos, he was forced to work at a variety of jobs. After teaching school for a year or two following his graduation, he went to Washington in 1932 as secretary to the congressman from his district. In 1935 the young Texan was appointed director of the National Youth Administration in his home state. Meanwhile, he had married Claudia (Lady Bird) Taylor. In 1937 he won a special election to fill a congressional vacancy and was regularly reelected thereafter. He ran for the United States Senate in 1948 and managed to win (by 87 votes) in an extraordinarily close election.

Johnson rose like a meteor in the Senate. His qualities of leadership so impressed powerful Democrats like Richard B. Russell that he was chosen as Senate minority leader in 1953. After the Democrats won the congressional elections of 1954, Johnson became majority leader in the upper house. Although the Texas Senator suffered a severe heart attack in 1955, he made a good recovery; by the late fifties he had become perhaps the most powerful Democrat in Washington. Johnson became a master of parliamentary maneuver, made effective use of "unanimous consent" agreements to limit debate, and was adept at applying and relaxing pressure on senators who were undecided or opposed on a particular question. He had an unlimited capacity for courtesies, flattering attentions, and small favors in his personal relations with his colleagues, and he also frequently used what some observers called "the treatment." Rowland Evans and Robert D. Novak have described the majority leader in action: "He moved in close, his face a scant millimeter from his target, his eyes widening and narrowing, his eyebrows rising and falling. From his pockets poured clippings, memos, statistics. Mimicry, humor, and the genius of analogy made the Treatment an almost hypnotic experience and rendered the target stunned and helpless."

Johnson's record in the Senate was neither liberal nor conservative, although the Texan had shown some pronounced conservative leanings in supporting Taft-Hartley, opposing Truman's civil rights program, and manifesting special concern for the oil and gas interests of the Southwest. At the same time, he was not basically ideological. He was, first and foremost, a professional politician. Still, his fundamental outlook had been enduringly shaped by his background and formative experiences. For one thing, he was a Southerner—a white Southerner who grew up in a depressed regional economy and society; his own experiences and observations as well as the attitudes and stereotypes he encountered among non-Southerners in Washington made him sensitive to his regional and cultural disadvantages. Whether or not he was influenced by Southern populism, he was imbued with real concern for the poor and the deprived, and he accepted the Populist prescription of positive governmental action as a means of restoring opportunity. The New Deal reinforced these convictions, and Johnson later would recall that FDR "was like a daddy to me." Although strongly influenced by his regional heritage, the Texan moved steadily toward a wider perspective. In 1960 he sought to portray himself as a Westerner as well as a Southerner, and his role as a conciliator and harmonizer in the Senate served to lessen his provincialism and to broaden his views.

A tall, powerfully built man, Johnson provided a sharp contrast to John F. Kennedy; one's rural, Southwestern background, small-college education, drawling speech, and backslapping demeanor seemed the antithesis of the other's Northeastern, metropolitan youth, Harvard training, eloquence, and urbanity. Johnson lacked his predecessor's graceful style on the speaker's platform, and his unadorned language and effusive rhetoric caused some sophisticated liberals to wince. Yet the Texan had a flair for the dramatic, and he was a man of enormous energy, drive, and determination. He was also a vain man, eager for approval and sensitive to criticism. He demanded total loyalty from his subordinates and delighted in petty revenge against those who crossed him.

Lyndon Johnson entered the White House with a great deal of congressional support and goodwill. "If the President decides that it would be nice to have a coast-to-coast tunnel," remarked Richard Rovere at the outset of the Eighty-ninth Congress (1965–1966), "he need only call in some engineers and lawyers to put the scheme in order, advise Congress of his wishes, and begin letting contracts." Relishing the whirligig of congressional action and his own role in the process from 1600 Pennsylvania Avenue, Johnson seemed to know every detail of the administration's program and every pressure that affected its disposition. He made a point, especially during his first year in office, of stressing his commitment to the realization of Kennedy's New Frontier. Congress and the public responded positively to the administration's articulation of these reform goals, as they did to the President's announcement of his own Great Society. Following his electoral triumph of 1964, Johnson amplified the Great Society and explained it in greater detail. Presenting his State of the Union message to Congress early in 1965, he outlined a far-reaching and unprecedented program of domestic reform.

Having achieved a series of spectacular successes during his first year in office, Johnson proceeded to guide through Congress the most impressive array of domestic reforms since the 1930s. The first session of the Eighty-ninth Congress (1965) was particularly productive. The coalition of Republicans and conservative Democrats, where it did appear in the House of Representatives roll call votes, was victorious only 25 percent of the time in 1965, as compared with 67 percent in 1963 and 1964 and 74 percent in 1961.[1] Harris and Gallup polls showed that two-thirds of the American people liked LBJ's performance in the White House. Then the Great Society began to slow down, and within a year polls revealed a mounting loss of confidence in the President extending almost uniformly across the range of his responsibilities.

The Quest for Equality

In his first address to Congress, in late November 1963, President Johnson called for "the earliest possible passage" of the Kennedy administration's civil rights bill, which had recently been reported favorably by the House Judiciary Committee. The new Chief Executive soon made it clear that he was totally committed to the enactment of this broad equal rights measure and that he was prepared to push on boldly to advance the cause with additional legislation and with executive action. "We have talked long enough in this country about equal rights," Johnson declared on November 27, 1963. "We have talked for one hundred years or more. It is time now to write the next chapter, and to write it in the books of law."

When the second session of the Eighty-eighth Congress began its work in January 1964, the Johnson administration mobilized all of its powers behind the effort to enact an omnibus civil rights statute. The threat of a discharge petition persuaded the House Rules Committee to clear H.R. 7152 for floor action by late January, and the bill was passed with strong bipartisan support on February 10, by a vote of 290 to 130. In steering the measure through the lower house, Emanuel Celler, the floor manager, was greatly assisted not only by liberal party members identified with the Democratic Study Committee but also by such Republican leaders as William H. McCulloch, the ranking minority member of the House Judiciary Committee. Thousands of people poured into Washington in early 1964 to press for congressional approval, and scores of national organizations participated in the movement through the Leadership Conference on Civil Rights.

Prospects for the passage of such far-reaching civil rights legislation

---

[1]Liberal Democratic strength in the House in the Eighty-ninth Congress also resulted in a revision of the rules in a way that gave the Speaker authority to bring legislation to the floor if blocked by the Rules Committee.

in the Senate were much less encouraging, given the strategic positions of Southern leaders in that body and the difficulty of overcoming filibusters. Southern senators hoped to bury the House-approved bill in James O. Eastland's Judiciary Committee, but administration leaders skillfully avoided that trap and persuaded the Senate on February 26 to place the measure directly on the upper chamber's calendar. Hubert H. Humphrey, who managed the drive for Senate passage, and other supporters of the proposed law succeeded in creating a strong coalition and in preventing its disruption as a result of partisan politics, an ever-present danger. Senate leaders of both parties and administration spokesmen carried on intensive negotiations in an effort to work out an agreement that would make it possible to halt debate and enact the bill. The pivotal figure in these negotiations was minority leader Everett M. Dirksen of Illinois. The administration undertook painstaking conferences with the minority leader, and so intensive were the discussions that, in the words of one White House aide, Johnson "never let him alone for thirty minutes." The Illinoisan slowly moved toward a compromise, and in mid-May, during the seventh week of floor debate, a package of compromise amendments was agreed to in these negotiations and incorporated into a "clean bill" to be offered as a substitute for H.R. 7152.

On June 10 the Senate adopted a cloture resolution by a vote of 71 to 29, and for the first time in history the upper house had voted to close debate on a civil rights bill. Senator Russell and his Southern colleagues had made a strategic error in demanding unconditional surrender. Had they sought an agreement with Republican moderates earlier in the debate, they might well have obtained significant concessions and seriously weakened the final enactment. Yet as Dirksen said, quoting words attributed to Victor Hugo, "Stronger than all the armies is an idea whose time has come." After cloture the Senate approved a few minor amendments, voted down a large number designed to weaken the measure, and passed the bill on June 19 by a roll call vote of 73 to 27. The House accepted the Senate version, and President Johnson signed it on July 2.

The Civil Rights Act of 1964 was the most sweeping affirmation of equal rights and the most comprehensive commitment to their implementation ever made by a United States Congress. The law contained new provisions to help guarantee Negro voting rights; assured access to public accommodations such as motels, restaurants, and places of amusement; authorized the federal government to bring suits to desegregate public facilities and schools; extended the life of the Civil Rights Commission for four years and gave it new powers; provided that federal funds could be cut off where programs were administered discriminatorily; required most companies and labor unions to grant equal employment opportunity; and authorized the Justice Department to enter into pending civil rights cases. Compliance was not universal, but the act was generally obeyed throughout the South, in part because of careful preparations by federal and local officials. A startling change in the daily behavior if not the thinking of millions of Southerners took place with incredible swiftness.

The administration soon decided to take advantage of the reform impulse in civil rights by seeking additional legislation in the field of voting rights, an area where the 1964 law was considered weak. Such ancient obstructions as literacy tests, discriminatory treatment by local officials, economic pressure, and intimidation were still prevalent in much of the South, particularly in the lower part of the region.

Early in 1965 Martin Luther King, Jr., launched a series of demonstrations that were centered in Selma, Alabama, to dramatize the absence of Negro voting rights in the Deep South. Dallas County, in which Selma is located, had a black majority, but only 325 Negroes were registered to vote as compared with 9,800 whites. In some other black belt counties not a single Negro was enfranchised. King announced plans for "a march on the ballot boxes throughout Alabama," moving from Selma to Montgomery, the state capital, fifty-four miles away. Governor George C. Wallace refused to permit such a march, and when the demonstrators tried to proceed without his approval, they were met with clubs and tear gas. The President finally stepped in, federalizing the Alabama National Guard, and the march was completed between March 21 and 25. The violent clashes that took place in the Selma area provoked national outrage and set the stage for congressional action on voting rights legislation.

Having become committed to the passage of a strong voting rights statute, the Johnson administration submitted a carefully developed proposal on March 17, 1965. From March until August, the voting rights coalition never lost its momentum. It was a bipartisan effort, with strong administration support and powerful assistance from the Leadership Conference on Civil Rights and other groups. After a compromise antipoll tax provision was approved, the Senate adopted a cloture motion on May 25—the second one in two years. The bill was passed on the following day. The House passed a similar measure on July 9, and after a conference committee worked out an agreement reconciling the differences between the two houses, the revised measure was approved in early August. The President signed it on August 6. "They came in darkness and they came in chains," he said of the first American blacks. "Today we strike away the last major shackle of those fierce and ancient bonds."

The Voting Rights Act of 1965 authorized direct federal action to enable Negroes to register and vote. It empowered the Attorney General to appoint federal examiners to supervise voter registration in states or voting districts where a literacy test or similar qualifying devices existed and where fewer than 50 percent of the voting age residents were registered or cast ballots in the 1964 presidential election.[2] Stiff penalties were provided for interference with voter rights. The Department of Justice moved quickly to implement the new statute. The act of 1965, the invalidation of the poll tax, and the "one man, one vote" principle handed down by the Supreme Court went a long way to democratize Southern— and American—politics. The number of black voters in the Southern states steadily increased as a result of these reforms and the work of such campaigns as the Southern Regional Council's Voter Education Project.

The Johnson administration brought many more blacks into important government jobs, and Johnson was the first President to appoint a Negro to his Cabinet and to the Supreme Court. Robert C. Weaver was named to head the new Department of Housing and Urban Development, while the famous NAACP attorney Thurgood Marshall was elevated from the federal circuit court to the nation's highest court. Johnson also pressed on, along with many civil rights leaders and organizations, to secure still more congressional action. In his State of the Union message of January 1966, the President urged the passage of legislation to prevent discrimination in jury selection, to guarantee the physical security of all citizens, and to outlaw discrimination in the housing field. The House of Representatives proceeded to pass this legislation, though the margin of victory on the housing title was very narrow; but the proposals failed in the Senate when efforts to adopt a cloture resolution were twice unsuccessful.

Black impatience and white resistance mounted even as the structure of legal segregation was being dismantled. Equality, many Negro leaders had come to realize, was only a mirage unless tangible opportunities for self-improvement could be created. Some of the basic problems facing American blacks were touched upon in *The Report of the National Advisory Commission on Civil Disorders* (1968). The work of a special commission appointed by President Johnson on July 27, 1967, and headed by Otto Kerner, a former Governor of Illinois, the report stated that "white racism is essentially responsible for the explosive mixture which has been accumulating in our cities since the end of World War II." The commission cited the growing concentration of Negroes in cities; the chronic discrimination and segregation in employment, education, and housing; the oppressive effects of ghetto life upon the young and the increase in crime, drug addiction, and welfare dependency; and the fact that 2 million "hard-core disadvantaged" urban blacks were making no significant economic gains.

---

[2]This brought the federal registration machinery to bear on seven states—Alabama, Alaska, Georgia, Louisiana, Mississippi, South Carolina, and Virginia—plus thirty-four counties in North Carolina and one county each in Arizona, Idaho, and Maine.

By early 1967 the civil rights movement appeared to have collapsed. While the urban riots raged out of control during the summer of 1967, the House of Representatives voted down rent subsidy and rat control legislation. The assassination of Martin Luther King on April 4, 1968, touched off the most widespread rioting that had yet occurred in Negro areas throughout the country and contributed further to black disillusionment and alienation. King's assassination did help bring the enactment of one additional civil rights measure during the Johnson years. The Civil Rights Law of 1968, which had been pending for more than two years, outlawed racial discrimination in the sale and rental of 80 percent of all American houses and apartments. It also imposed stringent criminal penalties on persons found guilty of interfering with anyone's civil rights. With the passage of the Open Housing Act of 1968, the right of American blacks to equal treatment in most aspects of the national life was established in law.

Lyndon B. Johnson was, as the black novelist Ralph Ellison has said, "the greatest American President for the poor and for the Negroes." Johnson, even more than Kennedy, contributed to the quickening pace of the civil rights movement during the 1960s and to the enormous progress made since World War II toward the goal of equal rights for all. Even so, the task of converting equal rights to truly equal opportunity was far from finished. Most white Americans were still opposed to open housing, the urban ghettos remained volatile, millions of blacks were working in menial jobs or were unemployed, and in the 1970s the nation seemed to have lost a sense of urgency about the terrible condition of its minorities.

The War on Poverty

Lyndon Johnson, like all modern American Presidents, was continually concerned with the effort to promote the nation's economic security and growth. He quickly embraced the Kennedy administration's tax reduction plan, which had passed the House of Representatives in September 1963, and pushed it through the Senate in February 1964, though without many of the tax reforms Kennedy had originally recommended. Johnson's sympathetic attitude toward business, as well as his early budgetary restraints, appealed to businessmen, and for a time, at least, he succeeded in bringing the business class into his broad-gauged coalition. The tax cut of 1964 seemed to work brilliantly, and even though the legislation favored established interests, a new principle of economic policy had been enacted. The continued expansion of the economy during 1964 and 1965, the steady decline of unemployment, and the marked increase of sales and profits lent support to the claims of the new public finance and justified the slash in excise taxes enacted by Congress in June 1965.

The Johnson administration also moved to help less fortunate

Americans in more direct ways. In 1966 the administration got Congress to raise the minimum wage from $1.25 to $1.60 an hour, effective in 1968. The Manpower Development and Training Act of 1964 was designed to train the unskilled or technologically displaced worker in new skills. Congress established a permanent food stamp program in 1964. Taking Kennedy's embryonic war on poverty plans, Johnson developed his own legislative program and gave it the impetus of his administration's all-out support. Poverty, LBJ asserted in his first State of the Union message, was a national problem against which his administration "here and now declares unconditional war."

Most Americans were slow to recognize the extent of poverty in the United States during the post-1945 period. Until 1964 the term "poverty" did not appear as a heading in the index of either the *Congressional Record* or the *Public Papers of the Presidents.* Yet in 1960 more than one-fifth of all American families—perhaps as many as 40 million people—were living on less than $4,000 a year, that is, below the official poverty line. Twice as many blacks as whites, relative to population, were the victims of poverty, but in chronically depressed areas like Appalachia as well as rural pockets and city slums all over the country there were millions of impoverished white people, as well as Indians, Mexican-Americans, and Puerto Ricans. Local welfare officials in San Antonio, Texas, for example, reported in 1967 that between 100,000 and 150,000 of that city's residents were suffering from hunger or malnutrition.

President Johnson submitted his specific recommendations to Congress on March 16, 1964. He requested an initial outlay of $962.5 million to support a variety of programs. The antipoverty bill encountered a good deal of opposition in Congress, especially from Republicans, who called it a partisan scheme to win votes in an election year. But once Johnson had made the proposal the "centerpiece" of his 1964 program, it was impossible to prevent its passage. Congress gave the administration virtually all that it asked, appropriating almost a billion dollars for the first year of the antipoverty war.

The Economic Opportunity Act of 1964 established ten separate programs to be administered by an Office of Economic Opportunity (OEO), which was given broad discretionary powers. The President appointed R. Sargent Shriver, director of the Peace Corps, to head the OEO. Many of the new programs were designed to help the young and to do so primarily by giving them opportunities for further education and training. Thus Head Start was a program for preschoolers, while Upward Bound was for college students. VISTA (Volunteers in Service to America) was intended to function as a domestic peace corps in behalf of the poor and disadvantaged. The most innovative and controversial part of the legislation was Title II, which called for community action programs to develop employment opportunities and improve performance and motivation by stipulating "maximum feasible participation" by the poor themselves.

In 1965, with the administration vigorously pursuing the road to the Great Society, the war on poverty was stepped up still further. Congress passed amendments to the 1964 legislation which more than doubled the first year's authorization. By 1966 the Office of Economic Opportunity was devoting about two-fifths of its budget to a variety of community action programs, another two-fifths to its youth programs, and most of its remaining funds to work experience projects. One of Johnson's major congressional accomplishments in 1965 was the passage of the Appalachian Regional Development Act, which had passed the Senate but failed to win House approval in 1964. Emphasizing economic development rather than welfare support, the act provided $1.1 billion in subsidies for highway construction, health centers, and resource development in a depressed region stretching from Pennsylvania to Alabama. Another 1965 statute, the Public Works and Economic Development Act, extended the same concept to other depressed areas.

The war on poverty began to slow down in 1966, as the administration became more engrossed in the struggle over Vietnam and as growing inflationary pressure resulted from the sharply increased defense expenditures. Congressional Republicans found new Democratic allies in their efforts to curb the Great Society's spending and social reform programs. A measure to overhaul the unemployment compensation system, for instance, was left languishing in conference as the session ended in 1966.

For all its call to arms and good intentions, the war on poverty during the 1960s was never given more than a fraction of the funds it needed. Its entire cost during the years of its most active support—1964–1967—was only $6.2 billion. Much of this money went to landlords and construction companies; to big corporations like International Telephone and Telegraph and Litton Industries that received contracts for antipoverty projects; and to construction of highways, airports, and other facilities which benefited the middle classes and the affluent much more than the needy. In the end, the Great Society did little for the central cities and their inhabitants, and the depressed rural areas received even less help from Washington. Many of the antipoverty projects were hastily initiated, there was the usual bureaucratic inertia and inefficiency, and the control exercised by local officials frequently prevented progress. There was also waste in the OEO undertakings, as well as a substantial amount of pork-barrel funds in such programs as those begun in Appalachia. The rent supplement provisions of the housing legislation of the mid-sixties were never really implemented.

Still, there were some gains, not all of which resulted from action by the national government. By the end of the 1960s, only 11 percent of American families received an annual income of less than $4,000, as compared with 22 percent at the beginning of the decade (this does not take into account the losses resulting from inflation). The antipoverty programs, as well as Medicare and increased social security benefits, did help many poor people, young Americans, and elderly folk. The effort to involve the poor in community action programs, while alarming to many local leaders and the subject of much criticism, did represent a new approach by government to the problem of poverty. Finally, the war on poverty did constitute a beginning, even if an extremely limited one, toward the solution of a great social ill in the United States.

Breakthroughs in Education and Health

One of the goals of the Great Society, proclaimed President Johnson in early 1965, was to improve the quality of American life. "We begin with learning," he said. "Every child must have the best education our nation can provide." Several factors had served to obstruct direct federal intervention in this area: the historic church-state issue, the conservative suspicion of increased governmental involvement in such matters, Southern congressional fear that a federal program would become an instrument of school desegregation, and the insistence of Representative Adam Clayton Powell and others that federal aid must be accompanied by the banning of racial discrimination in education. The Kennedy administration had mounted a new attack on the problem, but without much immediate success. Johnson's efforts in 1964 to secure the passage of direct federal-aid-to-education legislation were also unsuccessful.

When the first session of the Eighty-ninth Congress convened in January 1965, President Johnson was ready to submit a series of educational proposals. Some of these recommendations had originated in a presidential task force on education headed by John W. Gardner, president of the Carnegie Corporation. Assistant Secretary Wilbur J. Cohen and other HEW staff members had been working on the problem of the church-state issue as an obstacle to a general education statute, and both sides of the religious controversy seemed to have become more amenable to compromise. Johnson's consensus-building technique and his legislative skill were much in evidence on the educational front. The administration won the support of both the National Education Association and the National Catholic Welfare Conference for a new approach to federal aid based on the needs of individual students rather than assistance to schools per se.[3] Democratic leaders were able to push the

---

[3]The new formula centered on the child benefit instead of the school benefit concept, a distinction the federal courts had made during recent years. As early as 1947, in *Everson v. Ewing Township*, the Supreme Court had upheld a New Jersey law providing bus transportation for parochial school children because the benefit went to the individual rather than the school. Under the federal statute of 1965, aid would be given to all children, but public agencies would control the expenditure.

general education bill through Congress by April 1965, despite the opposition of conservatives who objected to the expenditure of federal funds and to the growing role of the national government in the field of education.

The Elementary and Secondary Education Act of 1965 was the first general federal aid to education law in American history. The act authorized the expenditure of over a billion dollars in federal funds for textbooks, library materials, special educational programs for adults and the handicapped, and the strengthening of state educational agencies. Large sums were to be devoted to improving the teaching of students in the urban slums and in impoverished rural areas. Private schools, whether religious or not, could benefit from this federal support in several ways, including educational television and the use of library materials.

Another feature of the Great Society was a wide-ranging program of aid to higher education. The Higher Education Act of 1965 expanded federal assistance to colleges and universities, providing scholarships and low-interest loans for students, aid to struggling colleges and community service programs, and grants for college libraries. The law made scholarships available to more than 140,000 capable but needy students and authorized a National Teacher Corps to work in poverty-stricken areas.

By mid-1965 resistance to federal aid to education had been shattered, and Congress was pouring more than $4 billion a year into all levels of the national education system. In 1966 Congress provided further massive infusions of federal aid, including $3.9 billion over a three-year period for colleges and universities and $6.1 billion for public schools in a two-year extension of the Elementary and Secondary Education Act. Although the lawmakers refused to appropriate funds in 1966 for the new Teacher Corps, they did approve several additional educational measures during the Ninetieth Congress. Meanwhile, the U.S. Office of Education issued broad new guidelines for the desegregation of schools, hospitals, and other medical facilities under Title VI of the Civil Rights Act of 1964. Lyndon Johnson liked to be called "the education President," and he deserved the label.

Johnson also achieved a dramatic breakthrough with the approval of Medicare in 1965. The final legislation was the product of fifteen years of refinement and liberalization since the first comprehensive medical care proposal had been made by the Truman administration. But like the educational enactments of the mid-sixties, it reflected the special circumstances and pressures associated with the Johnsonian Great Society. By the early 1960s, polls indicated that over two-thirds of the American people favored the idea. Organized labor, the elderly, and other groups increased the pressure for congressional approval. Johnson took up the cause in 1964, but while numerous expiring laws, including Hill-Burton hospital legislation, were extended and broadened that year, Medicare was defeated once again.

The Democratic landslide of 1964 went a long way toward settling the question. Practically the entire Democratic "class of '64" in the House—numbering sixty-five—was committed to Medicare. Johnson made the issue his top priority measure in 1965, and the administration's bill, introduced by Representative Cecil R. King and Senator Clinton P. Anderson, was appropriately numbered H.R. 1 and S. 1. The American Medical Association, sensing the swelling tide of support for congressional action, now presented its own legislative plan, calling for a program to be financed through private insurance companies. Congressional Republicans also introduced comprehensive medical care legislation, but they adhered to the voluntary concept and financing through insurance companies. Congress effectively resisted the lobbying of the AMA and other opponents of Medicare, in part by incorporating some features of the other proposals into the King-Anderson bill, which was considerably broadened in scope during the process. Both houses passed the bill by large majorities.

The $6.5 billion Medical Care Act of 1965 established two major health care programs for persons sixty-five or older. The basic plan, usually referred to as Medicare, would cover most hospital and nursing

Figure 21 LBJ Signs the Medicare Bill *(Lyndon B. Johnson Library)*

home costs, diagnostic studies, and home health care visits. It was to be compulsory, financed mainly by a payroll tax and administered by the Social Security System. The second health care program, called the supplementary plan, would be voluntary and was to be financed by monthly premiums from participants and by general revenue. It was designed to cover about 80 percent of the costs of a variety of health services, including doctors' bills. A little-noticed feature of the medical care act was the provision authorizing Medicaid, a program making federal funds available to the states to help cover medical expenses of the needy.

LBJ and the Urban Nation

The mounting problems of American cities provided a major focus for Lyndon Johnson's Great Society. The condition of the great American city had become extraordinarily precarious, as a *Newsweek* article in March 1969 suggests:

> Choking in air so polluted that it filters out a quarter of the sun's light; stifled by traffic jams; plagued by strikes that cripple essential services; victimized by muggers who fill the streets with fear, America's cities daily appear to confirm Thomas Jefferson's sour conviction that they would be "penitential to the morals, the health and the liberties of man."

During the sixties the Kennedy and Johnson administrations pushed hard for such programs as urban renewal, public housing, mass rapid transit, and water pollution control, and following the election of 1964, Congress enacted an unprecedented number of urban-oriented measures.

The assault on the slums drew the most attention, but Washington's response to the urban crisis was broad and varied. One approach was the community-centered character of the antipoverty programs. This approach sought to meet the sharp criticism of the traditional urban renewal process—charges, for example, that it involved haphazard and undemocratic destruction of communities, the forced relocation of families, and the replacement of older houses and buildings with high-rise apartment complexes. The Johnson administration also attempted to reduce the political fragmentation of metropolitan districts. The Housing and Urban Development Act of 1965, for example, authorized support for areawide planning, and during the following year Congress gave the newly created Department of Housing and Urban Affairs power to require the review by a locally appointed and financed regional council or planning board of all applications for federal funds from governmental units within a given metropolitan area. The elaborate housing law of 1965 not only extended the existing urban renewal programs but provided federal funds for community health and recreation centers and for urban beautification, grants to low-income homeowners for home repairs and improvements, and a controversial rent supplement program.

Part of the trouble in urban America was the result of inadequate, inefficient, and expensive transportation. Although public transit was cheaper, safer, and more efficient for the user, it was costly to provide and much less central to the economy than the automobile system, in which there was a huge existing investment. In 1964 Congress enacted a $375 million mass transit bill to aid in planning and developing areawide urban transit systems. The federal grants aimed at relieving the heavy traffic congestion in most major metropolitan areas were supplemented by appropriations in the Urban Mass Transportation Act of 1966. Congress also responded to another administration request in 1966 by creating a Cabinet-level Department of Transportation, with full responsibility for the development of a coordinated transportation system for the United States.

The most prominent feature of the administration's urban program was the Demonstration Cities and Metropolitan Area Redevelopment Act of 1966. This so-called "Model Cities" Act was designed to improve the quality and efficiency of urban life by authorizing $1.2 billion to be spent in slum areas for the improvement of housing, health, education, job training, recreational facilities, welfare, and transportation. Calling for an intensive attack on urban blight, the act sought to encourage slum clearance and rehabilitation in some sixty or seventy cities by covering up to 80 percent of the costs of planning and construction, to encourage metropolitan area planning, and to underwrite the building of new model communities by providing land development mortgage insurance.

A growing consumer movement in the second half of the sixties spurred the Johnson administration to sponsor other measures somewhat related to its urban programs. The Highway Safety Act and the Traffic Safety Act of 1966 allocated federal funds for state and local traffic safety programs and applied safety standards to automobile manufacturers. Ralph Nader's muckraking book, *Unsafe at Any Speed* (1965), and his research and lobbying played an important part in the enactment of these laws. The young lawyer soon became a full-time advocate of the public interest, investigating and criticizing numerous products, industries, and government agencies. Congress also took action in 1966 to broaden federal controls over the labeling and packaging of foods, drugs, cosmetics, and household supplies. The Consumer Credit Protection Act of 1968 established a Commission on Consumer Finance to oversee the operations of the consumer finance business and consumer credit transactions in general. The Truth in Lending Act, as it was popularly called, did not limit the charge for credit, but it did require lenders and creditors to give

their customers full, honest, and comparative information on the interest
rates they were paying—and on a uniform, annual basis.

"A prime national goal," the President told Congress in 1965, "must
be an environment that is pleasing to the senses and healthy to live in."
During the early postwar years little was said in Washington to suggest
that the purity of air and water, the pressure of population upon outdoor
open space, and the beauty of countryside and city were *national*
concerns. There was a growing awareness, however, of the environmental
implications of the postindustrial pattern of metropolitan growth; writers
like Rachel Carson and Barry Commoner warned of increasing ecological
dangers; and such groups as the Sierra Club began to attract some
political support in their battles for conservation and an end to the
wholesale destruction of the environment. President Kennedy endorsed
the idea of more federal spending for conservation and environmental
controls. By the time Johnson sent Congress the first presidential message
ever devoted to natural beauty, in February 1965, the national government had adopted or was in the process of adopting a long series of
measures designed to protect the environment.

According to President Johnson and Secretary of the Interior Stewart
L. Udall, the Eighty-eighth Congress was a "conservation Congress."
Among the conservation measures it passed was the National Wilderness Preservation Act of 1964, which incorporated federally held wilderness areas into a National Wilderness System. Congress also set up a
Land Conservation Fund in 1964 to provide for future state and federal
recreation area needs. Each year thereafter brought new legislation and
increased appropriations for conservation and environmental protection,
an enlargement of federal responsibilities in this field, and an intensified
attack on the problem through the formation of regional control agencies
and planning commissions. In 1965 Senator Edmund S. Muskie of Maine
and other congressional conservation advocates cooperated with the
administration to secure the passage of an important Water Quality Act.
The Solid Waste Disposal Act of 1965, the Clean Water Restoration Act
of 1966, and a variety of other enactments provided federal support for air
and water purification; for the construction of sewage and waste treatment plants; and for research, planning, and the establishment of mandatory standards and enforcement procedures.

Among the "working groups" Johnson created to develop Great
Society programs was one on "natural beauty." Appointed in July 1964,
this committee reported to the President during the following November.
Its recommendations included a highway beautification proposal. Known
as "Lady Bird's bill," because of the First Lady's identification with the
natural beauty campaign, the bill became the Highway Beautification Act
of 1965. It attacked the human-made blight that lined the country's
highways.

Despite the variety and scope of the Kennedy and Johnson attacks on the urban crisis, their programs did little to halt the deterioration of America's cities. The city-suburban conflict persisted, and the critical questions of race and metropolitan fragmentation remained largely unresolved. Many of the urban programs died before their impact could be felt, some were badly conceived, and others were destroyed by the conflicting and overlapping intraurban governments. Lack of money was also an acute problem.

Lyndon B. Johnson sponsored the most advanced program of social reform in the history of the Republic. His Great Society sought to correct old racial wrongs, to provide badly needed educational and medical services, to advance social justice by mounting a broad-based attack on poverty and urban blight, and to demonstrate man's capacity to master his environment. There were genuine successes in moving toward greater racial equality, in offering expanded educational opportunities and better health care, and in launching important federal programs in such areas as the war on poverty and environmental control. If the Great Society was a failure in many respects, it was nevertheless an audacious failure and one that could be a constructive legacy to Americans in future years.

SUGGESTIONS FOR FURTHER READING

Among the most useful works on the Johnson administration are Rowland Evans, Jr., and Robert D. Novak, *Lyndon B. Johnson: The Exercise of Power, a Political Biography** (1966); Jim F. Heath, *Decade of Disillusionment: The Kennedy-Johnson Years (1975);* and Hugh Sidey, *A Very Personal Presidency: Lyndon Johnson in the White House* (1968). Alfred Steinberg's *Sam Johnson's Boy: A Close-up of the President from Texas* (1968) fills in some of the needed background. Leonard Baker's *The Johnson Eclipse: A President's Vice Presidency* (1966) recounts a neglected story. For other books on the thirty-sixth President see Jack Bell, *The Johnson Treatment: How Lyndon B. Johnson Took Over the Presidency and Made It His Own* (1965); Louis Heren, *No Hail, No Farewell* (1970); Michael Davie, *LBJ: A Foreign Observer's Viewpoint* (1966); Eric F. Goldman, *The Tragedy of Lyndon Johnson** (1969); and Richard Harwood and Haynes Johnson, *Lyndon* (1973). Johnson's own views are presented in his *The Vantage Point: Perspectives of the Presidency, 1963–1969** (1971), and *Public Papers of the Presidents of the United States: Lyndon B. Johnson* (12 vols., 1965–1970). See also Claudia Alta (Taylor) Johnson, *A White House Diary* (1970).

Several books cited in Chapter 11 are valuable for the black revolution during the Johnson period. For other important volumes, see Benjamin Muse, *The American Negro Revolution: From Nonviolence to Black Power, 1963–1967** (1968), a convenient overview; Talcott Parsons and Kenneth B. Clark (eds.), *The Negro American** (1966), a comprehensive assessment by a number of writers; and August Meier and Elliott Rudwick (eds.), *Black Protest in the Sixties** (1970), a

*Available in paperback edition.

useful anthology of *New York Times* articles. *The Report of the National Commission on Civil Disorders** (1968) is an indispensable document for the urban riots of the sixties. Robert E. Conot's *Rivers of Blood, Years of Darkness** (1967) deals with the Watts riot of 1965. For other aspects of the black revolution, see Gary Orfield, *The Reconstruction of Southern Education: The Schools and the 1964 Civil Rights Act* (1969); Thomas R. Dye, *The Politics of Equality** (1971); and Charles Fager, *Selma 1965: The Town Where the South Was Changed* (1974).

In the larger realm of social reform Sundquist's *Politics and Policy** is extremely valuable for the Johnson period. A collection of critical articles is available in a volume edited by Marvin E. Gettleman and David Mermelstein, *The Great Society Reader: The Failure of American Liberalism** (1967). Among the helpful works on postwar poverty and the antipoverty campaign are Richard L. Morrill and Ernest H. Woldenberg, *The Geography of Poverty in the United States** (1971); Sar A. Levitan, *Federal Aid to Depressed Areas: An Evaluation of the Area Redevelopment Administration* (1964); Richard M. Elman, *The Poorhouse State: The American Way of Life on Public Assistance** (1966); and Chaim I. Waxman, *Poverty: Power and Politics** (1968).

Congress and the Nation, 1965–1968 (1969), by the Congressional Quarterly Service, is an invaluable reference work for the Johnson years.

Lyndon Johnson
and the Denouement
of Containment

.

Like all Presidents of the post-World War II period, Lyndon B. Johnson's administration was beset with a series of difficult international problems. "World affairs will continue to call upon our energy and courage," Johnson declared in his State of the Union message in January 1965. "But today we can turn increased attention to the character of American life." Unfortunately, however, there was to be little time after 1965 in which the administration could concentrate upon the task of advancing the Great Society at home. Although United States relations with the Soviet Union were improving when Johnson assumed the presidency, he also inherited a set of thorny foreign problems from John F. Kennedy. The Atlantic alliance was undergoing severe strain, the pressure for large-scale economic and social change in Latin America was steadily mounting, the Middle East remained in an unsettled and volatile condition, and like a small cloud on the horizon, the question of America's role in Southeast Asia would soon have to be decided.

The Pattern of American Policy in the Mid-1960s

An internationalist schooled in the struggles of World War II and the cold war, Johnson accepted implicitly the threat of international communism, the wisdom of containment, the need to live up to commitments to one's allies, and the special obligation to maintain an American role in the Far East. Following the President's overwhelming victory at the polls in 1964, his consciousness of the immense power at his disposal and his faith in his capacity to use it nourished his globalist pretensions and his determination to master intractable problems in the international arena.

Although the United States conflict with the Soviet Union and with "international communism" was no longer quite such an obsession by the mid-sixties, this dual conflict was still the single most important international factor in the shaping of American policy. There was some concern in Washington when Khrushchev was suddenly deposed in October 1964, but his successors, Leonid Brezhnev and Alexei N. Kosygin, soon revealed their desire for a continuation of peaceful coexistence. In 1964 the Americans and the Russians worked out arrangements for cultural exchanges involving teachers, researchers, and artists. They reached a joint understanding not to place nuclear warheads into orbit. They inaugurated direct air service between New York and Moscow and signed a new consular treaty establishing additional consulates in both countries. The invasion and occupation of Czechoslovakia by Russian troops in August 1968 in order to crush the liberalization program of Czech party leader Alexander Dubcek provoked strong criticism in the United States; but even this turn of events failed to disrupt the improved relations between the two great powers.

The Johnson administration also took up the cause of a nonproliferation treaty with the Soviet Union in 1965. Years of effort to reach an agreement to prevent the spread of nuclear weapons culminated in July 1968, with the signing of a nonproliferation treaty by the United States, the Soviet Union, Britain, and fifty-eight nonnuclear nations. The treaty forbade the transfer or control of nuclear weapons to any nation not possessing such devices; the nonnuclear nations agreed neither to manufacture nor to receive nuclear weapons.[1]

The Russo-American détente of the sixties did not mean that the two superpowers had abandoned their rivalry for the support of the unaligned nations and the Third World. The explosive situation in the Middle East made that clear. Following Israel's spectacular military victory in the Six Day War of 1967, the Arab nations aligned themselves more closely with the U.S.S.R. The Russians denounced Israel's "aggression," provided new military aid to their Arab friends, and dispatched naval forces into

---

[1]France and the People's Republic of China refused to enter into the agreement.

Figure 22   Kosygin and Johnson Confer at Glassboro State College, June 1967
(Lyndon B. Johnson Library)

the eastern Mediterranean to counter the U.S. Sixth Fleet. The UN was unable to bring the Arab-Israeli dispute much closer to a permanent settlement, and in later years the problem was further complicated by the guerrilla attacks carried out by bands of Palestinian refugees against the Israelis. President Johnson and Premier Kosygin made no real progress in dealing with the Middle East crisis when they held a series of friendly conversations at Glassboro State College, New Jersey, June 23–25, 1967.

In Western and Central Europe Johnson hoped to carry forward the Kennedy administration's plans for the strengthening of defense and trade relations within the Atlantic community. He made little progress, however, and the NATO alliance continued to lose cohesiveness as its members grew more independent of Washington. In early 1966 Charles de Gaulle announced that France would formally withdraw from the NATO military organization within three years, and the alliance's commands and installations were thus forced to leave French soil.[2] A bitter quarrel between Greece and Turkey over the relative political status of their respective nationals on the island of Cyprus also strained the Atlantic alliance.

The United States encountered similar difficulties in its efforts to promote further economic integration of the Atlantic community. France

[2]NATO command headquarters were subsequently shifted to Brussels.

blocked British membership in the Common Market, and the tariff negotiations made possible by the Trade Expansion Act of 1962 failed to produce a great trading area stretching from West Germany to Japan in which goods and services could move with relative freedom. In the bargaining preliminary to the so-called Kennedy Round negotiations within the General Agreement on Tariffs and Trade, the United States and the Common Market nations engaged in sharp debate over some issues. The completion of the Kennedy Round in 1967 did result in substantial reductions by both sides on a large number of items.

Meanwhile, American involvement in Africa grew larger. The United States replaced Belgium as the most powerful foreign element in the Congo, and after a left-wing nationalist attempt to overthrow the central government was repulsed by General Joseph D. Mobutu in 1964, United States influence with the Congolese increased still further. Another rebellion in 1967 and rising protest in the United States against further aid to Mobutu, coupled with the growing American preoccupation with Vietnam, limited Washington's initiatives in the Congo. The same was also true in other newly emerging countries.

During the campaign of 1964 Lyndon Johnson pictured himself as a peaceful and prudent President, in contrast to a warmongering and trigger-happy Barry Goldwater. The President talked about strengthening the United Nations, reducing cold war tensions, expanding economic aid to underdeveloped countries, increasing world trade, and employing patience and moderation in dealing with international crises. Yet Johnson also urged a powerful military system for the United States. By 1965, in fact, Secretary McNamara's energetic efforts to strengthen and broaden the nation's military posture were producing impressive results.

United States Ideals and Self-Interest in Latin America

While the United States in the twentieth century had emerged as one of the major world power centers, the vast region to its south remained a power vacuum. Lacking unity and political stability, Latin America was backward, agrarian, and undiversified in its economic life. It was a land of mass illiteracy, grinding poverty, and inadequate social services. Long dominated by foreign capitalists, local elites, and right-wing military dictatorships, most of the Latin American countries faced an enormous task of modernization. It was the challenge of the "revolution of rising expectations" in Latin America that eventually resulted in Kennedy's Alliance for Progress.

Johnson was determined to prevent a recurrence of Castroism in the Western Hemisphere, not only because of his commitment to the containment of communism, but also because of his keen awareness of the political use the Republican party had made of the Cuban situation during the early sixties. One indication of the administration's approach to Latin America came with the appointment of Thomas C. Mann as Assistant Secretary of State for Inter-American Affairs. Mann, a Texas lawyer and former Ambassador to Mexico, wanted above all else to stabilize Latin American politics, to protect the private interests of the United States in the area, and to wage a vigorous struggle against communism. Johnson and Mann took a hard line toward Castro's regime. They resisted Cuban pressure on the United States naval base at Guantanamo and maintained the economic boycott of the island.

President Johnson was confronted with his first foreign affairs crisis early in 1964 when long-festering anti-Americanism in Panama erupted into violence. In January 1964 controversy over the displaying of the American and Panamanian flags resulted in rioting, property destruction, and the loss of several lives. American troops finally were used to restore order. Meanwhile, President Roberto Chiari of Panama severed diplomatic relations with the United States and demanded a revision of the treaty of 1903 under which the Americans had built and operated the canal. Chiari also brought charges against the United States before the United Nations and the Organization of American States. The Johnson administration adopted a moderate position in dealing with the crisis, and with the encouragement of the OAS secret talks were held between representatives of the two countries, leading to some easing of tensions and a decision to discuss the Panamanian grievances in a more formal way. Internal upheavals in Panama and the seizure of power by a military junta in 1968 prevented the adoption of a new treaty during the Johnson years.

The major crisis in Johnson's Latin American diplomacy resulted from his precipitous decision in the spring of 1965 to send a contingent of United States Marines into the Dominican Republic, ostensibly to protect American lives and property. The government of Juan Bosch, a non-Communist intellectual and nationalist reformer, had been overthrown by a military coup in September 1963. In April 1965 an odd coalition of democrats, radicals, and junior military officers launched a countercoup with the object of restoring constitutional government under Bosch. A bloody struggle ultimately broke out in the streets of Santo Domingo. The American embassy in Santo Domingo and the State Department in Washington, which from the beginning had sided with the conservative military elements against the Bosch rebels, hastily urged the use of United States troops to stop the fighting.

On April 28, four days after the revolt began, Johnson sent in the Marines. They were followed during the next few weeks by more than 20,000 Army troops. The President defended the intervention by charging that the rebels had carried out mass executions, which proved not to have been the case. He also asserted that "people trained outside the Dominican Republic are seeking to gain control." Suspecting that the revolt was part of a larger conspiracy, probably masterminded by Castro, Johnson had acted decisively. "We don't expect to sit here on our rocking chairs with our hands folded and let the Communists set up any government in the Western Hemisphere," he explained. Once the American troops had restored some order, Washington sought to broaden the basis of its intervention by securing OAS support. The two sides finally accepted a cease-fire, and an interim government was agreed upon. More than a year after the revolt, on June 1, 1966, Joaquín Balaguer, a moderate, was chosen President in a peaceful election.

Johnson's police action and diplomatic moves had apparently accomplished their purpose. A strife-torn Caribbean republic had been stabilized, and the possible establishment of another Castrolike government in the Western Hemisphere had been prevented. Johnson could also claim to have supported the cause of free elections. Furthermore, the Dominican Republic venture appeared to confirm the promise of the Kennedy-McNamara strategy of flexible response. On the other hand, the intervention raised serious doubts about American intentions throughout Latin America and about Johnson's capacity for the wise and restrained exercise of power. It led to new charges of United States imperialism and United States support of right-wing dictatorships. It reinforced many long-standing Latin American fears and placed new strains on the relations between the United States and the nations to its south.

The Johnson administration's gunboat diplomacy in the Dominican Republic also threatened to undo the good it had accomplished through the Alliance for Progress. American support of the *Alianza* began to decline in the mid-sixties, and with Johnson's encouragement its initial ten-year timetable was lengthened to eighteen years. As American fears of Castro declined, United States appropriations for Latin American aid dropped. Furthermore, Alliance aid was not predicated, as originally intended, on local reforms. Although the United States had spent $9.2 billion on the Alliance program by 1969, so great was the population increase resulting from the high birthrate that the per capita increase in real productivity per year had amounted to only about 1.5 percent.

The United States continued to use the rhetoric of its democratic creed, even as it showed a willingness to cooperate with right-wing military leaders in many Latin American countries. President Johnson, for example, met with leaders from twenty Latin American nations at Punta del Este, Uruguay, in April 1967. But he was unable to overcome the ill effects of his Caribbean intervention two years before. Even the military regimes in some South American countries began to behave in strange and unpredictable ways. A military coup toppled the Peruvian government in the fall of 1968. The new government proceeded to nationalize the local subsidiary of Standard Oil, to capture United States fishing boats within 200 miles of its coast, and to establish diplomatic and commercial ties with the Soviet Union. Soon afterward, a new military government in Bolivia began to act in a somewhat similar manner.

Vietnam: The Making of a Quagmire

When Lyndon Johnson entered the White House in late November 1963, he hoped to continue John Kennedy's policies in Southeast Asia, as in other parts of the world. It was assumed that this would require only a limited American involvement, largely in the form of military advisers to instruct the South Vietnamese, and that the Communist threat in the region could be blunted with economic and military aid. When South Vietnam's National Liberation Front made overtures to General Duong Van Minh, head of the new Saigon government, for the possible negotiation of a cease-fire and a coalition government, Johnson asserted that "neutralization of South Vietnam would only be another name for a Communist take-over." He promised Minh "American personnel and material as needed to assist you in achieving victory." Later in the year LBJ declared, "I am not going to be the President who saw South Vietnam go the way China went."

The situation in South Vietnam became more uncertain in 1964, as the Vietcong enlarged its operations and the political instability in Saigon continued. In June 1964, when the Pathet Lao fired upon American planes making reconnaissance flights over Laos, the President ordered retaliatory air strikes against the rebel positions. American advisers continued to assist the Army of the Republic of Viet Nam (ARVN) in carrying out raids and acts of sabotage in the North. Furthermore, the U.S. Navy had begun to send destroyers on reconnaissance missions off the coast of North Vietnam. In early August the *U.S. Maddox* was attacked while on such a mission in the Gulf of Tonkin by North Vietnamese PT boats, and two days later the *Maddox* and a second destroyer were allegedly fired upon during a night so dark and rainy that the two United States ships could not even see each other. Johnson seized upon this encounter to broaden his discretionary authority in the Vietnam conflict. He ordered retaliatory air attacks against three North Vietnamese torpedo boat bases and an oil storage depot. More importantly, he asked Congress for a blanket authorization to use military force to defend the American position in Southeast Asia.

Congress speedily complied with the President's request. By August 25 the two houses had passed the Gulf of Tonkin Resolution with only two opposing votes being cast against the measure. The resolution authorized the President "to take all necessary measures to repel any armed attack against the forces of the United States and to prevent further aggression."

Despite the Gulf of Tonkin, Johnson continued to urge restraint in his public statements. He resisted pressures for the United States to begin bombing the North in the fall of 1964, even after a Vietcong mortar attack on an American base near Saigon in early November. Yet when Hanoi put out peace feelers soon after the November election, neither Johnson nor his advisers were interested in the kind of compromise solution that would likely have resulted from such peace negotiations. Nothing came of UN Secretary General U Thant's efforts during the following winter to bring the United States and North Vietnam to the conference table.

Having rejected negotiations, Johnson's problem was how to win the war in Vietnam. The position of South Vietnam—and of the United States—had steadily deteriorated. The Vietcong, receiving supplies and some military reinforcements from North Vietnam by way of the Ho Chi Minh trail through Laos, controlled great sections of the southern countryside. In Saigon seven different governments came to power in 1964 as one coup followed another. While the generals feuded in Saigon, there were student demonstrations, Buddhist protests, and other evidence of disunity among the South Vietnamese. Virtually all of the President's advisers on foreign affairs recommended an expansion of American military force in Vietnam. They believed that Hanoi was directing and controlling the Vietcong insurgency, and they were convinced that the demonstration of American military power north of the 17th parallel would persuade the North Vietnamese to withdraw. Once again, as so often in the past, American policy makers talked about the Munich appeasement analogy, the test-of-will hypothesis, and the need to maintain "our credibility vis-à-vis the Communists." Furthermore, North Vietnam was, in LBJ's pungent phrase, only a "raggedy-ass little fourth-rate country."

A fateful decision was made in the wake of an attack on February 6, 1965, by Vietcong guerrillas on an American military advisers' compound in Pleiku in the Central Highlands and on a nearby United States helicopter base. Johnson ordered an immediate reprisal raid on a North Vietnam barracks forty miles north of the Demilitarized Zone (DMZ). New incidents provoked similar reprisals later in the month, and on March 2 a systematic bombing campaign of the North began. Within a week Operation Rolling Thunder, as this campaign was called, was spreading destruction by dropping incendiary bombs containing napalm on North Vietnam's villages and countryside. "We seek no wider war," the President declared in a nationwide television address following the attack in Pleiku. "We want nothing for ourselves, only that the people of South Vietnam be allowed to guide their own country in their own way."

When Operation Rolling Thunder had no perceptible impact on the position of North Vietnam or the National Liberation Front, the Johnson

Figure 23 The Vietnam War, 1969 *(From A History of the American People, 2d ed., by Norman A. Graebner, Gilbert C. Fite, and Philip L. White. Copyright © 1970, 1975 by McGraw-Hill, Inc.)*

administration made another crucial decision. It committed American ground troops to the war in Vietnam. On April 1 Johnson authorized 3,500 Marines in Danang to take an offensive combat position. At the same time, the President sent 20,000 more men to Vietnam to join the 27,000 American soldiers already there. By the summer of 1965, the "advisory" role of the American military units had been abandoned; the mission of United States ground forces in Vietnam was changed from defense to offense. They also increased steadily in number. In July Johnson raised the troop level in Vietnam to 125,000 men, and by the end of 1965 more than 184,000 troops were stationed there.

While the United States was doing its best to force North Vietnam to end its support of the NLF and to recognize the independence of South Vietnam under an anti-Communist government, its leaders talked of peace. Thus in an important address at Johns Hopkins University on April 7, 1965, Johnson urged an end to the war on the basis of self-determination by the South and a massive United States investment of a billion dollars for the development of the rich Mekong Valley, a development in which North Vietnam would share. Reiterating the American commitment to the independence of South Vietnam, the Chief Executive made it clear that the United States "will not withdraw, either openly or under the cloak of a meaningless agreement." From time to time in the years that followed, beginning with an informal Christmas truce observed by both sides in December 1965, Washington launched other peace offensives.

In the meantime, the tempo of the war continually increased. By the spring of 1966, B-52 bombers were regularly conducting large-scale raids on North Vietnam, and in June of that year their strikes were extended to include oil installations and other targets near the major cities of Hanoi and Haiphong. The total number of American troops in Vietnam had grown to 385,000 by the end of 1966 and to more than 485,000 a year later. But escalation was a two-way street. North Vietnam responded to the American buildup by sending additional forces to the South, leading General William C. Westmoreland, the United States Commander in South Vietnam, to plead for more and more troops. By October 1967, 40 percent of America's combat-ready divisions, half of its tactical air power, and a third of its naval strength were involved in the Vietnam war.

The war developed into a costly stalemate. As American men and equipment poured into South Vietnam, it became clear that North Vietnam lacked the military power to drive the United States out of Southeast Asia. On the other hand, it eventually became equally apparent that the United States, in spite of its enormous military predominance, could neither prevent Communist infiltration into the South nor force the enemy to enter into what American leaders considered genuine negotiations. The United States carefully avoided an invasion of North Vietnam, fearing large-scale Chinese intervention as a consequence; but the American air assault above the 17th parallel was unprecedented in its severity. Yet this air war failed either to break the enemy's morale or to stop the flow of supplies to the Vietcong from the North.

General Westmoreland's ground strategy was no more successful than the United States air bombardment. Periodically he sent "search and destroy" missions through the countryside in an effort to demolish the Vietcong. The Americans also carried on a "pacification campaign" that was intended to win the loyalty of the South Vietnamese peasants. But neither the military operations nor the pacification programs accomplished their purpose. The NLF guerrillas would habitually fade away in the face of search and destroy sweeps, only to reappear and resume control as American and ARVN forces withdrew. Washington found some satisfaction in the greater stability of the Saigon government that resulted from Air Marshal Nguyen Cao Ky's accession to power as

Figure 24 American Marines on a Search and Destroy Mission, South Vietnam, October 1967 *(Defense Department Photograph)*

Premier in 1965. In 1967 a new constitution for South Vietnam was approved, and in an effort to display its democracy, the Saigon government held national elections in which Nguyen Van Thieu and Ky were selected as President and Vice President, respectively.

The war went on month after month. The employment of bombs, napalm, and defoliants wiped out whole villages and created thousands of refugees. In the absence of established battle lines, American officials measured progress not in the amount of territory won but by the number of enemy killed. By 1968 the "body count" in this numbers game had exceeded 400,000 of the enemy—surely an exaggerated figure.

Then, on January 31, 1968, came a surprise offensive in which the enemy launched powerful, simultaneous attacks against dozens of key cities and towns in South Vietnam. Days and even weeks of bitter fighting ensued before the enemy was finally dislodged. The "Tet offensive"—which took place during the celebration of Tet, the lunar new year—was the most destructive enemy attack of the war. The offensive inflicted heavy losses on United States and ARVN forces, though at a heavy cost to the Vietcong and North Vietnamese. Although Westmoreland described the all-out offensive as the "last gasp" of the enemy, he also requested that an additional 206,000 American troops be sent to Vietnam. The Tet offensive was, as Townsend Hoopes remarks, "the eloquent

Figure 25   U.S. Soldiers in the Streets of Hue, February 1968 *(Defense Department Photograph)*

counterpoint to the effusive optimism" that had long held sway in the White House and in the Pentagon. After years of heavy fighting in Vietnam, victory for the Americans and their allies seemed as remote as ever.

Antiwar Protest and the Lost Crusade

Defenders of Johnson's policies generally believed that the United States must contain Communist expansion in every part of the world. Accepting the logic of the domino theory, they endorsed the administration's promise to contain Communist aggression everywhere by fighting in Southeast Asia. They stressed Johnson's often-expressed willingness to negotiate a general withdrawal of "foreign" forces from the South, which the Communists continued to reject. Some "hawks," as supporters of the war were dubbed, disapproved of the President's approach as too limited and urged that a quick and total American victory should be sought.

Liberal critics of the American war in Vietnam, who were called "doves," pictured Johnson as too quick to resort to force. They tended to view the Vietnam conflict as fundamentally a civil war, and they questioned the administration's assumption that the North Vietnamese, in view of their traditional distrust of the Chinese, were pawns of Peking. They scoffed at the domino theory; charged the administration with exaggerating the Communist threat in Vietnam; called attention to the repressive, reactionary character of the Saigon government; objected to the massive aerial bombing of Vietnam; deplored the heavy loss of American life and the enormous cost of the war; and denied that the United States was advancing the cause of democracy or of a stable peace.

University students and professors were among the earliest critics of the American escalation, and antiwar protests called "teach-ins" were held on various campuses in the spring of 1965. Beginning at the University of Michigan in late March, the teach-ins quickly spread. During a two-day demonstration at Berkeley, California, 12,000 students heard such speakers as Dr. Benjamin Spock, the noted authority on baby care, Socialist leader Norman Thomas, and Dick Gregory, the well-known black comedian, condemn the government's policy in Vietnam. In mid-May a national teach-in was held in Washington, D.C., and during the following August representatives of various peace, civil rights, and church groups organized a National Coordinating Committee to End the War. This committee sponsored a series of mass demonstrations during the fall of 1965. The teach-ins and other campus demonstrations, while initially supported by only a small minority of students, were important because they helped make dissent respectable.

Antiwar sentiment also began to appear in some newspapers and journals of opinion, in radio and television commentaries, and in Congress. The first congressional doves were an intrepid little group of critics led by Wayne Morse, Ernest Gruening, and Gaylord Nelson, who risked their political future by opposing the administration's policy. But congressional opponents soon began to multiply in both houses following the great escalation of 1965. The most important defection from the President's cause was Senator J. William Fulbright. In January 1966 Fulbright's committee commenced televised hearings on the Vietnam situation, and this inquiry was followed by another set of hearings that probed the war's impact on Chinese affairs.

Many civil rights leaders, including Martin Luther King, Jr., eventually joined the peace ranks. King argued that Negroes were being called upon to make disproportionately large sacrifices in Vietnam and that the conflict there was undermining badly needed reforms at home. In April 1967 King led a march of over 100,000 people from New York's Central Park to UN headquarters in an antiwar demonstration. A few days earlier he had characterized the United States as "the greatest purveyor of violence in the world today." King's death in the early spring of 1968 completed the disillusionment that many blacks had begun to feel over the American war in Vietnam.

Much of the antiwar protest in the United States was based on moral considerations, including traditional pacifism and revulsion against the war's brutality. The corrupt and repressive regimes of Ky and Thieu seemed to make a mockery of American intervention in support of democracy and self-determination in Vietnam. Photography and television brought daily illustrations of the war's inhumanity into American homes: the death and maiming of United States soldiers, the killing of civilians by American military operations, the wholesale destruction of Vietnamese villages, the use of napalm and defoliants to ruin forests and crops, and the savage spoliation of an ancient culture by modern warfare. In March 1968, for example, an American platoon led by Lieutenant William Calley, Jr., indiscriminately machine-gunned and bayoneted more than 100 old men, women, and children in the South Vietnamese hamlet of My Lai.[3] One soldier later described the behavior of a friend on the scene that day:

> He was covered with smoke, his face streaked with it, and it looked like there was blood on him, too. You couldn't tell, but there was blood everywhere. Anyway, he was kneeling there holding this grenade launcher, and he was launching grenades at the hootches. A couple of times he launched grenades at groups of people. The grenades would explode, you know, KAPLOW, and then you'd see pieces of bodies flying around.[4]

While all of the major American religious groups were represented in the antiwar movement, young Catholic priests and nuns were notably outspoken in their dissent. One of the most active of the Catholic peace advocates was Father Philip Berrigan, a Josephite priest and a veteran of World War II. In late October 1967, Berrigan and three other men broke into a Baltimore draft office, drenched the board records with blood, and waited to be arrested. They were tried and sent to prison. During the following spring, while out on bail, Berrigan was joined by his brother Daniel, a Jesuit priest, and seven other Catholic priests and lay people in the destruction of draft records at Catonsville, Maryland. The "Catonsville Nine," as they came to be called, were tried, convicted, and sentenced to prison. These shocking acts provided one measure of the tumultuous changes taking place in American society as a consequence of the far-off war in Southeast Asia.

One of the effective forms of antiwar protest was the draft-resistance

---

[3] The American public did not learn of this massacre until two years later, when Calley was court-martialed and convicted. By that time, similar incidents had come to light, and the full meaning of the Vietnam war's impact upon the United States was beginning to be understood.

[4] Richard Hammer, *One Morning in the War: The Tragedy at Son My* (1970), p. 128.

movement. Increasing reliance upon the Selective Service System imposed an enormous burden of uncertainty, coercion, and risk upon young American men, especially those from the lower and lower-middle classes who were unable to attend college and obtain educational deferments. Draft card "turn-ins" began to occur, and the public burning of such cards became a dramatic means of refusing to fight in Vietnam. Thousands of young men exiled themselves to Canada or Europe in order to avoid military duty. Mass protests were held outside induction centers. In October 1967 some 50 thousand demonstrators conducted a spectacular march on the Pentagon, hated symbol of the United States war machine. Resistance eventually began to appear within the military. The desertion rate from the armed forces mounted, and sizable communities of American deserters developed in Canada, Sweden, and other Western European countries.

The continuing escalation of the war tended not only to polarize public opinion on the issue but also to radicalize a significant proportion of the antiwar protestors. According to such New Left groups as the Students for a Democratic Society (SDS), the war in Vietnam was an expression of fundamental ills in American society, including the oppression of nonwhite people, imperialism, and the capitalist drive for raw materials, markets, and investment opportunities.

Plagued by ghetto riots, campus unrest, rising inflation, and sharp divisions over the Vietnam war, Lyndon Johnson lost popularity rapidly after 1965. While 63 percent of the people approved of Johnson's handling of the Presidency at the beginning of 1966, only 44 percent did so in October of that year. The President's problems were complicated by what many Americans began to perceive as his duplicity—his "credibility gap." Johnson, hoping and believing that every new increase in the American military effort in Vietnam would bring victory into sight, persisted in his course for a long time. He lashed out at his critics, contemptuously referring to "some Nervous Nellies and some who will become frustrated and bothered and break ranks under the strain."

In the fall of 1967 the White House launched an energetic campaign to win renewed support for the war, and the Pentagon reiterated its confidence in an early military victory for the United States. But the administration's problems were steadily exacerbated. The President's neglect of the ambitious reform programs of the mid-sixties dissipated much of his support within the United States. The economy was in serious trouble by 1967, with the cost of the war going up drastically and the resulting inflation becoming more and more acute. Some of the administration's ablest Great Society architects, including Secretary John W. Gardner of HEW, resigned because of the President's absorption in Vietnam. Secretary of Defense McNamara, who had been instrumental in

Figure 26 President Johnson Visits Seoul, South Korea, October 1966 *(Lyndon B. Johnson Library)*

formulating the strategic and technological rationale for the American escalation, left office in November 1967, having become increasingly unhappy over United States policy in Vietnam and dubious as to its effectiveness.

Early in 1968 the administration was dealt a series of heavy blows. First came the seizure by North Korea of the *U.S. Pueblo,* an intelligence ship cruising off the North Korean coast. This incident created a new American crisis in the Far East and led to drawn-out negotiations that finally secured the release of the crew but not the ship almost a year later. The Tet offensive followed hard on the heels of the *Pueblo* affair, and for many Americans that psychological setback was the last straw. Then, on March 12, Senator Eugene J. McCarthy, an announced candidate for the Democratic presidential nomination in 1968, made a surprisingly strong showing in the New Hampshire primary, winning 42.4 percent of the votes to President Johnson's 49.5 percent. Private polls indicated that McCarthy would defeat Johnson in the forthcoming Wisconsin primary. Four days after the New Hampshire primary, Robert F. Kennedy entered the Democratic presidential race as an active candidate. It was obvious that the President's renomination would be bitterly challenged and that the party was confronted with a bruising intraparty fight in the coming months. The mood of the country had become intensely bitter, public opinion was polarized, much of the nation's youth had been politicized,

Johnson's popularity had sunk to a new low, and the President himself had become a divisive force in a badly fragmented nation.

Johnson finally heeded those who contended that the United States must abandon the search for a decisive victory in Vietnam. A high-level review of American policy, brilliantly conducted by Clark Clifford, the new Secretary of Defense, convinced Johnson that further escalation would not guarantee greater success. By 1968 the conflict in Vietnam had become the longest war in American history. It was also one of the bloodiest, having involved more casualties than the Korean war. It had cost almost $100 billion, had brought incalculable losses to the Vietnam people, and had become the least popular war in the nation's experience. In a major address to a national television audience on March 31, the President announced that he was restricting the bombing of North Vietnam and inviting Hanoi to discuss a settlement of the war. At the end of his speech, Johnson made an even more startling announcement. "I have concluded," he declared, "that I should not permit the Presidency to become involved in the partisan divisions that are developing in this political year. . . . Accordingly, I shall not seek, and I will not accept, the nomination of my party for another term as your President."

The Election of 1968: The Center Holds

Ho Chi Minh responded with unexpected promptness to Johnson's peace overture of March 31, and after weeks of painfully slow progress, the two sides managed to begin formal negotiations in Paris on May 10. Although the war thereafter lost some of its terrible intensity, the military operations dragged on month after month, while the peace talks soon bogged down in the quicksand of basic differences separating the negotiators. Meantime, the bitter social division and conflict within the United States showed no signs of diminishing. With the nation on the verge of social disintegration, its citizens turned to politics and the national elections that would be held in November.

The focus of interest during the first half of the year was the struggle going on in the Democratic party. Three contestants for the party's presidential nomination dominated the center of the stage in the hectic spring of 1968: Eugene J. McCarthy, Robert F. Kennedy, and Hubert H. Humphrey. McCarthy, a handsome, soft-spoken congressional liberal with a sharp wit and an intellectual bent, brought thousands of students actively into his campaign. As the "peace candidate," he appealed to many elements of the New Left, as well as to various other groups calling for a "new politics."

In announcing his candidacy on March 16, Senator Kennedy told a press conference in the Senate caucus room where his older brother had declared his candidacy eight years earlier: "I run to seek new policies,

policies to end the bloodshed in Viet Nam and in our cities, policies to close the gap that now exists between black and white, between rich and poor, between young and old in this country and around the rest of the world." Kennedy plunged into a characteristically energetic campaign. Charismatic, ambitious, and hard-driving, "Bobby" aroused either passionate approval or intense dislike; he appealed strongly not only to those who venerated the memory of his martyred brother but also to Negroes, the lower-middle classes, and urban ethnic groups, many of whom looked on him as a zealous champion.

Vice President Humphrey announced his candidacy on April 27. Having the tacit support of President Johnson, Humphrey could count on the backing of party leaders throughout the country. While the two Democratic Senators fought it out in the primaries, the Vice President proceeded to gather a large number of convention delegates in the nonprimary states. A reluctant defender of the administration's foreign policies, Humphrey was also closely identified with the civil rights acts of the mid-1960s and with other reforms of the Great Society.

Meanwhile, Kennedy's vigorous and well-financed campaign was picking up steam. In May the New York Senator defeated his Minnesota opponent in Indiana and Nebraska, but then received a setback at the end of the month when McCarthy won the Oregon primary. The two candidates turned to California for a final showdown in the June 4 primary where 174 convention votes were at stake. The Kennedy forces were elated when they won a narrow victory in California with a 46 to 42 percent edge in primary votes. Then came another of those incredible and bizarre acts of violence which seemed almost more than the American people could bear. Robert Kennedy was fatally shot early on June 5 as he was leaving a victory celebration being held in Los Angeles's Ambassador Hotel. The police seized a young Jordanian immigrant named Sirhan Bishara Sirhan, a confused Arab zealot who probably resented the New York Senator's support of Israel. Once again the nation paused, stunned and saddened, as funeral rites were held for a second Kennedy.

The Democratic party never really recovered in 1968 from the shock of Robert F. Kennedy's assassination. McCarthy attracted much, though by no means all, of Kennedy's more than 300 delegates, and he consistently led the Vice President in the public opinion polls. Yet McCarthy's quest for delegates was attended by many handicaps, including his own introspective and enigmatic personality, the image of his campaign as a "children's crusade," the fact that most professional politicians distrusted him, and the success Humphrey achieved among party regulars in lining up delegates.

The convention itself, which was held in Chicago's Amphitheater in late August, was a bitter affair. After an angry debate, a "peace" plank calling for "an unconditional end to all bombing in North Vietnam" was voted down in favor of an endorsement of the President's efforts to achieve "an honorable and lasting settlement." Humphrey was easily nominated on the first ballot. He decided upon Edmund S. Muskie, a respected Senator from Maine, as his running mate. The Democrats adopted a platform in keeping with their traditional liberalism, and in spite of the steamroller tactics sometimes employed by the Humphrey managers, the delegates abrogated the long-established unit rule, refused to seat the segregationist Mississippi delegation, and initiated an unprecedented democratization of delegate selection to take effect in 1972.

In the meantime, a drama of street violence unfolded in downtown Chicago. Some 10,000 antiwar youths had descended upon the city, including such elements of the New Left as the Youth International Party (Yippies), to demonstrate against Johnson's Vietnam policy. In the tense atmosphere that resulted, a series of acrimonious and bloody clashes took place between the youthful demonstrators and the city police, who operated under the tight control of Mayor Richard J. Daley, a powerful old-time political boss and strong Humphrey partisan. Given orders to restrict the organized activities of the protestors and whipped into a frenzy by taunts, obscenities, and showers of stones, the police went "berserk" and turned brutally on their tormentors with clubs, tear gas, and mace. A nationwide television audience watched in fascinated horror as scenes of party warfare and of mayhem in the streets followed each other.

Republicans were spared such fierce intraparty struggles and bitter differences as they prepared for the campaign of 1968. The party's leading candidate at the outset was Governor George W. Romney of Michigan, a dynamic businessman who had built the failing American Motors Company into a going concern before entering politics. While a series of forthright but undiplomatic statements on Vietnam and other issues had hurt Romney's prestige, he formally announced his candidacy in November 1967. New York's Governor Nelson A. Rockefeller, who had foresworn future presidential ambitions in 1965, once more became interested in heading the national ticket following his election to a third gubernatorial term in 1966. Still a third aspirant from the ranks of the Republican governors was Ronald Reagan of California, who had defeated Governor Edmund G. (Pat) Brown in 1966 by more than a million votes.

The fourth major candidate was Richard M. Nixon, who had undergone a remarkable rehabilitation following his humiliating defeat at the hands of Pat Brown in 1962. Nixon left California following his failure to win the governorship and joined a prominent New York law firm. But he remained active in Republican affairs, speaking and attending party meetings all over the country. He won the gratitude of hundreds of

Republican candidates and party leaders by his extensive efforts in the campaign of 1966.[5] Nixon did not formally announce his candidacy until February 1, 1968, but he had determined long before to undertake a strenuous campaign in most of the party primaries in order to demonstrate his popular support and to erase his loser's image. The New Hampshire primary brought forth the "new Nixon"—relaxed and confident, gracious and unhurried, seemingly without bitterness or rancor.

Nixon quickly established his dominance in the Republican contest for the presidential nomination. Romney abandoned his campaign two weeks before the New Hampshire election, while Rockefeller entered the race too late to mount an effective challenge to Nixon. Meanwhile, the former Vice President won a number of significant preferential primaries and steadily added to his delegate strength in nonprimary states. Nixon was concerned over the threat that Reagan posed in the South and in other conservative quarters, but he dealt with this potential barrier by holding private talks with a number of important Southern Republicans in Atlanta on May 31 and June 1. He assured such Republican leaders as Senator J. Strom Thurmond of South Carolina of his sympathy for their position on questions like school busing and law and order.

The Republican National Convention was held in Miami Beach, Florida, in early August. Nixon was nominated on the first ballot. To the surprise of most observers, he chose Governor Spiro T. Agnew of Maryland for second place on the ticket. Agnew was acceptable to conservatives like Thurmond, and the selection of the Governor, rather than a representative of the liberal wing of the party, was another indication of what became known as Nixon's "Southern strategy." The GOP platform emphasized an "all-out" campaign against crime, reform of the welfare laws, an end to inflation, and a stronger national defense. On Vietnam the platform promised to "de-Americanize" the war, to engage in "clear and purposeful negotiations," and not to accept "a camouflaged surrender."

The national campaign was well under way by early September. The Republicans, confident that they would be able to smash the divided Democrats, unleashed the most elaborate and expensive presidential campaign in United States history. Nixon campaigned at a deliberate, dignified pace, seeking to dramatize the nation's decline at home and abroad under two Democratic administrations. The Democratic campaign, by contrast, started very badly. The disastrous Chicago convention still hung like a pall over the party. The Democrats also faced a serious challenge from the third-party candidacy of Governor George C. Wallace of Alabama.

[5]The Republicans gained forty-seven House and three Senate seats in 1966, as well as eight governorships.

Increasingly unhappy with the Democratic party's national policies, Wallace finally organized what he labeled the American Independent party; he selected General Curtis E. LeMay, former Chief of the Strategic Air Command, to run with him on a national ticket. Well-financed by wealthy conservatives and many grass-roots donations, the new party was able to get itself listed on the ballots of all fifty states. Wallace developed surprising strength, not only among white Southerners but also among blue-collar groups and the lower-middle class in other regions, where there was often rising tension between white and black America. A short, pugnacious man with a quick wit and a folksy speaking style, Wallace liked to assert that there was not "a dime's worth of difference" between the two major parties. He promised a policy of victory in Vietnam and tough measures at home against dope users, hippies, and Communists.

Nixon, in a subtle way, appealed to many of the same fears and prejudices that Wallace aroused. But the Republican nominee's basic strategy was to seize the middle by stressing peace and healing, in contrast to the demagogic Wallace and the divided Democrats, whose failings Nixon promised to repair. Agnew, on the other hand, was given the task of capturing as much of the right as possible from Wallace. The Maryland Governor fulfilled this assignment with a series of blunt speeches, attacks on left-wing dissident groups, and racial slurs.

For the Republican party, Humphrey appeared to be an ideal opponent: he could not dissociate himself from his party's record in Washington without provoking a counterrevolution within the Democratic organization itself. Nevertheless, from the rock-bottom position his campaign had reached in September, Humphrey began to move upward. During October the Vice President's aggressive, underdog campaigning began to have an effect. Senator Muskie's low-keyed personality and calm and forceful style made him a distinct asset to the Democratic cause. Humphrey was searching for a way in which to take an independent line without actually repudiating President Johnson. He made what seemed to be a significant move in this direction in a televised speech in Salt Lake City on September 30. "As President," he declared, "I would stop the bombing of the North as an acceptable risk for peace." On November 1, just before the election, Johnson made a dramatic effort to get the stalled peace talks moving and to help his party win. He proclaimed a complete halt in the bombing of North Vietnam on that day.[6]

By early November the Humphrey surge had brought the Democrats

[6]Johnson also announced that the United States and North Vietnam had agreed that South Vietnam and the NLF could begin taking part in the peace talks. Unfortunately, the South Vietnam government, hoping no doubt for greater backing from a Republican administration in Washington, refused to join in the discussions, thereby neutralizing the Democratic advantage resulting from Johnson's action on November 1.

almost abreast of the Republican ticket in the public opinion polls. But Nixon won a narrow victory, receiving 31.7 million votes to 31.2 million for Humphrey and 9.9 million for Wallace. Nixon carried thirty-two states and 301 electoral votes, while Humphrey was successful in thirteen states with 191 electoral votes. Wallace carried five Southern states and received 46 electoral votes. Both houses of Congress remained in Democratic hands.

The Republicans obviously took advantage of the disarray and division in the Democratic party. Vietnam was clearly both an immediate cause of Democratic enervation and a catalyst and symbol of more widespread dissatisfaction with the party's programs and policies. Many youthful idealists sat out the campaign, a good many liberals failed to vote at all, support from various of the traditional Democratic components declined somewhat, and even the usually reliable black vote dropped 11 percent from 1964. The Democrats suffered defections from the South, from blue-collar workers, and from the left. The Republicans conducted a well-organized and well-financed campaign. Nixon solidified the "law and order" tendencies of the GOP center, and his Southern strategy enabled him to divide the South with Wallace, without subtracting much from his support in the Midwest and West. The public, it seemed, sought out the "decisive middle ground" in the politics of 1968, and as David S. Broder has remarked, the central paradox of the election is that, in a year of almost unprecedented violence, turmoil, and political oscillations, the electorate gave "a terribly conventional result."

The result was hardly conventional from the point of view of the Democratic party and President Johnson. In four years a Democratic presidential plurality of 16 million votes had evaporated. From 1965 on, the Johnsonian consensus had declined in a steady curve, its fragile structure shattered by war, inflation, racial strife, and widespread disillusionment with the leadership and personality of the President. Thus the election of 1968 was the final scene in the tragedy of Lyndon Johnson.

SUGGESTIONS FOR FURTHER READING

Several of the books previously cited, including those by Ambrose, LaFeber, O'Neill, Osgood, and Spanier, deal in part with the foreign policies of the Johnson administration. Philip L. Geyelin, *Lyndon B. Johnson and the World* (1969), is a general treatment. Edward Weintal and Charles Bartlett, *Facing the Brink: An Intimate Study of Crisis Diplomacy* (1967), is a journalistic account of Kennedy and Johnson leadership in foreign affairs. David Halberstam's *The Best and the Brightest** (1972) offers a critical assessment of several key presidential advisers in the areas of military strategy and diplomacy. William B. Bader's *The United States and the Spread of Nuclear Weapons** (1968) is useful on arms control.

*Available in paperback edition.

One of the best of the studies of Johnson's intervention in the Dominican Republic is Theodore Draper's *The Dominican Revolt: A Case Study in American Policy* (1968). For two good reports by journalists, see Dan Kurzman, *Santo Domingo: Revolt of the Damned* (1965), and Tad Szulc, *Dominican Diary** (1965). Jerome Slater, *The OAS and United States Foreign Policy* (1967), analyzes the operation of the inter-American organization.

The literature on Vietnam is vast and still growing. A good beginning place is Frances Fitzgerald, *Fire in the Lake: The Vietnamese and the Americans in Vietnam** (1972), which also considers Vietnamese politics and culture. Other valuable books include Bernard Fall, *The Two Viet-Nams: A Political and Military Analysis* (2d rev. ed., 1967); Robert Shaplen, *Road from War: Vietnam, 1965–1970** (1970); George M. Kahin and John W. Lewis, *The United States in Vietnam** (rev. ed., 1969); David Kraslow and Stuart H. Loory, *The Secret Search for Peace in Vietnam** (1968); Townsend Hoopes, *The Limits of Intervention: An Inside Account of How the Johnson Policy of Escalation in Vietnam Was Reversed** (1969); Chester L. Cooper, *The Lost Crusade: America in Vietnam** (1970); and Robert W. Tucker, *Nation or Empire: The Debate over American Foreign Policy** (1968).

J. William Fulbright, *The Arrogance of Power** (1966), is an important critique by the leading Senate critic of American policy in Vietnam. Norman Mailer, *Armies of the Night: History as a Novel, the Novel as History** (1968), is concerned with the march on the Pentagon in October 1967. Among critical works by revisionists on the left are Noam Chomsky, *American Power and the New Mandarins** (1969), and Richard J. Barnet, *Roots of War* (1972). On the war and United States brutality in Vietnam, see Don Oberdorfer, *TET** (1971); Seymour M. Hersh, *My Lai 4: A Report on the Massacre and Its Aftermath** (1970); and Richard Hammer, *One Morning in the War: The Tragedy at Son My** (1970). Kirkpatrick Sale, *SDS** (1973), throws light on the largest New Left organization.

Theodore H. White's *The Making of the President, 1968** (1969) is readable and informative. Lewis Chester, Godfrey Hodgson, and Bruce Page, *American Melodrama: The Presidential Campaign of 1968* (1969), is an absorbing account by three British journalists. For more restricted treatments, consult Joe McGinniss, *The Selling of the President, 1968* (1969); Jules Witcover, *The Resurrection of Richard Nixon* (1970); Witcover, *85 Days: The Last Campaign of Robert Kennedy** (1969); and Marshall Frady, *Wallace** (1968). Kevin Phillips, *The Emerging Republican Majority** (1969), offers an interesting analysis of the broader implications of Nixon's election in 1968. Richard M. Scammon and Ben J. Wattenberg, *The Real Majority** (1970), emphasizes the importance of the so-called "social issue" in contemporary American politics.

Chapter 14

The Nixon
Years Begin

Richard M. Nixon's victory in the election of 1968 and his inauguration as
the nation's thirty-seventh President on January 20, 1969, seemed to mark
the beginning of a new era in American politics. Yet the meaning of the
transfer of power in Washington was far from clear, and the prospects for
the new Republican era were uncertain. Nixon had not won a clear-cut
mandate; he was a minority President facing a Congress controlled by the
opposition party. The center he represented was apparently holding, but
there was widespread discontent over taxes, big government, bureaucracy, special privilege, and the war in Southeast Asia. Foreign affairs
reflected a similar ambiguity involving such developments as the emergence of the People's Republic of China as a third great power center, the
growing United States concern with Asia and the Third World, mounting·
opposition to foreign aid programs, and an upsurge of isolationist
sentiment.

The Return of Richard Nixon

Richard Milhous Nixon, the second of five sons in a hard-working Quaker
family, was born on January 9, 1913, in Yorba Linda, California, a farming

community in the southern part of the state. He grew up in nearby Whittier, was graduated from Whittier College, and attended the Duke University Law School in North Carolina, where he worked hard and compiled a good academic record. After receiving his law degree, he returned to Whittier to practice and in 1940 married a local schoolteacher named Thelma "Pat" Ryan. During World War II the young lawyer served as a naval supply officer in the South Pacific. After the war Nixon was presented with an opportunity to enter politics, and he made the most of his chance, unseating Congressman Jerry Voorhis with a hard-hitting and somewhat demagogic campaign in 1946. In Washington Nixon soon made a name for himself as a member of the House Committee on Un-American Activities. He moved up to the Senate in 1950 by defeating Helen Gahagan Douglas in another campaign characterized on Nixon's part by charges of radicalism and the use of guilt by association tactics. Two years later Senator Nixon was selected by General Eisenhower as his running mate on the Republican national ticket.

Nixon continued to be a controversial figure during his eight years as Vice President. His loss of the presidency by an eyelash in 1960 and his devastating defeat in the California gubernatorial election of 1962 set the stage for an incredible recovery and political vindication in 1968. Totally absorbed in political affairs, this intensely ambitious and rigorously disciplined man was determined to succeed. There was a streak of ruthlessness in his character, a tendency toward arrogance and self-righteousness, and the self-made man's emphasis upon the moral value of success. Basically a somewhat shy and introverted person, Nixon was also secretive, sensitive, and rather lonely—easily hurt, prone to lash back at his critics, always careful not to reveal too much of himself. He was neither charismatic nor eloquent, but in the troubled sixties he appealed to more and more Americans because he gave expression to, indeed he embodied, traditional American virtues and aspirations which millions of people continued to cherish and desperately wanted to maintain.

During the interim between his election and his inauguration, Nixon and Johnson cooperated in effecting a smooth transition in the presidency. The President-elect announced the makeup of his Cabinet in December. William P. Rogers, an urbane New York lawyer who had served as Attorney General under Eisenhower, was appointed Secretary of State. David M. Kennedy, a Chicago banker, was named Secretary of the Treasury, while Representative Melvin R. Laird, a hawkish member of the House Armed Services Committee from Wisconsin, took over as Secretary of Defense. Nixon's New York law partner and campaign manager, John N. Mitchell, became Attorney General. Two Harvard University professors were brought into the new administration as

Figure 27 Inauguration of the Thirty-seventh President, January 20, 1969 *(U.S. Army Photograph)*

Presidential advisers: Henry A. Kissinger in the area of national security and foreign affairs and Daniel P. Moynihan in the field of urban affairs and domestic policies.

Nixon sought to foster the spirit of moderation, and he pledged himself to put an end to inflated rhetoric and exaggerated promises emanating from the White House. Stressing organization with clearly defined lines of authority and areas of responsibility, the new President established the most elaborate array of assistants and councils in the history of the executive branch. Nixon was far more interested in international questions than in domestic problems, in part no doubt because his party's dominant constituency and orientation gave him somewhat greater latitude in that sphere. He carefully set about defusing the explosive tensions surrounding United States involvement in Vietnam. At the same time, there were signs that the Nixon administration would not drastically change Johnson's policies in Southeast Asia. The selection of Henry Cabot Lodge as chief negotiator in Paris and the retention of Ellsworth Bunker as Ambassador to Saigon were straws in the wind. Nixon's increasing reliance on the tough-minded Henry Kissinger, who emphasized stability as the goal of policy and military power as the most trusted instrument, provided another clue to the President's basic ideas on foreign policy.

Nixon's restrained and prudent course elicited general approval in the United States. Tensions subsided and the public mood changed, not to one of optimism as much as to one of relief over the passing of the bitter divisions associated with the Johnson administration. People seemed prepared to give the new administration a chance to end the war, unify the country, and formulate policies for the solution of troublesome social problems. In July 1969, while this mood persisted, *Apollo 11* landed on the moon after a long and dramatic flight. Americans everywhere felt a thrill of exultation as Commander Neil Armstrong and Colonel Edwin E. Aldrin made a perfect landing on the Sea of Tranquility and became the first earth men to walk on the moon.

The Persistence of Vietnam

President Nixon's most pressing task was to end the Vietnam war. Not only had he committed himself to the solution of the Vietnamese problem, but failure to end it, or at the very least to remove most American combat forces before 1972, might well drive him from the presidency. The United States position was that all outside forces should be withdrawn from South Vietnam and that the voters of that country should decide their future in internationally supervised elections. The North Vietnamese and the National Liberation Front insisted upon a complete withdrawal of American forces and the installation in Saigon of a coalition government that would include the NLF. The Thieu regime was fiercely resolved to continue as the dominant element in any postwar government, and the

Figure 28 Astronaut Edwin E. Aldrin, Jr., Walks on the Moon *(National Aeronautics and Space Administration)*

Figure 29 American Troops Move Up a Canal on a Search and Destroy Mission near Dong Tam, August 1969 *(U.S. Army Photograph)*

United States, while trying from time to time to persuade South Vietnam to moderate its position, was unwilling to sacrifice the existing government, which Washington associated with the right of self-determination for the South Vietnamese. Its survival thus became, to the United States, an essential requirement for a peace settlement.

A variety of proposals and counterproposals were presented as the peace talks dragged on. The talks frequently stalled and sometimes broke down completely, only to be resumed after a few weeks. The United States sought to convince the other side of its error in two ways. One was the process of "Vietnamization"—building up the ARVN forces and preparing them to take over an increasingly large part of the fighting. The other was the massive use of American air power, tactical and strategic, in direct support of ground operations and in attacks upon North Vietnamese supply routes, bases, and production centers.

The administration hoped to disarm its critics and to ease the antiwar tensions at home by a systematic reduction of United States combat troops in South Vietnam. The President announced in June 1969 that 25,000 men were being sent home without replacements, and in December 1969 he ordered the withdrawal of an additional 50,000 soldiers. The process continued until the number of American troops had declined from a high of 543,000 in the spring of 1969 to approximately 255,000 by May 1971. Meanwhile, monthly draft quotas were reduced, and the administration eventually reorganized the Selective Service System and replaced its unpopular director.[1] Nixon also outlined what became known as the Nixon Doctrine. The United States, he declared, would remain a Pacific power safeguarding Asia's peace; but the principal responsibility for Asian security and development must rest with the Asians themselves.

Despite the general disposition in the United States to give the administration time in which to work out a settlement in Vietnam and the widespread approval of troop reductions and such pronouncements as the Nixon Doctrine, antiwar feeling remained strong. In the fall of 1969 a series of antiwar demonstrations erupted throughout the country. Hundreds of rallies and mass observances were held on October 15, and a second "moratorium" staged a month later drew still larger crowds. Some 250,000 persons participated in a three-day demonstration in the national capital, with a "March against Death" proceeding from Arlington National Cemetery to Capitol Hill. President Nixon denounced the demonstrators in a television address on November 3, 1969, stated that he planned to remove all American ground forces from Vietnam (though he failed to be specific about such plans), and pleaded for more time. Vice President Agnew also spoke out sharply against the peace demonstrators, condemn-

---

[1]The complicated deferment system was replaced with a lottery, which would enable most young men to learn at the age of nineteen what the probability was of their having to enter the armed forces, either then or after completing college.

United States Military Forces in South Vietnam, 1965–1973

Year	Number
1965	184,300
1966	385,300
1967	485,600
1968	536,100
1969	475,200
1970	334,600
1971	157,800
1973*	23,500

*As of January 27, 1973, when the cease-fire agreement was signed.
Sources: United States Department of Defense, Office of the Secretary, Selected Manpower Statistics, annual and unpublished data; New York Times, Feb. 28, 1973.

ing them on one occasion as "an effete corps of impudent snobs who characterize themselves as intellectuals."

Then came the shock of Cambodia. In late April 1970, in a step long urged by United States military leaders, the President announced an American-South Vietnam invasion of Communist staging areas in Cambodia. The Cambodian "incursion" was also justified as necessary to prevent the Communists from taking over all of Cambodia. Addressing the American people on the evening of April 30, Nixon called the military move "indispensable" for the continuing success of his withdrawal program. The advancing troops, supported by powerful United States air forays, failed to uncover the elusive command headquarters of the enemy, but they located extensive Vietcong supply centers and huge stores of materials.

The Cambodian invasion triggered an outbreak of violence and turmoil in the United States. Just when Nixon was supposedly winding down the war, he had extended it to another country in Southeast Asia. The contradictions between Nixon's earlier claims for Vietnamization and his alarmist statements about powerful enemy forces threatening South Vietnam were especially disturbing to many Americans. Reaction to the President's announcement was notably violent on college and university campuses. In one of the demonstrations, at Kent State University in Ohio, a confrontation between students and National Guardsmen ended on May 4 with four students fatally shot and eleven others wounded.[2] Student protests soon forced more than 400 colleges and universities to close, and many of these institutions did not reopen until summer or fall.

The severe criticism of the Cambodian invasion and the upheaval it produced on college campuses shook the President. He agreed to talk to six Kent State students who had traveled to Washington, conferred with the presidents of eight universities, and asked Chancellor Alexander Heard of Vanderbilt University to serve as a special liaison between the universities and the White House. Still, Nixon's interest in placating his critics did not last long, partly perhaps because a good many Americans seemed to approve of his Cambodian policy and to oppose the antiwar protests. On May 8, 1970, for example, a group of protesting students in New York City was brutally attacked by helmeted construction workers who bludgeoned them with wrenches and clubs. Shouting "all the way, U.S.A.," the hard hats then marched on City Hall and raised the American flag.

[2]A report made subsequently by the President's Commission on Campus Unrest, while critical of actions by the student protestors at Kent State, condemned the casual issuance of live ammunition to guardsmen and denounced their "indiscriminate firing" as "unnecessary, unwarranted and inexcusable."

Nixon had not consulted or even informed Congress prior to announcing his move into Cambodia, and the congressional response to the invasion was sharp and critical. A bipartisan amendment to a military bill, sponsored by Senators Frank Church of Idaho and John Sherman Cooper of Kentucky, sought to require the President to withdraw all American troops from Cambodia by June 30, 1970, and to forbid any new strikes into that country. Although weakened by changes, the measure was adopted by the Senate on June 30. Late in 1970 Congress voted to deny funds for any further United States ground operations in Cambodia and repealed the Tonkin Gulf resolution. Meanwhile, Senators Mark Hatfield of Oregon and George S. McGovern of South Dakota proposed an amendment that would have required the withdrawal of all American troops from Vietnam by the end of 1971.

The progress of Vietnamization was tested in February 1971, when South Vietnamese troops invaded Laos, which had long been subjected to heavy air bombardment by United States bombers. Assuming that a major offensive by the South Vietnamese army was now feasible, American leaders approved a large-scale ARVN offensive, with strong United States air support, in an attempt to cut the Ho Chi Minh trail in eastern Laos, the vital supply route for men and materials flowing south from North Vietnam. The offensive went badly for the invaders. Communist forces outflanked the South Vietnam units, destroying some of them and forcing others into headlong retreat. In the meantime, the Vietcong challenged the pacification efforts in South Vietnam, shelling cities and raiding villages that were assumed to be invulnerable to attack.

The invasion of Laos provoked new antiwar protests, and in April 1971 demonstrators were back in Washington. The reaction against the Laotian venture was heightened when Americans began to learn that approximately 25,000 South Vietnamese civilians had been killed and 100,000 wounded during the past two years of fighting. The public awareness of the massacres of Vietnam civilians by United States servicemen was intensified by the military trial of Lieutenant William L. Calley, Jr., which began at Fort Benning, Georgia, in November 1970. On March 29, 1971, a court composed of six Army officers found Calley guilty, personally, of the premeditated murder of at least twenty-two unarmed civilians. He was sentenced to life imprisonment.[3]

The Nixon administration countered the antiwar protests and criticisms of its policies in Vietnam with a combination of rebuffs to the peace advocates and a continuation of the troop withdrawals. Yet as the war ground on, there was a growing loss of credibility in administration

---

[3]Calley's conviction was reversed by a federal court in 1974 because of major flaws in his prosecution under military law.

policies and pronouncements concerning Vietnam. These doubts were increased by the publication, in June 1971, of excerpts from the so-called Pentagon Papers. Daniel Ellsberg, a military analyst who had worked for the Defense Department, had photocopied a massive study of United States involvement in Vietnam that had been commissioned by the Pentagon. Ellsberg made these documents available to the press. The Pentagon Papers not only suggested that the Kennedy and Johnson administrations had made a fairly steady effort to widen the American role in the Vietnam war, but they also revealed the government's lack of candor in explaining certain details of this policy to the public.

In March 1972 the Communists launched their heaviest offensive since the Tet campaign four years earlier. With most of the American ground forces gone and the burden of defense on the South Vietnamese troops, the enemy soon overran Quangtri province in the north, made strong advances in the central and southern sections, and inflicted heavy losses on the ARVN units before the situation was stabilized and some of the lost ground was recovered. With his Vietnamization program in jeopardy, Nixon again resorted to drastic action. Contending that the Communist offensive violated the implicit understanding under which President Johnson had halted the bombing of North Vietnam in 1968, Nixon ordered renewed attacks north of the DMZ, first with sporadic retaliatory raids and then with sustained air bombardments. In a television address on May 8, the President announced an even bolder move— the mining of Haiphong and other North Vietnamese ports.

By this time, the war had assumed a surrealistic quality. As one staff officer remarked, "Often it reminded me of the caucus race in 'Alice in Wonderland.' Everyone runs in circles, no one really gets anywhere, and when the race is over, everybody gets a medal."[4]

The Nixon Presidency and Domestic Problems

In domestic affairs the thirty-seventh President was also confronted with pressing problems. While Nixon failed to launch any bold new programs during the first part of his Presidency, he made a special effort to identify his administration with the "silent majority" and "middle America," as against militants, radicals, and youthful dissenters. After a brief period of amicability, Nixon's relations with Congress worsened as partisan tensions increased and recurrent deadlocks occurred. The Chief Executive frequently succeeded in dominating the Democratically controlled Congress by masterful timing, skillful maneuvering, and effective presenta-

[4]Quoted in William L. O'Neill, *Coming Apart: An Informal History of America in the 1960's* (1971), pp. 405–406.

tion of his case through television and other media. One of Nixon's first triumphs was the approval of the antiballistic missile program originally sponsored by the Johnson administration. Despite strong opposition, Congress authorized an ABM system by a narrow margin in the summer of 1969.

One area in which Nixon hoped to effect substantial change was the composition of the Supreme Court. He was eager to add "strict constructionists" to the tribunal and to overcome the liberal majority that had dominated the Warren Court. The President thought the Court had swung too far in the liberal direction under Chief Justice Warren, and thus he threw his weight on the side of the wide-ranging criticism of Supreme Court decisions in such fields as civil rights, school prayers, and obscenity cases.

President Nixon's first appointment to the Supreme Court was Warren E. Burger, who was named Chief Justice when Warren retired in June 1969. Burger, a respected conservative who had served as a court of appeals judge, was readily confirmed by the Senate. This was not the case with Clement F. Haynsworth, Jr., whom Nixon appointed to replace Abe Fortas in 1969.[5] Haynsworth, a federal circuit court judge from South Carolina, was strongly opposed by several civil rights groups and labor organizations because of his conservative opinions. It was also charged that he had owned stock in a company involved in litigation before his court. A furious debate broke out over the nomination, and in November 1969 the Senate voted 55 to 45 against his confirmation. Much annoyed by this rebuff, Nixon then submitted the name of G. Harrold Carswell, a Floridian who had recently been appointed to the Fifth Circuit Court of Appeals. Carswell was not only open to the charge of having been a racist earlier in his career, but his record on the bench was decidedly mediocre and he had been frequently overruled on appeal. The Senate rejected Carswell by a vote of 51 to 45. In his next effort Nixon succeeded. The Senate, in May 1970, unanimously approved the nomination of Harry A. Blackmun, a federal judge from Minnesota known for his judicial scholarship.

The conservatism of the Burger Court was further strengthened in the fall of 1971 when Justice Black died and Justice Harlan resigned. Nixon replaced them with two staunch conservatives: Lewis F. Powell, a

[5]Fortas resigned in May 1969 after it was learned that he had received an annual stipend from a family foundation established by promoter Louis Wolfson, who was subsequently sent to prison for illegal stock manipulation. Ironically, President Johnson had nominated Fortas as Chief Justice in June 1968, when Warren indicated his desire to retire. The nomination was severely criticized in the Senate on the ground that Justice Fortas was a "crony" of the President and had violated judicial ethics by continuing to act as a White House adviser. Fortas finally asked Johnson to withdraw his nomination.

well-known Virginia lawyer, and Assistant Attorney General William H. Rehnquist of Arizona. Thus within three years Nixon had been able to transform the High Court, and before the end of his first term the new conservative majority had begun to chip away at some of the Warren Court's rulings, particularly in criminal law decisions. Nevertheless, the Court did not entirely reverse the humane precedents laid down under Chief Justice Warren. In *Furman v. Georgia* (1972), the Court advanced to a new liberal position by holding capital punishment unconstitutional as "cruel and unusual," except when the law made it mandatory.

Nixon also tried in other ways to identify himself as a champion of law and order. His administration made greater use of wiretapping and other electronic surveillance of organized crime, obtained increased support for the Law Enforcement Assistance Administration, and sponsored a special District of Columbia Criminal Justice bill which Congress finally passed in 1970. Other new statutes, including the organized crime law of 1970, limited immunities under the Fifth Amendment, permitted a judge to lengthen the sentence of a dangerous criminal, and provided the death penalty for bombings involving loss of life.

The Nixon administration's approach to civil rights and the condition of blacks was clearly meant to implement his Southern strategy. The Department of Justice, in sharp contrast to its position under Kennedy and Johnson, opposed the extension of the Voting Rights Act of 1965, proposing unsuccessfully to replace it with a uniform national law. The administration also attempted to slow the pace of school desegregation in the South. In 1969 HEW relaxed its policy against five school districts in South Carolina and flip-flopped in handling litigation involving thirty-three Mississippi school districts (after having earlier approved desegregation plans for the fall term).[6]

President Nixon defended his administration's civil rights policies in a comprehensive statement issued in March 1970. He announced that he would ask Congress for $1.5 billion to improve education in racially impacted areas and to help school districts meet problems caused by court-directed desegregation. But Nixon emphasized the distinction between *de jure* segregation based on discriminatory laws and *de facto* segregation based on residential patterns, and he promised that "transportation beyond normal geographical school zones for the purpose of achieving a racial balance will not be required." In January of the following year the President announced his firm opposition to federal efforts to "force integration of the suburbs," calling such measures "counterproductive, and not in the interest of race relations."

[6]The Supreme Court eventually overruled the delaying action in the Mississippi case, and in *Alexander v. Holmes County* (1969) Chief Justice Burger, speaking for a unanimous Court, declared that "the obligation of every school district is to terminate dual school systems at once and to operate now and hereafter only unitary schools."

One of the administration's boldest domestic proposals was its plan for the revision of the nation's welfare programs. Strongly influenced by Daniel Patrick Moynihan, the President sent Congress a message in August 1969 recommending "the transformation of welfare into 'workfare,' a new work-rewarding system." Instead of the existing federal welfare grants, the government under the Nixon-Moynihan Family Assistance Plan (FAP) would make a cash payment to guarantee a prescribed minimum income level—$1,600 a year for a family of four in which there was no wage earner. Such a family could also receive food stamps valued at $820 a year. Nixon's welfare reform proposal created quite a stir, and during the controversy that followed the measure's introduction it was attacked by both the right and the left. The House passed a bill containing the basic features of the Nixon program in 1970, but the Senate Finance Committee failed to report it. A new and somewhat more ambitious version of the measure was approved by the House in June 1971, but the Senate remained divided over the issue. Thus the FAP was not enacted during Nixon's first term, and the President himself, sensing the deep middle-class resentment against welfare recipients, eventually abandoned the scheme.

President Nixon looked to the midterm elections of 1970 for popular endorsement and legislative support of his program. Nixon and Agnew joined other Republican leaders in conducting a strenuous campaign that year. Agnew had emerged as an outspoken and controversial champion of the administration, and in numerous speaking engagements he lashed out at dissident college students, critics of American involvement in Vietnam, radicals, hippies, and network television commentators, whom he described as "a tiny and closed fraternity of privileged men" biased toward the Eastern establishment. Nixon took a more elevated road, but he too assumed the familiar role of partisan campaigner. The outcome was extremely disappointing to the administration: while the Democrats lost two seats in the Senate, they gained nine in the House.

When the new Congress convened in January 1971, Nixon urged its members to prepare the way for "a New American Revolution." The President's extravagant rhetoric on this occasion was somewhat reminiscent of the so-called "new federalism" he had first enunciated to Congress in the summer of 1969. The most substantial result of the new federalism was "revenue sharing," which Nixon repeatedly advocated and formally presented in his State of the Union message in January 1971. In order to halt the steady enlargement of the central government and return more responsibilities to the local communities, the plan would eliminate a number of specific federal programs and substitute general-purpose grants to the states and cities to administer as they thought best. Revenue sharing soon became mired in controversy, but it was eventually approved, in October 1972, as the State and Local Fiscal Assistance Act.

The act provided for the sharing of $30.2 billion in federal revenue over a five-year period, with $5.2 billion to be allocated in 1972 on the basis of two-thirds to local governments and one-third to the states. Local officials soon began to complain that the new system, which coincided with drastic reductions or freezes in various federal programs, was likely to worsen rather than relieve their revenue plight.

The administration's timid approach to conservation and environmental issues reflected its probusiness orientation and the fact that the principal polluters were large corporations in such industries as automobiles, aviation, and petroleum. Most environmentalists opposed Nixon's efforts to win continued support for the development of a supersonic transport (SST), and in this case the President suffered a setback when the Senate, under the leadership of William Proxmire of Wisconsin, voted against further appropriations for the SST in December 1970. Nixon had appointed Walter J. Hickel of Alaska as Secretary of the Interior, and surprisingly Hickel became something of an environmentalist. He halted drillings in the Santa Barbara Channel after a severe oil spill, persuaded the Justice Department to prosecute the Chevron Oil Company for polluting the Gulf of Mexico, took firm action to protect the Florida Everglades from a proposed jet airport, and held up construction of the trans-Alaskan oil pipeline that threatened the native tundra, before being fired in November 1970.

Perhaps the most pressing domestic problem facing Richard Nixon was the mounting inflation, which had intensified during the last years of the Johnson administration. The cost of living rose more than 7 percent in 1969, and it continued to go up at a high rate. Nixon realized the importance of halting inflation, but he was limited in dealing with the problem by his conservative economic philosophy. The administration's anti-inflation program at first revolved around tighter credit and a cut in government spending. The Federal Reserve Board raised interest rates so sharply during the first six months of 1969, however, that many businessmen became alarmed, and the tight money policy was relaxed in the fall. Nixon's attempt to reduce federal expenditures proved equally unsuccessful; the budget was increased every year, and there were large annual deficits ($23 billion in fiscal 1971, for example). The President's program for the ABM, space exploration, and continued involvement in Vietnam wiped out any economies he managed to make in health, education, and housing.

In May 1970 the Dow-Jones index of stock prices dropped from almost 1,000 to below 700. During the following month the Penn Central Railroad went bankrupt. Corporate profits, industrial production, automobile sales, and new construction slipped. Someone coined the word "Nixonomics" to describe the curious combination of lagging output and soaring prices. With the economy still sluggish and the price index continuing to rise, Nixon finally adopted a new economic policy. In a television address on August 15, 1971, he announced that, under authority previously given him by Congress (which he had vowed never to use!), he was freezing all wages, prices, and rents for ninety days. In an effort to improve the position of the dollar abroad, he cut its tie with gold and permitted it to "float" freely in foreign exchange. He imposed a 10 percent surtax on a wide list of imported goods and requested Congress to change the tax laws as a stimulus to industry. He established a Cost of Living Council headed by Secretary of the Treasury John B. Connally to administer the new program. In December 1971, at an international monetary conference held in Washington, the United States agreed to reduce the exchange value of the dollar by about 12 percent and to drop the 10 percent import surtax in return for increases in the exchange rate of foreign currencies and other trade concessions. Phase Two of the President's plan was initiated in November 1971, with the introduction of a system of controls administered by a price commission and a pay board.

Nixon's new economic policy was only partially successful. The rate of inflation declined to 3.2 percent during the first year of the policy's operation, wages were generally held within the 5.5 percent increase, and production rose substantially. But food prices went up at a 4.2 percent rate, unemployment did not drop below 5.5 percent, and American trade deficits continued to be large.

Old Approaches and New Initiatives Abroad

Although Nixon seemed to appreciate the need to change the nation's overextended and overbearing international posture, his basic instincts were those of the cold warrior. As the *New York Times* observed after two years of the Nixon administration, "President Nixon has labored to protect and to perfect the foreign-affairs concepts of the last two decades against the widespread disenchantment with Vietnam and against the allure of insular doctrines." Nixon was consistently able to dominate Congress in dealing with international affairs.[7] He also moved quickly to centralize the most critical aspects of foreign policy formulation and implementation within the White House.

The tentative steps Kennedy and Johnson had taken toward a détente with the Soviet Union were endangered during the late 1960s by the Vietnam war and the tense situation in the Middle East. Nixon hoped to ease tensions between the two superpowers through a mutual agreement

---

[7]Nixon's reliance upon Henry A. Kissinger in the formulation and conduct of his personal diplomacy worried some congressmen. Several senators publicly warned that Kissinger exerted far more influence in the shaping of American diplomacy than did Secretary William P. Rogers. Unlike the Secretary of State, Kissinger could not be summoned before congressional committees to explain and defend his policies. As the President's personal adviser, he was able to invoke executive immunity.

to limit strategic nuclear weapons. He expressed great satisfaction over the Senate's approval of the Nuclear Nonproliferation Treaty in March 1969, and during the following November he unilaterally renounced American use of biological warfare and chemical weapons except for defense. The Strategic Arms Limitation Talks (SALT) were resumed in Helsinki, Finland, in November 1969. The two cold war antagonists agreed in 1971 to modernize and strengthen their hot-line communications link. More important was the breakthrough that came in August 1971, when the Russians offered new guarantees to keep the access routes open into Berlin from West Germany, in exchange for an Allied promise to reduce the city's political significance for the West and allow a Russian consulate in Berlin. While moving to ease the conflict over Berlin, Brezhnev suggested the possibility of a general settlement in Central Europe under which NATO and the Warsaw Pact allies would reduce their forces. Nixon responded positively to this overture.

In the Middle East the Russians had begun to supply the Arabs with new military resources soon after the swift Israeli triumph in the war of 1967. Although committed to the defense of Israel, the Nixon administration delayed sending additional arms to the Israelis, while negotiating with the Soviet Union and Egypt on a plan calling for Israeli withdrawal from the occupied territories in return for recognition of Israel's right to exist and to use the Suez Canal and other waterways. The United States did help to obtain an Israeli-Egyptian cease-fire along the Suez, but Secretary Rogers's efforts to secure a more permanent settlement were unsuccessful. Soviet intrigue in Egyptian affairs eventually caused President Anwar El-Sadat, in a surprise move in July 1972, to expel all Russian technicians and military advisers from Egypt, a step that somewhat reduced American anxieties about the Middle East. The United States had earlier used its influence to prevent a Middle East explosion when Palestinian commandos attacked the forces of Jordan's moderate King Hussein. Despite the intervention by Syria on the side of the rebels, Hussein's air force soon subdued the attackers.

Farther to the east, the United States suffered a diplomatic setback when it became involved in a new crisis between India and Pakistan. When the Pakistan government attempted to suppress a nationalistic rebellion in East Bengal, India intervened in behalf of the Bengali rebels. Washington supported Pakistan, hoping that India would be deterred from going to war against Pakistan and that the Soviet Union would decide not to support India in any such war. When the Bengali nationalists won their independence and became the new state of Bangladesh, the Russians emerged with enhanced prestige in South Asia.

In general the United States under Nixon demonstrated little tolerance toward political change in the developing nations. The limits of its tolerance were determined by the expected consequences of such change.

Latin America illustrated Nixon's approach to the Third World. Governor Nelson A. Rockefeller, who made a special investigation for the President in 1969, emphasized serious problems and deficiencies in the Latin American economies and called for greater United States assistance in strengthening them. President Nixon, like his predecessors, counted on extensive private United States investments in such developing regions as Latin America, but Washington could not control the investment policies of the large multinational corporations, which became relatively less interested in such uncertain areas. Terrorism and guerrilla activities increased in Venezuela, Colombia, Guatemala, and Bolivia, and in 1970 Salvador Allende, the head of the Socialist party in Chile, won the presidency of that country as a coalition candidate of the left-wing parties. Allende was the first avowed Marxist to come to power in the Western Hemisphere through free elections. He soon began to nationalize the large United States investments in Chile (most notably the copper industry), opened diplomatic relations with Cuba, and signed a trade agreement with the Soviet Union. Allende's government was overthrown in 1973, and later revelations implicated the CIA in helping create the climate for the coup d'etat.

In 1971 President Nixon achieved a startling new departure in the established policy toward the People's Republic of China. The turnabout in United States-Chinese relations came as the People's Republic was emerging from a prolonged period of political and social upheaval. In April 1971 the Chinese leaders unexpectedly invited the American champion table tennis team, then playing in Japan, to visit mainland China. Significantly, this friendly gesture was made just at the time that the U.S.S.R. was convening a Communist party congress to line up opposition against the People's Republic. In any case, the United States accepted the invitation, and the table tennis players went to China in May, thus becoming the first group of Americans to visit the mainland since 1949.

When the Chinese overtures came in the spring of 1971, Washington quickly responded, not only by accepting Peking's invitation, but also by relaxing United States trade and travel restrictions against the People's Republic. Then, in mid-July 1971, the President informed the American people that Kissinger had just returned from a secret trip to Peking and that he himself had accepted an invitation to visit China sometime before May 1972. The State Department, during the following month, let it be known that the United States would no longer oppose the admission of the People's Republic to the United Nations.[8]

[8]When the General Assembly convened in October, the American proposal of a "two-China" policy was rejected, and the Assembly voted, 76 to 34, to admit the Peking government and to oust Taiwan. The People's Republic thus replaced Nationalist China on the UN Security Council as well as in the General Assembly.

President and Mrs. Nixon, accompanied by a large number of advisers and journalists, began their spectacular visit to the Far East by landing at the Peking airport on February 21, 1972. They remained in China for a crowded week of ceremonial functions, high-level talks, and visits to other parts of the country. The concrete results of Nixon's series of conferences with Premier Chou En-lai were not very impressive, but as a symbolic event in the effort to establish more normal relations the meetings were extremely significant. Nixon seemed to agree that Taiwan was really part of China and that American forces would eventually leave Formosa, as tensions "in the area" subsided. In a joint statement following their discussions, Nixon and Chou discussed other areas of agreement and wider contacts in such fields as science, sports, and culture. A delegation of Chinese doctors soon visited the United States, the Chinese bought ten Boeing 707 transport planes and $50 million worth of American grain, and early in 1973 the two countries agreed to exchange diplomatic missions.

The Chinese adventure had another consequence as well: it contributed to a new détente with the Soviet Union. Nixon's visit to Peking made Soviet leaders suspicious of American and Chinese motives in arranging such an unprecedented meeting. As for the Nixon administration, it had sought since 1969 to promote greater harmony with the U.S.S.R. in the SALT meetings, in Berlin, and in the Middle East. Rapprochement with the Soviet Union might also contribute to a settlement in Southeast Asia, while strengthening the President's position at home and in the election campaign of 1972. In May Nixon made his second sensational trip abroad in 1972—a visit to the Soviet Union.

After several days of talks with Leonid Brezhnev and other Russian leaders, President Nixon came home with a number of signed agreements. The Moscow summit meeting focused on an arms limitation treaty and a series of agreements concerning trade, scientific and space cooperation, and environmental problems. Nixon was unable to negotiate a comprehensive trade agreement, but the two nations did establish a joint commission to discuss this question in detail. Later in the year a harvest shortage led the Russians to make a large purchase of American wheat. The arms limitation agreements Nixon signed in Moscow represented the consummation of the first phase of the SALT efforts. One of these agreements was a treaty on defensive weapons limiting the building of antiballistic missile systems to two sites in each country. On the more difficult question of offensive weapons, an interim agreement was signed placing a five-year freeze on the number of strategic offensive weapons in both arsenals, including ICBMs, modern ballistic missile submarines, and submarine-launched missiles. Senator Henry M. Jackson charged that the nuclear arms agreements conceded too much to the Russians, and he succeeded in securing a proviso that in any future accords the United States would not accept any inferiority to the U.S.S.R.[9] Otherwise, the Nixon arms limitation agreements won overwhelming congressional approval.

By the late summer of 1972, the Nixon administration had reason to be pleased with its foreign policy initiatives of the past year. American leaders could even be hopeful about the final ending of the long American involvement in the Vietnam war. In August 1972 the last American ground combat unit in Vietnam was deactivated, leaving fewer than 40,000 United States military men in the country. Although the Paris peace talks remained deadlocked, secret meetings between Henry Kissinger and the principal North Vietnam diplomats, Xuan Thuy and Le Duc Tho, had been held with growing frequency in 1972. On October 8, Tho made a significant concession in these talks. No longer insisting on a new government in Saigon, he offered to accept an internationally supervised cease-fire and promised to release American prisoners of war in return for the withdrawal of United States forces from Vietnam. Kissinger quickly accepted these terms. The Hanoi government soon announced that a nine-point agreement would shortly be signed.

Nixon's Triumph: The Election of 1972

Despite President Nixon's initiatives on the economic front and in the international sphere, his political prospects were not altogether favorable as the election year 1972 opened. Nixon and other Republican leaders could not forget their party's congressional setback in 1970. Senator Edmund S. Muskie, the favored Democratic presidential candidate, had pulled even with the President in public opinion polls. The Vietnam war dragged on, inflation had not been brought under control, and although public discourse had become less strident, controversy and division continued to dominate American life.

The favorite presidential possibility among most Democrats during the early part of Nixon's Presidency was Senator Edward M. Kennedy of Massachusetts, the surviving Kennedy brother and the recently chosen party whip in the upper house. Not only did Kennedy have the advantage of his famous family name, but he had also proved, to the surprise of many observers, to be an able Senator, a strong campaigner, and a popular figure both with party regulars and with Democratic liberals. While driving back from a party on Chappaquiddick Island, off Martha's

[9]The agreement on offensive weapons provided for a five-year freeze at the current missile levels—1,054 land-based and 635 sea-based missiles for the United States, 1,550 land-based and 740 sea-based missiles for the Soviet Union. The apparent Russian superiority was misleading, since the American multiple, separately targetable warheads (MIRVs) gave the United States a substantial advantage.

Vineyard, on the night of July 18, 1969, Kennedy was involved in a tragic accident that suddenly altered his prospects for 1972. The car he was driving careened off a bridge, and a young woman with him was drowned in the submerged vehicle, despite his efforts to rescue her. These circumstances and Kennedy's inexplicable failure to report the accident until the following morning raised many questions in the public mind,[10] damaged the Senator's reputation, and removed the Democrats' best hope for 1972.

After Kennedy became unavailable, Senator Muskie emerged as the Democratic front-runner. But the Senator from Maine was forced to share the Democratic center with Hubert H. Humphrey, who had reentered the Senate in January 1971. A third aspirant from the Senate was George S. McGovern of South Dakota, a liberal and an early opponent of the war in Vietnam. One other Democrat cast a long shadow over the contest for the party's presidential nomination in 1972— Governor George C. Wallace. There were several minor candidates: Senator Henry F. Jackson of Washington, the peppery black congresswoman Shirley Chisholm of New York, and Mayor John V. Lindsay of New York (who had recently left the Republican party to affiliate with the Democrats).

Senator Muskie continued to lead the field of Democratic hopefuls until early 1972, when his drive lost momentum and the middle ground he had cultivated so well suddenly became untenable. Although Muskie won the New Hampshire primary, his performance there was unimpressive, and during the next few weeks his campaign failed to arouse genuine enthusiasm. With Muskie's decline, Humphrey's prospects brightened somewhat even though he suffered in many quarters as a result of his identification with the Johnson administration and the ill-fated Chicago convention of 1968. The most notable primary campaigns were those of McGovern and Wallace, the candidates of the left and right, respectively. Starting from far back in the pack, the South Dakota Senator won a series of primary victories in states like Wisconsin, Massachusetts, and New York. Wallace likewise demonstrated impressive strength, sweeping several Southern primaries as well as such Northern states as Michigan and Maryland. Then, as he rattled "the eyeteeth of the Democratic party," fate intervened: the Governor was critically wounded by a gunman while campaigning in Maryland on May 15.[11] Left paralyzed from

---

[10]Kennedy explained his nine-hour delay in reporting the accident as a result of the shock and confusion he had experienced. The Senator then made a televised statement to the people of Massachusetts in which he asked them to let him know whether or not they wished him to remain in the Senate. Not surprisingly, this emotional appeal elicited a heavy majority in favor of Kennedy's continuing in office and running for reelection in 1970.

[11]Wallace's would-be assassin was an unstable young "loner" from Milwaukee named Arthur Bremer. Immediately apprehended and later indicted and tried, Bremer was sentenced to life imprisonment.

the waist down, he was unable to continue his campaign for the Democratic nomination. Thereafter, McGovern advanced rapidly to a dominant position, defeating Humphrey in the important California primary and winning that state's 271 delegate votes.

The composition and conduct of the Democratic National Convention, which convened in Miami Beach, Florida, on July 10, also favored McGovern. The South Dakota Senator himself, as chairman of a Democratic reform committee, had taken a leading part in liberalizing the rules under which convention delegates were selected. It was now stipulated that the composition of each delegation must "reasonably" reflect that state's relative proportion of women, minorities, and young people—all groups with which McGovern was strong. The reform faction was able to establish control of the convention, and McGovern was easily nominated on the first ballot. Senator Thomas F. Eagleton of Missouri, a liberal, a Catholic, and a friend of organized labor, was selected by McGovern as his running mate. In his acceptance speech McGovern pleaded with Americans to "come home"—to abandon their imperialistic ambitions, turn their energies to their pressing domestic problems, subordinate their differences, and renew the idealism and faith of the American dream.

The Republicans were spared the internecine conflict that took place within the Democratic party during the first half of 1972. President Nixon was in an unassailable political position by the spring of the election year, and the GOP convention, opening on August 21 at Miami Beach, brought few surprises. Although Nixon had been challenged in the primaries by Representative Paul N. "Pete" McCloskey, Jr., of California, a liberal who opposed the Vietnam war, and Representative John Ashbrook of Ohio, a conservative who was unhappy with the administration's economic policies and with its rapprochement with the Communist powers, he was overwhelmingly renominated on the first ballot. Vice President Agnew was also nominated for a second term. The President, in the midst of much pageantry, rhetorical acclaim, and a galaxy of movie stars and other celebrities, called for "a new America bound together by our common ideals."

Although Nixon was strongly favored to win in November, McGovern's preconvention appeal seemed to reveal a widespread desire among Americans for new approaches and new solutions to national problems. Unfortunately for Democratic hopes, McGovern's campaign failed to capture the public imagination or to carry forward the momentum of the Miami Beach convention. The South Dakotan ran into bad luck soon after his nomination when it was revealed that his attractive young running mate, Senator Eagleton, had been hospitalized on three occasions during the 1960s for "nervous exhaustion and fatigue" and had undergone brief psychiatric treatment for "depression." McGovern, who had not known about Eagleton's hospitalization, at first supported the Missouri Senator, but as the pressure for his removal from the ticket mounted, the Democratic leader capitulated and asked his colleague to withdraw. McGovern then selected R. Sargent Shriver, a former director of the Peace Corps and brother-in-law of Senator Kennedy, to replace Eagleton.

Having identified himself as an uncompromising and forthright progressive in the battle for the Democratic nomination, Senator McGovern discovered that he could not easily change direction and move into the vitally important center. Many long-time party stalwarts were unhappy because of the new Democratic rules, which they associated with McGovernism. The Democratic nominee's demand for immediate United States withdrawal from Vietnam disturbed some Democrats, while his promise to cut $30 billion from the Pentagon budget alarmed thousands of defense workers. Labor leaders were unhappy with McGovern's labor record, and many of the union spokesmen disliked the Senator's dovish position on Vietnam. His desire to grant amnesty to those who had fled the country or otherwise evaded military service upset others.

The strife-torn Democrats and McGovern's image as a candidate of the left gave President Nixon a decided advantage, and his campaign succeeded in attracting the votes of millions of dissatisfied Democrats and independents. The country was relatively tranquil, and, in contrast to the widespread pessimism of early 1971, the public assessment of the state of the nation was rather favorable. Although Nixon remained in seclusion for the most part, the Republicans were able to mount an impressive campaign on the basis of a huge election fund.

McGovern and Shriver campaigned hard, but they made little headway. The Democratic standard-bearer urged the need for changes in the tax laws to ease the burden on disadvantaged groups, pledged himself to cut the huge defense budget, and advocated better programs in education, health, and welfare. The Senator also hit hard at the alleged corruption associated with the Nixon administration. Some McGovernites suspected that a large contribution to the Nixon campaign by the International Telephone and Telegraph Company was linked to the favorable settlement of an antitrust suit against ITT in 1971, and that a sizable sum contributed by the dairy interests was related to an increase in the price support of milk. McGovern and his associates cited the break-in, on June 17, at the Washington headquarters of the Democratic National Committee. Five men had been apprehended in the party headquarters located in the office and apartment building known as the Watergate, including two former White House aides and a member of the Committee to Re-elect the President. They were charged with breaking and entering, planting wiretaps and electronic bugging devices, and stealing and photographing documents. Administration spokesmen dismissed the Watergate break-in as "a third-rate burglary attempt" of little importance.

The election results confirmed the polls, which had shown President Nixon ahead all the way. In fact, Nixon won by a landslide, receiving 47.1 million popular votes to McGovern's 29.1 million and carrying every state except Massachusetts and the District of Columbia. With 60.8 percent of the popular vote (a percentage surpassed only by Lyndon Johnson in 1964) and 521 electoral votes, Nixon made the best showing of any Republican presidential nominee in history. The Democrats, in the face of Nixon's one-sided margin, retained control of both houses of Congress.[12] Nixon thus became the first President in the United States history to begin two terms with an opposing Congress.

The extensive ticket splitting and the Democratic congressional victories in 1972 suggested that millions of voters were less attracted to Nixon than they were distrustful of McGovern. Only 55 percent of the electorate bothered to vote, a lack of enthusiasm that raised doubts about the validity of Kevin Phillips's idea of an emerging Republican majority. McGovern had been wrong in assuming that the center would not hold, and in the aftermath of the 1972 election most Democratic politicians lost little time in moving to middle ground. Nevertheless, the election promised some long-range benefits for a revitalized Democratic party. It held out some hope for a new direction and the emergence of a renewed political coalition in which young people, students, professional people, and suburban housewives as well as traditional elements would play a role.

SUGGESTIONS FOR FURTHER READING

The literature on Richard M. Nixon and his first administration is uneven and for the most part impressionistic. Rowland Evans, Jr., and Robert D. Novak, *Nixon in the White House: The Frustration of Power** (1971), is a useful account by two well-known journalists. Garry Wills, *Nixon Agonistes: The Crisis of a Self-Made Man** (1970), is a stimulating and wide-ranging study. The historian Bruce Mazlish reveals some understanding of the thirty-seventh President in his book, *In Search of Nixon: A Psychohistorical Inquiry** (1972). Earl Mazo and Stephen Hess offer a sympathetic account of the pre-presidential period in *Nixon: A Political Portrait** (1968). For Nixon's comeback and altered style, see Jules Witcover, *The Resurrection of Richard Nixon* (1970), and Paul Hoffman, *The New Nixon** (1970). *Congress and the Nation, 1969–1972* (1973), by the Congressional Quarterly, is a valuable reference work.

Among the books that throw light on the problems facing the first Nixon

[12]The Democrats lost twelve House seats but gained two Senate seats. The new party alignment gave the Democrats an advantage of 57 to 43 in the Senate and 242 to 192 in the House. The Democrats also won two new governorships and led in this category thirty-one to nineteen.

*Available in paperback edition.

administration are Kermit Gordon (ed.), *Agenda for the Nation* (1969); President's Commission on Campus Unrest, *Campus Unrest** (1970); I. F. Stone, *The Killings at Kent State: How Murder Went Unpunished** (1971); Harland B. Moulton, *From Superiority to Parity: The United States and the Strategic Arms Race, 1961–1971* (1972); and John Newhouse, *Cold Dawn: The Story of SALT* (1973). For other aspects of Nixon's foreign policy, see David Landau, *Kissinger: The Uses of Power* (1972); Robert E. Osgood and others, *Retreat from Empire? The First Nixon Administration* (1973); Henry Brandon, *The Retreat of American Power** (1973); and Lloyd C. Gardner (ed.), *The Great Nixon Turnaround: America's New Foreign Policy in the Post-Liberal Era** (1973).

The administration's sudden shift in economic policy is described by Roger L. Miller's *The New Economics of Richard Nixon: Freezes, Floats, and Fiscal Policy* (1972) and Leonard Silk's *Nixonomics: How the Dismal Science of Free Enterprise Became the Black Art of Controls** (1972).

Several works cited in the previous chapter are useful for an understanding of the background of the election of 1972. Other significant studies are Theodore H. White, *The Making of the President, 1972** (1973); Robert Sam Anson, *McGovern: A Biography* (1972); Jules Witcover, *White Knight: The Rise of Spiro Agnew* (1972); and David S. Broder, *The Party's Over: The Failure of Politics in America** (1972).

Chapter 15

The Crisis of Confidence: America in the 1970s

Bolstered by his great electoral triumph of 1972, Richard Nixon began his second term in the White House with a new sense of power and assurance. On the international front he completed the settlement of the Vietnam war and strengthened his administration's cooperative relationship with mainland China and the Soviet Union. In domestic affairs Nixon moved forthrightly toward a conservative position, and he quickly concentrated more power over the domestic arena within the White House, as he had earlier concentrated power over foreign affairs in the presidency. But the new administration had scarcely begun before it encountered a series of challenges and setbacks which ultimately shattered the President's confidence, destroyed his capacity to govern effectively, and forced his resignation in August 1974. Meanwhile, as the seventies unfolded, Americans still clung to their historic ideals but were less confident than ever before of their ability to master either their private lives or their public affairs.

The Second Nixon Administration—Confusion in the Void

At the outset of his second term, Nixon reorganized his Cabinet and made new appointments to many other upper-level positions in the executive branch. Henry A. Kissinger continued to play a leading role in the administration's foreign policy, and when William P. Rogers resigned in the fall of 1973, Kissinger assumed his position as Secretary of State. Relying heavily on such aides as H. R. "Bob" Haldeman and John D. Ehrlichman, Nixon seemed to increase his isolation in the White House, much to the displeasure of some Republican leaders. He held few press conferences, preferring to deliver prepared addresses to national television audiences.

The second Nixon administration got off to a good start in foreign affairs. A formal settlement of the Vietnam war was finally negotiated. In mid-December 1972, with the agreement so confidently predicted in late October still unrealized, the President ordered the resumption of massive bombing and mining attacks on North Vietnam, apparently as a tactical move to put pressure on the enemy to assume a more conciliatory position. These assaults resulted in heavy United States losses of aircraft and airmen, and they were soon suspended north of the 20th parallel. But in January 1973 Kissinger and Le Duc Tho resumed intensive negotiations in Paris, and a formal accord was signed on January 27. The peace agreement provided for the complete withdrawal of all United States troops and military advisers from Vietnam within sixty days; for the dismantling of all United States military bases; for the return within sixty days of all prisoners of war held by both sides; for the withdrawal of all foreign troops from Laos and Cambodia; and for the maintenance of a demilitarized zone at the 17th parallel to serve as a provisional dividing line between North and South Vietnam, with the reunification question to be settled by peaceful means.

In general, foreign policy promised to be more subdued during the 1970s. "The time has passed," Nixon declared in his second inaugural address, "when America will make every other nation's conflict our own, or make every other nation's future our responsibility, or presume to tell the people of other nations how to manage their own affairs." America's longest and most unpopular war was over, all United States combat forces had left Vietnam by the end of March 1973, and the Americans who had been prisoners of war came home to rejoin their families. In the meantime, the administration ended the draft, thus removing the prospect of compulsory military service for the first time in a quarter-century. Nixon and Kissinger talked not only of strengthening their rapprochement with the great Communist powers, but also of reassuring their NATO allies and of making 1973 the "year of Europe." Nevertheless, American prestige and influence in Europe and in many other parts of the world were not restored. The fighting in Vietnam continued, and United States bombers, operating out of Thailand, kept up their bombing raids on Cambodia until Congress adopted an amendment prohibiting the use of any funds for bombing or other military action in either Cambodia or Laos.

The administration's domestic policies reflected the President's sweeping electoral conquest of 1972. Although Nixon refrained from directly attacking the reform programs instituted by Johnson and Kennedy, he made clear his intention of establishing more conservative domestic policies. He gave up altogether on his own programs for welfare reform and health insurance. He dismissed the liberal and forthright Theodore M. Hesburgh as chairman of the Civil Rights Commission. He used his veto power more freely, disapproving congressional measures providing for environmental control, hospital construction, the establishment of child day-care centers, and the like. The administration began to dismantle the Office of Economic Opportunity. Its budget proposals, while providing generously for defense and aerospace development, slashed funds for welfare, medical services, housing, and manpower programs.

Nixon now assumed a tough stance in dealing with Congress. One of his tactics was to impound billions of dollars appropriated by Congress for social services; that is, the President simply refused to spend congressional appropriations larger than he wanted, contending that it was his prerogative to exercise this kind of executive discretion. Several federal courts eventually ruled that the Chief Executive had exceeded his authority in impounding certain federal funds and eliminating some federal programs. Another source of presidential-congressional contention was the administration's assertion of the doctrine of executive privilege—the privilege not to make its documents accessible to Congress or to refuse to testify before congressional committees.

The erratic performance of the economy confronted the administration with a continuing problem in 1973 and 1974. On January 11, 1973, Nixon suddenly terminated most wage and price controls and substituted reliance on "voluntary cooperation." Phase Three, as the new economic program was labeled, worked badly. Food prices skyrocketed, and such items as rents, fuel, and manufactured goods rose rapidly in cost. In June the President acknowledged the failure of Phase Three by imposing a sixty-day ban on all price increases except for food products at the farm level. The American dollar also suffered further humiliation in the foreign money markets in 1973, and on February 12 Nixon announced a second devaluation of the dollar—this time by about 10 percent.

In August 1973 the administration introduced a system of moderate controls allowing price adjustments. Since food prices were unfrozen before Phase Four was instituted, the cost of living continued to climb. Nixon's countermeasures were limited. A tight money policy was followed by the Federal Reserve System. The President also signed a new price support measure designed to increase domestic farm production, thus reversing the restrictive programs introduced in the 1930s. The economic situation worsened during the winter of 1973–1974 when the country suddenly found itself in the midst of a fuel crisis. Inflation during the first half of 1974 increased at an annual rate of over 11 percent, unemployment mounted once more, and the gross national product for the first quarter actually declined at a rate of 5.8 percent.

Watergate: The Making of a Scandal

To the surprise of most Americans, the burglary of the Democratic National Committee headquarters in mid-June 1972 did not fade out of public consciousness, despite the limited impact it had on the campaign of 1972. The trial of the seven defendants in January 1973 set off a startling chain of developments and revelations which eventually revealed that Watergate was part of a larger effort involving covert and illegal activities to influence the outcome of the election in 1972. It also developed that a systematic effort had been made to cover up the administration's involvement in the Watergate affair. By the spring of 1973 the outlines of an unprecedented political scandal were emerging.

The Watergate trials began in Washington on January 8, 1973. Five of the men arrested for the crime pleaded guilty as charged. The other two—G. Gordon Liddy, counsel for the Committee to Re-elect the President (CRP), and James W. McCord, security officer for CRP—were tried and convicted. The presiding judge, John J. Sirica, pressed the defendants to tell all they knew about the incident, and during the trial he made it clear that he thought they were withholding information. In late March, shortly before Sirica pronounced the sentences in the case, he revealed that McCord had informed him that perjury had been committed at the trial, that the defendants had been under pressure to plead guilty and divulge nothing, and that people in the White House or higher up in the reelection committee had been involved in the Watergate break-in and bugging. A Washington grand jury began to investigate these charges.

McCord's revelations exposed the cover-up operation and set off a succession of further disclosures in the Watergate affair. Much of the story was brought to light through the probing inquiries of persistent journalists, particularly those employed by the *Washington Post* and the *New York Times*. It quickly became evident that some of the President's aides and former advisers were willing to divulge information in the hope that they could gain immunity or partial immunity from prosecution. Thus Jeb Stuart Magruder, a former special assistant to Nixon and later deputy director of CRP, was reported to have implicated John N. Mitchell and John W. Dean III, Counsel to the President, in the Watergate intrusion and subsequent efforts to buy the silence of the convicted conspirators. Dean himself informed the press that the Nixon administration had decided to make him the "scapegoat" in the affair, and he charged that Haldeman and Ehrlichman had supervised the whole Watergate cover-up. On May 10, 1973, a New York grand jury indicted Mitchell and former Secretary of Commerce Maurice H. Stans for conspiracy to defraud the United States and to obstruct justice.[1] Meanwhile, a Senate committee considering the nomination of L. Patrick Gray to be Director of the Federal Bureau of Investigation[2] also uncovered evidence linking Presidential aides with Watergate. Gray, who eventually asked that his name be withdrawn from consideration, admitted that he had destroyed certain documents relating to the Watergate incident.

On April 27, Judge W. Matthew Byrne, who was presiding at the trial of Daniel Ellsberg for stealing and making public the Pentagon Papers, reported that two of the men convicted in the Watergate case had burglarized the office of Ellsberg's psychiatrist's files on Ellsberg. On May 11 Judge Byrne dismissed all charges against Ellsberg and his codefendant, Anthony Russo, on grounds of improper government conduct.[3] John D. Ehrlichman later reported that Nixon had ordered him to reinforce the FBI investigation of the leaks that led to the publication of the Pentagon Papers. Ehrlichman then assembled the "plumbers" to stop such leaks, and some of them were subsequently involved in the Ellsberg case and in the Watergate affair. The plumbers also bugged the telephones of several journalists and government officials suspected of giving certain information to the press.

When the Watergate disclosures began early in 1973, the administration first tried to ignore the mounting furor; but it soon became defensive and gradually acknowledged the involvement of certain White House aides. On April 30 the President made a nationwide television address on Watergate. Flanked by a bust of Lincoln and a photograph of his family, Nixon accepted official "responsibility" for the Watergate events and

[1]They were charged with accepting $200,000 in cash for the Nixon campaign of 1972 from a financier named Robert L. Vesco, who at the time was being sued by the Securities and Exchange Commission in a $224 million securities fraud case. Mitchell was alleged to have interceded with the SEC in Vesco's behalf. Mitchell had directed the activities of the Committee for the Re-election of the President until his resignation soon after the Watergate break-in, while Stans had been chairman of the CRP finance committee. A jury ultimately acquitted both men of these charges.

[2]FBI Director J. Edgar Hoover died in May 1972.

[3]The judge did not refer to another defense complaint: two conversations Byrne had with Ehrlichman during the trial about the possibility of Byrne's becoming the next FBI Director. The judge refused to consider the matter while the trial was in progress.

asserted that "there can be no whitewash at the White House." Yet he
denied any foreknowledge of these events or any part in their cover-up,
declaring that there had been an effort "to conceal the facts both from the
public—from you—and from me." He announced the resignations of
Ehrlichman and Haldeman, but described them as "two of the finest
public servants it has been my privilege to know." Nixon implied that
John Dean had, for reasons of his own, masterminded the entire
Watergate cover-up and kept the Chief Executive in the dark about the
whole affair.

Nixon soon made another move to strengthen his position in the eyes
of the nation. He issued a long written statement to the press on May 22,
declaring, first, that he had no intention of resigning, as some reports had
suggested he might. He acknowledged, for the first time, that there had
been extensive White House involvement in the plumbers' activities and
in the subsequent cover-up. The President conceded that some "highly
motivated individuals" may have been engaged in "specific activities that
I would have disapproved had they been brought to my attention," and he
admitted that there were apparently "wide-ranging efforts" to limit the
investigation or to conceal the possible complicity of members of the
administration and of the campaign committee. But he denied any
personal involvement or knowledge in all areas except certain limited
"national security" matters, which he tried clearly to distinguish from
Watergate.

Under pressure to authorize the selection of an independent Special
Prosecutor, Nixon agreed to such a course, and Attorney General Elliot
L. Richardson chose Professor Archibald Cox of the Harvard Law
School for this task. While Cox set about his work, another inquiry into
Watergate was getting under way on Capitol Hill. The Senate had voted
on February 7 to establish a seven-man select committee to investigate
the Watergate break-in and other campaign election violations. The
committee, headed by Senator Sam J. Ervin, Jr., of North Carolina, began
its public hearings on May 17. During the weeks and months that
followed, the committee heard a parade of witnesses, including Mitchell,
Stans, Dean, Haldeman, Ehrlichman, McCord, and Magruder. J. Fred
Buzhardt, Special Counsel to the President, presented a memorandum in
which he claimed that John Dean was "the principal actor in the
cover-up." The Ervin committee hearings, televised by the national
networks, assumed the character of a great dramatic spectacle in the
summer of 1973.

The committee—and the American people—learned that various
individuals connected with the Nixon administration and the Presidential
campaign committee had been involved in burglary, bugging, spying on
the sex lives of political opponents, and other "dirty tricks," destruction
of evidence, blackmail, perjury, and pledges of executive clemency to

Figure 30 The Watergate Hearings (*Congressional Quarterly, Inc.*)

buy silence. It was also disclosed that an attempt had been made after the initial Watergate arrests to put the FBI off the trail by implying that secret CIA activities might be uncovered if the search were continued. Dean told the committee that the President had known of the attempted cover-up almost from the beginning. It was also learned, from Dean's testimony, that the White House had maintained a "Political Enemies Project," and that the "enemies" on this list were to be subjected to income tax audits and other kinds of harassment.

Another sensational discovery revealed that the Secret Service, on Nixon's orders, had made regular tape recordings of everything said in the Presidential offices and on the Presidential telephones. The Ervin committee sought access to these Presidential tapes for several specified days, as did Special Prosecutor Cox. The White House denied those requests, however, on the grounds of executive privilege and the principle of separation of powers. The Senate committee and the Special Prosecutor then asked the courts to issue a subpoena for the tapes, and in the hearings that ensued before Judge Sirica the President's lawyers argued that the subpoenas should not be granted.

After the Ervin committee recessed, President Nixon on August 15 made another television speech on Watergate. He also issued a supplementary statement to the press. He denied once again that he had any knowledge of or complicity in the Watergate burglary or cover-up. Nixon also defended his decision not to release the disputed tapes. He said he had ordered an investigation soon after the Watergate break-in, and he repeated his earlier assertion that he had not known of a cover-up until March 1973. He appealed to the nation to leave Watergate to the courts and to turn to such pressing concerns as foreign affairs and inflation.

A variety of other revelations in 1973 cast the President in an unfavorable light. Some of these disclosures and allegations involved money. The dairy industry, for example, contributed heavily to the Nixon campaign fund in 1972, presumably in return for the imposition of selective import quotas and an increase in milk price supports. Nixon had paid federal income taxes of only $792.81 in 1970 and $878.03 in 1971, about what a person with an income of $8,500 a year would have paid.[4] Rumors of huge federal expenditures for repairs and construction at the President's private homes in San Clemente, California, and Key Biscayne, Florida, were finally confirmed, after first being denied by the General Services Administration. The administration suffered still further setbacks. After Judge Sirica ordered that the disputed White House tapes be turned over to him for review, a Presidential assistant told the judge that two of the tapes (possibly the most important ones) had never existed.

In the early fall of 1973, another crisis in Washington momentarily diverted the public's attention from the Watergate scandal, but this new development represented a further blow to the reeling Nixon administration. The Watergate disclosures had not involved Vice President Agnew in any way, but in August 1973 he was informed that a federal grand jury in Baltimore was probing his connection while Governor of Maryland with certain alleged kickbacks to state and Baltimore County officials. The Vice President vigorously denied these allegations, and as rumors of his probable indictment spread, he spoke out sharply in maintaining his innocence. But in a dramatic move on October 10, Agnew resigned the vice-presidency and pleaded *nolo contendere* to a charge of income tax evasion. His lawyers had earlier engaged in plea bargaining with the prosecutors. The judge fined Agnew $10,000 and gave him a suspended prison sentence, thus bringing down the most outspoken "law and order" champion in the administration. President Nixon, following the provisions

---

[4]Nixon had made large deductions as a result of giving his Vice-Presidential papers to the National Archives. It was later revealed that the deed transferring the papers was not signed until several months after the expiration of the law permitting such deductions. The President eventually agreed to pay $467,000 in back taxes.

of the Twenty-fifth Amendment, soon nominated Gerald R. Ford, Republican leader in the House of Representatives, to succeed Agnew, and both houses readily confirmed his nomination.

Shortly after Agnew's resignation, another major development occurred in the Watergate case. It grew out of the efforts by the Ervin committee and Archibald Cox to subpoena nine Presidential tapes. When the President refused to comply with the subpoenas, Ervin and Cox sought an order from Judge Sirica to force their release, and after hearing arguments from both sides, Sirica in late August ordered the President to turn over the tapes and related documents to him for review, after which he would provide the grand jury with the relevant material from these sources. The White House appealed Sirica's decision to the Circuit Court, which upheld the district judge on October 12. Seeking to avoid an appeal to the Supreme Court, Nixon and his advisers then sought a "compromise" with the Ervin committee and the Special Prosecutor. They offered to provide a summary of the nine tapes, which Senator John C. Stennis of Mississippi could "authenticate" after listening to the tapes in question. Senator Ervin apparently agreed to this proposal at first, but Cox rejected it on the ground that no trial court would accept summaries of evidence when the full evidence existed. On October 19 Nixon directed Cox "to make no further attempts by judicial process to obtain the tapes, notes, or memoranda of presidential conversations." Cox refused to accept this order, at which point the President directed Attorney General Richardson to fire the Special Prosecutor. Richardson resigned rather than carry out this order, as did Deputy Attorney General William D. Ruckelshaus. But the next man down the line, the Solicitor General, fired the Special Prosecutor.

The "Saturday night massacre," coming only hours before the deadline for filing an appeal with the Supreme Court, shocked the country and immediately stimulated talk of impeachment in Congress.[5] One White House spokesman described the reaction to the President's defiant action as a "firestorm." This was doubtless one reason Nixon soon abandoned his adamant position on the White House tapes and directed his attorneys to inform Sirica that the White House would comply with the judge's order. Some observers suspected, however, that Nixon had contrived a way to get rid of Cox, possibly because his careful investigation was likely to implicate the President. There was also criticism in some quarters of Nixon's decision, on the night of October 24, to order a worldwide alert of American military units as a result of a new outbreak

---

[5]Forty-four Watergate related bills and resolutions were introduced in the House of Representatives on October 23 and 24—twenty-two calling for impeachment of the President or for an investigation of impeachment procedures. The House Judiciary Committee began an impeachment inquiry on October 30.

of war in the Middle East. The Chief Executive's credibility had sunk so low that some people interpreted the alert as a desperate ploy to divert attention from Nixon's domestic difficulties. The President finally held a televised press conference in an effort to improve his standing in the eyes of the public. He named Leon Jaworski, a respected Houston lawyer, to succeed Cox as Special Prosecutor in the Watergate case and Senator William B. Saxbe of Ohio to replace Richardson as Attorney General.

As the year ended, Watergate was still very much in the news. Although the Ervin committee had completed most of its investigation, its final report had not yet been made. Jaworski and his staff were continuing their quiet but methodical probe, including an effort to obtain access to additional White House tapes. Perhaps of even greater significance was the full-fledged impeachment inquiry being undertaken by the House Judiciary Committee. George Gallup's polls indicated that Nixon's popularity had dropped from a high of 68 percent early in 1973 to a mere 27 percent a year later.

The Energy Crisis and the Environment

Most Americans were worried and aggravated during the winter of 1973–1974 by a more immediate problem than Watergate. The United States was suddenly hit by an acute fuel shortage, particularly of gasoline. The possibility of inadequate fuel supplies first became meaningful to Americans soon after Egypt and Syria attacked Israel on *Yom Kippur,* October 6, 1973. Within two weeks of the resumption of war in the Middle East, the Arab nations announced an outright ban on oil exports to the United States, the major supplier of arms to Israel; the embargo would apparently remain in effect until the Israeli forces withdrew from the territories occupied in 1967 and 1973.[6] This would deprive the United States of a million barrels of oil a day.

Neither President Nixon nor Congress had done much to anticipate the energy shortage, but in November Congress passed the Emergency Petroleum Allocation Act. It provided for a mandatory allocation program of available fuel supplies within thirty days, with additional time being granted for the allocation of gasoline and products already being allotted under the administration's plan of distribution. Early in December William E. Simon took over as director of the administration's new omnibus energy agency. While warning of higher fuel prices, Simon stated that gasoline rationing would be employed only as a last resort.

[6]The fighting was inconclusive, and a truce was soon arranged under the auspices of the United States and the Soviet Union. Secretary of State Kissinger's persistent diplomacy finally produced a tentative agreement between the two sides in the spring of 1974. Although the Arab nations then lifted their oil embargo, a permanent settlement of the Middle East dispute continued to elude mediators.

Congress enacted certain other energy legislation in late 1973, including the Trans-Alaska Oil Pipeline bill. The act cleared the way for the construction of a 789-mile pipeline, to be built by a consortium of seven oil companies at an estimated cost of $4.5 billion. The pipeline was designed to carry oil from the North Slope to the southern Alaskan port of Valdez, from whence it would be transported by tanker to West Coast ports. By 1980, the sponsors of the bill predicted, the pipeline would be supplying the United States with 2 million barrels of oil a day. In December Congress completed action on a measure instituting daylight saving time on a year-round basis, an innovation expected to save as much as $1^{1}/_{2}$ percent of the nation's fuel consumption during the winter months.

Both the legislative and the executive branches of the national government were preoccupied with the energy crisis during the winter of 1973–1974. An avalanche of proposed laws descended upon Congress, and in his State of the Union message on January 30, 1974, President Nixon declared that "the number one legislative concern must be the energy crisis." Nixon urged the development of "reliable new energy sources," but he also cautioned Americans to adjust "to the fact that the age of unlimited supplies of cheap energy is ended." The administration proposed a five-year research program costing $10 billion, which Senator Henry M. Jackson, the Senate's chief authority in the energy field, criticized as altogether inadequate. In late February Congress passed the Emergency Energy bill, only to have the President veto the measure on March 6. The legislation would have resulted in a substantial rollback in domestic crude oil prices. Opponents of this provision argued that it would discourage petroleum companies from exploring and drilling for new wells. While the debate continued, fuel prices rose spectacularly.

Meanwhile, Americans tried to conserve energy. The country shifted to daylight saving time early in January, the President and other leaders urged people to turn their thermostats down to 68 degrees, and Congress established a national speed limit of 55 miles an hour. Citizens everywhere suffered from a gasoline shortage unknown in the United States since the grim days of World War II. "The scene is the same in one area after another," the *U.S. News & World Report* noted late in the winter: "scores, even hundreds of cars, stretching as far as the eye can see, winding around corners, creating traffic jams. Inside the cars are drivers trying—not always with success—to control their tempers as they spend an hour or more waiting their turn at the gasoline pumps." Many people expressed their exasperation and resentment to their congressmen. "As an average American housewife," one Floridian wrote Senator Lawton Chiles, "I am fighting mad. I've had it with the high prices for food, the chicanery of Watergate and now the so-called gasoline shortage."

The Federal Energy Office under William Simon moved clumsily to allocate gasoline and other scarce fuels among the states and regions of the country. Several states resorted to various types of rationing their gas supplies, but the Nixon administration, continuing to blame the Arab oil embargo for the crisis, steadfastly opposed federal rationing. Gradually, by the early spring of 1974, the fuel shortage began to ease. One of the contributing factors was the success of voluntary efforts to conserve heating fuel, which eventually made it possible to begin refining more gasoline. The winter in most parts of the country providentially turned out to be exceedingly mild.

There was widespread suspicion in the United States that the giant petroleum concerns were reaping inordinate profits from the energy crisis and that they might even have conspired to cause it. The great oil companies operated with the advantage of concentrated economic resources and technological expertise. They maintained powerful political lobbies in Washington and the state capitals. The National Petroleum Council, made up entirely of industry representatives, served as the Department of Interior's official advisory body on all aspects of oil policy. For the past fourteen years United States oil producers had demanded and obtained restrictive quotas on petroleum products. The industry enjoyed a 22 percent depletion allowance on domestic and foreign operations. In addition, for more than two decades American petroleum companies had been permitted by the federal government to use the royalties they paid to foreign producing countries to offset, dollar for dollar, their United States taxes. "A small group of businessmen," the economist James Patterson wrote early in 1974, "could, and did, decide to let gasoline demand catch up with refining capacity in the United States while expanding refining capacity at a breakneck rate over the rest of the world." The profits of American petroleum companies were up 61 percent in the last quarter of 1973, as compared with a similar period a year before.

The fuel crisis led to much discussion of "alternative energy." There was even talk of solar power and fusion power, although the development of such projects on a large scale did not appear to be realistic possibilities in the near future. On the other hand, a boom in coal and domestic fuel production seemed certain during the next few years. Whatever course the search for energy took, it was likely to be surrounded with difficulties. National policy apparently assumed that increased energy use was desirable, and by sponsoring long-term investment to meet expected needs, government action probably would reinforce existing patterns of energy demand.

The energy crisis of the 1970s also evoked the image of an economic "catastrophe." Some Americans expressed fear that economic growth would soon have to be curtailed, that it would be necessary to place a ceiling on the nation's historic trend of industrial and business expansion. The American economy used 5.8 billion tons of materials in 1971—28 tons for every man, woman, and child—and almost all of these materials and energy resources came from virgin sources.

Even more disturbing was the growing awareness of the fact that United States economic growth was accompanied by unwanted side effects, including a steady decline in the quality of the air and water, a series of human-made disasters of ecological imbalance, and widening alarm over the imminent destruction of the natural environment. In its first report the Council on Environmental Quality observed that the Santa Barbara oil spill early in 1969 showed the nation how one accident could temporarily devastate a large area. "Since then," the report continued, "each environmental issue—the jetport project near Everglades National Park, the proposed pipeline across the Alaskan wilderness, the worsening blight of Lake Erie, the polluted beaches off New York and other cities, smog in mile-high Denver, lead in gasoline, phosphates in detergents, and DDT—flashed the sign to Americans that the problems are everywhere and affect everyone." *U.S. News & World Report* estimated in 1970 that it would cost $71 billion within the next five years to clean up the American environment.

By this time the environment and its degradation had emerged as a compelling public issue. Television brought pictures of ecological disaster into every American home, politicians began to discuss the problems of environmental collapse, a new vocabulary of words like ecology and population explosion entered everyday speech, and such scientists as Barry Commoner began to argue that "the proper use of science is not to conquer nature, but to live in it." The growing importance of ecological issues reflected a profound change in public consciousness. Thus the long period of uncritical public accommodation to the automobile was apparently coming to an end, and the motorcar was increasingly being conceived as a major social problem rather than a historically progressive instrument for change in America.

The Impeachment of a President

The dramatic succession of revelations and confrontations in the Watergate affair dominated public affairs in the United States in 1973 and 1974. By the beginning of the latter year, the issue of overwhelming importance in the Watergate case had become President Nixon's possible involvement in the scandal. The focus of the Watergate inquiry had become a movement to impeach the President. What had seemed unthinkable during the early stages of the various investigations into the matter had become a realistic possibility, especially in the aftermath of the notorious Saturday night massacre in October 1973. The House Judiciary Committee, under the chairmanship of Peter W. Rodino, Jr., of New Jer-

sey, was formally considering impeachment charges against the Chief
Executive.

Public reaction to the firing of Archibald Cox in the fall of 1973 was
so hostile that the President had agreed to turn over the disputed tapes to
Judge Sirica. But a week later the White House informed the court that
two of the nine subpoenaed tapes were missing and that another of the
specified conversations had never been recorded. Three weeks later it
was further revealed that one of the other tapes contained an eighteen-
minute gap in a conversation between Nixon and H. R. Haldeman on June
20, 1972—three days after the Watergate break-in. Embarrassed White
House spokesmen tried to explain the gap as resulting from an accidental
erasure by the President's secretary, Rose Mary Woods, but a panel of
electronics experts reported to Sirica, after studying the tape, that
"someone" had deliberately erased it in at least five efforts.

With only 27 percent of the American people approving his performance as Chief Executive, Nixon launched "Operation Candor" in
November 1973. This bid for public support through speeches and travel
to various parts of the country served only momentarily to improve the
President's image. Even the traditional bases of his support—the business
community, middle-of-the-road and conservative Republicans, and the
South—seemed to be eroding. Congress had learned to say "no" to the
White House. The *Congressional Quarterly* reported that the executive
branch had got its way on only 50.6 percent of the legislative votes on
which it had expressed its wishes in 1973, as compared with 66 percent in
1972 and 77 percent in 1970.

Both Leon Jaworski and the House Judiciary Committee requested
further evidence from the White House, including a large number of
recorded conversations between the President and his subordinates.
Nixon adamantly refused to provide this information, arguing that to do
so would infringe upon executive privilege and interfere with the stability
and authority of the presidency. Nixon's strategy was to delay, to assert
that the President was unimpeachable in the absence of explicit proof of
serious criminality, and to refuse to surrender evidence that could either
provide such proof or demonstrate his innocence. On April 11 the
Judiciary Committee voted 33 to 3 to issue a subpoena ordering the Chief
Executive to deliver the tapes of forty-two Presidential conversations
within two weeks. A week later the Special Prosecutor subpoenaed
sixty-four White House tapes for his own use.

Nixon decided, in a carefully staged move, to make public edited
transcripts of thirty-one of the forty-two tapes demanded by the House
committee.[7] Having provided the committee with what he described as

[7]Nixon's attorneys stated that the other eleven tapes were missing or had never been
recorded.

voluminous materials, the President made it clear that there would be no further White House disclosures concerning Watergate. Before the transcripts were released, James D. St. Clair, the President's top lawyer, had given the press an account of the transcripts; the White House had also approached key Republican leaders and lined up television programs in an effort to blitz the media. Nixon took his "case" for the Watergate transcripts directly to the people in a televised speech on April 29, 1974. He projected a forceful and controlled image, and as a TV "presentation" his address seemed to be a success. The bulky transcripts—1,308 pages in length—were made public on May 1. Although cleansed of profanity ("expletive deleted") and filled with sections marked "unintelligible," the transcripts were published in several editions and read by millions of people. They did not have the effect the President had evidently intended, for at crucial points such as the conversation involving Nixon, Haldeman, and Dean on March 21, 1973, they contained talk of extortion, blackmail, cover-ups, hush money, and other desperate measures.

President Nixon's Watergate transcripts, Eric Sevareid of CBS remarked, "constitute a moral indictment without known precedent in the story of American government." The *Wall Street Journal* thought the transcripts "reveal a flawed mentality." Leaders of the Republican party and long-time Nixon supporters in the press voiced dismay at the quality of the President's thinking and leadership. The President's authority, as the *New York Times* noted, was "visibly disintegrating."

Still, Nixon held on. His recalcitrance finally led Jaworski, in a cogent letter to the Senate Judiciary Committee on May 20, to point out that he had been personally assured by General Alexander M. Haig, Jr., Nixon's chief aide, that the White House recognized his right as Special Prosecutor to seek any evidence he considered necessary, including that in the President's personal possession. Ten days later the Supreme Court agreed to Jaworski's request that it rule directly on Nixon's refusal to turn over the sixty-four subpoenaed tapes for use in the approaching trials of leading Watergate defendants. It was revealed in early June that the grand jury which indicted those persons involved in the Watergate cover-up had also named the President as an "unindicted co-conspirator." This prompted the White House to ask the Supreme Court to hear arguments about whether the grand jury had overstepped its authority in this instance. The Court agreed to hear such arguments. At about the same time, the House Judiciary Committee voted 37 to 1 to issue still another subpoena for tapes, calling on the President to produce, by June 10, forty-five Watergate-related conversations held between November 15, 1972, and June 4, 1973. Nixon refused to comply. In June two more former Presidential assistants—Charles W. Colson and Herbert W. Kalmbach—pleaded guilty and were convicted for their involvement in the Watergate affair.

The beleaguered President was apparently determined to ride out the worsening Watergate storm. His tactics were those of "fighting," "counterattacking," "toughing it out," and resorting insistently to his international role in an effort to vindicate himself at home. In mid-June, hard on the heels of Secretary of State Kissinger's successful negotiations in arranging a military disengagement between Syria and Israel, Nixon made a well-publicized five-day visit to the Middle East in search of a more lasting peace. The Nixon entourage was delighted with the reception given the President, and it almost seemed that the exhilarating pre-Watergate days had returned. In late June and early July Nixon made another spectacular visit to the Soviet Union.

In early July the President's chances of escaping impeachment appeared to be improving. But there was a recurrent phenomenon in the Watergate affair: every time the outlook for Nixon brightened, a series of new developments served to renew the storm. The second week of July brought a spate of new disclosures and setbacks for the White House. John Ehrlichman was convicted by a federal court of having authorized the 1971 break-in of Ellsberg's former psychiatrist.[8] The House Judiciary Committee released a mass of Presidential transcripts and other evidence indicating that the transcripts approved and released by Nixon with such fanfare in the spring had been edited to make the President's involvement appear less extensive than it was. A 2,500-word segment of a March 22, 1973, conversation had been left out entirely. In that conversation Nixon had told his aides: "I want you all to stonewall it, let them plead the Fifth Amendment, cover up or anything else, if it'll save it—save the plan."

The Senate Watergate committee published its final report at about this time. While refraining from making charges that would interfere with the impeachment procedure or the Watergate trials, the Ervin committee expressed alarm over indications that people in high office were indifferent to public morality and operated "on the belief that the end justifies the means, that the laws could be flaunted to maintain the present Administration in office."[9] A few days later, on July 24, the Supreme Court ruled 8 to 0 that the President must turn over the sixty-four subpoenaed tapes to Judge Sirica so that whatever relevant material they contained could be used by the Special Prosecutor.

The final scenes of the Watergate drama were now enacted. The House Judiciary Committee held six days of nationally televised debate in late July, and the committee members adopted three articles of impeach-

[8]Nixon had testified, in a written statement, on Ehrlichman's behalf. By August 1974, fourteen of Nixon's former administrative or campaign aides and twenty-one other men had pleaded guilty or had been convicted for crimes related to Watergate.
[9]The committee recommended broad legislative reforms "to safeguard the electoral process and to provide the requisite checks against the abuse of executive power."

ment. The committee recommended that the President be impeached by the House of Representatives for obstruction of justice in the Watergate cover-up, for general abuse of his powers, and for refusing to comply with its subpoenas for White House tapes. Several Republican members voted for impeachment, and virtually all informed observers agreed that Nixon would be impeached by the House. In a surprise move on August 5, the President made public the transcripts of three of the tapes recently surrendered to Sirica. The three conversations took place between Nixon and Haldeman on June 23, 1972—six days after the Watergate break-in— and they showed that the President had sought to use the CIA to slow the FBI investigation of the crime. Thus Nixon was involved in the cover-up almost from the beginning. He acknowledged that he had monitored the "damaging" tapes in May 1974 and had kept the information from the Judiciary Committee as well as his lawyers. Many influential Republicans now joined the call for Nixon's resignation or impeachment. It was clear that he would have to stand trial in the Senate for "high crimes and misdemeanors."

The nation waited while Richard Nixon made his decision. Addressing a nationwide television audience on the evening of August 8, Nixon announced that he would resign the presidency on the following day. He made no mention of Watergate, admitting nothing beyond misjudgment and the erosion of his "political base." But behind "the dazzling succession of events of this most extraordinary week in American political history," as the *New York Times* put it, "lies one fact of surpassing importance: the long and unmistakable drift toward concentration of power in the hands of one elected official, the President of the United States, has been stopped." At noon on August 9, Vice President Gerald R. Ford was sworn in as the nation's thirty-eighth President.[10] "Our long nightmare is over," he declared. "Our Constitution works. Our great republic is a government of laws and not of men."

Watergate was unquestionably the most serious political scandal in American history. But the Watergate crimes were more than that: they constituted an attempt to use government power to subvert the political process in the broadest sense of the term. This audacious venture involved a cover-up by conspirators in such high places that they were in position to manipulate the investigation that should have ferreted them out. Senator Jacob Javits of New York referred to Watergate as "a symptom of political decadence," and few thoughtful Americans could doubt that the scandal was in some measure a reflection of the nation's

---

[10]Soon afterward Ford nominated Governor Nelson A. Rockefeller for the vice-presidency, and after extended consideration Congress voted in December to confirm the nomination.

Figure 31 President Ford and Soviet Secretary General Brezhnev in Vladivostok, November 1974 (*David Hume Kennerly, the White House*)

social environment and cultural themes. The problem of moral leadership was suggested by the refusal of nearly all of those who appeared before the Ervin committee to accept responsibility for their acts. Coming to power after a decade of disorder, turmoil, and violence, profoundly fearful of the frightful conditions abroad in the land, the President's men felt themselves justified in employing the most extraordinary means to ensure Nixon's reelection. Morality was relative, and what was ethical depended upon the situation. Watergate was also rooted in a cold war mentality that justified the most dubious activities to overcome a single totalitarian enemy. Thus Watergate was only the other side of the clandestine operations of the cold war, the falsified records, and the Cambodian bombings.

Watergate sparked a reconsideration of political ethics, mounting distrust of intelligence activities, a searching reappraisal of federal power, and widespread criticism of the vast authority lodged in the executive branch in Washington. The shadow of the President's impeachment stimulated discussion of how to restore the balance between the legislative and executive branches and how to prevent future abuses of power by the White House. There were indications that Congress might be moving to reassert its authority, despite the characteristic lack of unity and basic purpose in the Democratic majority.[11] One corrective step was the passage over Nixon's veto of the War Powers Act, limiting presidential ability to commit troops abroad by executive action. There were also other signs of reform vigor, among them the activities of public-interest groups like Common Cause and the network of Nader organizations. An Associated Press survey in the late spring of 1974 showed that twenty-one states had adopted political reforms in 1974 establishing ethics commissions, regulating campaign spending and lobbying, and requiring the disclosure of campaign contributions.

The Crisis of Confidence and the American Future

By the early 1970s a deep crisis of the spirit had settled over America, accompanied by a pervasive pessimism unknown in the United States since the depths of the Great Depression. A series of enervating events contributed to this sense of foreboding. As community organizer Saul Alinsky remarked in 1969, "Every time you turn around, there's a crisis of some sort. You have the black crisis, the urban crisis—it's just one goddam crisis after another. It's just too much for the average middle-class Joe to take." The widespread repudiation, especially by the young, of long-established norms and values heightened the mood of anxiety and despair. External threats constituting a "civilizational malaise" further undermined American confidence. Robert L. Heilbroner wrote, in *The Human Prospect* (1974), that "we are entering a period in which rapid population growth, the presence of obliterative weapons, and dwindling resources will bring international tensions to dangerous levels for an extended period."

The American experience in Vietnam, more than any other aspect of the nation's contemporary history, demonstrated the limits of United States power, destroyed a large part of the public's confidence in the country's capacity to deal with foreign and domestic problems, and bruised the national spirit as had no other development in the twentieth century. Then came Watergate, which made Americans acutely aware of the fragility of their political institutions, deepening the doubts that had already entered the public consciousness. The events of the late sixties and early seventies showed how difficult it was to apply political solutions to social problems. The frightful outbreak of prison violence at Attica, New York, in September 1971 was only one example of the seemingly

[11]Watergate as well as the worsening economic situation probably contributed to Democratic successes in the midterm elections of 1974. The Democrats picked up 43 House seats and 3 senatorships, increasing their totals to 291 in the House and 61 in the Senate.

endless social problems which Americans had made little headway in solving.[12] The Attica revolt set off a national debate, not only about the problem of rising crime rates but about the whole system of American justice as well.

The loss of assurance in the United States stemmed in considerable part from some hard realities, one of which was the crisis of the national economy. The cost of living rose over 8 percent in 1973, and during the following year its galloping gait reached 12 percent. The gross national product actually declined in 1974, a condition that would have proved demoralizing only a short time before. Unemployment continued to be a problem, reaching 6.5 percent by late 1974 and 9 percent by the spring of 1975. The mounting cost of living confronted more and more people with a drastic loss of purchasing power. The United States economy was far less self-contained than it had been before World War II, and many Americans began to fear that their capitalist system would not function if most of Europe and Asia should abolish free enterprise, as appeared likely. Faith in the "new economics" had also been shaken, including the assumption that capitalism would manifest a steady trend to economic growth and that its undesirable results—poverty, unemployment, social neglect—could be adequately dealt with by governmental intervention. Most Americans still adhered to the idea that growth was indispensable, but a strong movement was clearly under way to modify the measurements of growth to take into account such factors as social costs.

Although racial tensions seemed to subside somewhat during the early 1970s, the reality of inequality was everywhere apparent in America. The black community was one of the principal victims of the reaction that had set in against radicalism, and of the reaction's instrumentality, the Nixon administration. Black Americans were hard hit by the severe inflation, the high unemployment rates in their ranks, and the contraction of the welfare system. Crime, drug addiction, and bad housing made life in slum areas almost intolerable for millions of blacks and Puerto Ricans. Genuine school integration in Northern cities was delayed by the resistance of white parents to busing and the Supreme Court's increasing tolerance of racial imbalances in school systems.[13] The end of the "Second Reconstruction" was punctuated, in the early seventies, by

---

[12]A thousand inmates of the state prison in Attica—mostly minority group members—revolted on September 9, 1971, seizing thirty-three guards as hostages and demanding a long list of concessions. When negotiations failed to end the uprising, state troopers and deputy sheriffs stormed the prison and subdued the prisoners on September 13. Nine hostages and twenty-nine inmates were killed. Many prison officials around the country criticized the way the revolt was handled by New York authorities.

[13]In July 1974 the Supreme Court prohibited, by a 5 to 4 decision, busing into the suburban Detroit school districts. This ruling appeared to be a reversal of the long trend that began with the *Brown* decision of 1954.

a debate among scholars over the alleged genetic inferiority of blacks.

If the civil rights movement had lost its momentum, one group complaining about its discriminatory treatment showed signs of new vitality. Stimulated by the civil rights movement, student protests, and antiwar demonstrations, as well as the new "sexual revolution," a movement for women's liberation came into being. It was manifested in a variety of feminist organizations, protests, and campaigns. In 1966 Betty Friedan, author of one of the first important literary expressions of postwar feminism, *The Feminine Mystique* (1963), and several other women founded the National Organization of Women (NOW) to support new governmental policies and new social arrangements to help liberate women. NOW worked for the enforcement of the Civil Rights Act of 1964, which had prohibited job discrimination based on sex as well as on race and religion. The National Women's Political Caucus, organized in 1971, undertook to lobby for women's rights within both major parties. On August 26, 1970—the fiftieth anniversary of the ratification of the Woman Suffrage Amendment—feminists conducted a "Strike for Equality," with a big parade in New York City and smaller demonstrations in numerous other cities. The demonstrators emphasized such objectives as equal opportunity for women in jobs and education, free twenty-four-hour child-care centers, and free abortions on demand.

The reformers made some notable gains. New York enacted a liberal abortion law in 1970, and several other states made their abortion statutes less restrictive despite the strong opposition of the Catholic church and certain other groups. In January 1973 the Supreme Court held abortions to be legal during the first six months of pregnancy. The women's liberationists also advocated an amendment to the United States Constitution guaranteeing equality of rights. Congress responded by passing an Equal Rights Amendment, and it began its way through the state capitals in the spring of 1972. Meanwhile, universities, business institutions, and the professions began to employ more women, in part because of the pressure exerted by Washington. Even so, there was much evidence of tokenism in the acceptance of women, just as there was in the case of blacks and other minorities.

American women, like the depressed racial minorities, felt the social and emotional consequences of inequality. But the ramifications of inequality extended through much of the rest of the nation's society as well. For example, many blue-collar workers, trapped in unpleasant jobs with no hope of advancement, experienced a growing sense of frustration and alienation. The runaway inflation of the seventies hit many moderate-income Americans very hard, especially the large number of people (almost 40 percent of the total population) who stood above the poverty line but below the median family income ($9,870 in 1970). "After years of feeling himself a besieged minority," *Newsweek* reported in 1969,

Figure 32   The National Organization for Women Pickets the White House, May 1969
(*United Press International Photo*)

"the man in the middle—representing America's vast white middle-class majority—is giving vent to his frustrations, his disillusionment—and his anger."

The consequences of inequality in America were exacerbated by the weakening social fabric. Many old sources of stability such as the small towns and rural areas were lost in the years following World War II. In the cities much of the group cohesion and close-knit family life of the ethnic communities disappeared, despite the revival of ethnic consciousness in politics. Increasingly, the old sense of rootedness in the United States was lost as a generalized feeling of out-of-placeness became characteristic. The cultural fragmentation of America was producing a society of many different and sometimes competing conceptual worlds and life-styles. This new pluralism had its virtues, but as Peter Schrag has written, it made all Americans feel at one time or another that they were "refugees of time and identity, if not of place."

The crisis of confidence that overtook the United States in the 1970s reflected a remarkable change in the American outlook. One significant shift in attitude was related to America's place in the world: in the late sixties and early seventies isolationism grew rapidly, while internationalist support dropped to a post-1945 low. Reporting in October 1969 on an extensive national survey, *Newsweek* suggested that the average American was more deeply troubled about his country's future than at any time since the 1930s. But the malaise went deeper still, to fundamental questions like the sanctity of work, the stability of the family, and the threat to such "familiar totems" as premarital chastity, the notion of postponing gratification, and filial gratitude for parental sacrifice.

Nevertheless, the grand American experiment in the search for liberty and security was far from finished as the nation approached the bicentennial of its independence. It remained unbelievably rich and powerful, with a vigorous and inventive population, an extraordinarily well-developed economy, and a social order that retained enormous stability in spite of the challenges and disappointments of the last decade. There was still hope that the nation's vast resources and lofty ideals would enable its people to deal more successfully with the age-old problems of poverty, human rights, environmental deterioration, and the loss of community.

SUGGESTIONS FOR FURTHER READING

The Watergate scandal is illuminated by two installments published in the *New York Times Magazine,* July 22, 1973, and January 13, 1974, and the Congressional Quarterly's two-volume *Watergate: Chronology of a Crisis** (1973–1974). *All the President's Men** (1974), by Bob Woodward and Carl Bernstein, is a fascinating account of the Watergate cover-up and the press's role in the early Watergate disclosures. Lewis Chester and others, *Watergate: The Full Inside Story* (1973), is one of several early books on the scandal. Three other works that provide useful background for an understanding of Watergate are Arthur M. Schlesinger, Jr., *The Imperial Presidency* (1973); Peter Schrag, *Test of Loyalty: Daniel Ellsberg and the Rituals of Secret Government* (1974); and Delmar D. Dunn, *Financing Presidential Campaigns** (1972). See also Theodore H. White, *Breach of Faith: The Fall of Richard Nixon* (1975).

S. David Freeman, *Energy: The New Era* (1974), explores the origins of the fuel crisis and offers a blueprint for future action. Lawrence Rocks and Richard P. Runyon, *The Energy Crisis** (1972), is a devastating assessment of the federal government's failure to cope with the intensifying energy problem. Among the helpful books dealing with the environment and the environmental movement are Frank Graham, Jr., *Since Silent Spring** (1970); John C. Esposito, *Vanishing Air: The Ralph Nader Study Group Report on Air Pollution** (1970); James Ridgeway, *The Politics of Ecology** (1970); Gene Marine, *America the Raped: The Engineering Mentality and the Devastation of a Continent* (1969); J. Clarence Davies, III, *The Politics of Pollution** (1970); Paul R. Ehrlich and Anne Ehrlich, *Population, Resources, Environment: Issues in Human Ecology* (1970); and Robert Disch (ed.), *The Ecological Conscience: Values for Survival** (1970).

Judith Hole and Ellen Levine, *Rebirth of Feminism** (1971), is a history of the first decade of the growing movement to eliminate sexism in the United States. Various aspects of the cultural crisis of the sixties and seventies are treated in Theodore Roszak, *The Making of a Counter Culture** (1969); Charles A. Reich,

*Available in paperback edition.

The Greening of America* (1970); Alvin Toffler, *Future Shock** (1970); Philip E. Slater, *The Pursuit of Loneliness: American Culture at the Breaking Point** (1970); Patricia Cayo Sexton and Brendan Sexton, *Blue Collars and Hard-Hats: The Working Class and the Future of American Politics** (1971); Seymour Martin Lipset, *Rebellion in the University* (1972); Kirkpatrick Sale, *SDS** (1973); Irwin Unger and Debi Unger, *The Movement: A History of the American New Left, 1959–1972** (1974); Ron E. Roberts, *The New Communes: Coming Together in America* (1971); and Laurence R. Veysey, *The Communal Experience: Anarchist and Mystical Counter-Cultures in America* (1973).

Index

National Association for the Advancement of
    Colored People (NAACP), 86, 201
National Catholic Welfare Conference, 221
National Coordinating Committee to End the
    War, 241
National Council of the Churches of Christ, 153
National defense, U.S.: following World War II,
    8–10
    in the 1950s, 91, 177–178
National Defense Education Act (NDEA) of
    1958, 86, 149
    NDEA legislation, 150
National Education Association, 221
National Farm Workers' Association, 141
National Geographic, 160
National Liberation Front (NLF), 97, 187–188,
    235–239, 249n., 255, 258–259
National Organization of Women (NOW), 295
    illustration, 296
National Petroleum Council, 286
National Review, quoted, 155
National Science Foundation, 48
National Security Act (1947), 9
National Security Council, 10, 28, 52
    (*See also* NSC 68)
National Security Resources Board, 10
National Teacher Corps, 222
National Wilderness Preservation Act (1964), 226
National Women's Political Caucus, 295
National Youth Administration, 212
Nationalist China, 15, 30, 51–52, 58, 61, 94
    96–97, 99, 267n.
Nationalist movements in Asia, 50
Natural Gas Act (1938), amendment to, 78
Negroes, 3, 128–130, 154, 175, 219, 241, 262,
    294–295
    and black protest movement, 136–140, 198–202,
        214–218
    black writers, 166–167
    and school desegregation, 85–86
    and urban ghettos, 132, 217
    as voters, 33, 44, 67, 83, 216–217, 250
Nehru, Jawaharlal, 104
Nelson, Gaylord, 241
Neutralism in Third World, 102
New Deal, 2, 34, 35, 38, 40, 43, 44, 48, 62, 66, 69,
    70, 77, 191, 197, 213
New Deal coalition, 33, 67
New Frontier, 176, 191–205, 213
    (*See also* Kennedy, John F.)
New Hampshire primary:
    1952, 64, 65
    1956, 82
    1968, 244
    1972, 270
New Left, 243, 245, 247
New Look in foreign policy and defense, 90
New Republic, 38
New Theology, 154
New towns, 132–133
New York City Ballet, 162
New York Herald Tribune, quoted, 53
New York Philharmonic Orchestra, 161
New York Times, 43, 71, 144, 159, 265, 278, 289
New Yorker, 103
Newman, Paul, 158
Newspapers, American, 159
Newsweek, quoted, 224, 295–296
Newton, Huey P., 140
Niebuhr, Reinhold, 152
Nixon, Richard M.:
    background of, 252–253

Nixon, Richard M.:
    in campaign of 1952, 63, 65–67
    in campaign of 1968, 247–250
    character of, 173, 253
    and economic policies, 110, 264–265, 277–278
    and election of 1960, 172–174
    and election of 1972, 269–273
    first term as President, 253–269
    and foreign policy initiatives, 265–269, 290
    and Hiss case, 60, 207
    inauguration as President, illustration, 254
    move to impeach, 283–284, 287–291
    resigns presidency, 275, 291
    second term, 275–278
    tax difficulties and other problems, 282
    as Vice President, 81–82, 101, 253
    and Watergate, 279–284
Nixon, Thelma Ryan (Pat), 101, 253, 268
Nixon administration, 121, 150
    domestic policies, 260–265
    foreign policies, 265–269
Nixon Doctrine, 257
Nixonomics, 264
North Atlantic Council, 26
North Atlantic Treaty Organization (NATO),
    26–27, 52, 58, 64, 92–93, 96, 98, 102–103, 106,
    177–178, 181, 183, 189, 209, 231, 266, 276
North Carolina Agricultural and Technical
    College, 138
North Korea, 52–58, 244
North Vietnam, 95, 97, 187, 209, 235–240, 245,
    249, 255–256, 260, 276
Novak, Robert D., 212
NSC 68, 28, 52, 91
    (*See also* National Security Council)
Nuclear energy, international control of, 16
Nuclear Nonproliferation Treaty of 1968, 230,
    266
Nuclear Test Ban Treaty (1963), 185
Nuclear testing, 82, 104, 184
Nuremberg trials, 11

O'Connor, Flannery, 166
O'Donnell, Peter, 207
Office of Economic Opportunity (OEO), 219–220,
    277
Office of Price Administration (OPA), 5, 7
Office of War Mobilization and Reconversion, 7
O'Hara, John, 165
Oldenburg. Claes, 164
Ole Miss (University of Mississippi) and
    Meredith case, 199–200
Oligopoly, 115
    (*See also* Economic concentration)
"One man, one vote" principle, 217
O'Neill, Eugene, 165
O'Neill, William L., quoted, 203
Op art, 163–164
Open Housing Act of 1968, 218
Operation Candor, Watergate and, 288
Operation Rolling Thunder in Vietnam, 236
Oppenheimer, J. Robert, 73
Organization of American States (OAS), 27–28,
    183, 186, 233–234
Organized labor (*see* Labor unions)
Osgood, Robert E., quoted, 185
Oswald, Lee Harvey, 203–204

Pacification campaign in Vietnam, 238
Panama, relations with U.S., 101, 233
Parker, Charlie, 158
Parks, Rosa, 137